SEMIOTICS AND LINGUISTIC STRUCTURE

Truth and Denotation

The Notion of Analytic Truth

Toward a Systematic Pragmatics

Intension and Decision

Belief, Existence, and Meaning

Logic, Language, and Metaphysics

Events, Reference, and Logical Form

Whitehead's Categoreal Scheme and Other Papers

Peirce's Logic of Relations and Other Studies

SEMIOTICS AND LINGUISTIC STRUCTURE

A PRIMER OF PHILOSOPHIC LOGIC

R. M. Martin

State University of New York Press
Albany, 1978

P
99
M 36

First published in 1978 by
State University of New York Press
Albany, New York 12246

© 1978 State University of New York
All Rights Reserved

Made and printed in the United States of America

Library of Congress Cataloging in Publication Data

Martin, Richard Milton.
    Semiotics and linguistic structure.

    1. Semiotics.   2. Language and logic.
3. Structural linguistics.   I. Title.
P99.M36   149′.94   78-6873
ISBN 0-87395-381-9

To each and every reader who finds herein
anything in any way philosophically or
linguistically clarificatory.

"The . . . tendency to discard or neglect the Logic which aimed at the philosophical study of thought and knowledge, and to worship at the shrines of the formalists, symbolists, analysts, and positivists . . . would be disastrous if it were anything more than a temporary phenomenon. But I venture to think that it is only a case of 'reculer pour mieux sauter'. Like phases of transition in the history of music, it may well prove beneficial to the study of Logic in the end. For ultimately, one can hardly doubt, there will be a return to the study of philosophical logic—a return by students enriched with a greater knowledge and command of the technical means of expressing their meaning."

H. Joachim, *The Nature of Truth*

CONTENTS

Preface   xi

Part A. SEMIOTICS   1
I.   Virtual Classes, Identity, and Descriptions   3
II.   Virtual Relations   21
III.   Individuals, Parts, and Wholes   41
IV.   Events, States, Acts, and Processes   57
V.   Words and Expressions   73
VI.   Reference and Acceptance   99
VII.   Prolegomena to Mathematics   123

Part B. LINGUISTIC STRUCTURE   145
VIII.   Harris's Systems of Report and Paraphrase   147
IX.   On Generative Semantics   185
X.   Some Prepositional Relations   205
XI.   Prepositional Protolinguistics I   217
XII.   Prepositional Protolinguistics II   245
XIII.   Some Temporal Adverbs   273
XIV.   'Now'   289
XV.   The Very Idea of a Logical Form   299

Index   319

PREFACE

The discovery or invention—it need not be decided which—of the *quantifiers*, by Frege and Peirce, is surely one of the greatest steps forward in the history of logic. The little phrases 'for all x' and 'for some x' (or 'there exists at least one x such that'), for all their disarming simplicity, carry an incredible burden upon their shoulders. For one thing, the *traditional deductive logic*, the whole theory of syllogistic inference, no mean achievement by itself, can be given a proper systematic treatment in terms of them. For a second, they permeate *the language of mathematics* (either intuitionistic or classical) in a most fundamental way, and must be fully characterized before the structure of that language can be made clear. And since mathematics in turn is used in the language of *empirical science*, at least wherever counting and measurement are needed, quantifiers play there a most fundamental role also. Thirdly, they lead us directly to the portals of *ontology*. As soon as we ask what entities our variables of quantification are taken to range over, we become sensitive to issues of almost perennial interest in metaphysics and in the history of philosophy. In fact, the quantifiers have become one of our best instruments with which to formulate divergent metaphysical views and with which to explore to the depths issues and arguments constituting philosophical history. A philosopher is, after all, known by the quantifiers he keeps.

The truth-functional notions embodied in 'not', 'and', 'or', 'if---then' and 'if and only if' are, of course, presupposed. These five notions together with the universal and particular (or existential) quantifiers constitute the basic notions of logic in the modern sense—*first-order logic*, as it is now commonly called. Sometimes identity is added, in which case we speak of first-order logic with *identity*. This subject has now been before the learned world for nearly a century, and is almost universally recognized today as providing the pivotal core of theory needed for handling the most common modes of valid reasoning in the sciences and elsewhere.

Nonetheless, it is also almost universally recognized that this standard pivotal core must be extended in various ways if it is to be adequate to the various philosophical demands made upon it. Some philosophic logicians think that a *higher-order logic* must be added; others a *set theory* in some one or other of its various axiomatizations, together with a theory of *models*. Still others favor the *calculus of individuals* (Leśniewski's *mereology* or theory of the part-whole relation) as the most appropriate and helpful next step. Some favor a systematic *semiotics* or *metalogic* comprising a *syntax* and *semantics*, and perhaps also a *pragmatics* as well. Others want a logic gained by incorporating a theory of *grammatical tense* into it. Some think that extensions into *modal* logic are the most appropriate, including perhaps a *deontic* and *epistemic* logic as well. Some think a *many-valued* logic is needed. These various ways of extending the basic quantificational logic are by no means mutually exclusive, however, and various combinations are not only possible but are being actively cultivated at the moment. But not all of these extensions are on a par, and there are strong reasons for preferring the standard first-order logic, extended to include a metalogic or semiotics formulated on its basis. The calculus of individuals may then be added, as well as a method for handling *events*, resulting in an *event logic*.

The historically first attempt to develop a systematic semiotics or pragmatics in a sufficiently coherent form for the purposes of structural linguistics and philosophical analysis was the author's *Toward a Systematic Pragmatics* (1959). In that little book the relation of *acceptance* played a fundamental role. In the present book a host of other pragmatical relations are introduced, including many heretofore characterized in a purely syntactical or semantical way. Of particular interest and importance is a pragmatical relation of *reference*. A theory of events, acts, states, processes, and the like, is then developed, of such breadth as to lead immediately to the characterization of linguistic structure. Although in part technical, actually the characterization here is probably the simplest yet known, presupposing only first-order logic without sets or models. But first some further prefatory comments.

Logic is to the linguistic philosopher, it seems, what mathematics is to the empirical scientist. One can do a good deal of science without using numbers, that is, without counting or measurement, but a point is soon reached at which such procedures are not only highly desirable but in practice indispensable. In philosophy one can do a good deal without the self-conscious use of modern logic, but at a certain level of sophistication one finds such use extraordinarily helpful in practice and well-nigh indispensable in principle in providing the necessary theoretic framework or substructure. This book thus contains quite as much a treatise on philosophic method as it does a brief sketch of formal logic and metalogic. These latter, if construed in a suitably narrow sense, may in fact be called 'philosophic logic', providing for just the theories thought to be of greatest philosophic utility and relevance.

Logic is of course of particular interest for the study of natural language. Every sentence of English is a lesson in logic, Mill wrote with some truth. He should have noted also that every formula of logic is a lesson for the student of language. The study of logical form has played a significant role in both subjects since antiquity and great progress has been made in it in recent years. Yet few philosophers of natural language avail themselves of what is now known. Many of them even today write as though no progress had been made in its study since before the time of Peirce and Frege. Even the new linguistics has not yet come to terms with it. "Decades have been wasted," the late Uriel Weinreich noted, because linguists have not paid sufficient attention to recent work in logic.

Philosophic logic must of course be construed in a sense sufficiently wide to include a systematic semiotics in the form of a metalogic. In fact it is due to advances in this latter that the

subject has come of age. Without an explicit metalogic, philosophic logic reduces to first-order logic, a part of the content of
Volume I of Whitehead and Russell's epoch-making *Principia
Mathematica*. Of course that content is of astonishing richness
when suitably reformulated in accord with modern standards of
rigor, and when suitable nonlogical constants are added as undefined and postulates concerning them laid down.

Metalogic or semiotics conveniently divides, following Peirce,
Carnap, and Charles Morris, into syntax, semantics, and pragmatics. This honored triumvirate has been questioned by some,
but no clear or compelling reasons seem to have emerged for its
overthrow. What is important is rather its *unification*. Both
syntax and semantics play an important role in what follows, but
pragmatics will emerge as far and away the most interesting.
Some philosophers question the need for introducing an explicit
pragmatics; others think its inclusion essential. In any case, it
will be dealt with here not only as a necessary adjunct, but as providing the very heart of the subject. Both syntax and semantics
will emerge only in a pragmatized form. Metalogic, as thus conceived, is itself an extension of the elementary, first-order logic
already mentioned. Richer, nonelementary areas of metalogic
have been developed in recent years, mostly by mathematicians,
but it is not clear that these are needed outside of mathematics.
Most of what they achieve, for philosophical and linguistic
purposes anyhow, can be provided in more elementary terms.

This book is thus devoted entirely to elementary formal logic
and metalogic, and their applications to language. In particular,
then, as already hinted at, there will be no concern with so-called
higher logic or mathematical set theory (or the model theory
based on it). There are several reasons for this omission. Properly
these subjects belong more to mathematics than to linguistic
philosophy. Also they all presuppose, if developed formally,
essentially the more elementary logic here. In addition, set theory
as usually interpreted introduces philosophically obscure and
suspect entities, a charge to which even its proponents themselves
are sensitive. Also the view (due in part to Tarski) is now wide-
spread that set theory has utterly failed to provide adequate

foundations for mathematics, the very purpose for which it was designed. It would seem doubtful therefore that it will succeed in providing adequate foundations for anything else, in particular for exact philosophy and the systematic study of natural language.

Attention being devoted here entirely to the classical two-valued theories of truth-functions, quantifiers, and identity, with syntax, semantics, and pragmatics built upon their basis, there will be no concern with alternative forms of logic, so-called three-valued (or, more generally, n-valued) logics, modal logics, intuitionistic logics, and the like. The view is that whatever is valuable in these alternatives can be achieved more readily within the classical framework by suitable extensions. Strictly there is only one logic, which, however, can be extended variously for specific purposes as needed. "One God, one country, one logic," in the stunning phrase of Whitehead.

The first-order or elementary point of view is pressed in this book, not as far as possible perhaps, but a good deal further than is usually supposed possible. The reader may find himself surprised to see how much can be achieved on so narrow a basis. God made first-order logic and all the rest is the handiwork of man.

Event logic has been mentioned only in passing. 'Event' is construed here in a very broad sense so as to include states, acts, and processes of all kinds as well as various complexes of them. The fundamentals of event logic are to be explored rather more thoroughly than has been done heretofore. The subject is conceived so widely as to embrace the whole of elementary logic and metalogic. In fact philosophic logic here is in effect identified with event logic in a rather extended form.

There is a good deal of concern throughout with matters of notation. This is thought to be essential for clarity, and the use of symbols is becoming increasingly common in all logico-philosophical and logico-linguistic writing. A good deal of preliminary concern is needed to distinguish carefully between the symbol and what the symbol stands for. This distinction of use and mention is often difficult to maintain and a good deal of vigilance is needed to do so. Some readers may think that the use of symbolism here is excessive, especially in the later chapters. The use of it in the early ones will not be questioned and is now standard in handling such material. Once the reader is familiar with the symbolism of the earlier chapters, however, it seems eminently natural to extend it to the expanded material later. Not to do so would be to suggest too sharp a dichotomy in the nature of the subjects treated. There is no such dichotomy *de re* and hence it is not clear why some think there should be *de dicto*. Also the symbolism used throughout is of an extremely simple kind. It is for the most part either an adaption of that of *Principia Mathematica* itself or mere abbreviated English words suggestive of what is being symbolized. With such notational aids, there is gain in explicitness, precision, and clarity, and no loss in perspicuity.

An old German saying has it that *Gott wohnt im Detail*. The philosopher is sometimes put off by the thousand and one little notational details he finds in symbolic writing. He complains that there is too much overelaboration, too many trees, so that he is lost in the forest. This is perhaps regrettable, but the fact is that philosophy in our time is becoming increasingly technical in all its branches. With increased technicality goes extensive symbolization, and the day is already at hand when philosophy cannot, in the words of Peirce, do without an "immense technical vocabulary." There is surely no better way of keeping one's technical vocabulary straight than by the prudent use of a wise symbolism.

Philosophic logic is becoming more and more intimately associated with the study of the logical forms of sentences of natural language. No account of the former therefore could achieve its aim without providing a rather extensive theory of the latter. This is accomplished in the later portions of the book, in which the study of logical form is shown to be at the very center of structural linguistics. The book thus divides conveniently into two parts, the first, Part A, being concerned with semiotics or philosophic logic proper, and the second, Part B, with its applications to the study of linguistic structure.

The material of Part A is cumulative, each chapter built upon the preceding ones. Presupposing the theory of the truth-functional connectives and quantifiers, we go on, in Chapter I, to the theory of *virtual classes*, *identity*, and *descriptions*. The theory of *virtual relations* is then developed rather fully in Chapter II. The use of virtual classes and relations will be of help throughout in compensating for not admitting real ones. The hallmark of real ones is that they are taken as values for variables, virtual ones never. Chapters I and II are merely introductory and place more or less familiar material in a somewhat new setting. In Chapter III a suitable adaptation of the calculus of individuals or mereology is presented. Chapter IV is devoted to a sketch of event logic in the narrower sense. In Chapter V the rudiments of logical syntax are presented in a pragmatized form. And in Chapter VI, the foundations of a pragmatized semantics are given. Chapter VII is devoted to some *prolegomena for mathematics*, and it will be of interest to see how arithmetic, geometry, and analysis (theory of real numbers) can be handled without presupposing the strong devices of set theory.

The first seven chapters, those of Part A, are somewhat technical. To keep the exposition at a minimum—the chapters are intended after all only as a kind of breviary—only a few examples from natural language are given. However, this defect is overcome in the later chapters, those of Part B, which are more discursive and exploratory, and concerned entirely with natural language. In Chapter VII, Zellig Harris's *systems of report and paraphrase* are discussed in some detail, and it is shown how logical forms for the kinds of sentences considered may be provided upon the basis of the preceding event logic. And for good measure, in Chapter IX, a similar discussion is presented of some features of George Lakoff's *generative semantics*. In Chapter X, a considerable simplification of the theory of logical form of VII–IX is presented by considering *some prepositional relations*, such as To, From, By, With, and so on. In terms of these the material of the preceding chapters may be given an especially simple and economical structure. The theory of prepositions is carried forward in XI and XII in close connection with an examination of relevant parts of the monumental *A Grammar of Contemporary English* by Randolph Quirk and associates. In XIII there is study of the logic of some *temporal adverbs* and XIV is devoted in particular to 'now'. Finally, in XV, the very notion as to what a *logical form* is is discussed in some detail.

Another way of describing the material of this book is as follows. It is often said—and indeed justly—that the standard first-order logic of quantifiers is not adequate for the philosophic tasks expected of it. It needs extension in various directions, as already noted, into higher-order logic or set theory, into mereology, tense logic, metalogic, model theory, modal, deontic, or epistemic logics, or into event logic. These topics constitute modern logic at the intermediate level, as it were, beyond that of an introductory text but not yet at the level of technicality of professional mathematics. Almost all treatments of them to date, however, are such as to presuppose higher logic or set theory fundamentally, and thus to require very powerful assumptions of a mathematical kind. A distinguishing feature of the present book is that all of these topics are treated in novel ways without such a presupposition and with no loss of depth or comprehensiveness. In this way philosophic logic takes on a new dignity of its own.

Event logic is thought to consist of the minimum of extensions of first-order logic required for exhibiting the structures of sentences of natural language. Nothing less will suffice, surely, nor, it would seem, is anything more needed that cannot be accommodated within this framework. The material of the first seven chapters, those of Part A, which presupposes first-order logic with identity, constitutes thus the minimum of semiotical theory needed for structural linguistics, the minimum of what every linguist and philosopher, linguistic or otherwise, may profitably know of formal logic and semiotics. The later chapters, those of Part B, exhibit this minimum *in usu*.

The main features of this book are, by way of summary, as follows. (1) It contains the most extensive exposition of the logic of virtual classes and relations to be found to date in the literature. (2) It contains an especially simple formulation of the theory of the part-whole relation as confined to individuals (mereology), where only first-order logic without sets is presupposed. (3) It contains a sketch of a novel and urgently needed event logic on a first-order basis, apparently the only one of its kind to be found anywhere. (4) It contains the formulation of a pragmatized, conceptualistic syntax differing in important respects from previous characterizations of syntax. (5) It contains a formulation of a pragmatic theory of reference of the most extensive kind yet developed, embracing the notions of traditional semantics as well as a theory of pronouns and demonstratives. (6) It contains a novel philosophical theory as to the nature of mathematics, providing for some fragments of geometry and for the arithmetic of real numbers on the basis of a suitable extension of the theory of reference. (7) It examines in detail some of the significant recent discussions by eminent linguists of problems concerned with the logical forms of sentences of natural language. And (8) it contains a sketch of a novel theory of prepositional relations, which provides an especially simple theory of logical form of far-reaching generality. (9) Structural linguistics and modern logic are thus seen to be much more intimately interrelated than seems heretofore to have been recognized. (10) The treatment throughout is elementary in the sense of presupposing only first-order logic without sets. Hence in a very immediate sense this book contains presumably the simplest and most readily accessible account of philosophic logic and the theory of logical form yet available.

Familiarity with the rudiments of first-order logic are presupposed. Readers familiar also with the theory of virtual classes and relations may skip immediately to Chapter III, and those familiar with mereology or the logic of individuals, directly to Chapter IV. The Chapters I–III nonetheless are thought useful as prolegomena, for they place more or less familiar material in just the form needed for the sequel. Readers impatient of logical detail or already familiar with the essentials of event logic may even wish to skip ahead directly to Part B.

The author wishes to thank New York University, Northwestern University, and the National Science Foundation, Grant No. GS-37954, for support of the research reported in this volume, as well as (the late) Professors Rudolf Carnap and

Aron Gurwitsch, and also Professor Henry Hiż, for some helpful discussions. Thanks are due also to the D. Reidel Publishing Co., the Yale University Press, Walter de Gruyter and Co., and the editors of *Theoretical Linguistics* for permission to reproduce or rework some material originally published by them.

PART A

SEMIOTICS

CHAPTER I

VIRTUAL CLASSES, IDENTITY, AND DESCRIPTIONS

Let us consider a specific logical system to be used as a basis for various extensions to follow. This system is in essentials a rather famous and historically important one, namely, that due to Paul Bernays as a reformulation of the material of *Principia Mathematica*.[1] Because detailed presentations of this material or its equivalent are readily available, a brief outline here will suffice.

The system is presumed to contain some primitive *n*-place predicates and some primitive individual constants. In addition, let '$\sim$' and '$\vee$' be the primitive sentential connectives, standing for negation and disjunction respectively. By definition the other connectives may then be introduced as follows.

D1.　　$\ulcorner(A \supset B)\urcorner$　abbreviates　$\ulcorner(\sim A \vee B)\urcorner$,

D2.　　$\ulcorner(A \cdot B)\urcorner$　abbreviates　$\ulcorner\sim (\sim A \vee \sim B)\urcorner$,

---

1. See especially, in addition to *Principia Mathematica* itself, P. Bernays, "Axiomatische Untersuchungen über des Aussagen-Kalküls der *Principia Mathematica*," *Mathematische Zeitschrift* 25 (1926): 305–320, and D. Hilbert and W. Ackermann, *Principles of Mathematical Logic* (New York: Chelsea Publishing Co., 1950), for the historically first expositions of this system.

and

D3. $\ulcorner(A \equiv B)\urcorner$ abbreviates $\ulcorner((A \supset B) \cdot (B \supset A))\urcorner$.

Boldface italic letters are used throughout as informal syntactical variables for expressions. In particular, '*A*', '*B*', with or without accents or numerical subscripts, are used for formulae, and '*x*', '*y*', and '*z*', with or without accents or numerical subscripts, for terms, that is, for variables or individual constants. Note the special use of quasi-quotes or corners enclosing contexts containing a boldface letter.[2]

Universal quantifiers are written with parentheses in the usual fashion as $\ulcorner(x)\urcorner$, where *x* is a variable. The existential quantifier is then introduced as follows.

D4. $\ulcorner(Ex)\urcorner$ abbreviates $\ulcorner\sim (x) \sim\urcorner$, where *x* is a variable.

The definition schemata *D1–D4* are not by themselves of any particular interest. They became so only when coupled with axioms and rule of inference. Axioms, rules, and definitions are in fact so closely interwoven that definitions alone are, strictly speaking, meaningless. Without the axioms and rules the behavior of the primitive logical and nonlogical constants is not fixed. Likewise, without the convenient abbreviations provided by the definitions, the axioms are often so long and cumbrous as to be unintelligible.

Let Frege's compound symbol '⊢' be used now in the metalanguage for 'is provable', i.e., 'is a theorem'.[3] Thus '⊢ *A*' reads 'the sentence *A* is provable'. Further, the '⊢' will be taken in such a way as to absorb the single quotation marks or quasi-quotes

2. See W. V. Quine, *Mathematical Logic*, revised edition (Cambridge: Harvard University Press, 1951), pp. 33–37. Consider again $\ulcorner(\sim A \lor B)\urcorner$. This is not strictly to be regarded as the expression consisting of '(' followed by '$\sim$' followed by '*A*' (which is a boldface italic letter) followed by ' $\lor$ ' and so on, as it would be if the single quotes were being used in their usual sense. It is to be rather the expression consisting of '(' followed by ' $\sim$ ' followed by *A* (which is a formula) followed by ' $\lor$ ' followed by *B* followed by ')'.

3. See especially G. Frege, *Grundgesetze der Arithmetik*, Vol. 1 (Jena: 1893), p. 9.

around the context to which it applies. Thus '⊢ $(A \lor \sim A)$'
is to express that $\ulcorner(A \lor \sim A)\urcorner$ is provable.

Just as definition schemata were given above, each providing
an infinity of particular definitions, so *axiom schemata* will now
be given, each providing for an infinity of axioms. If an axiom
schema is prefixed by '⊢', the result will be a *rule* or *metaaxiom*
to the effect that every instance of that schema is provable. In
this way, all the axioms are regarded as provable, as immediately
provable, we might say.

The *metaaxioms* for the present formulation of first-order
logic are the following.

R1.   ⊢ $(A \lor A) \supset A$.

R2.   ⊢ $A \supset (A \lor B)$.

R3.   ⊢ $(A \lor B) \supset (B \lor A)$.

R4.   ⊢ $(A \supset B) \supset ((C \lor A) \supset (C \lor B))$.

R5.   ⊢ $(x)A \supset B$, if B differs from A only in containing
free occurrences of a variable or occurrences of a term wherever
there are free occurrences of the variable x in A.

R6.   ⊢ $(x)(A \lor B) \supset (A \lor (x)B)$, if there are no free
occurrences of the variable x in A.

The two *Rules of Inference* are *Modus Ponens* and the *Rule
of Generalization*.

MP.   If ⊢ A and ⊢ $(A \supset B)$, then ⊢ B.

Gen.   If ⊢ A then ⊢ $(x)A$, where x is a variable.

It is well known that on this basis the full, classical, first-order
theory of the truth-connectives and quantifiers is forthcoming.
At the very head then of the list of logico-philosophical principles to be given in this book are those of first-order logic.
These are presupposed as the *sine qua non* of everything that
follows.

Let us go on now to extend the foregoing in two directions.
On the one hand, a notation will be introduced for the theory of
virtual classes, and on the other, a primitive '=' for the *identity*

of individuals. On the basis of the theory of identity, a foundation is laid for the theories of *selective* and *singular descriptions.* These two extensions are merely the first to be made, more to follow with the introduction of further primitives in later chapters.

A. ABSTRACTION

A notation for the notion of one-place abstraction may now be introduced.

One could, if one wished, introduce

$\ulcorner\{y3B\}x\urcorner$ as an alternative notation for A, if (i) x is a term, (ii) y is a variable not occurring freely in A but occurring freely n times ($n \geqq 0$) in B, and (iii) B is like A except in containing free occurrences of y in place of some or all of the n free occurrences of x in A.

Although this stipulation or "definition" is not strictly an abbreviation, it does introduce a useful alternative notation. Let 'Q' be a one-place predicate and 'R' a two-place one. Then

$$\text{‘}\{y3Qy\}x\text{’}$$

may be written in place of 'Qx', or

$$\text{‘}\{y3Ryz\}x\text{’}$$

in place of 'Rxz'. Also

$$\text{‘}\{y3(Qy \lor \sim (Ez)Rzy)\}x\text{’}$$

may be written in place of

$$\text{‘}(Qx \lor \sim (Ez)Rzx)\text{’}.$$

Thus

(1) $\qquad\qquad\text{‘}\{y3(Qy \lor \sim (Ez)Rzy)\}\text{’}$

is allowed to occur in the position of a one-place predicate.

The '϶', the *inverted epsilon*, is Peano's symbol for abstraction.[4] In essentially the notation of *Principia Mathematica*,

$$\text{'}\hat{y}(Py \ \vee \ \sim (Ez)Rzy)\text{'}$$

is sometimes used in place of (1), with a somewhat similar meaning. Some writers prefer rather

$$\text{'}(\lambda y)(Py \ \vee \ \sim (Ez)Rzy)\text{'}$$

or

$$\text{'}\{y\!:\!(Py \ \vee \ \sim (Ez)Rzy)\}\text{'}.$$

Here the original notation of Peano is retained, together with the braces.

An expression of the form $\ulcorner\{x϶A\}\urcorner$, where x is a variable and A a formula, is a *one-place abstract*. It should be noted that if the above definition is adapted, one-place abstracts are in no way a part of the primitive notation. They can always be eliminated at will. In practice, however, they are useful in providing interesting alternative notations. Also it will be shown later that one-place abstracts (containing no free variables) together with the one-place primitive predicates are the most important kinds of expressions that may be said to *denote*. For this reason it is convenient to include '϶' as an additional primitive sign.

Let now '϶', '{', and '}' be added to the primitive notation. The definition of 'formula' needed is then as follows.

1. Any n-place primitive predicate followed by n terms (variables or individual constants) is a formula.
2. If A is a formula, so is $\ulcorner\sim A\urcorner$.
3. If A and B are formulae, so is $\ulcorner(A \ \vee \ B)\urcorner$.
4. If A is a formula and x is a variable, $\ulcorner(x)A\urcorner$ is a formula.
5. If B is a formula, y a variable, and x a term, then $\ulcorner\{y϶B\}x\urcorner$ is a formula.

---

4. See G. Peano, *Formulaire de Mathématiques* (Paris: Gauthier-Villars, 1901), p. 1.

B.   SOME PRINCIPLES

The rules *R1–R6* above are now to be extended to include the following *Principles of One-Place Abstraction.*

Abst.   ⊢ $\{y3B\}x \equiv A$, if (etc., as in the definition given above).

Every occurrence of a variable y in $\ulcorner\{y3B\}\urcorner$ is now to be regarded as *bound.* Note that in expressions of the form $\ulcorner\{y3B\}\urcorner$ the variable y may or may not occur freely in B. If it does, all well and good. If it does not, the abstract is said to be *vacuous.* Also B may contain terms other than y. If B contains no free variables other than y, the abstract $\ulcorner\{y3B\}\urcorner$ is said to stand for a *virtual class.* If B does contain free variables other than y, the abstract $\ulcorner\{y3B\}\urcorner$ stands rather for a *virtual-class function.* (The phrase 'stands for' here is somewhat loose and will be made precise in a later chapter.) A virtual-class function is like a virtual class except that the expression standing for it contains at least one free variable.

An occurrence of an abstract in a formula A is said to be *free* if every occurrence of a free variable in that abstract is also a free occurrence of that variable in A. Thus, for example, the exhibited occurrence of $\ulcorner\{x3A\}\urcorner$ is free in

$$\ulcorner(z)(\{x3A\}z \supset B)\urcorner$$

but not in

$$\ulcorner(y)(z)(\{x3A\}z \supset B)\urcorner,$$

if x, y, and z are distinct variables and z is not free in A but y is. (Any occurrence of x in a context $\ulcorner(x)A\urcorner$ or $\ulcorner\{x3A\}\urcorner$ is of course understood to be that of a variable.)

One-place abstracts containing no free variables behave very much like the primitive one-place predicate constants. Thus they may be referred to as *defined* one-place predicate constants. In fact all defined predicate constants may be introduced as abstracts.

Formulae of the form '$\{y3\text{--}y\text{--}\}x$' may conveniently be read as 'the entity x is a member of the virtual class of x's such that

--y--'. Because virtual classes behave very much as real classes do, the use of 'is a member of' here seems appropriate. Here '--y--' is understood to be any formula of the language containing 'y' as a free variable. An alternative notation for '$\{y3$--y--$\}x$' could thus be

$$\text{'}x \ \varepsilon \ \{y3\text{--}y\text{--}\}\text{'},$$

where 'ε' reads as is customary 'is a member of'.

Virtual classes are virtual merely because they are in no wise values for variables. Classes, sets, or relations taken as values for variables in a given formalism are said to be *real*. Strictly of course there are no virtual classes and all talk about them is merely a *façon de parler*.[5]

It might be thought more perspicuous to write '$\{y3(\text{--}y\text{--})\}$' with parentheses added, rather than '$\{y3\text{--}y\text{--}\}$'. Note, however, that the conventions of parentheses implicit in the definition of 'formula' above are such that the additional parentheses would not be needed unless '--y--' is an atomic formula or the negation of one. Thus one writes '$\{x3Qx\}$' and '$\{x3\sim Qx\}$' but '$\{x3(Qx \lor Rxy)\}$', '$\{x3(Qx \supset Qx)\}$', and so on. If these conventions are borne in mind, no lack of perspicuity will result and parentheses around atomic formulae A or the negations of such in contexts $\ulcorner\{x3A\}\urcorner$ will not be needed.

Hereafter let the boldface letters '$\boldsymbol{F}$', '$\boldsymbol{G}$', and '$\boldsymbol{H}$' be used as informal syntactical variables for one-place abstracts and primitive predicate constants. Also the Roman letters 'F', 'G', and 'H' will be used occasionally for specific virtual classes themselves.

A few important laws concerning virtual classes and virtual-class functions are the following.

TA1. $\vdash \{x3A\}y \equiv A$, if x does not occur freely in A.

TA2. $\vdash \{x3(A \lor B)\}y \equiv (\{x3A\}y \lor \{x3B\}y)$.

TA3. $\vdash \{x3\sim A\}y \equiv \sim \{x3A\}y$.

TA4a. $\vdash \{x3(y)A\}z \equiv (y)\{x3A\}z$, if x and y are distinct variables and z is a term distinct from y.

5. Cf. the author's "The Philosophical Import of Virtual Classes," in *Belief, Existence, and Meaning* (New York: New York University Press, 1969), pp. 123–135.

TA1 is the *Principle of Vacuous Abstraction.* According to *TA2*, an entity y is a member of a virtual class $\{x3(\text{--}x\text{--} \vee ..x. .)\}$ if and only if it is a member of $\{x3\text{--}x\text{--}\}$ *or* a member of $\{x ..x. .\}$. And similarly, according to *TA3*, an entity y is a member of $\{x3\sim \text{--}x\text{--}\}$ if and only if it is *not* a member of $\{x \text{--}x\text{--}\}$. *TA2* and *TA3* are *Abstractual Principles of Disjunction* and *Negation* respectively. *TA4a* is an *Abstractual Principle of Quantification.* It states, in a special case, that an entity z is a member of the virtual class $\{x3(y)\text{--}y\text{--}x\text{--}\}$ if and only if for all y, z is a member of the virtual-class function $\{x3\text{--}y\text{--}x\text{--}\}$. (Here '$\text{--}y\text{--}x\text{--}$' is any formula of the language containing 'y' and 'z' as free variables.) *TA4a* may be generalized as follows.

TA4b. $\vdash \{x3(y_1)...(y_n)A\}z \equiv (y_1)...(y_n)\{x3A\}z$, if x, $y_1, ... ,y_n$ are distinct variables and z is a term distinct from them.

C. SUMS, PRODUCTS, AND NEGATIVES

A few interesting notions concerned with virtual classes and virtual-class functions may now be introduced.

First there is the notion of identity.

D5. $\ulcorner F = G \urcorner$ abbreviates $\ulcorner (x)(Fx \equiv Gx) \urcorner$, if x is a variable not free in F or G.

Note that the right-hand side, the definiens, of this definition is not unique, for x can be taken as any variable not free in F or G. Actually then there are here infinitely many definientia, one for each choice of a variable in the range of 'x'. They are all of course equivalent. If a unique definiens is desired here, it may be achieved by stipulating a linear or alphabetic ordering of the variables. The first could be 'x', then 'y', then 'z', then 'x'', then 'x_1', then 'y'', then 'y_1', and so on. Then the x of the definiens of *D5* could be required to be the alphabetically first variable not free in F or G. Let the convention be adopted that hereafter in any definition or definition schema any variables exhibited in the definiens but not in the definiendum are to be understood in the order of occurrence as the alphabetically first, second, and so on, variable not free in the definiendum. 'x' will be used for the first, 'y' for the second, and so on.

Note that the identity sign '$=$' here is significant only as between abstracts. Only later will the identity sign be introduced as significant between terms for individuals.

The following are various principles covering virtual-class identity.

TA5. ⊢ $\{x3A\}$ = $\{y3B\}$, if x and y are distinct variables and A differs from B only in containing free occurrences of x wherever and only where there are free occurrences of y in B.

TA6. ⊢ $\{x3Fx\}$ = F, if the variable x does not occur freely in F.

TA7. ⊢ $(x)(A \equiv B) \equiv \{x3A\} = \{x3B\}$.

TA8. ⊢ $F = F$.

TA9. ⊢ $F = G \supset (A \supset B)$, if there are just n ($n \geq 1$) occurrences of F in A, and B differs from A only in containing free occurrences of G in one or more of those places where there are free occurrences of F in A.

TA10. ⊢ $F = G \supset G = F$.

TA11. ⊢ $(F = G \cdot G = H) \supset F = H$.

A virtual class F is said to be *included* or *contained* in a virtual class G, if every member of F is a member of G. Thus,

D6. $\ulcorner F \subset G \urcorner$ is short for $\ulcorner (x)(Fx \supset Gx) \urcorner$. ($x$ here is the alphabetically first variable not free in F or G, in accord with the convention.)

The following principles now clearly hold.

TA12. ⊢ $(x)(A \supset B) \equiv \{x3A\} \subset \{x3B\}$.

TA13. ⊢ $(F \subset G \cdot G \subset F) \equiv F = G$.

TA14. ⊢ $F \subset F$.

TA15. ⊢ $(F \subset G \cdot G \subset H) \supset F \subset H$.

TA16. ⊢ $(Fx \cdot F \subset G) \supset Gx$.

Hereafter, in expressions of the forms $\ulcorner (x)(Fx \lor Gx) \urcorner$ or $\ulcorner \{x3(Fx \lor Gx)\} \urcorner$ and the like, it is to be understood that x

has no free occurrences in F or G. Also when virtual classes are spoken of, virtual-class functions are to be included as special cases.

Let us consider now the Boolean algebra of virtual classes. Given virtual classes F and G, there is the *logical sum* or *union* of them containing as members the members of F together with those of G. Thus one may let

> *D7.* $\ulcorner(F \cup G)\urcorner$ abbreviate $\ulcorner\{x \ni (Fx \vee Gx)\}\urcorner$.

According to this definition, an entity x is a member of the virtual class (or virtual-class function) $(F \cup G)$ if and only if it is a member of F or a member of G.

Similarly the *logical product* or *intersection* of two virtual classes may be introduced. Thus

> *D8.* $\ulcorner(F \cap G)\urcorner$ abbreviates $\ulcorner\{x \ni (Fx . Gx)\}\urcorner$.

The logical product of F and G thus is the virtual class of all entities x such that x is an element of F and also an element of G.

The *negative* or *complement* of a virtual class F consists of just those entities that are not members of it. Thus

> *D9.* $\ulcorner - F\urcorner$ may abbreviate $\ulcorner\{x \ni \sim Fx\}\urcorner$.

Also there are two special virtual classes to note, the *universal* class and the *null* one. The universal class consists of all entities and the null one contains none at all. Thus

> *D10.*   'V' may abbreviate $\ulcorner\{x \ni (Qx \vee \sim Qx)\}\urcorner$

and

> *D11.*   'Λ' may abbreviate ' $- V$'.

The universal virtual class V consists of all entities x such that $(Qx \vee \sim Qx)$ where 'Q' is a primitive one-place predicate constant, thus indeed of all entities whatsoever. The null virtual class is the negative of V and thus contains no entities. Clearly

> *TA17.* $\vdash (x)Vx$

and

> *TA18.* $\vdash \sim (Ex)\Lambda x$.

D. THE LOGIC OF CLASSES

The full logic of virtual classes is at hand with the foregoing notions.

First there are laws covering the logical sums and products as follows.

TA19. $\vdash (F \cup G)x \equiv (Fx \lor Gx)$,
TA20. $\vdash (F \cap G)x \equiv (Fx \cdot Gx)$;

Commutative Laws:

TA21. $\vdash (F \cup G) = (G \cup F)$,
TA22. $\vdash (F \cap G) = (G \cap F)$;

Associative Laws:

TA23. $\vdash ((F \cup G) \cup H) = (F \cup (G \cup H))$,
TA24. $\vdash ((F \cap G) \cap H) = (F \cap (G \cap H))$;

and *Distributive Laws*:

TA25. $\vdash (F \cup (G \cap H)) = ((F \cup G) \cap (F \cup H))$,
TA26. $\vdash (F \cap (G \cup H)) = ((F \cap G) \cup (F \cap H))$.

In addition, the following obtain.

TA27. $\vdash ((F \cap G) \subset H) \cdot (F \cap H) \subset G) \equiv$
$(F \cap G) = (F \cap H)$.
   TA28. $\vdash F = (F \cup F)$.
   TA29. $\vdash F = (F \cap F)$.
   TA30. $\vdash (F \subset G \cdot F \subset H) \equiv F \subset (G \cap H)$.
   TA31. $\vdash F \subset G \supset F \subset (G \cup H)$.
   TA32. $\vdash F \subset G \supset (F \cap H) \subset G$.
   TA33. $\vdash F \subset G \supset (F \cup H) \subset (G \cup H)$.
   TA34. $\vdash F \subset G \supset (F \cap H) \subset (G \cap H)$.
   TA35. $\vdash F \subset (F \cup G)$.
   TA36. $\vdash (F \cap G) \subset F$.
   TA37. $\vdash (F \subset G \cdot H \subset J) \supset (F \cup H) \subset$
$(G \cup J)$.
   TA38. $\vdash (F \subset G \cdot H \subset J) \supset (F \cap H) \subset$
$(G \cap J)$.
   TA39. $\vdash (F \subset G \cdot H \subset G) \equiv (F \cup H) \subset G$.

$TA40.$ $\vdash F \subset G \equiv (F \cup G) = G.$
$TA41.$ $\vdash F \subset G \equiv (F \cap G) = F.$
$TA42.$ $\vdash F = (F \cup (F \cap G)).$
$TA43.$ $\vdash F = (F \cap (F \cup G)).$
$TA44.$ $\vdash (F \subset G \lor H \subset G) \supset (F \cap H) \subset G.$

The converse of *TA44* does not hold.

$TA45.$ $\vdash (F \subset G \lor F \subset H) \supset F \subset (G \cup H).$

Here also the converse does not obtain.
Concerning negatives there are the following theorems.

$TA46.$ $\vdash (x)(-Fx \equiv {\sim} Fx).$
$TA47.$ $\vdash {\sim} F = -F.$
$TA48.$ $\vdash F = --F.$
$TA49.$ $\vdash F \subset G \equiv -G \subset -F.$
$TA50.$ $\vdash F \subset -G \equiv G \subset -F.$
$TA51.$ $\vdash F = G \equiv -F = -G.$
$TA52.$ $\vdash F = -G \equiv -F = G.$
$TA53.$ $\vdash -(F \cup G) = (-F \cap -G).$
$TA54.$ $\vdash -(F \cap G) = (-F \cup -G).$

Covering the universal and null virtual classes the following laws hold.

$TA55.$ $\vdash {\sim} V = \Lambda.$
$TA56.$ $\vdash F \subset V. \ \Lambda \subset F.$
$TA57.$ $\vdash F = V \equiv V \subset F.$
$TA58.$ $\vdash F = \Lambda \equiv F \subset \Lambda.$
$TA59.$ $\vdash (x)Fx \equiv F = V.$
$TA60.$ $\vdash {\sim} (Ex)Fx \equiv F = \Lambda.$
$TA61.$ $\vdash (F \cup -F) = V.$
$TA62.$ $\vdash (F \cap -F) = \Lambda.$
$TA63.$ $\vdash (F \cup V) = V.$
$TA64.$ $\vdash (F \cap V) = F.$
$TA65.$ $\vdash (F \cup \Lambda) = F.$
$TA66.$ $\vdash (F \cap \Lambda) = \Lambda.$
$TA67.$ $\vdash F \subset G \equiv (-F \cup G) = V.$
$TA68.$ $\vdash F \subset G \equiv (F \cap -G) = \Lambda.$
$TA69.$ $\vdash (x)A \equiv \{x3A\} = V.$
$TA70.$ $\vdash {\sim} (Ex)A \equiv \{x3A\} = \Lambda.$

We see, with this peroration of principles, that the theory of virtual classes is surprisingly powerful. It has been argued elsewhere (in *Belief, Existence, and Meaning*) that the virtual-class theory suffices for most of the purposes of set theory itself, as long as one remains outside of mathematics. Mathematics will be handled in a quite new way, in Chapter VII. Thus it may be that the theory of virtual classes may suffice for mathematics also. In any case, there can be no doubt but that the theory is much more powerful than is generally supposed.

E. IDENTITY OF INDIVIDUALS

The identity sign '=' has been introduced above, in *D5*, as significant only between expressions for virtual classes. Now '=' is introduced primitively as significant between terms (individual constants or variables). The '=' is thus ambiguous, but no harm can arise from this. One can always tell from the context which usage is intended.

The definition of 'formula' in §A must be extended now once more to accommodate '='. Thus the following clause is now added.

6.   If x and y are terms, $\ulcorner x = y \urcorner$ is a formula.

Also the following *Principles of Identity* are to be added to *R1–R6*, *MP*, *Gen*, and *Abst*.

IdR1. $\vdash x = x$.

IdR2. $\vdash x = y \supset (Fx \supset Fy)$.[6]

The following are the most important principles concerning identity.

TId1. $\vdash x = y \supset (x = z \supset y = z)$.
TId2. $\vdash x = y \equiv y = x$.
TId3. $\vdash \sim x = y \equiv \sim y = x$.
TId4. $\vdash x = y \supset (y = z \supset x = z)$.

6. Cf. D. Hilbert and P. Bernays, *Grundlagen der Mathematik*, Vol. I (Berlin: Springer, 1934), pp. 164–177.

TId5.　　$\vdash x = z \supset (y = z \supset x = y)$.

TId6a.　　$\vdash \sim x = y \supset (\sim x = z \vee \sim y = z)$.

TId6b.　　$\vdash (Fx \cdot \sim Fy) \supset \sim x = y$.

TId7.　　$\vdash Fy \equiv (x)(x = y \supset Fx)$.

TId8.　　$\vdash Fy \equiv (Ex)(x = y \cdot Fx)$.

TId9.　　$\vdash (x)(\sim x = y \supset Fx)$　　$((x)Fx \vee$
$(\sim Fy \cdot (x)(z)(\sim x = z \supset (Fx \vee Fz)))$.

TId10.　　$\vdash (Ex)(\sim x = y \cdot Fx) \equiv ((Ex)Fx \cdot$
$(Fy \supset (Ex)(Ez)(\sim x = z \cdot Fx \cdot Fz)))$.

TId11.　　$\vdash (Ex)(y)(\sim y = x \supset Fy) \equiv (x)(y)(\sim x = y \supset (Fx \vee Fy))$.

TId12.　　$\vdash (x)(Ey)(\sim y = x \cdot Fy) \equiv (Ex)(Ey)(\sim x = y \cdot Fx \cdot Fy)$.

Throughout *TId7* et seq. the *x*, *y*, and so on, are to be understood as distinct variables with just the exhibited occurrences. Thus, in *TId7*, there are to be no free occurrences of *x* in *F*.

TId7 and *TId8* are especially useful laws. *TId7* says in effect that an entity *y* is a member of a given virtual class *F* if and only if every entity identical with *y* is a member of it. Similarly *TId8* says that *y* is a member of *F* if and only if some entity identical with *y* is a member of it.

The '=' has been taken here as a logical primitive. Under suitable circumstances, however, it may be defined in terms of the primitive predicates available. Thus suppose that there are only the two primitive predicates 'Q' and 'R', as above, and that 'Q' is one-place and 'R' of two places. The atomic formulae are then of the forms

$$\ulcorner Qx \urcorner \quad \text{and} \quad \ulcorner Rxy \urcorner,$$

where *x* and *y* are any terms. Then, the '=' may be introduced in context as follows.

$\ulcorner x = y \urcorner$ abbreviates $\ulcorner (Qx \equiv Qy) \cdot (z)(Rxz \equiv Ryz) \cdot (z)(Rzx \equiv Rzy) \urcorner$, if *z* is the alphabetically first variable distinct from *x* and *y*.

The effect of this definition, it should be noted, is to allow *x* to be replaced by *y* in all atomic contexts. Of course Q here is not to be either universal or null, nor may R be—(see below,

(II,B).) If Q and R were universal the definiens here would always hold for, then

$$\vdash (x)(y)((Qx \equiv Qy) \cdot (z)\text{---etc.---}).$$

In practice of course the primitive predicates are not to be taken as either universal or null, for otherwise they could readily be defined.

F. SELECTIVE DESCRIPTIONS

Let us turn for a moment to the so-called *selector operator* as a prelude to formulating the Russellian theory of definite descriptions.

Let

D12. $\ulcorner G(\varepsilon F) \urcorner$ abbreviate $\ulcorner (Ex)Fx \cdot (x)(Fx \supset Gx) \urcorner$.

The phrase '(εF)', to take an instance, may be read 'any selected entity in (or that is a member of) F', and an entire context '$G(\varepsilon F)$' may be read 'any selected entity in F is a member of G'. The 'ε' here is in effect a selector operator. To say that any selected entity in F is in G is to say that there is an F and every F is a G, no matter how selected.

The following theorems obtain.

TSel1. $\vdash (Ex)Fx \equiv F(\varepsilon F)$.
TSel2. $\vdash (x)Fx \equiv \sim -F(\varepsilon - F)$.

These are of interest in showing that the quantifiers may be expressed wholly in terms of 'ε'. To say that there is an F is to say in effect that any selected entity in F is in F. And to say that every entity is in F is to say in effect that it is not the case that any selected entity in $-F$ is in $-F$.

A Rule of *Existential Instantiation* may now be expressed by means of 'ε'.

TSel3. If $\vdash (Ex)Fx$, then $\vdash F(\varepsilon F)$.

And a Rule of *Existential Generalization* may be given as follows.

TSel4. If $\vdash (Fy \vee F(\varepsilon F))$, then $\vdash (Ex)Fx$.

The following law is of interest in showing that the order in which two ε-expressions are taken is indifferent.

TSel5.   ⊢ $\{x3\{y3A\}(\varepsilon G)\}(\varepsilon F) \equiv \{y3\{x3A\}(\varepsilon F)\}(\varepsilon G)$, if *x* and *y* are distinct variables perhaps having free occurrences in *A* but not in *F* or *G*.

G.   SINGULAR DESCRIPTIONS

The Russellian notion of a singular description, here rendered as a phrase of the form 'the one entity *x* in *F*', is very closely allied to that of a selective description. In the case of a singular description one and only one entity is described and said to be in a given virtual class. In the case of a selective description, there may be more than one such entity. Thus an additional clause is needed here to assure that there is *at most* one entity being described.

Thus without further ado,

D13. $\ulcorner G(\imath F)\urcorner$ may abbreviate $\ulcorner (G(\varepsilon F) \; . \; (x)(y)((Fx \; . \; Fy) \supset x = y))\urcorner$.

The added clause here, the uniqueness condition, is to the effect that there is at most one entity in *F*, that is, that if both *x* and *y* are in *F*, for any *x* and *y*, they are identical.[7]

The following definitions are of interest in providing the effect of predicates for *existence*.

D14a. $\ulcorner E!F\urcorner$ ⎫
D14b. $\ulcorner E!(\varepsilon F)\urcorner$ ⎬ abbreviate $\ulcorner (Ex)Fx\urcorner$.
D14c. $\ulcorner E!(\imath F)\urcorner$ abbreviates $\ulcorner (E!(\varepsilon F) \; . \; (x)(y)((Fx \; . \; Fy) \supset x = y))\urcorner$.

All three definienda are to the effect that such and such exists. Thus *D14a* provides for the idiom 'the virtual class *F* exists', *D14b* for 'any selected entity in *F* exists', and *D14c* for 'the one entity in *F* exists'. The first two are defined merely as '$(Ex)Fx$'.

---

7. Cf. of course *14 of *PM* itself.

The uniqueness condition is added to the definiens of the third. The following theorems are immediate.

TDscrp1.   ⊢ $G(\imath F) \supset G(\varepsilon F)$.
TDscrp2.   ⊢ $E!(\imath F) \supset (E!(\varepsilon F) \,.\, E!F)$.
TDscrp3.   ⊢ $E!(\imath F) \equiv (Ex)(Fx \,.\, (y)(Fy \supset y = x))$.

(Here *x* and *y* are to be understood of course as distinct variables.)

TDscrp4.   ⊢ $G(\imath F) \equiv (Ex)(Gx \,.\, (y)(Fy \equiv y = x))$.

TDscrp5.   ⊢ $\{x3\{y3A\}(\imath G)\}(\imath F) \equiv \{y3\{x3A\}(\imath F)\}(\imath G)$,

if (etc., as in *TSel5*).

TDscrp6.   ⊢ $\{x3\{y3A\}(\varepsilon G)\}(\imath F) \equiv \{y3\{x3A\}(\imath F)\}(\varepsilon G)$,

if (etc., as in *TSel5*).

CHAPTER II

VIRTUAL RELATIONS

A fairly comprehensive theory of virtual classes was developed in the preceding chapter, together with the theory of the identity of individuals and of selective and singular descriptions. Let us go on now to the theory of virtual relations. The latter are of course, like virtual classes, in no way real in the sense of being values for variables. Even so, a strong and workable theory of them may be developed, and with no further strengthening of the primitive vocabulary or axiomatic framework. This is an interesting circumstance. The theory of virtual relations becomes wholly absorbed in the theory of virtual classes, more specifically, of that of virtual-class functions, where the abstract contains at least one free variable.

A.   RELATIONAL ABSTRACTS

The only abstracts introduced thus far are one-place abstracts. Clearly, however, in order to provide for the theory of virtual relations, abstracts of more than one place are needed. These may be introduced in terms of one-place abstracts as follows.

D15a. $\ulcorner\{xy3A\}zw\urcorner$ abbreviates $\ulcorner\{x3\{y3A\}w\}z\urcorner$, if x and y are distinct variables and z and w are any terms.

D15b. $\ulcorner\{xyz3A\}x'y'z'\urcorner$ abbreviates $\ulcorner\{x3\{y3\{z3A\}$ $z'\}y'\}x'\urcorner$, if x, y, and z are distinct variables and x', y', and z' are any terms.

And so on, for abstracts of still higher degree.

Note that $\ulcorner\{y3A\}\urcorner$ here stands for, in the interesting cases, a virtual-class function, for A then contains a free occurrence of x also. If A contains a free variable other than x or y, the two-place abstract $\ulcorner\{xy3A\}\urcorner$ then also stands for a virtual-relation function.

The following are *Principles of Relational Abstraction*, and are consequences of *Abst.*

TRelAbst1. $\vdash \{xy3B\}zw \equiv A$, if (i) z and w are terms, (ii) x and y are distinct variables not occurring freely in A, and (iii) B is like A except in containing free occurrences of x and y respectively in place of some or all of the free occurrences of z and w (if any) in A.

TRelAbst2. $\vdash \{xyz3B\}x'y'z' \equiv A$, if (etc., as required).

And so on.

For the present let attention be confined to dyadic virtual relations, and let the boldface letters '$\mathbf{R}$', '$\mathbf{S}$', and '$\mathbf{T}$' be used as informal syntactical variables for two-place abstracts or primitive predicates. Also occasionally the Roman italic letters 'R', 'S', and 'T' may be used to stand for specific dyadic virtual relations.

The following principles are similar to the corresponding principles in the theory of virtual classes.

TR1. $\vdash \{zw3A\}xy \equiv A$, if z and w do not occur freely in A.

TR2. $\vdash \{zw3(A \lor B)\}xy \equiv (\{zw3A\}xy \lor \{zw3B\}xy)$.

TR3. $\vdash \{zw3\sim A\}xy \equiv \; \sim \{zw3A\}xy$.

TR4. $\vdash \{zw3(u)A\}xy \equiv (u)\{zw3A\}xy$, if u is a variable distinct from x, y, z, and w.

The relations of *identity* and *subsumption* (or inclusion) between dyadic virtual relations may be introduced as follows.

D16a. $\ulcorner R = S \urcorner$ abbreviates $\ulcorner (x)(y)(Rxy \equiv Sxy) \urcorner$.

D16b. $\ulcorner R \subset S \urcorner$ abbreviates $\ulcorner (x)(y)(Rxy \supset Sxy) \urcorner$.

The following theorems are then immediate.

TR5. $\vdash \{xy3A\} = \{zw3B\}$, if A is like B except in containing free occurrences of x and y respectively wherever and only where there are free occurrences of z and w in B.

TR6. $\vdash \{xy3Rxy\} = R$, if x and y do not occur freely in R.

TR7. $\vdash (x)(y)(A \equiv B) \equiv \{xy3A\} = \{xy3B\}$.

TR8. $\vdash R = R$.

TR9. $\vdash R = S \supset (A \supset B)$, if (etc., as required).

TR10. $\vdash R = S \equiv S = R$.

TR11. $\vdash (R = S . S = T) \supset R = T$.

TR12. $\vdash (x)(y)(A \supset B) \equiv \{xy3A\} \subset \{xy3B\}$.

B. THE LOGIC OF DYADIC RELATIONS

A Boolean algebra or logic of virtual classes was formulated above. In a similar way now the logic of dyadic virtual relations may be developed. Thus the logical sum or union and the logical product or intersection of virtual dyadic relations may be introduced as follows.

D17. $\ulcorner (R \cup S) \urcorner$ abbreviates $\ulcorner \{xy3(Rxy \vee Sxy)\} \urcorner$.

D18. $\ulcorner (R \cap S) \urcorner$ abbreviates $\ulcorner \{xy3(Rxy . Sxy)\} \urcorner$.

And also the negative or complement, and the universal and null dyadic relations.

D19. $\ulcorner -R \urcorner$ abbreviates $\ulcorner \{xy3 \sim Rxy\} \urcorner$,

D20. 'V' abbreviates $\ulcorner \{xy3(x = x . y = y)\} \urcorner$,

and

D21. 'Λ' abbreviates '−V'.

Analogous to *TA13–TA70* there are now corresponding principles for virtual relations. These need not be listed, but let them be referred to, should need arise, as *TR13–TR70*.

Thus *TR28*, for example, reads:

$$\vdash R = (R \cup R),$$

and *TR66*:

$$\vdash (R \cap \Lambda) = \Lambda.$$

Note that the various Boolean signs are now ambiguous. Thus '$\cup$' may stand for the operation of summation of virtual classes or for that of virtual dyadic relations. The usage intended, however, will always be clear from the context. The identity sign '$=$' is now three-way ambiguous, and is significant as between individuals, virtual classes, and virtual dyadic relations. Again, however, the usage intended will always be clear from the context.

C. DOMAINS, COUNTERDOMAINS, AND FIELDS

All the notions concerning dyadic virtual relations introduced thus far are analogous to corresponding notions in the theory of virtual classes. The most interesting notions concerning virtual relations, however, are those that have no such analogues. Let us consider now the most important of these.

Consider the totality or virtual class of all entities that bear R to something. The virtual class of fathers, for example, contains just those persons who bear the father-of relation to someone. Such a virtual class is said to be the *domain* of the dyadic relation in question. Thus one lets

D22. $\ulcorner D'R \urcorner$ abbreviate $\ulcorner \{x \exists (\mathrm{E}y)Rxy\} \urcorner$.

Similarly the *counterdomain* or *converse domain* of R is the virtual class of entities to which something or other bears R. Thus,

D23. $\ulcorner \mathrm{C}'R \urcorner$ abbreviates $\ulcorner \{x \exists (\mathrm{E}y)Ryx\} \urcorner$.

The counterdomain of the relation father-of consists of all people, for everyone has a father.

Finally, the *campus* or *field* of a relation is the virtual-class sum of its domain and counterdomain.

D24. $\ulcorner C'R \urcorner$ abbreviates $\ulcorner (D'R \cup Q'R) \urcorner$.

The following principles are of interest.

TR71. $\vdash Rxy \supset (D'Rx . Q'Ry)$.
TR72. $\vdash C'Rx \equiv (Ey)(Rxy \lor Ryx)$.
TR73a. $\vdash D'R = Q'R \supset D'R = C'R$.
TR73b. $\vdash Q'R \subset D'R \equiv D'R = C'R$.
TR73c. $\vdash D'R \subset Q'R \equiv Q'R = C'R$.
TR74a. $\vdash D'(R \cap S) \subset (D'R \cap D'S)$.
TR74b. $\vdash Q'(R \cap S) \subset (Q'R \cap Q'S)$.
TR74c. $\vdash C'(R \cap S) \subset (C'R \cap C'S)$.

The converses of *TR74a–74c* do not hold.

TR75a. $\vdash D'(R \cup S) = (D'R \cup D'S)$.
TR75b. $\vdash Q'(R \cup S) = (Q'R \cup Q'S)$.
TR75c. $\vdash C'(R \cup S) = (C'R \cup C'S)$.
TR76. $\vdash R \subset S \supset (D'R \subset D'S . Q'R \subset Q'S)$.

D. CONVERSES AND RELATIVE PRODUCTS

The *converse* of a dyadic virtual relation R is the relation that holds between entities y and x whenever R holds between x and y. The usual symbol for the converse is '$\smile$' used as a prefix. Thus one may let

D25. $\ulcorner \smile R \urcorner$ abbreviate $\ulcorner \{yx \ni Rxy\} \urcorner$.

If R is the relation between people of being younger than, $\smile R$ is the relation of being older than. Where '$<$' stands for the relation between integers of being less than, '$\smile <$' (which may be abbreviated as '$>$') stands for the relation of being greater than.

The following principles concerning converses hold.

TR77a. $\vdash Q'R = D'\smile R$.
TR77b. $\vdash D'R = Q'\smile R$.

$TR77c.$ $\vdash C^{t}R = C^{\cdot\smile}R.$

$TR78.$ $\vdash R = \smile S \equiv S = \smile R.$

$TR79.$ $\vdash \smile\smile R = R.$

$TR80a.$ $\vdash \smile(R \cap S) = (\smile R \cap \smile S).$

$TR80b.$ $\vdash \smile(R \cup S) = (\smile R \cup \smile S).$

$TR81.$ $\vdash \smile -R = -\smile R.$

$TR82a.$ $\vdash \smile V = V.$

$TR82b.$ $\vdash \smile \Lambda = \Lambda.$

$TR83.$ $\vdash R \subset S \equiv \smile R \subset \smile S.$

The *relative product* of dyadic virtual relations R and S is the relation that stands between entities x and y whenever x bears R to some entity that bears S to y. Thus

$D26.$ $\ulcorner(R/S)\urcorner$ abbreviates $\ulcorner\{xy\exists(Ez)(Rxz \, . \, Szy)\}\urcorner.$

Let R be the relation of father-of and S that of mother-of. Then (R/S) is the relation of being the maternal grandfather-of. (R/R) is the relation of being paternal grandfather-of. The relation of being a grandfather-of is the sum $((R/R) \cup (R/S))$. The relation of being a grandparent-of is $(((R/R) \cup (R/S)) \cup ((S/S) \cup (S/R)))$.

The following principles concerning relative products obtain.

$TR84.$ $\vdash \smile(R/S) = (\smile S/\smile R).$

$TR85.$ $\vdash ((R/S)/T) = (R/(S/T)).$

$TR86a.$ $\vdash (S/(T \cap R)) \subset ((S/T) \cap (S/R)).$

$TR86b.$ $\vdash ((S \cap T)/R) \subset ((S/R) \cap (T/R)).$

Note that the converses of $TR86a$ and $TR86b$ do not hold.

$TR87a.$ $\vdash (S/(T \cup R)) = ((S/T) \cup (S/R)).$

$TR87b.$ $\vdash ((S \cup T)/R) = ((S/R) \cup (T/R)).$

$TR88.$ $\vdash (R \subset T \, . \, S \subset U) \supset (R/S) \subset (T/U).$

E. RELATIONS WITH LIMITED FIELDS

Of interest are virtual relations whose domains or counter-domains are restricted to just certain classes of entities. One might wish to limit the field of the father-of relation to just living persons, or one might wish to limit its domain to married persons over thirty. There are three notions to consider here, as follows.

D27a. $\ulcorner(F \!\restriction\! R)\urcorner$ abbreviates $\ulcorner\{xy3(Fx \; . \; Rxy)\}\urcorner$.

D27b. $\ulcorner(R \!\restriction\! F)\urcorner$ abbreviates $\ulcorner\{xy3(Rxy \; . \; Fy)\}\urcorner$.

D27c. $\ulcorner(F \!\restriction\! R \!\restriction\! G)\urcorner$ for $\ulcorner\{xy3(Fx \; . \; Rxy \; . \; Gy)\}\urcorner$.

The following principles hold.

TR89. $\vdash ((R \!\restriction\! F) \!\restriction\! G) = (R \!\restriction\! (F \cap G))$.

TR90. $\vdash ((R \!\restriction\! F)/S) = (R/(F \!\restriction\! S))$.

TR91. $\vdash (R \!\restriction\! (F \cup G)) = ((R \!\restriction\! F) \cup (R \!\restriction\! G))$.

TR92a. $\vdash \mathbf{C}`R \subset F \supset (R \!\restriction\! F) = R$.

TR92b. $\vdash \mathbf{C}`R \subset F \supset (S/(F \!\restriction\! R)) = (S/R)$.

TR93. $\vdash \smile(R \!\restriction\! F) = (F \!\restriction\! \smile R)$.

TR94a. $\vdash D`(F \!\restriction\! R) = (F \cap D`R)$.

TR94b. $\vdash \mathbf{C}`(R \!\restriction\! G) = (G \cap \mathbf{C}`R)$.

TR95. $\vdash F \subset \mathbf{C}`R \supset \mathbf{C}`(R \!\restriction\! F) = F$.

TR96. $\vdash \mathbf{C}`R \subset F \equiv (R \!\restriction\! F) = R$.

Where both the domain and counterdomain are restricted to the same virtual class, the following notation is useful.

D27a. $\ulcorner(R \!\restriction\! F)\urcorner$ abbreviates $\ulcorner(F \!\restriction\! R \!\restriction\! F)\urcorner$.

Then

TR97. $\vdash (x)(y)((R \!\restriction\! F)xy \equiv (Rxy \; . \; Fx \; . \; Fy))$.

TR98a. $\vdash C`R \subset F \equiv (R \!\restriction\! F) = R$.

TR98b. $\vdash (R \!\restriction\! F) = (R \!\restriction\! (F \cap C`R))$.

TR99. $\vdash (R \!\restriction\! C`R) = R$.

F. RELATA AND VIRTUAL CLASSES OF SUCH

The notion of a singular description has already been introduced. Especially interesting are descriptions of the one entity that bears a given relation to an entity. 'The father of Joseph' is an example, as is 'the positive square root of 2'. In general one may let

D28. $\ulcorner(R`x)\urcorner$ abbreviate $\ulcorner(\imath\{y3Ryx\})\urcorner$.

If R is the relation of father of, $(R'x)$ is the father of x. Note that '$(R'x)$' here is merely an abbreviation for a singular description. The following principles hold.

> $TR100a.$ $\vdash \{z \mathbin{3} x = z\}(R'y) \equiv (z)(Rzy \equiv z = x).$
> $TR100b.$ $\vdash \mathrm{E}!(R'y) \equiv (\mathrm{E}x)(z)(Rzy \equiv z = x).$
> $TR100c.$ $\vdash \mathrm{E}!(R'y) \supset (\{z \mathbin{3} x = z\}(R'y) \equiv Rxy).$

Next consider the virtual class of all entities that bear a given relation to an entity x. Thus

> $D29a.$ $\ulcorner F\ \vec{R}\ x \urcorner$ may abbreviate $\ulcorner F = \{y \mathbin{3} Ryx\} \urcorner$.

And similarly

> $D29b.$ $\ulcorner F\ \bar{R}\ x \urcorner$ may abbreviate $\ulcorner F = \{y \mathbin{3} Rxy\} \urcorner$.

If R is the relation of lover of, then if $F\ \vec{R}\ x$ then F is the virtual class of x's lovers. If R is the relation of father-of, then if $F\ \bar{R}\ x$ then F is the class of x's children.

The following theorems clearly hold.

> $TR101a.$ $\vdash (x)(F\ \vec{R}\ x \equiv F\ \vec{S}\ x) \equiv R = S.$
> $TR101b.$ $\vdash (x)(F\ \bar{R}\ x \equiv F\ \bar{S}\ x) \equiv R = S.$
> $TR102a.$ $\vdash (R \subset S\ .\ F\ \vec{R}\ x\ .\ G\ \vec{S}\ x) \supset F \subset G.$
> $TR102b.$ $\vdash (R \subset S\ .\ F\ \bar{R}\ x\ .\ G\ \bar{S}\ x) \supset F \subset G.$
> $TR103.$ $\vdash (F\ \vec{R}\ x\ .\ F\ \vec{S}\ x) \equiv F\ (\overrightarrow{R \cap S})\ x.$
> $TR104.$ $\vdash (F\ \vec{R}\ x \vee F\ \vec{S}\ x) \equiv F\ (\overrightarrow{R \cup S})\ x.$
> $TR105.$ $\vdash F\ \overrightarrow{-R}\ x \equiv -F\ \vec{R}\ x.$

Next comes the interesting notion of a *plural descriptive function*, namely, the virtual class of all entities that bear a given relation to some member of a given virtual class.

> $D30.$ $\ulcorner R``F \urcorner$ abbreviates $\ulcorner \{x \mathbin{3} (\mathrm{E}y)(Rxy\ .\ Fy)\} \urcorner$.

If F is the virtual class of Oxford dons, and R is the relation of being married to, then $R``F$ is the virtual class of the wives of Oxford dons.

The following theorems clearly obtain.

> $TR106a.$ $\vdash R``F \subset \complement'R.$
> $TR106b.$ $\vdash \breve{R}``F \subset \complement'R.$

TR107.	$\vdash F \subset G \supset R``F \subset R``G.$
TR108.	$\vdash R``(F \cup G) = (R``F \cup R``G).$
TR109a.	$\vdash D`R = R``\Box`R.$
TR109b.	$\vdash \Box`R = \smile R``D`R.$
TR110.	$\vdash R``F = R``(F \cap \Box`R).$
TR111.	$\vdash R``\Lambda = \Lambda.$
TR112.	$\vdash D`(R/S) = R``D`S \,.\, \Box`(R/S) = \smile S``\Box`R.$
TR113.	$\vdash (R/S)``F = R``S``F.$

G.   UNIT CLASSES AND CARDINAL PAIRS

A virtual class containing just one member is a *unit* class. More particularly, the virtual class whose only member is some given entity x is the unit class of x. For this notion one may let

D31a.   ⌜$\{x\}$⌝ abbreviate ⌜$\{y \ni y = x\}$⌝.

Clearly then the following hold. (Because these principles concern virtual classes only, they are numbered as abstraction theorems with an 'A'.)

TA71a.	$\vdash \{x\}y \equiv y = x.$
TA71b.	$\vdash \{x\}x.$
TA72.	$\vdash Fx \equiv \{x\} \subset F.$
TA73.	$\vdash \sim Fx \equiv (\{x\} \cap F) = \Lambda.$
TA74.	$\vdash x = y \equiv \{x\} = \{y\}.$
TA75.	$\vdash (\sim F = \Lambda \,.\, F \subset \{x\}) \equiv F = \{x\}.$

The virtual class whose only members are x and y is the *dual* class or *cardinal pair* of x and y.

D31b.   ⌜$\{x,y\}$⌝ abbreviates ⌜$(\{x\} \cup \{y\})$⌝.

Clearly

TA76.	$\vdash \{x,y\}z \equiv (z = x \lor z = y).$
TA77.	$\vdash \{x,y\} = \{y,x\}.$
TA78.	$\vdash \{x,y\}x \,.\, \{x,y\}y.$
TA79.	$\vdash x = y \equiv \{x,y\} = \{x\}.$

And similarly the *triple* virtual class x, y, and z is the class whose only members are x, y, and z.

D31c. $\ulcorner\{x,y,z\}\urcorner$ abbreviates $\ulcorner(\{x,y\} \cup \{z\})\urcorner$,

and so on.

H.   ORDERED PAIRS

According to *TA77* a cardinal pair is not ordered. A virtual ordered pair differs from a cardinal pair in that its members, so to speak, are given an order in some fashion or other. For this notion,

D32a. $\ulcorner\langle x,y\rangle\urcorner$ may abbreviate $\ulcorner\{zw\exists(z = x \,.\, w = y)\}\urcorner$.

The order here is established by the order of z and w in the relational abstract.

Concerning ordered pairs there are the following fundamental principles.

TR114. $\vdash \langle x,y\rangle zw \equiv (z = x \,.\, w = y)$.
TR115. $\vdash \langle x,y\rangle = \langle z,w\rangle \equiv (x = z \,.\, y = w)$.
TR116. $\vdash \langle x,y\rangle = \langle z,w\rangle \equiv \langle y,x\rangle = \langle w,z\rangle$.
TR117. $\vdash \sim x = y \supset \sim \langle x,y\rangle = \langle y,x\rangle$.
TR118. $\vdash (D'R = \{x\} \,.\, \mathbb{C}'R = \{y\}) \equiv R = \langle x,y\rangle$.
TR119. $\vdash Rxy \equiv \langle x,y\rangle \subset R$.
TR120. $\vdash (\sim R = \Lambda \,.\, R \subset \langle x,y\rangle) \equiv R = \langle x,y\rangle$.
TR121. $\vdash R \subset (\langle x,y\rangle \cup \langle z,w\rangle) \equiv (R = \Lambda \vee$
$R = \langle x,y\rangle \vee R = \langle z,w\rangle \vee R = (\langle x,y\rangle \cup \langle z,w\rangle))$.

Ordered triples, quadruples, and so on, may be provided for in similar fashion. One may let

D32b. $\ulcorner\langle x,y,z\rangle\urcorner$ abbreviate $\ulcorner\{x'y'z'\exists(x' = x \,.\, y' = y \,.\, z' = z)\}\urcorner$,

and so on.

Ordered pairs are the smallest non-null virtual relations just as unit classes are the smallest non-null virtual classes. Thus an ordered pair $\langle x,y \rangle$ may also be referred to as the unit dyadic relation of x and y. And similarly with ordered triples, and so on.

It is useful also to have a notation for the virtual relation between entities x and y determined by the circumstance that x is in a given virtual class F and y in G. Thus

D33.　⌜$(F{\uparrow}G)$⌝　may abbreviate　⌜$\{xy\exists(Fx \, . \, Gy)\}$⌝.

$(F{\uparrow}G)$ may be regarded as the *Cartesian product* of F and G. Concerning this notion the following principles obtain.

TR122a.　⊢ $(F{\uparrow}G) = (F{\upharpoonright} \lor {\upharpoonright}G)$.
TR122b.　⊢ $(F{\upharpoonright}R{\upharpoonright}G) = (R \cap (F{\uparrow}G))$.
TR123.　⊢ $(D{}^{\iota}R \subset F \, . \, \mathcal{Q}{}^{\iota}R \subset G) \equiv R \subset (F{\uparrow}G)$.
TR124.　⊢ $-(F{\uparrow}G) = ((-F{\uparrow}G) \cup (F{\uparrow}-G) \cup$
$(-F{\uparrow}-G))$.
TR125.　⊢ $((F{\uparrow}G) \cap (F'{\uparrow}G')) = ((F \cap F'){\uparrow}$
$(G \cap G'))$.
TR126.　⊢ $\smile(F{\uparrow}G) = (G{\uparrow}F)$.
TR127.　⊢ $(F{\uparrow}G) = \Lambda \equiv (F = \Lambda \lor G = \Lambda)$.
TR128.　⊢ $\langle x,y \rangle = (\{x\}{\uparrow}\{y\})$.

I.　ONE-MANY, MANY-ONE,
AND ONE-ONE RELATIONS

Let us reflect now upon some further kinds of virtual relations of interest.

A dyadic virtual relation R is said to be *one-many* provided, given any y, at most one entity bears R to it. Thus

D34.　⌜$(1{\rightarrow}\text{Cls})R$⌝　abbreviates　⌜$(x)(y)(z)((Rxy \, . \, Rzy)$
$\supset x = z)$⌝.

The father-of relation is one-many, for example, because each person has at most one father.

A relation is said to be *many-one* provided given any x, x bears R to at most one entity.

D35.　⌜$(\text{Cls}{\rightarrow}1)R$⌝　abbreviates　⌜$(x)(y)(z)((Rxy \, . \, Rxz)$
$\supset y = z)$⌝.

Finally, a relation R is *one-one* provided it is both one-many and many-one.

D36. $\ulcorner(1{\to}1)R\urcorner$ abbreviates $\ulcorner((1{\to}\text{Cls})R$. $(\text{Cls}{\to}1)R)\urcorner$.

The relation of being legally married to (at a given time) in a monogamous society is clearly one-one.

The following important theorems obtain.

TR129a. $\vdash (1{\to}\text{Cls})R \equiv (\text{Cls}{\to}1)\breve{\ }R$.

TR129b. $\vdash (1{\to}1)R \equiv (1{\to}1)\breve{\ }R$.

TR130a. $\vdash ((1{\to}\text{Cls})R$. $S \subset R) \supset (1{\to}\text{Cls})S$.

TR130b. $\vdash ((\text{Cls}{\to}1)R$. $S \subset R) \supset (\text{Cls}{\to}1)S$.

TR130c. $\vdash ((1{\to}1)R$. $S \subset R) \supset (1{\to}1)S$.

TR131a. $\vdash (1{\to}\text{Cls})R \supset (1{\to}\text{Cls})(R \cap S)$.

TR131b. $\vdash (\text{Cls}{\to}1)R \supset (\text{Cls}{\to}1)(R \cap S)$.

TR131c. $\vdash (1{\to}1)R \supset (1{\to}1)(R \cap S)$.

TR132a. $\vdash ((1{\to}\text{Cls})R$. $(1{\to}\text{Cls})S) \supset (1{\to}1)(R \cap \breve{\ }S)$.

TR132b. $\vdash ((\text{Cls}{\to}1)R$. $(\text{Cls}{\to}1)S) \supset (1{\to}1)(R \cap \breve{\ }S)$.

TR132c. $\vdash ((1{\to}\text{Cls})R$. $(\text{Cls}{\to}1)S) \supset (1{\to}1)(R \cap S)$.

TR133a. $\vdash ((1{\to}\text{Cls})R$. $(1{\to}\text{Cls})S$. $(\text{Œ}`R \cap \text{Œ}`S) = \Lambda) \supset (1{\to}\text{Cls})(R \cup S)$.

TR133b. $\vdash ((\text{Cls}{\to}1)R$. $(\text{Cls}{\to}1)S$. $(\text{D}`R \cap \text{D}`S) = \Lambda) \supset (\text{Cls}{\to}1)(R \cup S)$.

TR133c. $\vdash ((1{\to}1)R$. $(1{\to}1)S$. $(\text{C}`R \cap \text{C}`S) = \Lambda) \supset (1{\to}1)(R \cup S)$.

TR134a. $\vdash ((1{\to}\text{Cls})R$. $(1{\to}\text{Cls})S) \supset (1{\to}\text{Cls})(R/S)$.

TR134b. $\vdash ((\text{Cls}{\to}1)R$. $(\text{Cls}{\to}1)S) \supset (\text{Cls}{\to}1)(R/S)$.

TR134c. $\vdash ((1{\to}1)R$. $(1{\to}1)S) \supset (1{\to}1)(R/S)$.

TR135a. $\vdash (1{\to}\text{Cls})R \supset (\{z3x = z\}(R`y) \equiv Rxy)$.

TR135b. $\vdash (\text{Cls}{\to}1)R \supset (\{z3y = z\}(\breve{\ }R`x) \equiv Rxy)$.

TR136. $\vdash (1{\to}1)\langle x,y \rangle$.

TR137. $\vdash (\text{Cls}{\to}1)R \supset (R``F \cap R``G) = R``(F \cap G)$.

TR138. $\vdash ((1{\to}\text{Cls})R$. $F \subset \text{D}`R) \supset R``\breve{\ }R``F = F$.

J. REFLEXIVITY, SYMMETRY, AND TRANSITIVITY

Virtual dyadic relations may be further classified, in another fashion, as follows.

First a relation R is said to be *reflexive*, if x bears R to itself, for any x in the field of R.

D37. ⌜Refl R⌝ abbreviates ⌜$(x)(C'R\ x\ \supset\ Rxx)$⌝.

The relation of being the same age as between men is reflexive. Also the relation of being less than or equal to among integers.

Next, a relation R is *irreflexive* if x does not bear x to itself, for any x in the field of R.

D38. ⌜Irrefl R⌝ abbreviates ⌜$(x)(C'R\ x\ \supset\ \sim Rxx)$⌝.

The relation of father-of among human persons is irreflexive, and so also the relation of weighing less than among gross physical objects.

Similarly virtual relations may be classified as *symmetric* or *asymmetric* as follows.

D39. ⌜Sym R⌝ abbreviates ⌜$(x)(y)(Rxy\ \supset\ Ryx)$⌝.
D40. ⌜Asym R⌝ abbreviates ⌜$(x)(y)(Rxy\ \supset\sim Ryx)$⌝.

Clearly the relation of being parallel to between lines is symmetric, whereas the father-of relation is asymmetric.

Likewise virtual relations may be classified as *transitive* or *intransitive*.

D41. ⌜Trans R⌝ abbreviates ⌜$(x)(y)(z)((Rxy\ .\ Ryz)$ $\supset Rxz)$⌝.

D42. ⌜Intrans R⌝ abbreviates ⌜$(x)(y)(z)((Rxy\ .\ Ryz)$ $\supset\ \sim Rxz)$⌝.

The relations of being parallel to and of being the same age as are transitive. The relations of being father-of among people or successor-of among integers are intransitive.

Next a relation is *totally reflexive* if for any x it holds between x and itself.

D43. ⌜TotRefl R⌝ abbreviates ⌜$(x)Rxx$⌝.

And *totally irreflexive* if it does not hold between any x and itself.

D44. $\ulcorner$TotIrrefl $R\urcorner$ abbreviates $\ulcorner(x)\sim Rxx\urcorner$.

Note that not all relations need be either reflexive or irreflexive, nor symmetric or asymmetric, nor transitive or intransitive, nor totally reflexive or totally irreflexive. But there are some interesting connections among these various kinds of relations, as shown by the following principles.

TR139. $\vdash$ TotRefl $R \equiv$ (Refl R . D'$R = $ V).
TR140. $\vdash$ (Trans R . Sym R) $\supset$ Refl R.
TR141. $\vdash$ Asym $R \equiv$ Irrefl (R/R).
TR142. $\vdash$ Asym $R \supset$ Irrefl R.
TR143. $\vdash$ (Trans R . Asym R) $\equiv$ (Trans R .
Irrefl R).
TR144. $\vdash$ Sym $R \equiv$ Sym $\smile R$.
TR145. $\vdash$ (Asym R . $S \subset R$) $\supset$ Asym S.
TR146. $\vdash$ Irrefl (R/R) $\supset$ Irrefl R.
TR147. $\vdash$ (Trans R . Irrefl R) $\supset$ Irrefl (R/R).

K. SERIES

Some further kinds of virtual relations are the following.

A relation is regarded as *connected* if it or its converse holds between any two individuals in its field. Thus

D45. $\ulcorner$Connex $R\urcorner$ may abbreviate $\ulcorner(x)(y)((C'R\ x$. C'$R\ y) \supset (x = y \lor Rxy \lor Ryx))\urcorner$.

And a relation is then *serial* if and only if it is irreflexive, transitive, and connected.

D46. $\ulcorner$Ser $R\urcorner$ abbreviates $\ulcorner$(Irrefl R . Trans R . Connex $R)\urcorner$.

It is regarded as *antisymmetric* or *partially symmetric* if (in effect) it is asymmetric for distinct individuals. Thus

D47. $\ulcorner$PSym $R\urcorner$ may abbreviate $\ulcorner(x)(y)((Rxy$. $\sim x = y) \supset \sim Ryx)\urcorner$.

Finally, a relation is regarded as a *partial ordering* if it is reflexive, transitive, and partially symmetric, and a *simple ordering* if it is a partial ordering and is connected.

D48. ⌜POrd R⌝ abbreviates ⌜(Refl R . Trans R . PSym R)⌝

and

D49. ⌜SOrd R⌝ abbreviates ⌜(POrd R . Connex R)⌝.

The following principles show how these kinds of virtual relations are interconnected.

TR148. ⊢ Ser R ≡ (Asym R . Trans R . Connex R).

TR149. ⊢ Ser R ≡ (Connex R . Irrefl (R/R) . Irrefl $((R/R)/R)$).

TR150. ⊢ Ser R ⊃ (D‘R = Λ ∨ (Ex)(Ey)($\sim x = y$. D‘R x . D‘R y)).

TR151. ⊢ POrd R ⊃ (R/R) = R.

TR152. ⊢ SOrd R ≡ (Refl R . Trans R . PSym R . Connex R).

TR153. ⊢ SOrd R ≡ SOrd ⌣R.

TR153. ⊢ SOrd R ≡ SOrd ⌣R.

TR154. ⊢ SOrd R ⊃ D‘R = Ɑ‘R.

TR155. ⊢ (SOrd R . C‘R x . C‘R y . $\sim x = y$) ⊃ (Rxy ≡ $\sim Ryx$).

TR156. ⊢ (SOrd R . S ⊂ R . Refl S . Connex S) ⊃ SOrd S.

TR157. ⊢ (SOrd R . $(x)(y)(Sxy$ ≡ $(R⌊F)xy))$ ⊃ SOrd S.

L. TRIADIC RELATIONS

Some fundamental notions in the theory of triadic relations may now be considered very briefly.

The basic definition *D15b* of three-place abstraction and the principle *TRelAbst2* have already been given. A basis for the theory of triadic relations is thus at hand. Identity and inclusion as relations between triadic relations may be introduced in obvious fashion, just as for dyadic relations, but with three arguments. And similarly for the Boolean notions. Thus principles (numbered *in absentia TR158–TR227*) analogous to *TR1–TR70* may easily be proved.

More interesting notions emerge only when domains, counterdomains, and so on, are brought in. In the case of a triadic relation, there is a domain, a *middle* domain, and a counterdomain. Let 'U' and 'W' be used now as informal variables for three-place abstracts, and 'U' and 'W' to stand for virtual triadic relations. Then

D50a. $\ulcorner D'U \urcorner$ may abbreviate $\ulcorner \{x3(Ey)(Ez)Uxyz\} \urcorner$,

D50b. $\ulcorner M'U \urcorner$ may abbreviate $\ulcorner \{y3(Ex)(Ez)Uxyz\} \urcorner$,

and

D50c. $\ulcorner \text{Ⅎ}'U \urcorner$ may abbreviate $\ulcorner \{z3(Ex)(Ey)Uxyz\} \urcorner$.

The campus of a triadic relation is then the logical sum of the three.

D50d. $\ulcorner C'U \urcorner$ abbreviates $\ulcorner (D'U \cup (M'U \cup \text{Ⅎ}'U)) \urcorner$.

Extended principles (*TR228–TR233 in absentia*) analogous to *TR71–TR76* may now be proved.

Let G be the triadic relation of giving so that '$Gxyz$' expresses that x gives y to z. D'G is then the virtual class of givers, M'G is that of gifts, and Ⅎ'G is that of recipients of gifts.

A dyadic relation has only one converse. A triadic relation has five, however, depending upon the order of the arguments.[1] Thus

D51a. $\ulcorner \overset{1}{\smile}U \urcorner$ may abbreviate $\ulcorner \{xyz3Uxzy\} \urcorner$,

D51b. $\ulcorner \overset{2}{\smile}U \urcorner$ abbreviates $\ulcorner \{xyz3Uyxz\} \urcorner$,

D51c. $\ulcorner \overset{3}{\smile}U \urcorner$ abbreviates $\ulcorner \{xyz3Uyzx\} \urcorner$,

D51d. $\ulcorner \overset{4}{\smile}U \urcorner$ abbreviates $\ulcorner \{xyz3Uzxy\} \urcorner$,

---

1. Cf. C. S. Peirce, *Collected Papers* (Cambridge: Harvard University Press, 1931–1958), Vol. III, 317.

and

D51e. $\ulcorner\overset{5}{\smile}U\urcorner$ abbreviates $\ulcorner\{xyz3Uzyx\}\urcorner$.

The order in which these are defined is of course arbitrary.

Consider again the relation G of giving. $\overset{1}{\smile}$G is the relation among x, y, and z of x's giving z a gift y; $\overset{2}{\smile}$G is the relation of a gift x's being given by y to z; $\overset{3}{\smile}$G, that of x's receiving a gift z from y; $\overset{4}{\smile}$G, that of a gift x's being given by z to y; and $\overset{5}{\smile}$G, that of z's giving y to x. These are of course all quite distinct relations, and a suitable notation is needed to distinguish them.

It is of interest to note the following principles.

TR234a. $\vdash D'U = D^{\cdot\overset{1}{\smile}}U = M^{\cdot\overset{2}{\smile}}U = \mathsf{G}^{\cdot\overset{3}{\smile}}U = M^{\cdot\overset{4}{\smile}}U = \mathsf{G}^{\cdot\overset{5}{\smile}}U.$

TR234b. $\vdash M'U = \mathsf{G}^{\cdot\overset{1}{\smile}}U = D^{\cdot\overset{2}{\smile}}U = D^{\cdot\overset{3}{\smile}}U = \mathsf{G}^{\cdot\overset{4}{\smile}}U = M^{\cdot\overset{5}{\smile}}U.$

TR234c. $\vdash \mathsf{G}'U = M^{\cdot\overset{1}{\smile}}U = {}^{\cdot\overset{2}{\smile}}U = M^{\cdot\overset{3}{\smile}}U = D^{\cdot\overset{4}{\smile}}U = D^{\cdot\overset{5}{\smile}}U.$

TR234d. $\vdash C'U = C^{\cdot\overset{1}{\smile}}U = C^{\cdot\overset{2}{\smile}}U = C^{\cdot\overset{3}{\smile}}U = C^{\cdot\overset{4}{\smile}}U = C^{\cdot\overset{5}{\smile}}U.$

Principles (*TR283–TR288 in absentia*) analogous to *TR78–TR83* are provable for each kind of converse. In addition the following principle *inter alia* is not without interest.

TR289. $\vdash U = \overset{5\ 1\ 4}{\smile\smile\smile}U . U = \overset{3\ 5\ 2}{\smile\smile\smile}U . U = \overset{4\ 3\ 5}{\smile\smile\smile}U.$

For triadic relations there are eight relative products.

D52a. $\ulcorner(W/_1U)\urcorner$ abbreviates $\ulcorner\{xyz3(Ex')(Wxyx' . Uyx'z)\}\urcorner$,

D52b. $\ulcorner(W/_2U)\urcorner$ abbreviates $\ulcorner\{xyz3(Ex')(Wxyx' . Ux'y'z)\}\urcorner$,

D52c. $\ulcorner(W/_3U)\urcorner$ abbreviates $\ulcorner\{xyz3(Ex')(Ey)(Wxyx' . Ux'y'z)\}\urcorner$,

D52d. $\ulcorner(W/_4U)\urcorner$ abbreviates $\ulcorner\{xyz3(Ex')(Ey')(Wxyx' . Uy'x'z)\}\urcorner$,

D52e. $\ulcorner(W/_5U)\urcorner$ abbreviates $\ulcorner\{xyz3(\mathrm{E}x')(\mathrm{E}y')$
$(Wxx'y'$. $Ux'yz)\}\urcorner$,
D52f. $\ulcorner(W/_6U)\urcorner$ abbreviates $\ulcorner\{xyz3(\mathrm{E}x')(\mathrm{E}y')$
$(Wxx'y'$. $Uy'yz)\}\urcorner$,
D52g. $\ulcorner(W/_7U)\urcorner$ abbreviates $\ulcorner\{xyz3(\mathrm{E}x')(\mathrm{E}y')$
$(Wxx'y'$. $Uyx'z)\}\urcorner$,
D52h. $\ulcorner(W/_8U)\urcorner$ abbreviates $\ulcorner\{xyz3(\mathrm{E}x')(\mathrm{E}y')$
$(Wxx'y'$. $Uyy'z)\}\urcorner$.

Also there are of course various kinds of mixed relative products of triadic with dyadic relations. For example, the relation among x, y, and z where x gives y to the father of z is a certain relative product of the giving relation with that of being the father-of.

Let '$Jxyz$' express that x is jealous of y's affection for z. Then '$(G/_6J)xyz$' expresses that x gives something to someone who is jealous of y's affection for z. '$(J/_3G)xyz$' expresses that x is jealous of y's affection for someone who gives something to z. '$(G/_2J)xyz$' expresses that x gives y to someone of whom someone is jealous because of his affection for z. And so on.

A notation for triadic relations with limited domains, middle domains, counterdomains, and fields may easily be given.

Similarly various descriptions analogous to '(R^cx)' may be defined.

D53a. $\ulcorner U^{1c}xy\urcorner$ abbreviates $\ulcorner(\imath\{z3Uzxy\})\urcorner$,
D53b. $\ulcorner U^{2c}xy\urcorner$ abbreviates $\ulcorner(\imath\{z3Uxzy\})\urcorner$,

and

D53c. $\ulcorner U^{3c}xy\urcorner$ abbreviates $\ulcorner(\imath\{z3Uxyz\})\urcorner$.

$G^{1c}xy$ is the giver of x to y; $G^{2c}xy$ is the gift given y by x; and $G^{3c}xy$ is the recipient of x's gift y.

Enough has been shown to see how the theory of triadic virtual relations may be developed within the preceding framework. Nothing new in principle emerges, merely many notions of interest wherever triadic relations are needed in practice.

In similar fashion we could go on to the theory of quadratic relations, and so on, but this scarcely seems necessary at this point. The entire theories of relations of higher degree, of polyadic relations, may be developed on the preceding framework. No doubt some extremely interesting notions would emerge if the subject were to be developed in detail.

A predicate for virtual-relation existence has not been introduced. By analogy to *D14a* we may let

D54a. 　　⌐E!*R*⌐　abbreviate　⌐(E*x*)(E*y*)*Rxy*⌐,

D54b. 　　⌐E!*U*⌐　abbreviate　⌐(E*x*)(E*y*)(E*z*)*Uxyz*⌐,

and so on. Clearly then

TR290. 　　⊢ E!*R* ≡ E!D'*R* ≡ E!ᗡ'*R*.

TR291. 　　⊢ E!*U* ≡ E!D'*U* ≡ E!M'*U* ≡ E!ᗡ'*U*.

The 'E!' is of course now multiply ambiguous, but the usage intended is always clear from the context.

For specificity, suppose k is the degree of the predicate of greatest degree admitted as a primitive. Every primitive predicate has a degree and since only a finite number is admitted, there must be such a k. In practice we may think of the theory of virtual relations as developed only for relations of degree n where $2 \leq n \leq k$. Although this supposition is not necessary, it will facilitate some subsequent definitions in later chapters.

This much must suffice for our brief sketch of the theory of virtual relations. It is interesting to emphasize again that the entire theory is merely a development of quantification theory with the addition of identity and one-place abstraction. All the foregoing principles are thus provable solely on the basis of *R1–R6*, *Abst*, *IdR1–IdR2*, *MP*, and *Gen*. It is perhaps surprising that so much can be gotten out of so little. Also it is of interest to observe that all of the theory has been provided without the use of real classes or relations. Again, it is surprising that so much can be achieved without them, for they are usually thought indispensable for the foregoing theory.

CHAPTER III

INDIVIDUALS, PARTS, AND WHOLES

The word 'individual' has been used above as the most general term for whatever objects are taken as values for variables. Nothing has been said about the internal structure of individuals, nor of the relations they may bear each other. Especially important among such relations is that of *part-to-whole*. Traditionally the so-called *calculus of individuals* has been concerned with this relation, and the calculus of individuals is now to be added to the preceding framework. Surely this calculus is of great interest philosophically and in fact is almost always needed in philosophical analyses of almost any kind.[1]

---

1. See especially H. S. Leonard and N. Goodman, "The Calculus of Individuals and Its Uses," *The Journal of Symbolic Logic* 5 (1940):45–55; Appendix E by A. Tarski in J. H. Woodger, *The Axiomatic Method in Biology* (Cambridge: Cambridge University Press, 1937); and N. Goodman, *The Structure of Appearance* (Cambridge: Harvard University Press, 1951), pp 42–51.

A.   PART-TO-WHOLE

Let 'P' hereafter be significant primitively so that 'Pxy' is a formula expressing that the individual x is a part of the individual y.

To the preceding definition of 'formula' (in I, A and E) the following clause is now added.

7.   If x and y are terms, $\ulcorner Pxy \urcorner$ is a formula.

Just as one must be very clear about identity, so one must be very clear as to just what is assumed concerning the relation of part-to-whole. Just as *IdR1–IdR2* give the fundamental properties of identity, so now various rules concerning P are to be given. The first of these is the *Principle of Total Reflexivity for P*.

IndR1.   ⊢ TotRefl P.

The next is the *Principle of Transitivity for P*.

IndR2.   ⊢ Trans P.

And the third is the *Principle of Partial Symmetry for P*.

IndR3.   ⊢ PSym P.

The following theorem then immediately obtains.

TInd1.   ⊢ $Pxy \equiv (z)(Pzx \supset Pzy)$.

An individual x is said to be a *proper part* of an individual y if and only if Pxy but not Pyx. Thus

DInd1.   'PP' abbreviates $\ulcorner \{xy \mathbf{3}(Pxy \ . \ \sim Pyx)\} \urcorner$.

Clearly then the following hold.

TInd2.   ⊢ TotIrrefl PP.
TInd3.   ⊢ Trans PP.
TInd4.   ⊢ Asym PP.
TInd5a.   ⊢ $(PPxy \ . \ Pyz) \supset PPxz$.
TInd5b.   ⊢ $(PPxy \ . \ Pyz) \supset Pxz$.
TInd5c.   ⊢ $(Pxy \ . \ PPyz) \supset PPxz$.
TInd5d.   ⊢ $(Pxy \ . \ PPyz) \supset Pxz$.
TInd5e.   ⊢ $(PPxy \ . \ PPyz) \supset Pxz$.

Note of course that the other combination does not in general obtain.

TInd5f.   ⊢ ∼ $(x)(y)(z)((Pxy \ . \ Pyz) \supset PPxz)$.

Consider next the notion of a *unit* or *atomic* individual. Let

DInd2.   'At' abbreviates ⌜$\{x3(\sim \ (y)Pxy \ . \ (y)((\sim$
$(z)Pyz \ . \ Pyx) \supset Pxy))\}$⌝.

According to this definition, an individual x is an atom, or is atomic, if and only if the following two conditions hold: (i) it is not the case that it is a part of every individual, and (ii) given any y that is a part of x but is not a part of every individual, then x is a part of it.

The following principles hold concerning atoms.

TInd6a.   ⊢ $(At \ x \ . \ At \ y) \supset (Pxy \equiv x = y)$.
TInd6b.   ⊢ $(At \ x \ . \ At \ y) \supset (Pxy \equiv Pyx)$.
TInd6c.   ⊢ ∼ $At \ x \supset ((y)Pxy \ \lor \ (Ey)(\sim \ (z)Pyz \ .$
$PPyx))$.

Two individuals are said to *overlap* if and only if they contain a common atomic part.

DInd3.   'O' abbreviates ⌜$\{xy3(Ez)(At \ z \ . \ Pzx \ .$
$Pzy)\}$⌝.

And they are said to be *discrete* if and only if they do not overlap.

DInd4.   'D' abbreviates ⌜$\{xy3\sim Oxy\}$⌝.

Governing O and D the following principles obtain.

TInd7.   ⊢ Sym O.
TInd8.   ⊢ $(x)(z)((At \ z \ . \ Pzx) \supset Oxx)$.
TInd9.   ⊢ ∼ Trans O . ∼ Intrans O.
TInd10.   ⊢ $(x)(z)((At \ z \ . \ Pzx) \supset \ \sim Dxx)$.
TInd11.   ⊢ Sym D.

B. ATOMIC SUMMATION

Every individual, however simple or complex, may be regarded as composed or built up of atoms. In a real sense, each individual may be regarded as the sum of its atomic parts. It is convenient therefore to introduce primitively a notation for the idiom 'the sum of all atomic individuals x such that $--x--$', where '$--x--$' is a sentential function of the one variable 'x'. Let '$(x1---x--)$' be used now for this idiom. The '1' here is of course not the numeral for the integral number one, but for an operation of *atomic summation*.

Let the notion of *term* now be extended to include expressions of the form $\ulcorner(x1A)\urcorner$ where x is a variable and A of course a formula. To make this statement is easy enough, but actually it requires a further extension in the definition of 'formula'. These new expressions are allowed now to be terms and formulae of course are allowed to contain them. Also the definition of 'term' now requires reference to formulae. Because of these complications, let us start afresh and remind ourselves of what now the formulae and terms are allowed to be. In other words, the following stipulations are adopted.

1.   Any n-place, nonlogical, primitive predicate followed by n terms is a formula, for $1 \leq n \leq k$, where k is the degree of the primitive predicate of highest degree admitted.

2.   If A is a formulae, so is $\ulcorner \sim A \urcorner$.

3.   If A and B are formulae, so is $\ulcorner(A \lor B)\urcorner$.

4.   If A is a formula and x a variable, $\ulcorner(x)A\urcorner$ is a formula.

5.   If A is a formula, y a variable, and x a term, then $\ulcorner\{y3A\}x\urcorner$ is a formula.

6.   If x and y are terms, then $\ulcorner x = y \urcorner$ is a formula.

7.   If x and y are terms, then $\ulcorner Pxy \urcorner$ is a formula.

8.   If A is a formula and x a variable, then $\ulcorner(x1A)\urcorner$ is a term.

9.   If x is a variable or primitive individual constant, then it is a term.

These nine stipulations are to be taken together simultaneously as providing a recursive or inductive definition of 'formula' and 'term'. (For a more rigorous definition, see Chapter V below.)

Of course 'A', 'B', and so on, are now to be understood as informal syntactical variables for formulae in this extended sense, and 'x', 'y', and so on, for terms in this extended sense.

But as a result of these definitions, the abstracts are also now extended, and 'F', 'G', and so on, must be allowed to range over them in this extended sense. Hence of course $R1$–$R6$, $IdR1$–$IdR2$, $Abst$, $IndR1$–$IndR3$, Gen, and MP are all now extended accordingly. Also the notion of a bound variable must be extended. Thus, for example, all occurrences of x in a context $\ulcorner(x1A)\urcorner$ are now regarded as bound. Also an occurrence of a term $\ulcorner(x1A)\urcorner$ in a formula B is now said to be a free occurrence of $\ulcorner(x1A)\urcorner$ provided every free occurrence of a variable in $\ulcorner(x1A)\urcorner$ is also a free occurrence of that variable in B. Also $R5$ now reads:

$\vdash (x)A \supset B$, where B is like A except in containing an individual constant, free occurrences of a variable, or free occurrences of an expression of the form $\ulcorner(y1C)\urcorner$ wherever there are free occurrences of x in A.

Governing atomic summation certain principles are needed. The first is the *Principle of Atomic Sums as Parts*,

$IndR4.$ $\quad \vdash P(x1Fx)y \equiv (x)((\text{At } x \, . \, Fx) \supset Pxy)$,

and the second is the *Principle of Atomic Sums as Wholes*,

$IndR5.$ $\quad \vdash Px(y1Fy) \equiv (y)((\text{At } y \, . \, Pyx) \supset Fy)$.

The following principles help to characterize atomic summation.

$TInd12a.$ $\quad \vdash Px(y1Pyx)$.
$TInd12b.$ $\quad \vdash P(y1Pyx)x$.
$TInd12c.$ $\quad \vdash x = (y1Pyx)$.
$TInd13.$ $\quad \vdash (x1A) = (y1B)$, if B differs from A only in containing free occurrences of y wherever and only where there are free occurrences of x in A.
$TInd14a.$ $\quad \vdash (x)(A \supset B) \supset P(x1A)(x1B)$.
$TInd14b.$ $\quad \vdash (x)(A \equiv B) \supset (x1A) = (x1B)$.
$TInd15.$ $\quad \vdash \text{At } x \supset (Px(y1(A \vee B)) \equiv (Px(y1A) \vee Px(y1B)))$.
$TInd16.$ $\quad \vdash \text{At } x \supset (Px(y1\sim A) \equiv \sim Px(y1A))$.
$TInd17.$ $\quad \vdash (z)Px(y1A) \equiv Px(y1(z)A)$.

These principles are comparable with analogous theorems concerning abstraction. Also

TInd18. $\quad \vdash Pxy \equiv (z)((At\ z\ .\ Pzx) \supset Pzy).$

TInd19. $\quad \vdash x = y \equiv (z)((At\ z \supset (Pzx \equiv Pzy)).$

C. BOOLEAN ELEMENTS

It should be recalled that all expressions of the form $\ulcorner(x1\text{--}x\text{--})\urcorner$ are now regarded as terms where $\ulcorner\text{--}x\text{--}\urcorner$ is a sentential form containing x as a free variable. By filling in the blanks here in various ways all manner of special terms may be introduced. Thus various Boolean elements may now be introduced.

In particular expressions for *sums* and *products* may be defined as follows.

DInd5. $\quad \ulcorner(x \cup y)\urcorner$ abbreviates $\ulcorner(z1(Pzx \vee Pzy))\urcorner$

and

DInd6. $\quad \ulcorner(x \cap y)\urcorner$ abbreviates $\ulcorner(z1(Pzx\ .\ Pzy))\urcorner.$

Thus $(x \cup y)$ is the individual consisting of all atoms that are parts of x or of y, and $(x \cap y)$, of all atoms that are parts of both x and y. These notions are of course comparable to the Boolean sums and products of virtual classes and virtual relations.

In a similar fashion the *negative* of each individual is admitted. Just as there is a negative to each virtual class or relation, so is there a negative to each individual. Thus

DInd7. $\quad \ulcorner -x \urcorner$ may abbreviate $\ulcorner(y1 \sim Pyx)\urcorner.$

The negative individual $-x$ is the sum of all atoms that are not parts of x, in other words, all the rest of the cosmos, the entire cosmos excluding x.

Consider now the individual $(x1x = x)$, the sum of all self-identical atoms. Clearly such an individual comprises everything. It may be regarded as the "world" or "cosmic" individual. Let

DInd8. $\quad$ 'W' abbreviate $\ulcorner(x1x = x)\urcorner.$

Just as the universal virtual class V is identical with $\{x3x = x\}$, although not by definition, so is the world individual here identified with $(x1x = x)$.

Similarly there is a null individual, the sum of all atoms such that $\sim x = x$. Thus

DInd9.   'N'   may abbreviate   '$-W$'.

Again, just as the null virtual class Λ is identical with $\{x3\sim x = x\}$, so the null entity may be taken as either $-W$, or, equivalently, as $(x1 \sim x = x)$.

D.   EXISTENCE PRINCIPLES

Little has been said thus far as to what is assumed to exist. Clearly, however, the following principles now all hold in virtue of *IdR1*.

TInd20a. $\vdash (Ex)x = (y1A)$.
TInd20b. $\vdash (Ex)x = (y \cup z)$.
TInd20c. $\vdash (Ex)x = (y \cap z)$.
TInd20d. $\vdash (Ex)x = -y$.
TInd20e. $\vdash (Ex)x = W$.
TInd20f. $\vdash (Ex)x = N$.

These various existence principles, although strong, are in no way surprising. Just as in arithmetic given any two integers m and n the sum $(m + n)$ is assumed to exist, so here, given any two individuals x and y their sum $(x \cup y)$ is assumed to exist. And similarly for products and negatives.

To complete the list of existence principles, two other assumptions are needed, the *Principle of Atomic Parts* and the *Principle of Non-Nullity*.

IndR6. $\vdash \sim x = N \supset (Ey)(At\ y\ .\ Pyx)$.
IndR7. $\vdash \sim (x)x = N$.

Every non-null individual has at least one atomic part, and not all individuals are null.

Various Boolean principles may now be proven on the basis of these definitions and principles, in particular, principles analogous to *TA21 et seq.* with 'P' supplanting '$\subset$'. In addition, the following may be noted.

TInd21a. $\vdash (\mathrm{E}x)\mathrm{At}\ x.$

TInd21b. $\vdash\ \sim x = -x.$

TInd21c. $\vdash\ \sim \mathrm{W} = \mathrm{N}.$

TInd22a. $\vdash (x)A \supset (x1A) = \mathrm{W}.$

TInd22b. $\vdash\ \sim (\mathrm{E}x)A \supset (x1A) = \mathrm{N}.$

TInd23a. $\vdash x = \mathrm{N} \equiv (y)\mathrm{P}xy.$

TInd23b. $\vdash x = \mathrm{W} \equiv (y)\mathrm{P}yx.$

TInd24. $\vdash (x \cap -y) = \mathrm{N} \equiv \mathrm{P}xy.$

TInd25a. $\vdash\ \sim (\mathrm{E}x)\mathbf{G}x \supset\ \sim \mathbf{G}\mathrm{N}.$

TInd26a. $\vdash \mathrm{VN} . \mathrm{VW}.$

TInd26b. $\vdash\ \sim \Lambda\mathrm{N} .\ \sim \Lambda\mathrm{W}.$

TInd27a. $\vdash x = \mathrm{N} \supset\ \sim \mathrm{At}\ x.$

TInd27b. $\vdash x = \mathrm{N} \equiv (y)(\mathrm{P}yx \supset y = \mathrm{N}).$

TInd27c. $\vdash x = \mathrm{N} \supset\ \sim (\mathrm{E}y)(\mathrm{At}\ y . \mathrm{P}yx).$

TInd27d. $\vdash (\sim \mathrm{At}\ x .\ \sim x = \mathrm{N}) \supset (\mathrm{E}y)(\sim y = \mathrm{N} . \mathrm{PP}yx).$

TInd28a. $\vdash (x)\sim \mathrm{ON}x.$

TInd28b. $\vdash (x)\mathrm{DN}x.$

TInd29. $\vdash (\sim x = \mathrm{N} .\ \sim \mathrm{At}\ x) \supset (\mathrm{E}y)(\mathrm{At}\ y . \mathrm{P}yx .\ \sim (x \cap -y) = \mathrm{N}).$

TInd30. $\vdash (\sim x = \mathrm{N} .\ \sim \mathrm{At}\ x) \supset (\mathrm{E}y)(\mathrm{E}z)(\sim y = z . \mathrm{At}\ y . \mathrm{At}\ z . \mathrm{P}yx . \mathrm{P}zx).$

TInd31. $\vdash (\sim x = \mathrm{N} .\ \sim \mathrm{At}\ x .\ \sim (\mathrm{E}y)(\mathrm{E}z)(\mathrm{At}\ y . \mathrm{At}\ z . \mathrm{P}yx . \mathrm{P}zx .\ \sim y = z .$
$(w)((\mathrm{At}\ w . \mathrm{P}wx) \supset (w = y \lor w = z)))) \supset$
$(\mathrm{E}y)(\mathrm{E}z)(\mathrm{E}w)(\mathrm{At}\ y . \mathrm{At}\ z . \mathrm{At}\ w . \mathrm{P}yx . \mathrm{P}zx . \mathrm{P}wx .$
$\sim y = z .\ \sim z = w .\ \sim y = w).$

TInd32. $\vdash (x)(\sim x = \mathrm{N} \supset \mathrm{OW}x).$

TInd33. $\vdash (x)(\sim x = \mathrm{N} \supset\ \sim \mathrm{DW}x).$

E.   EXISTENCE PREDICATES

With the null entity available, another predicate for existence may be defined, in addition to those given by *D14a, D14b, D14c,* and *D54a* and *D54b*. One may let

DInd10.   ⌜E!x⌝ abbreviate ⌜$\sim\ x\ =\ $N⌝,

so that x exists if and only if x is not the null entity.

Care should be taken hereafter to distinguish amongst the following:

$$⌜E!F⌝,$$
$$⌜E!R⌝,$$
$$⌜E!(\varepsilon F)⌝,$$
$$⌜E!(\imath F)⌝,$$

and now

$$⌜E!x⌝.$$

All of these uses of 'E!' are in effect predicates for existence of different kinds. Virtual-class and virtual-relation existence are very different from individual existence, and this latter is now of three kinds, depending upon whether the argument is a term (a variable or an individual constant or an expression of the form ⌜$(x1A)$⌝), or an expression of the form ⌜(εF)⌝ or ⌜$(\imath F)$⌝.

First let us consider some principles based on *DInd10* and then go on to reflect upon some stronger senses of existence. Clearly

TInd34.   ⊢ (E!x ∨ E!y) ⊃ E!(x ∪ y).
TInd35.   ⊢ (Ez)(At z . Pzx . Pzy) ⊃ E!(x ∩ y).
TInd36.   ⊢ (E!x . $\sim\ x\ =\ $W) ⊃ E!$-x$.
TInd37a.   ⊢ E!W.
TInd37b.   ⊢ $\sim$ E!N.

Suppose now that every member x of F is such that E!x. F need not then exist in the sense of having members but only in having all its members (if any) exist. Such a virtual class might be said to have *perexistence*. Thus

DInd11a.   ⌜PerE!F⌝ may abbreviate ⌜$(x)(Fx$ ⊃ E!$x)$⌝.

Similarly

DInd11b. ⌜PerE!R⌝ may abbreviate ⌜(x_1) ...
$(x_n)(Rx_1 ... x_n \supset (E!x_1 . E!x_2 . .... . E!x_n))$⌝, where R is
an *n*-place primitive predicate or an *n*-place abstract.

As a matter of fact, the virtual classes or relations for which
the primitive predicates stand almost always are such as to
exist in the sense of having members or relata. If they did not
they would not be of much interest. Their role would be completely usurped by reference to the null virtual class, the null
virtual dyadic relation, and so on, instead. Even so, that they
exist need not be explicitly assumed, for the nonlogical axioms
are usually such that this follows. Now that the null individual
is available, however, it is interesting to note that all the virtual
classes or relations for which the primitive predicates stand
should be such also as to *perexist*. The null individual should
not be assumed to have any nonlogical properties, so to speak,
but only those laid down in the calculus of individuals. Thus
the following additional *Principle of Perexistence* is needed.

IndR8. ⊢ PerE!R, where R is any *n*-place primitive
predicate.

Clearly the null individual is not to weigh so many grams, it is
not to be green or yellow, it is not to be beautiful or good, and
so on.

A still stronger kind of existence for a virtual class or relation
can now be defined if it both exists and perexists. This may be
called 'total existence'. Thus

DInd12a. ⌜TotE!F⌝ may abbreviate ⌜(E!F .
PerE!F)⌝,

and

DInd12b. ⌜TotE!R⌝ abbreviates ⌜(E!R . PerE!R)⌝, if
R is an *n*-place primitive predicate or an *n*-place abstract.

Note that

TInd38a. ⊢ E! V . ~ PerE! V . ~ TotE!V.
TInd38b. ⊢ ~E!Λ . PerE!Λ . ~ TotE!Λ.

TInd39.   ⊢ TotE!At.

TInd40.   ⊢ (E!x . $F = \{x\}$) ⊃ TotE!F.

TInd41a.   ⊢ E!$\{N\}$. ∼ PerE!$\{N\}$.

TInd41b.   ⊢ TotE!(V ∩ −$\{N\}$).

Also now that the null individual is available, both selective and singular descriptions may take on a new look if desired. Descriptions, either selective or singular, that fail to describe for one reason or another may be regarded in effect as describing the null individual. Thus in place of *D12*, we could now have

D12'.   ⌜$G(\varepsilon F)$⌝ abbreviates ⌜((TotE!F . $(x)(Fx$ ⊃ Gx)) ∨ (∼ TotE!F . GN))⌝.

A given (εF) then is a member of G if and only if F totally exists and every member of F is a member of G, or F does not totally exist in which case the null individual is a member of G.

Similarly in place of *D13*, we could have now

D13'.   ⌜$G(\imath F)$⌝ for ⌜((TotE!F . $(x)(Fx$ ⊃ Gx). $(x)(y)((Fx . Fy)$ ⊃ $x = y$)) ∨ ((∼ TotE!F ∨ ∼ $(x)(Fx$ ⊃ Gx) ∨ ∼ $(x)(y)((Fx . Fy)$ ⊃ $x = y$)) . GN))⌝.

There are two further interesting notions of descriptional existence to consider, where the individual or individuals described are required to be non-null. Thus

DInd13a.   ⌜TotE!(εF)⌝ may abbreviate ⌜(E!(εF) . PerE!F)⌝ or ⌜TotE!F⌝,

and

DInd13b.   ⌜TotE!($\imath F$)⌝ may abbreviate ⌜(E!($\imath F$) . PerE!F)⌝.

Clearly then

TInd42.   ⊢ TotE!(ε−$\{N\}$).

TInd43.   ⊢ (E!x . $F = \{x\}$) ⊃ TotE!($\imath F$).

TInd44.   ⊢ TotE!(εAt).

F.   FUSIONS AND NUCLEI

Two additional notions in the calculus of individuals are of interest, that of the *fusion* and of the *nucleus* of a virtual class. The former notion is also of great utility in all manner of applications.

Given a virtual class F, its fusion is the sum of all atoms that are parts of members of F. Thus

DInd14. $\ulcorner(\text{Fu}\,{}^{\backprime}F)\urcorner$ abbreviates $\ulcorner(x1(\text{E}y)(Fy \;.\; Pxy))\urcorner$.

And the nucleus of F is the sum of all atoms that are parts of *all* members of F.

DInd15. $\ulcorner(\text{Nu}\,{}^{\backprime}F)\urcorner$ abbreviates $\ulcorner(x1(y)(Fy \supset Pxy))\urcorner$.

Fusions and nuclei are analogous to logical sums and products of virtual classes. The fusion of F is in fact the logical sum of all members of F. The nucleus is rather the logical product of those members. Clearly now

TInd45. $\vdash x = (\text{Fu}\,{}^{\backprime}F) \equiv (y)(\text{At } y \supset (Pyx \equiv (\text{E}z) (Fz \;.\; Pyz)))$.

TInd46. $\vdash x = (\text{Nu}\,{}^{\backprime}F) \equiv (y)(\text{At } y \supset (Pyx \equiv (z) (Fz \supset Pyz)))$.

TInd47. $\vdash x = (\text{Fu}\,{}^{\backprime}F) \equiv (y)(\text{At } y \supset (Dyx \equiv (z) (Fz \supset Dyz)))$.

TInd48. $\vdash x = (\text{Fu}\,{}^{\backprime}F) \equiv (y)(\text{At } y \supset (Oyx \equiv (\text{E}z) (Fz \;.\; Oyz)))$.

TInd49a. $\vdash (x \cup y) = (\text{Fu}\,{}^{\backprime}\{x,y\})$.

TInd49b. $\vdash (x \cap y) = (\text{Nu}\,{}^{\backprime}\{x,y\})$.

TInd49c. $\vdash x = (\text{Fu}\,{}^{\backprime}\{x\}) \;.\; x = (\text{Nu}\,{}^{\backprime}\{x\})$.

TInd50. $\vdash -x = (\text{Fu}\,{}^{\backprime}\{y3(\text{At } y \;.\; \sim Pyx)\})$.

TInd51a. $\vdash \text{W} = (\text{Fu}\,{}^{\backprime}\text{V}) \;.\; \text{W} = (\text{Nu}\,{}^{\backprime}\Lambda)$.

TInd51b. $\vdash \text{N} = (\text{Fu}\,{}^{\backprime}\Lambda) \;.\; \text{N} = (\text{Nu}\,{}^{\backprime}\text{V})$.

TInd52. $\vdash \sim F = \Lambda \supset P(\text{Nu}\,{}^{\backprime}F)(\text{Fu}\,{}^{\backprime}F)$.

TInd53. $\vdash \sim F = \Lambda \equiv \text{E}!(\text{Fu}\,{}^{\backprime}F)$.

TInd54a. $\vdash F \subset G \supset P(\text{Fu}\,{}^{\backprime}F)(\text{Fu}\,{}^{\backprime}G)$.

TInd54b. $\vdash F = G \supset (\text{Fu}\,{}^{\backprime}F) = (\text{Fu}\,{}^{\backprime}G)$.

TInd55a. $\vdash \text{W} = (\text{Fu}\,{}^{\backprime}\text{At})$.

TInd55b. $\vdash \text{N} = (\text{Nu}\,{}^{\backprime}\text{At})$.

TInd56.   ⊢ At $x \supset (Fx \equiv Px(\mathrm{Fu}`F))$.
TInd57.   ⊢ $Fx \supset Px(\mathrm{Fu}`F)$.

G.   SOME ALTERNATIVES

The way in which the calculus of individuals is formulated here is by no means the only one. There are many alternatives, a few of which may now be mentioned.

Expressions of the form $\ulcorner(x1A)\urcorner$ were taken as primitives above, in particular as terms. This is not essential, however, and *IndR4* and *IndR5* could be transformed into definitions, in effect defining occurrences of expressions of the form $\ulcorner(x1A)\urcorner$ as arguments of 'P'. Other contexts of occurrence could then be introduced by definitions *in usu*. For this one could let

$$\ulcorner x = (y1A)\urcorner \quad \text{abbreviate} \quad \ulcorner(Px(y1A) \ . \ P(y1A)x)\urcorner,$$

and

$$\ulcorner F(x1A)\urcorner \quad \text{abbreviate} \quad \ulcorner(Ey)(y = (x1A) \ . \ Fy)\urcorner.$$

And, more generally,

A   may abbreviate $\ulcorner(Ex_1)...(Ex_n)(x_1 = (y_11A_1) \ . \ . \ . \ . \ .$
$x_n = (y_n1A_n) \ . \ B)\urcorner$, where *B* contains occurrences of $x_1, \ldots ,$
x_n as distinct free variables, no bound variable of *B* is free in
$A_1, \ldots , A_n$, and *A* differs from *B* only in containing free
occurrences of $\ulcorner(y_11A_1)\urcorner, \ldots , \ulcorner(y_n1A_n)\urcorner$ respectively wherever there are free occurrences of $x_1, \ldots , x_n$ in *B*.

If these definitions are adopted, the actual development of the theory is somewhat complicated, and further existence assumptions are needed.

Both of the formulations above are such as to admit atoms and all the Boolean elements. Further alternatives arise by not admitting atoms but retaining all Boolean elements. Or one can drop some of the Boolean elements, in particular N, and thus admit only certain restricted products. If N is rejected then of course any individual $(x \cap -x)$ must be excluded also.

The formulations with atoms and Boolean elements seems the most natural, however, and also the most useful in applications. In particular N is a rather interesting kind of individual and will be given some important roles to play subsequently. Thus it seems desirable to retain it here. Also expressions of the form $\ulcorner(x\,1A)\urcorner$ have been taken as primitives because later in Chapter VI they will be regarded as expressions that *refer* in essentially the same way that individual constants do—provided, that is, that they contain no free variables. However there is nothing sacrosanct about the formulation above and others could also be made to work also provided that N is retained in some fashion.

H.   QUANTIFICATION AND
THE NULL INDIVIDUAL

With the null individual available, it is of interest to reflect for a moment upon quantification and the null domain.

A method of developing quantification theory without existence assumptions has been suggested by several writers. In particular it amounts to ruling out all theorems of the form

$$\ulcorner(Ex)(Qx \ \vee \ \sim Qx)\urcorner$$

and the like as principles of quantification.

Another method of providing for quantification without existence assumptions is available if the null individual be regarded as the only individual in the null domain. The null individual does not exist and hence its presence does not amount to an existence assumption.

All the theorems of standard quantification theory remain intact even if the domain of individuals taken as values for variables is empty. For now

$$\ulcorner(Ex)(Qx \ \vee \ \sim Qx)\urcorner$$

need not say anything about any existing individual but only about N. And the law

$$\ulcorner(x)Qx \ \supset \ (Ex)Qx\urcorner$$

states merely that if every individual is in Q, then something is, namely, N.

It might be thought strange to allow N to be "in" the empty domain. Perhaps, but no more strange than to admit N in the first place, and no more strange really than to admit a null virtual class or *n*-adic relation. The null individual does not exist, and the empty domain is empty of all existing individuals.[2]

2. Cf the author's "Of Time and the Null Individual," *The Journal of Philosophy* 62 (1965): 723–736. For some penetrating further comment, see James Scoggin, *Reference and Ontology*, in preparation.

CHAPTER IV

EVENTS, ACTS, STATES, AND PROCESSES

In the preceding chapter some steps were taken towards an analysis of the internal structure of individuals in terms of the relation of part to whole. Nothing further was said as to how individuals may be subdivided, as to what basic kinds there may be, and as to how these are all interrelated. Especially important here, of course, to name only a few, are concrete and physical objects, linguistic signs or expressions, mental and linguistic acts or occurrences, events, states, processes, and the like, and geometric objects, numbers, and entities and virtual classes and relations taken in intension. Of whatever entities there are, not all need be taken as fundamental, for some are merely special kinds of others.

The word 'event' may be taken with either a narrower or wider extension. The narrower extension would comprise only acts, states, processes, and the like, together with all complexes of them. The wider extension would comprise in addition all physical or "substantial" individuals or objects together with all sums, products, and so on, of them. Not too much significance resides in mere labels, and 'event' could be used in the same very wide sense 'individual' is. For the present, however, it is events in the narrower sense that are of special interest, events in the sense of happenings, acts, states, and processes.

In this chapter a sketch of a logical analysis of the internal structure of events taken in the narrower sense is presented. Precisely what linguistic forms are needed in the handling of them? How can these forms be provided on the basis of the foregoing? And what principles, in addition to the foregoing, are needed to characterize them?

A. EVENT-DESCRIPTIVE PREDICATES

The first step in reflecting upon the inner structure of events, acts, states, and processes is to consider a new kind of predicate, the so-called *event-descriptive* predicates. Events may then be regarded as the kinds of entities these predicates significantly apply to.

Suppose one wishes to say that an event is of such and such a kind, say an event of Caesar's speaking in the Forum. Let 'S' be a nonlogical predicate such that 'Scf' expresses that Caesar speaks in the Forum. Here 'c' and 'f' are specific individual constants for Caesar and the Forum respectively. To say that Scf is to say merely that Caesar speaks in the Forum, nothing else. However, he may speak in the Forum many times, sometimes in the morning, sometimes in the afternoon, sometimes more eloquently than at others, and so on. To provide for sentences expressing such circumstances, it is convenient to distinguish different acts or events, all of which could be described by saying that they are acts or events of *Caesar's-speaking-in-the-Forum*.

Let a new one-place predicate

$$'\langle S,c,f \rangle'$$

be formed now and regarded as applicable to an event e, so that

$$'\langle S,c,f \rangle e'$$

expresses that e is an event, one perhaps out of many, of Caesar's speaking in the Forum.

Note that the order in which the two arguments of 'S' are taken is important. To say 'Scf' is not after all to say 'Sfc', that the Forum speaks in Caesar. So here '$\langle S,c,f \rangle$' is a very different predicate from '$\langle S,f,c \rangle$'. Hence the use of the '$\langle$' and '$\rangle$' to indicate order is appropriate. And no ambiguity can ever result between an ordered couple or triple and so on (as introduced by *D32a*, etc.) and an event-descriptive predicate, for one of the factors of the latter must always be a virtual class or relation. Further, the event-descriptive predicates are significant with only one argument, whereas expressions for ordered couples are significant with two arguments, ordered triples three, and so on.

Not all predicates giving rise to an event-descriptive predicate need be of two places. Consider 'Demosthenes orates'. Let 'Od' express this symbolically in obvious fashion. Here too there are many different occasions of Demosthenes' orating. The formula

$$\text{'}\langle O,d \rangle e\text{'}$$

expresses that *e* is one of them.

And of course there are event-descriptive predicates arising from higher polyadic relations. Let 'Sbcf' express that Brutus stabs Caesar in the Forum. Then

$$\text{'}\langle S,b,c,f \rangle e\text{'}$$

expresses that *e* is a Brutus-stabbing-Caesar-in-the-Forum event.[1]

To the variables 'x', 'y', and so on, of the preceding chapters, let us now add 'e', 'e_1', 'e'', and so on, as variables for this new kind of entity. For perspicuity it is often convenient to use special kinds of variables for special kinds of entities. (Later special variables for linguistic expressions including numbers will be introduced.) To distinguish the two kinds of entities we may let 'Obj x' express primitively that x is an individual or object and 'Ev e' that e is an event. Ordinarily we will not write 'Obj e' or 'Ev x', although such locutions are significant,

---

1. For further preliminary discussion, see the author's *Belief, Existence, and Meaning*, pp. 191–211; *Logic, Language, and Metaphysics* (New York: New York University Press, 1971), pp. 101–116; and *Events, Reference, and Logical Form* (Washington, D.C.: The Catholic University of America Press, forthcoming).

the use of the variables 'e', and so on, being merely an informal convenience.

The calculus of individuals extends now to events, so that $\ulcorner Pee'\urcorner$, and the various locutions definable in terms of it, are now significant. The entire theory of the preceding chapter is thus extended to apply now to events and the like. Of course some slight technical changes must be made in the formal material there now that 'Obj' and 'Ev' are new primitives. But these pose no difficulty. We merely insert clauses of the form $\ulcorner Ev\ e\urcorner$ or take them as hypotheses, wherever needed. And similarly for $\ulcorner Obj\ x\urcorner$ with respect to the formulae and definitions of the preceding chapter. We have then both a calculus of individuals and a calculus of events, and both will be seen to be useful as we go on.

The only predicates of events thus far considered are the event-descriptive predicates. However, there are all manner of other predicates applicable to events also. One stabbing of Caesar may be more *violent* than another, one kissing of Portia more *passionate* than another, one reading of Sappho's *Ode to Aphrodite* more *beautiful* than another, and so on. Thus predicates 'MV', 'MP', and 'MB' are needed to express such circumstances, as two-place predicates of events. Also various further one-place predicates of events may be introduced, and these may be either primitive or defined.

Now that events and the like are explicitly under discussion, it is also appropriate to introduce a primitive predicate for the relation of being *temporally before* or *earlier than*. Let 'B' be this predicate so that 'Be_1e_2' expresses that e_1 is earlier than e_2 in an appropriate sense to be fixed axiomatically below.

Note that some of the individual constants admitted may now be such as to name events or sums of such. Consider, for example, 'World War II'. Usually constants for events are abbreviations for singular descriptions. Even 'World War II' is probably best construed as short for 'the second World War', an ordinal notion being involved here—see Chapter VII. Similarly 'the Punic Wars', 'the death of Socrates', 'the assassination of Caesar', and so on, are clearly singular descriptions for certain events or complexes of such.

To make explicit the full structure of the language, consider again the syntactical notions of 'formula' and 'term' required, now that event-descriptive predicates are incorporated in the language. The full simultaneous definition of 'formula' and 'term', in the metalanguage, is now as above in (III, B), but with the following additional clauses.

10. If x and y are terms, $\ulcorner Bxy \urcorner$ is a formula.

11. If $x_1, \ldots, x_n$, and y are terms and R is an n-place primitive predicate, $\ulcorner \langle R, x_1, x_2, \ldots, x_n \rangle y \urcorner$ is a formula, for $1 \leq n \leq k$.

12. If x and y are terms, $\ulcorner \text{Obj } x \urcorner$ and $\ulcorner \text{Ev } x \urcorner$ are formulae.

Although the vocabulary at hand is one of very considerable richness, further extensions still have to be made later to provide for syntax, semantics, and some portions at least of mathematics.

Throughout the foregoing the predicate in an atomic formula has always occurred to the left of the argument constant(s) or variable(s). This seems the most appropriate order where only logical theory is under consideration. However, in applications to natural language, it is more perspicuous to allow the argument terms to occur first. Hence we may often wish to write '$\langle c,S,f \rangle$' or '$\langle b,S,c,f \rangle$' and the like as alternative notations for '$\langle S,c,f \rangle$' or '$\langle S,b,c,f \rangle$'. And even '$\langle d,O \rangle$' for '$\langle O,d \rangle$'. Wherever such notations are used they are to be understood as mere alternatives for the official one.

Hereafter we let 'R' and 'S', with or without numerical subscripts, be used for primitive n-place predicates, and not just for two-place primitive or defined predicates as above.

B. EVENT IDENTITY

With the admission of a realm of events with event variables ranging over them, some further principles of identity are to be added to *IdR1* and *IdR2* in (I,E) above. In particular, we have the following.

EvId1. $\vdash e_1 = e_2 \supset (\textbf{EDP } e_1 \supset \textbf{EDP } e_2)$, where **EDP** is any event-descriptive predicate.

EvId2a. $\vdash x = y \supset (\langle F,x\rangle e \supset \langle F,y\rangle e)$,

EvId2b. $\vdash x = y \supset (\langle x,R,z\rangle e \supset \langle y,R,z\rangle e)$,

EvId2c. $\vdash x = y \supset (\langle z,R,x\rangle e \supset \langle z,R,y\rangle e)$,

and so on. Also clearly

EvId2d. $\vdash F_1 = F_2 \supset (\langle F_1,x\rangle e \supset \langle F_2,x\rangle e)$,

and

EvId2e. $\vdash R = S \supset (\langle x,R,x_1, \ldots ,x_n\rangle e \supset$ $\langle x,S,x_1, \ldots ,x_n\rangle e)$, for $n \geqq 1$.

It is evident from the material in (I, C and E) above that the appropriate principles concerning event identity are forthcoming with the assumption of these new laws. They are in effect mere extensions of *IdR2.* But of course they provide only necessary conditions for identity, not a sufficient one. This latter can be given only after the full primitive vocabulary is at hand with a suitable method of handling intentionality. (Cf. the comments at the end of XI below.)

C. SOME PRINCIPLES

Some fundamental principles characterizing the event-descriptive predicates may now be given.

First there is a *Principle of Event-Existence.*

EvR1. $\vdash xRx_1 \ldots x_n \equiv (Ee)\langle x,R,x_1, \ldots ,x_n\rangle e$.

Where $xRx_1 \ldots x_n$ there may of course be many events of the kind described here, but the principle requires only that there is at least one.[2]

Further, wherever '$xRx_1 \ldots x_n$' holds, any event of the kind described by the corresponding event-descriptive predicate must be distinct from the various "subjects." Hence a *Principle of Distinctness* holds.

---

2. Cf. H. Reichenbach, *Elements of Symbolic Logic* (New York: The Macmillan Co., 1947), p. 271.

EvR2. $\vdash \langle x,R,x_1, \ldots, x_n \rangle e \supset (\sim e = x . \sim e = x_1 \ldots \ldots \sim e = x_n).$

Clearly the null event—call it 'NE'—is not to be regarded as described by any event-descriptive predicate. This is required by the *Principle of Non-Nullity.*

EvR3. $\vdash$ **EDP** $e \supset$ E!e, where **EDP** is any event-descriptive predicate not containing 'NE'.

Further, only events are described event-descriptively. Thus we have a *Principle of Eventhood.*

EvR4. $\vdash$ **EDP** $e \supset$ Ev e.

Next there is the *Principle of Inverse Variation.*

EvR5. $\vdash (R \subset S . \sim S \subset R) \supset (\langle x,R,x_1, \ldots, x_n \rangle e \supset (\text{E}e')(\langle x,S,x_1, \ldots, x_n \rangle e' . \text{PP}ee')).$

If an *n*-adic relation R is properly included in another *n*-adic relation S, then any $\langle x,R,x_1, \ldots, x_n \rangle$-event has as a proper part some $\langle x,S,x_1, \ldots, x_n \rangle$-event.[3]

There is also a *Principle of Decomposition.*

EvR6. $\vdash (R = (S_1 \cap \ldots \cap S_n) . \sim S_1 = S_2 . \sim S_1 = S_3 \ldots \ldots \sim S_{n-1} = S_n . \langle x,R,x_1, \ldots, x_k \rangle e) \supset (\text{E}e_1)\ldots(\text{E}e_n)(e = (e_1 \cup \ldots \cup e_n) . \sim e_1 = e_2 . \sim e_1 = e_3 \ldots \ldots \sim e_{n-1} = e_n . \langle x,S_1,x_1, \ldots, x_k \rangle e_1 \ldots \ldots \langle x,S_n,x_1, \ldots, x_k \rangle e_n),$ for $n \leq 2, k \leq 2.$

If R may be decomposed into a product of *n* distinct relations, then if e is an $\langle x,R,x_1, \ldots, x_k \rangle$-event there are *n* distinct events $e_1, \ldots, e_n$ of which e is the logical sum, each e_i ($1 \leq i \leq k$) being an $\langle x,S_i,x_1, \ldots, x_k \rangle$-event.

A few comments are in order. Recall that the R's and S's here are primitive predicate constants, not defined ones. Further they are all to be regarded as non-null and non-universal—otherwise there would not be much point in having them as primitives. Thus these rules are somewhat more restricted than they might appear. They do not cover Boolean compounds of

3. Cf. the discussion in "*Events*" in *Events Etc.*

relations, for example, to be considered in a moment. We could restrict these rules still further, to allow the *R*'s and *S*'s to be just certain predicates and not others—for example, to stand for relations giving rise to just "generic events" or something of the sort—but this seems hardly necessary. According to *EvR1*, then, every *n*-adic primitive relation gives rise to a corresponding state or event or whatever, even the relations P, B, and identity.

Note that the "subjects" of an event e, that is, the x, x_1, . . . , x_n where $\langle x,R,x_1, . . . ,x_n \rangle e$, might themselves be events. But if so, they must all be distinct from e itself. This is stipulated by *EvR2*. There is no need to admit forms such as '$\langle e,R \rangle e$', '$\langle x,R,e \rangle e$', and the like, and it is not even clear what significance if any could attach to them. And in any case they are for the present not needed.[4]

EvR3 serves merely to exclude the null event NE from having any **EDP** apply to it. The NE cannot be described event-descriptively. Note, however, that there may well be events having it as one of its subjects. Thus, for example, by *EvR1* we have that $(Ee)\langle NE,=,NE \rangle e$, that there is an identity state going from NE to itself, but the e here will then exist, by *EvR3*, in the sense of not being identical to NE.

The Principle of Inverse Variation, *EvR5*, stipulates that relational proper inclusion varies inversely with the proper-part relation between events. If every teaching is a loving, then any state or act of person p's teaching person q has as a proper part a state of p's loving q. This principle helps to characterize the relation P as between events. And so also does *EvR6*, the Principle of Decomposition, which helps us to see how complex events are built up out of simpler ones.

Note that in *EvR6* only primitive predicates are allowed to occur. The structure of complex events is thus to be understood by reference to those primitives. A thesis of relativity to language is herewith invoked, the structure of events being describable only relative to the linguistic resources available. Each complex primitive event, so to speak, may be decomposed into component

---

4. Cf., however, the author's "On the Whiteheadian God," in *Whitehead's Categoreal Scheme and Other Papers* (The Hague: Martinus Nijhoff, 1974).

primitive events of which it is the logical sum. The decomposition can be carried out as far as one wishes so long as primitive predicates are available. This way of arranging the matter seems to give a very natural way of interrelating the logical products of relations with logical sums of events.

There are of course other ways of decomposing events, in terms of place and time. Thus we may arrive ultimately at momentary events, or at events at a point but spread over time, or at point events themselves. This kind of decomposition need not be considered here, however, depending as it does on physical details concerning space, time, and spatio-temporal location. It seems hardly necessary to explore the depths of relativity theory as a prolegomenon to structural linguistics. And anyhow it is doubtful whether any satisfactory issue of such exploration has yet been achieved that is logically sound. Note incidentally that even point events can be further decomposed into atomic ones, if the language contains the requisite predicates. A point event might thus be something like a palimpsest, consisting of several atomic events superimposed upon each other at the same place and time, but still distinguishable from each other by appropriate event-descriptions.

In addition to the foregoing, we assume the obvious *Principle of Sorthood*,

$EvR7.$ $\vdash \text{Obj } x \equiv \sim \text{Ev } x,$

that objects and events constitute two mutually exclusive sorts or domains.

A few consequences of these principles are as follows.

$TEv1.$ $\vdash x R x_1, \ldots, x_n \supset (Ee)(E!e \; . \\ \langle x, R, x_1, \ldots, x_n \rangle e).$

$TEv2a.$ $\vdash \langle x, R, x_1, \ldots, x_n \rangle e \supset E!e.$

$TEv2b.$ $\vdash \sim \langle x, R, x_1, \ldots, x_n \rangle NE.$

$TEv3a.$ $\vdash (R \subset S \; . \; \langle x, R, x_1, \ldots, x_n \rangle e) \supset (Ee')(Ee'') \\ (\langle x, S, x_1, \ldots, x_n \rangle e' \; . \; e = (e' \cup e'')).$

$TEv3b.$ $\vdash R = S \equiv (e)(x_1) \ldots (x_n)(\langle x, R, x_1, \ldots, x_n \rangle e \\ \equiv \langle x, S, x_1, \ldots, x_n \rangle e).$

$TEv4.$ $\vdash \text{Obj } x \lor \text{Ev } x.$

D.   THE BEFORE-THAN RELATION

As fundamental principles concerning the relation B the following are needed.[5] The first is the *Principle of Asymmetry for* B.

EvR8.   ⊢ Asym B.

The next two principles are *Interrelational Principles for* P *and* B.

EvR9.   ⊢ (Ev e_1 . Ev e_2 . $(e)((E!e . Pee_1) \supset \sim B e_1 e_2)) \supset (e)(Be_2 e \supset Be_1 e)$.

EvR10.   ⊢ (Ev e_1 . Ev e_2 . $(e)((E!e . Pee_1) \supset \sim Bee_2)) \supset (e)(Bee_2 \supset Bee_1)$.

In accord with the first of these, if event e_2 is earlier than no non-null part of event e_1, then e_1 bears B to every event that e_2 does. And according to the second, if no non-null part of event e_1 is earlier than event e_2, then every event earlier than e_2 is also earlier than e_1.

The next two rules are *Principles of B for Atomic-Event Sums.*

EvR11.   ⊢ Ev $e' \supset (B(e1Fe)e' \equiv (e)((At e . Ev e . Fe) \supset Bee'))$.

EvR12.   ⊢ Ev $e' \supset (Be'(e1Fe) \equiv (e)((At e . Ev e . Fe) \supset Be'e))$.

These two principles are of course comparable in some respects with *IndR4* and *IndR5* and with their analogues in the calculus of events.

An additional principle is needed to assure that NE and WE (the world event) are excluded from the campus of B. This is the *Principle of Exclusion.*

EvR13.   ⊢ $\sim$ C'B NE . $\sim$ C'B WE.

Clearly nothing should be allowed to bear B to NE or to WE nor should NE or WE be allowed to bear B to anything.

---

5. Cf. R. Carnap, *Introduction to Symbolic Logic and Its Applications* (New York: Dover Publications: 1958), p. 213 ff.

A few consequences are as follows.

TEv5a.	⊢ TotIrrefl B.
TEv5b.	⊢ Trans B.
TEv6a.	⊢ $(Be_1e_2 \cdot Pe_3e_2) \supset Be_1e_3$.
TEv6b.	⊢ $(Pe_1e_2 \cdot Be_2e_3) \supset Be_1e_3$.
TEv7a.	⊢ $(Be_1e_2 \cdot Pe_3e_1 \cdot Pe_4e_2) \supset Be_3e_4$.
TEv7b.	⊢ $(Pe_1e_2 \cdot Be_3e_1 \cdot Be_2e_4) \supset Be_3e_4$.
TEv8.	⊢ $Be_1e_2 \supset (\sim Pe_1e_2 \cdot \sim Pe_2e_1)$.

It should be noted also that only events bear B to one another, so that we need also the *Principle of Limitation for* B.

EvR14.   ⊢ $Be_1e_2 \supset (Ev\ e_1 \cdot Ev\ e_2)$.

And similarly a *Principle of Limitation for* P is needed.

EvR15.   ⊢ $Pe_1e_2 \supset ((Obj\ e_1 \cdot Obj\ e_2) \lor (Ev\ e_1 \cdot Ev\ e_2))$.

In addition there are two *Principles of Atomicity*, that atomic sums of atomic objects are objects, and that atomic sums of atomic events are events.

EvR16.   ⊢ Obj $(x1(At\ x \cdot Obj\ x \cdot Fx))$.

EvR17.   ⊢ Ev $(e1(At\ e \cdot Ev\ e \cdot Fe))$.

Note, incidentally, the ambiguous use of '*F*', and so on, for virtual classes of objects or for virtual classes of events. And similarly for '*R*', and so on, which may stand for virtual relations between or among objects, or between or among events, or for relations between or among all manner of mixtures thereof.

We need not for present purposes develop any further the theory of the B-relation. However, it may be convenient to have available a few definable notions as follows. We let

DEv1.   ⌜e_1 TO e_2⌝ abbreviate ⌜(Ev e_1 . Ev e_2 . $((e_1 = WE \cdot \sim e_2 = NE) \lor (\sim e_1 = NE \cdot e_2 = WE) \lor (\sim e_1 = NE \cdot \sim e_2 = NE \cdot \sim e_1\ B\ e_2 \cdot \sim e_2\ B\ e_1)))$⌝.

An event *temporally overlaps* with an event provided neither is the NE and neither bears B to the other, or provided one is the

WE and the other not the NE. In this way it is assured that the NE bears TO to no event and that every event bears TO with the WE.

Next we let

DEv2. $\ulcorner e_1$ TP $e_2 \urcorner$ abbreviate $\ulcorner$(Ev e_1 . Ev e_2 . $\sim e_1 =$ NE . $\sim e_2 =$ NE . $(e)(e$ TO $e_1 \supset e$ TO $e_2))\urcorner$.

Thus event e_1 is a *temporal part* of event e_2 provided neither is the NE and any event that temporally overlaps e_1 temporally overlaps e_2 also. Thus every event other than the NE is a TP of the WE. And finally an event is a *moment* or is momentary just where it is not the NE and is a temporal part of all its non-null temporal parts.

DEv3. $\ulcorner$Mom $e \urcorner$ abbreviates $\ulcorner$(Ev e . $\sim e =$ NE . $(e')((\sim e' =$ NE . e' TP $e) \supset e$ TP $e'))\urcorner$.

This notion is of course analogous to, but to be distinguished from, that of an atomic event.

Concerning moments two additional rules are needed, one of them being akin to *IndR6* and its analogue for events. These are the *Principle of Momentary Temporal Parts* and the *Principle of Existence for Moments.*

EvR18. $\vdash$ (Ev e . E!e) $\supset$ (Ee')(Mom e' . e' TP e).

EvR19. $\vdash$ (Ee)Mom e.

Thus there are assumed to be moments, and every non-null event has momentary temporal parts.

The assumption of moments, like that of atomic objects and events, is not needed strictly, and most of what we do with them can be done in other ways without them. However, it is very convenient technically to have them available, as we shall see again and again as we go on.

E.   BOOLEAN NOTIONS

Certain Boolean event-descriptive predicates may now be defined if desired, in particular, sums, products, and negations.

Thus

DEv4. $\ulcorner\langle x,(R \cup S),x_1,\ldots,x_n\rangle\urcorner$ may abbreviate
$\ulcorner\{e3(\langle x,R,x_1,\ldots,x_n\rangle e \vee \langle x,S,x_1,\ldots,x_n\rangle e)\}\urcorner$,

DEv5. $`\langle x,(R \cap S),x_1,\ldots,x_n\rangle$'   may abbreviate
$\ulcorner\{e (\langle x,R,x_1,\ldots,x_n\rangle e . \langle x,S,x_1,\ldots,x_n\rangle e\}\urcorner$,

and

DEv6. $\ulcorner\langle x,-R,x_1,\ldots,x_n\rangle\urcorner$ may abbreviate $\ulcorner\{e3$
$(\text{Ev } e . \sim \langle x,R,x_1,\ldots,x_n\rangle e . \sim e = x . \sim e = x_1 \ldots . \sim e = x_n)\}\urcorner$.

To complete the list of Boolean predicates,

DEv7. $\ulcorner\langle x,V,x_1,\ldots,x_n\rangle\urcorner$ may abbreviate $\ulcorner\{e3$
$\langle x,(R \cup -R),x_1,\ldots,x_n\rangle e\}\urcorner$,

and

DEv8. $\ulcorner\langle x,\Lambda,x_1,\ldots,x_n\rangle\urcorner$ may abbreviate $\ulcorner\{e3$
$(\text{Ev } e . \sim \langle x,V,x_1,\ldots,x_n\rangle e . \sim e = x . \sim e = x_1 \ldots . \sim e = x_n)\}\urcorner$,

where **R** is some one primitive $(n + 1)$-adic predicate containing no free variables picked out in advance.

Restricted Boolean laws may now be proved. In particular observe of course that

TEv9a. $\vdash (e)((\text{Ev } e . \sim e = x . \sim e = x_1 . \ldots . \sim e = x_n) \supset \langle x,V,x_1,\ldots,x_n\rangle e)$.

TEv9b. $\vdash \sim (Ee)(\langle x,\Lambda,x_1,\ldots,x_n\rangle e . \sim e = x . \sim e = x_1 \ldots . \sim e = x_n)$.

TEv9c. $\vdash \sim x R x_1 \ldots x_n \equiv (e)((\text{Ev } e . \sim e = x . \sim e = x_1 \ldots . \sim e = x_n) \supset \langle x,-R,x_1,\ldots,x_n\rangle e)$.

F. ACTS, STATES, AND PROCESSES

Sometimes verbs are classified into action verbs, state verbs, and process verbs, somewhat roughly as follows. Process verbs are supposed to indicate change of state in some way or other. Examples are 'becomes', 'grows', 'increases', 'loses', 'gains', 'dies', and so on. State verbs indicate some continuous unchanging state, examples being 'sleeps', 'remains', 'anticipates', 'believes', and so on. Action verbs, on the other hand, indicate an action on the part of some subject upon or with respect to some object or objects. Examples are 'eats', 'kills', 'kisses', 'utters', and so on. The three kinds of verbs are by no means mutually exclusive, nor for that matter jointly exhaustive.[6] Actually, the matter is rather complicated, and we cannot hope to unlock fully its mysteries here. But let us look at it a little more closely as follows.

What now, we may ask, are states? The only answer possible—within the present framework—is that they are events of a certain kind. Consider an event e, say, of Jason's sleeping. No matter how e is partitioned into beginning and end slabs, so to speak, both parts may be described as events of Jason's sleeping. And similarly for other examples. In general, then, it seems, an event may be said to be a continuous *state* relative to x's being a member of a given virtual class F as follows.

$DEv9.$ $\ulcorner e$ St $x,F \urcorner$ abbreviates $\ulcorner (\langle x,F \rangle e$. $(e_1)(e_2)$ $((e = (e_1 \cup e_2)$. $Be_1 e_2$. $\sim (Ee_3)(Be_1 e_3$. $Be_3 e_2)) \supset (\langle x,F \rangle e_1$. $\langle x,F \rangle e_2))) \urcorner$.

This definition is perhaps not too bad as a first attempt. In any case, let it suffice for the present.

In the foregoing definition and hereafter 'F' and 'R' and so on will be used for definable as well as primitive predicates.

Clearly then

$TEv10.$ $\vdash e$ St $x,F \supset \sim e$ St $x,-F$.

$TEv11.$ $\vdash (e$ St x,F . e St $x,G) \supset e$ St $x,(F \cap G)$.

$TEv12.$ $\vdash (e$ St $x,F \vee e$ St $x,G) \supset e$ St $x,(F \cup G)$.

$TEv13.$ $\vdash e$ St $x,F \supset (E!e$. Ev $e)$.

$TEv14.$ $\vdash$ Ev $e \supset e$ St x,V.

$TEv15.$ $\vdash \sim (Ee)($Ev e . e St $x,\Lambda)$.

A process, on the other hand, involves change of state, usually of an object. This change should be describable in terms of

6. Cf. O. Jespersen, *The Philosophy of Grammar* (London: Allen and Unwin, 1924).

a relation holding between two states, one at the beginning of the process and one at the end. Further, the process should be continuous in just one direction, so to speak, and should not waver back and forth. At least the simplest process will have this property. Perhaps the following will serve, preliminarily anyhow, as a definition. The definiendum is to read 'e is a process with respect to R as confined to states of x's being F'.

DEv10.　⌜e Proc R,x,F⌝ abbreviates ⌜$(e$ St x,F . $(e_1)(e_2)((e_1$ P e . e_2 P e . e_1 St x,F . e_2 St $x,F) \supset (e_1$ R e_2 $\equiv$ e_1 B $e_2)))$⌝.

Consider again a state e of Jason's sleeping. Suppose it is such that of any two sleeping-parts of it one bears B to the other if and only if it is less deep (or sound) than it. The state e is then a process of Jason's coming to sleep more soundly. It might also be a process with respect to becoming more dream-like, of becoming taller (if Jason grows in his sleep), and so on.

Concerning process we have the following elementary principles.

TEv16.　⊢ e Proc $R,x,F \supset \sim e$ Proc $R,x,-F$.

TEv17.　⊢ e Proc $R,x,F \supset \sim e$ Proc $-R,x,F$.

TEv18.　⊢ $(e$ Proc R,x,F . e Proc $R,x,G) \supset e$ Proc $R,x,(F \cap G)$.

TEv19.　⊢ $(e$ Proc R,x,F . e Proc $S,x,F) \supset e$ Proc $(R \cap S),x,F$.

TEv20.　⊢ $(e$ Proc $R,x,(F \cup G)$. $(e$ St $x,F \vee e$ St $x,G)) \supset (e$ Proc $R,x,F \vee e$ Proc $R,x,G)$.

TEv21.　⊢ e Proc $R,x,F \supset ($Ev e . E!$e)$.

TEv22.　⊢ $\sim (Ee)($Ev e . $(e$ Proc $R,x,V \vee e$ Proc $R,x,\Lambda))$.

The word 'act' may be used as the most general word for events where some agency is involved. Also there is always a direct object of the action, something acted upon, although there need not always be explicit reference to it. We can say that Brutus kills without saying whom he kills. Thus the relation for an act must always be at least dyadic. Also with a complete listing of primitive predicates, some of them may be picked out as standing for generic relations of action. Thus we may let

DEv17. $\ulcorner e$ Act $x,R\urcorner$ abbreviate $\ulcorner (\mathrm{E}x_1)$. . . $(\mathrm{E}x_n)\langle x,R,x_1, \ldots ,x_n\rangle e\urcorner$, where R is an $(n + 1)$-place predicate for a generic relation of action.

As further event principles, there are then the following.

TEv23. $\vdash$ (Ev e . $\sim$ e Act $x,-R$) $\supset$ e Act x,R.

TEv24. $\vdash$ e Act $x,(R \cap S)$ $\supset$ (e Act x,R . e Act x,S).

TEv25. $\vdash$ e Act $x,(R \cup S)$ $\equiv$ (e Act x,R $\vee$ e Act x,S).

TEv26. $\vdash$ e Act x,R $\supset$ (Ev e . E!e).

TEv27. $\vdash$ Ev e $\supset$ e Act $x,$V.

TEv28. $\vdash$ $\sim$ (Ee)(Ev e . e Act x,Λ).

The foregoing comments are by no means intended to provide a full account of acts, states, and processes. At best these definitions are mere tentative suggestions that may be helpful. And in any case, these notions will scarcely be used in the sequel. The situation is rather the other way around. The material of the sequel, especially that of Part B, will no doubt be needed for any thorough analysis of these notions.

We have in this chapter the beginnings, it is hoped, of an exact logic of events. The subject is still in its infancy, but even so, there is enough here to provide a basis for handling the pragmatical notions of Chapters V, VI, and VII, and to help get us started on the voyage of discovery of linguistic structure in Part B.

CHAPTER V

WORDS AND
EXPRESSIONS

In logic and the philosophy of language human beings figure primarily as users of language. It is they who use linguistic expressions for various purposes. Of course human beings do all manner of other interesting things also, but it is especially their use of language that is of concern here. And when language is spoken of in this context, it is not the whole of it that is referred to but only bits of it, words and phrases, sentences and texts, and these bits seem best construed as actual verbal or other utterances, sounds, ink marks, or whatever. Linguistic expressions may thus be identified with actual entities in the world, or *sign events*.[1]

There is another view, that linguistic expressions should be identified rather with *sign designs* or *shapes*. This latter view is the more usual one and has dominated metalogical theory right

---

1. Cf. N. Goodman and W. V. Quine, "Steps toward a Constructive Nominalism," *The Journal of Symbolic Logic* 12 (1947): 105–122; W. V. Quine, *Mathematical Logic*, pp. 295–305; and the author's *Truth and Denotation* (Chicago: University of Chicago Press, 1958), pp. 70–97 and 227–245.

up to the present writing. Shapes, however, may be regarded merely as virtual classes of sufficiently similar sign events, so that they need not be neglected in the theory here.

As soon as the sign events of a given language are under discussion, one enters the domain of logical *syntax*. In syntax interest is focussed entirely on the words and expressions of the language and how they are interrelated with one another, how longer expressions are built out of shorter ones, and so on. The subject is thus rather narrow, and is of interest primarily as a necessary prologomenon to semantics and the theory of reference. These latter in fact presuppose syntax fundamentally.

A. SHAPE-DESCRIPTIVE PREDICATES

The first step in formulating the syntax of a language is to list the kinds of syntactical primitive predicates needed. Because the linguistic expressions of the language are sign events, and these in turn clearly a kind of event, the kinds of syntactical predicates needed are a special kind of predicate applicable to sign events. These are the *shape-descriptive predicates.*[2]

Expressions or sign events are concrete happenings of some kind in the natural world. But of course they are used by human beings for linguistic purposes. And all manner of entities may be used for such purposes. There is not in nature some one fixed class of entities picked out and labelled unto eternity 'sign events'. Expressions are rather whatever the human being uses as such, and in using them he makes them behave in prescribed ways. He pays them overtime and makes them behave as he wishes. Strictly then, anything at all, excepting N and W, and NE and WE, may be taken as an expression provided it behave in the proper way. What determines the proper way? The rules

---

2. The shape-descriptive predicates here bear some kinship with Wilfrid Sellars's use of dot quotes. See, for example, his *Philosophical Perspectives* (Springfield, Illinois: Charles C. Thomas, 1967), p. 311.

of the language at hand, the syntactical and semantical rules together, as will be seen in what follows.

The formulation of syntax to be given is a pragmatized one, in the sense that the user is brought in right at the start. Thus in a way the distinction between syntax and pragmatics is blurred, the former becoming merely a branch of the latter. More specifically, expressions are to be relativized to the user of language. It is the user who regards certain entities or events as signs and uses them as such. His behavior, or use, of these expressions is linguistically "correct" or not only if his use accords with the rules.

Let us consider now the entire language system of the preceding chapters as object language in order to develop its syntax. The *syntactical metalanguage* that results is then merely one more extension or specialization of first-order logic.

Left and right parentheses play an important role in the notation of the object language. They are used to help express universal quantification and tag along primitively with ' $\vee$ ' in the contexts $\ulcorner(A \ \vee \ B)\urcorner$. What, now, more precisely are left parentheses? Well, anything whatsoever the user wishes to regard as such and use as such. Let

$$\text{'}p \ LP \ e\text{'}$$

express primitively now, in the syntax language, that person p takes the entity e to be, or to function or to behave as, a left parenthesis. And similarly

$$\text{'}p \ RP \ e\text{'}$$

expresses that person p takes e to be or to function as a right parenthesis. Of course suitable principles concerning 'LP' and 'RP' have to be laid down axiomatically, but before this is done a full list of the syntactical predicates needed will be given.

The full primitive vocabulary of the foregoing system consists of: '(', ')', '$\sim$', '$\vee$', '$=$', '$\exists$', '{', '}', 'P', '1', 'B', '$\langle$', '$\rangle$', primitive nonlogical predicates and individual constants, and variables. The variables and the primitive nonlogical predicates and constants will be considered in a moment. For the others, let

> 'p Tilde e',
> 'p Vee e',
> 'p Id e',
> 'p Invep e',
> 'p LB e',
> 'p RB e',
> 'p Pee e',
> 'p One e',
> 'p Bee e',
> 'p LHD e',
> 'p RHD e',
> 'p EV e',

and

> 'p OBJ e',

express primitively, respectively, that user p takes e to be a *tilde*, a *vee* ('∨'), an *identity sign*, an *inverted epsilon* ('3'), a *left brace* ('{'), a right brace ('}'), a 'P', a '1', a 'B', a *left half-diamond*, a *right half-diamond*, an 'Ev', or an 'Obj'.

To simplify let all the nonlogical primitive predicates be written officially now as 'Q', 'Q'', 'Q''', and so on. And let all variables be officially written as 'x', 'x''', 'x'''', and so on, and all primitive individual constants as roman 'a', 'a''', and so on. In addition to the foregoing, let then

> 'p Quew e',
> 'p Ex e',
> 'p Ay e',

and

> 'p Ac e',

express that person or user p takes e to be a 'Q', and 'x', and 'a', or an accent (''), respectively.

Note that no shape-descriptive predicate for the commas in object-language expressions such as $\ulcorner \langle x, R, x_1, \ldots, x_n \rangle \urcorner$ is provided for. Since no ambiguity can result, let such object-language predicates be presumed written officially hereafter without commas.

Clearly now person p takes e as a *primitive sign* or *character* of the system if and only if he takes e as one or the other of the kinds listed.

DSyn1. ⌜p Char e⌝ abbreviates ⌜$(p$ LP e ∨ ... ∨ p Ac $e)$⌝.

Here of course ⌜LP pe⌝, and so on, could be written in place of ⌜p LP e⌝. Because of the special importance attached to the user, however, it seems best to exhibit the variable or parameter for him to the left of the shape-descriptive relational predicate. This usage makes for greater ease in reading and will be followed hereafter.

The use of the variable 'p' has crept in here surreptitiously. This again is a merely informal extension of the list of variables, the 'p' suggesting 'person'. When further such variables for persons are needed, 'p_1', 'p_2', and so on, as well as 'p''', 'p'''', and so on, may be used. Also the variable 'e' has been used here for sign events. Of course these latter are special kinds of events, so that such usage is eminently justified. Again, however, because of the special importance attached to sign events hereafter, it will be appropriate to use a new style of variable for them, say, 'a', 'b', 'c', and 'd' with or without accents or numerical subscripts. To summarize, then. The four styles of variables used hereafter are 'x', 'y', and so on, for individuals (or objects), 'e', and so on, for individuals or events including states, acts, processes, and the like, 'p', and so on, for human persons, and 'a', and so on, for sign events, more particularly, for the sign events of the object language under discussion. The word 'entity' will be used almost always (or at least primarily) hereafter for either object-language individuals or events. Human persons are regarded as a special—very special!—kind of object. And in order to keep the specifically metalinguistic part of the metalanguage (that is, the part of the metalanguage not containing the object language or a translation of such) quite separate, the sign events are regarded as constituting an altogether new kind of entity over and above the object-language events and individuals.

B.   CONCATENATION

The *concatenate* of two expressions is usually regarded as the compound expression of the two put end to end in proper orientation to one another. Given two expressions b and c user p forms a third expression a as the concatenate of b with c. Thus concatenation here is to be handled in terms of a *quadratic* relation.

Let

$$\text{`}p \ C \ abc\text{'}$$

express primitively in the syntax language that user p takes the expression a to be the result of concatenating b with c. For this to hold, it is not required that p bring b and c together in some fashion or write them end to end or even explicitly exhibit them to someone else. All that is required is that p bring them together at least conceptually and regard a as the result. Perhaps where $p \ C \ abc$, p merely performs a *Gedankenexperiment*—no matter. The important thing is that howsoever p takes his concatenates he does so in a fashion consistent with the principles of syntax.[3]

Useful are the following definitions.

DSyn2a.   ⌜$p \ C \ abcd$⌝ abbreviates ⌜$(Ea')(p \ C \ a'cd \ . \ p \ C \ aba')$⌝,

DSyn2b.   ⌜$p \ C \ abcda'$⌝ abbreviates ⌜$(Eb')(p \ C \ b'cda' \ . \ p \ C \ abb')$⌝,

and so on.

What now are the sign events or expressions of the language? Clearly all the entities taken as characters together with all

---

3. Some of the content of this chapter developed out of conversations with the late Rudolf Carnap.

concatenates. Thus

DSyn3. ⌜*p* SgnEv *a*⌝ may abbreviate ⌜(*p* Char *a* ∨ (E*b*)(E*c*)*p* C *abc*)⌝.

One more primitive predicate is required for the relation of *being longer than.* This too is to be handled in a pragmatized form. Let

'*p* Lngr *ab*'

express primitively that *p* takes the inscription *a* to be *longer than b* in the sense of having a greater number of characters. This is a straightforward enough notion.

A relation of being *equally long* likewise is needed. But

DSyn4. ⌜*p* EqLng *ab*⌝ may abbreviate ⌜(*p* SgnEv *a* . *p* SgnEv *b* . ∼ *p* Lngr *ab* . ∼ *p* Lngr *ba*)⌝.

With this array of notions available, all the basic ones needed for logical syntax are at hand.

C. FUNDAMENTAL PRINCIPLES

The fundamental principles of syntax, governing the shape-descriptive predicates, 'C', and 'Lngr', may now be given as follows.

The first is the *Principle of Character Discreteness.*

SynR1. ⊢ ((*p* LP *a* . *p* RP *b*) ∨ (*p* LP *a* . *p* Tilde *b*) ∨ . . . ∨ (*p* Ex *a* . *p* Ac *b*)) ⊃ D*ab*.

Here all possible combinations are to be filled in place of the '. . .', so that this principle stipulates in effect that if *p* takes *a* and *b* as characters of different shapes, then *a* and *b* are discrete.

The *Principle of Character Existence* is to the effect that there is at least one entity *p* takes to be an LP, at least one as an RP, and so on.

SynR2. ⊢ (E*a*)*p* LP *a* . (E*a*)*p* RP *a* . . . . . (E*a*)*p* Ac *a*.

Also if p takes a as a left parenthesis, then p also takes as a left parenthesis any part of a that he takes as a sign event. And similarly for characters of the other kinds.

SynR3. $\vdash ((p \text{ LP } a \text{ . } p \text{ SgnEv } b \text{ . P}ba) \supset p \text{ LP } b)$
. . . . . $((p \text{ Ac } a \text{ . } p \text{ SgnEv } b \text{ . P}ba) \supset p \text{ Ac } b)$.

This is the *Principle of Characters as Ultimate Linguistic Units*.
It is also assumed that no entity taken to be a sign event is null. This is the *Principle of Non-Nullity for Sign Events*.

SynR4. $\vdash p \text{ SgnEv } a \supset \text{E}!a$.

The next principle, the *Principle of Simplicity of the Characters*, is to the effect that the user takes no character as a concatenate.

SynR5. $\vdash p \text{ Char } a \supset \sim (\text{E}b)(\text{E}c)p \text{ C } abc$.

Clearly if p takes a as the concatenate of b and c, he does not then take a as the concatenate of c with b. This is required by the *Principle of Quasi-Asymmetry for C*.

SynR6. $\vdash p \text{ C } abc \supset \sim p \text{ C } acb$.

Also if $p \text{ C } abc$ then p takes b and c as sign events.

SynR7. $\vdash p \text{ C } abc \supset (p \text{ SgnEv } b \text{ . } p \text{ SgnEv } c)$.

This is the *Principle of Concatenates as Sign Events*. It follows from *DSyn3* of course that

TSyn1. $\vdash p \text{ C } abc \supset p \text{ SgnEv } a$.

A very important principle is the following, the *Principle of Concatenational Identity*.

SynR8. $\vdash (p \text{ C } a_1b_1c_1 \text{ . } p \text{ C } a_2b_2c_2) \supset (a_1 = a_2 \equiv ((b_1 = b_2 \text{ . } c_1 = c_2) \vee (\text{E}d)(p \text{ C } c_1dc_2 \text{ . } p \text{ C } b_2b_1d) \vee (\text{E}d) (p \text{ C } b_1b_2d \text{ . } p \text{ C } c_2dc_1)))$.

This principle seems somewhat complicated, but actually it is merely rather compact. It can be unpacked, so to speak, by noting the following consequences.

TSyn2a. $\vdash (p \text{ C } abc \text{ . } p \text{ C } dbc) \supset a = d$,
TSyn2b. $\vdash (p \text{ C } a_1b_1c_1 \text{ . } p \text{ C } a_2b_2c_2 \text{ . } p \text{ C } c_1dc_2 \text{ . }$
$p \text{ C } b_2b_1d) \supset a_1 = a_2$,

TSyn2c. $\vdash (p \ \mathrm{C} \ a_1b_1c_1 \ . \ p \ \mathrm{C} \ a_2b_2c_2 \ . \ p \ \mathrm{C} \ b_1b_2d \ . \ p \ \mathrm{C} \ c_2dc_1) \supset a_1 = a_2,$
TSyn2d. $\vdash (p \ \mathrm{C} \ ab_1c_1 \ . \ p \ \mathrm{C} \ ab_2c_2) \supset ((b_1 = b_2 \ . \ c_1 = c_2) \vee (\mathrm{E}d)(p \ \mathrm{C} \ c_1dc_2 \ . \ p \ \mathrm{C} \ b_2b_1d)).$

Observe that *TSyn2b* and *TSyn2c* are in effect *Principles of Associativity for Concatenation*.

The *Principle of Concatenational Existence* is as follows.

SynR9. $\vdash (p \ \mathrm{SgnEv} \ a \ . \ p \ \mathrm{SgnEv} \ b) \supset (\mathrm{E}c)p \ \mathrm{C} \ cab.$

This is of course a very strong existence principle, to the effect that there is something c which p takes to be the concatenate of any two entities a and b that he takes as sign events. This something c may be a and b strung end to end in proper orientation to one another, but it need not be. Strictly p can take c as anything at all, provided that he uses it in the proper way as a concatenate of a and b.

The next principle is the *Principle of Shapes*. For the statement of it the following definition-schema is useful. Let

DSyn5. $\ulcorner p \ (S_1 \frown \ldots \frown S_n) \ a \urcorner$ abbreviate $\ulcorner (\mathrm{E}b_1). \ldots (\mathrm{E}b_n)(p \ S_1 \ b_1 \ . \ \ldots \ . \ p \ S_n \ b_n \ . \ p \ \mathrm{C} \ ab_1 \ldots b_n) \urcorner$, where $S_1, \ldots, S_n$ are any primitive shape-descriptive predicates, and $n = 2, 3, \ldots .$

Thus, for example,

'$p \ (\mathrm{LP} \frown \mathrm{Ex} \frown \mathrm{RP}) \ a$' abbreviates '$(\mathrm{E}b_1)(\mathrm{E}b_2)(\mathrm{E}b_3)(p \ \mathrm{LP} \ b_1 \ . \ p \ \mathrm{Ex} \ b_2 \ . \ p \ \mathrm{RP} \ b_3 \ . \ p \ \mathrm{C} \ ab_1b_2b_3)$'.

The Principle of Shapes now reads as follows.

SynR10. If $\vdash (a)(p \ S \ a \supset Fa)$, for all S where S is any primitive shape-descriptive predicate or any predicate $\ulcorner(S_1 \frown \ldots \frown S_n)\urcorner$ of the kind defined in *DSyn5*, then $\vdash (a)(p \ \mathrm{SgnEv} \ a \supset Fa)$.

Next, some principles are required governing 'Lngr'. The first is the *Principle of Quasi-Transitivity for Lngr*.

SynR11. $\vdash (p \ \mathrm{Lngr} \ ab \ . \ p \ \mathrm{Lngr} \ bc) \supset p \ \mathrm{Lngr} \ ac.$

Also there is a *Principle of Limitation for Lngr*.

SynR12. $\vdash p \ \mathrm{Lngr} \ ab \supset (p \ \mathrm{SgnEv} \ a \ . \ p \ \mathrm{SgnEv} \ b).$

A *Principle of Characters as the Shortest Sign Events* is needed,

SynR13.   ⊢ *p* Char *a* ⊃ ∼ (E*b*)*p* Lngr *ab*,

as well as a *Principle of Characters as Equally Long*,

SynR14.   ⊢ (*p* Char *a* . *p* Char *b*) ⊃ ∼ *p* Lngr *ab*.

Finally, a *Principle of Concatenational Length*, to the effect that concatenates are always taken to be longer than their components but not longer than themselves.

SynR15.   ⊢ *p* C *abc* ⊃ (*p* Lngr *ab* . *p* Lngr *ac* . ∼
p Lngr *aa*).

D.   SOME CONSEQUENCES

A few interesting syntactical principles, logical consequences of *SynR1–SynR15*, may be listed as follows.

TSyn3.   ⊢ *p* Char *a* ⊃ *p* SgnEv *a*.
TSyn4.   ⊢ (*p* Char *a* . *p* SgnEv *b* . P*ba*) ⊃ *p*
Char *b*.
TSyn5.   ⊢ *p* C *abc* ⊃ (E!*a* . E!*b* . E!*c*).
TSyn6.   ⊢ (*p* SgnEv *a* . *p* SgnEv *b*) ⊃ (∼ *p* C *aaa* .
∼ *p* C *abb* . ∼ *p* C *aba* . ∼ *p* C *aab*).
TSyn7.   ⊢ *p* C *abc* ⊃ (∼ *p* C *bac* . ∼ *p* C *bca* .
∼ *p* C *cab* . ∼ *p* C *cba*).
TSyn8a.   ⊢ (*p* C *abc* . *p* C *cda'*) ⊃ *p* C *abda'*.
TSyn8b.   ⊢ (*p* C *abc* . *p* C *bda'*) ⊃ *p* C *ada'c*.
TSyn9a.   ⊢ *p* SgnEv *a* ⊃ ∼ *p* Ingr *aa*.
TSyn9b.   ⊢ *p* Lngr *ab* ⊃ ∼ *p* Lngr *ba*.
TSyn10.   ⊢ (*p* Char *a* . *p* Char *b*) ⊃ *p* EqLng *ab*.
TSyn11.   ⊢ *p* EqLng *ab* ⊃ *p* EqLng *ba*.
TSyn12.   ⊢ (*p* EqLng *ab* . *p* EqLng *cd*) ⊃ *p*
EqLng *ac*.
TSyn13.   ⊢ (*p* Char *a* . ∼ *p* Char *b* . *p* SgnEv *b*) ⊃
∼ *p* EqLng *ab*.
TSyn14.   ⊢ ((*a*)(*p* Char *a* ⊃ F*a*) . (*a*)(*b*)(*c*)((*p* SgnEv
a . *p* SgnEv *b* . F*a* . F*b* . *p* C *cab*) ⊃ F*c*)) ⊃
(*a*)(*p* SgnEv *a* ⊃ F*a*).

TSyn15.   ⊢ ((*a*)(*p* Char *a* ⊃ *Fa*) . (*a*)(*b*)(*c*)((*p* SgnEv *a* . *p* Char *b* . *Fa* . *p* C *cab*) ⊃ *Fc*)) ⊃ (*a*)(*p* SgnEv *a* ⊃ *Fa*).

E.   'FORMULA'

On the basis of the foregoing, exact definitions may be given of the various syntactical notions that have been used in the preceding chapters only informally. Among these are notions such as 'variable', 'individual constant', 'term', 'predicate constant', 'formula', and the like. Let us reflect upon just these and then go on to others in the next section.

What now officially is a variable? Well, an '*x*' or an '*x*'' and so on taken by *p*. The 'and so on' phrase here is supposed to cover any *string of accents*. What now is a string of accents? Let

DSyn6.   ⌜*p* AcStr *a*⌝ abbreviate ⌜(*p* SgnEv *a* . (*b*)((*p* Char *b* . P*ba*) ⊃ *p* Ac *b*))⌝.

Thus *p* may be said to take *a* as a *string of accents* provided he takes *a* as a sign event and also that he takes as an accent every part *b* of *a* that he takes as a character. A variable now officially is any entity taken by *p* to be an '*x*' or an '*x*' concatenated with a string of accents.

An indefinite, perhaps even infinite, number of variables is needed in the object language, whereas only a finite number of primitive predicates is ordinarily admitted. For specificity, let it be supposed that there are only two primitive predicate constants, say 'Q' and 'Q'', of one and two places, respectively. The number of primitive individual constants is left open. We may suppose these also to be infinite in number and all written as '*a*', '*a*'', and so on. Then

DSyn7.   ⌜*p* InCon *a*⌝ may abbreviate ⌜(*p* Ay *a* ∨ (E*b*)(E*c*)(*p* Ay *b* . *p* AcStr *c* . *p* C *abc*))⌝,

and

DSyn8.   ⌜*p* PrimPredCon *a*⌝ abbreviate ⌜(*p* Quew *a* ∨ *p* (Quew⌢Ac) *a*)⌝.

Also a *term* now is an expression taken by *p* as either a Vbl or an InCon.

DSyn9. 　 ⌜*p* Trm *a*⌝ 　abbreviates 　⌜(*p* Vbl *a* ∨ *p* InCon *a*)⌝.

Note that expressions of the form ⌜(*x*1*A*)⌝ are not included among terms for the moment. These will be provided for later.

If the admission of an infinite number of primitive individual constants is thought excessive, the definiens for ⌜*p* InCon *a*⌝ may be given by enumeration instead.

Some definitions of a slightly different kind may now be given. An expression is said to be taken by *p* to *begin b* where *a* and *b* are identical and are both taken by *p* to be sign events or where *p* takes *b* to be the concatenate of *a* with some *c*. Thus

DSyn10. 　 ⌜*p* Bgn *ab*⌝ 　abbreviates 　⌜((*p* SgnEv *a* . *p* SgnEv *b* . *a* = *b*) ∨ (E*c*)*p* C *bac*)⌝.

And under similar appropriate circumstances, *a* may be taken by *p* to *end b*. Thus

DSyn11. 　 ⌜*p* Ends *ab*⌝ 　abbreviates 　⌜((*p* SgnEv *a* . *p* SgnEv *b* . *a* = *b*) ∨ (E*c*)*p* C *bca*)⌝.

Then *a* is taken by *p* to be a (continuous) *segment* of *b* provided *a* is taken by *p* to end some *c* taken by *p* to begin *b*. Thus

DSyn12. 　 ⌜*p* Seg *ab*⌝ 　abbreviates 　⌜(E*c*)(*p* Ends *ac* . *p* Bgn *cb*)⌝.

An expression *a* is said to be taken by *p* to be *like b* under the circumstances given in the definiens of the following.

DSyn13. 　 ⌜*p* Like *ab*⌝ 　abbreviates 　⌜(*p* EqLng *ab* . (*c*)(*d*)((*p* EqLng *cd* . *p* Bgn *ca* . *p* Bgn *db*) ⊃ (E*e*)(E*e*′)(*p* Ends *ec* . *p* Ends *e*′*d* . ((*p* LP *e* . *p* LP *e*′) ∨ ... ∨ (*p* Ac *e* . *p* Ac *e*′)))))⌝.

Expressions *a* and *b* are taken to be alike, or like each other, to speak roughly, when the left-most character of one is of the same kind as the left-most character of the other, the second character of one is of the same kind as the second character of the other (in left-to-right order), and so on.

Recall now *DSyn5* above, which may be extended slightly as follows. Let

DSyn14. $\ulcorner p \ (S_1 \frown \ldots \frown S_n) \ a \urcorner$ abbreviate $\ulcorner (Eb_1) \ldots$ $(Eb_n)(p \ S_1 \ b_1 \ \ldots \ldots \ p \ S_n \ b_n \ . \ p \ C \ ab_1 \ldots b_n) \urcorner$, where each S_i is either a shape-descriptive predicate or a term, and if S_i is a term then $\ulcorner p \ S_i \ b_i \urcorner$ is to be taken as $\ulcorner p \ Like \ S_i b_i \urcorner$ for $1 \leq i \leq n$.

The use of *DSyn14* is of help in formulating the following definition, of the notion of being taken as an *atomic formula*.

DSyn15. $\ulcorner p \ AtFmla \ a \urcorner$ abbreviates $\ulcorner (Eb)(Ec)(Ed)$ $(p \ Trm \ b \ . \ p \ Trm \ c \ . \ p \ Trm \ d \ . \ (p \ (Quew \frown b) \ a \ \vee$ $p \ (Quew \frown Ac \frown b \frown c) \ a \ \vee \ p \ (b \frown Id \frown c) \ a \ \vee \ p \ (Pee \frown b \frown c)$ $a \ \vee \ p \ (Bee \frown b \frown c) \ a \ \vee \ p \ (LHD \frown b \frown RHD \frown c) \ a \ \vee \ p$ $(LHD \frown b \frown Quew \frown RHD \frown c) \ a \ \vee \ p \ (LHD \frown b \frown Quew \frown$ $Ac \frown c \frown RHD \frown d) \ a)) \urcorner$.

Note that this definition is in effect one by enumeration, all kinds of atomic sentences being provided for *seriatim*.

Another closely related notion is needed, that of a *quasi-atomic formula*.

DSyn16. $\ulcorner p \ QuasiAtFmla \ ae_1e_2e_3d_1d_2d_3 \urcorner$ abbreviates $\ulcorner (p \ Vbl \ d_1 \ . \ p \ Vbl \ d_2 \ . \ p \ Vbl \ d_3 \ . \ (Eb)(Ec)(Ed)((p \ Trm$ $b \ \vee \ p \ (LP \frown d_1 \frown One \frown e_1 \frown RP) \ b) \ . \ (p \ Trm \ c \ \vee \ p$ $(LP \frown d_2 \frown One \frown e_2 \frown RP) \ c) \ . \ (p \ Trm \ d \ \vee \ p \ (LP \frown d_3 \frown$ $One \frown e_3 \frown RP) \ d) \ . \ (p \ (Quew \frown b) \ a \ \vee \ p \ (Quew \frown Ac \frown$ $b \frown c) \ a \ \vee \ p \ (b \frown Id \frown c) \ a \ \vee \ p \ (Pee \frown b \frown c) \ a \ \vee \ p \ (Bee \frown$ $b \frown c) \ a \vee \ b \ (LHD \frown b \frown RHD \frown c) \ a \ \vee \ p \ (LHD \frown b \frown Quew \frown$ $RHD \frown c) \ a \ \vee \ p \ (LHD \frown b \frown Quew \frown Ac \frown c \frown RHD \frown d) \ a))) \urcorner$.

Observe that the quasi-atomic formulae may contain expressions of the form $\ulcorner (x \ 1 A) \urcorner$, occurrences of which are not allowed in atomic formulae proper. In the cases where e_1, e_2, and e_3 are taken to be formulae, then of course a is also. Thus the quasi-atomic formulae need not all be formulae. The definiendum here expresses that p takes a to arise from e_1, e_2, e_3 (with respect respectively to the variables d_1, d_2, d_3) by replacing the terms of atomic formulae by expressions whose shape-descriptions are '$(LP \frown d_1 \frown One \frown e_1 \frown RP)$', '$(LP \frown d_2 \frown One \frown e_2 \frown RP)$', and '$(LP \frown$

d_3⌢One⌢e_3⌢RP)'. Such a procedure is *quasi-atomic formulization*.

An expression *a* is said to be taken by *p* to be a *negative* of *b* provided *p* takes *a* to be *b* prefixed by a Tilde.

DSyn17. ⌜*p* Neg *ab*⌝ abbreviates ⌜*p* (Tilde⌢*b*) *a*⌝.

In analogous fashion, *p* may be said to take *a* as the *disjunction* of *b* and *c*,

DSyn18. ⌜*p* Disj *abc*⌝ abbreviates ⌜*p* (LP⌢*b*⌢Vee⌢ *c*⌢RP) *a*⌝,

as a *generalization* of *b*,

DSyn19. ⌜*p* Gen *ab*⌝ abbreviates ⌜(E*c*)(*p* Vbl *c* . *p* (LP⌢*c*⌢RP⌢*b*) *a*)⌝,

or as an *abstraction* of *b*,

DSyn20. ⌜*p* Abst *ab*⌝ abbreviates ⌜(E*c*)(E*d*)(*p* Vbl *c* . *p* Trm *d* . *p* (LB⌢*c*⌢Invep⌢*b*⌢RB⌢*d*) *a*)⌝.

These definitions are useful in leading up to the definition of 'formula', the formulae being built up recusively from atomic ones by negation, disjunction, generalization, and abstraction— provided the quasi-atomic ones are also accommodated some-how, as they will be in a moment.

That *a* is taken by *p* to be a *framed ingredient* of *b* is defined as follows.

DSyn21. ⌜*p* FrIng *ab*⌝ abbreviates ⌜(∼ (E*c*)(*p* Seg *ca* . *p* (LP⌢RP) *c*) . (E*d*)(*p* Seg *db* . *p* (LP⌢RP⌢*a*⌢LP⌢ RP) *d*))⌝.

And that *a* is taken by *p* to be *prior* to *b* in *c*, as follows.

DSyn22. ⌜*p* Pr *abc*⌝ abbreviates ⌜(E*d*)(*p* Bgn *dc* . *p* FrIng *ad* . *p* FrIng *ac* . *p* FrIng *bc* . ∼ *p* FrIng *bd*)⌝.

These two definitions are useful in enabling us to achieve the effect of a recursive definition of 'formula' and related notions. Note that *a* is taken as a framed ingredient of *b* if it contains no segment of the form '()' but occurs in *b* flanked on both sides by expressions of the form '()'. The use of '()' serves to frame *a* on both sides, as it were. And *a* is taken to be prior to *b* in *c* provided both *a* and *b* are taken as framed ingredients of *c* and there is some beginning segment of *c* of which *a* is taken as a framed ingredient but *b* not.

What, now, is a formula? The answer is: any expression *a* taken by *p* to be a framed ingredient of some *b*, every framed ingredient of which is taken by *p* to be either atomic or to arise from prior formulae by negation, disjunction, generalization, abstraction, or quasi-atomic formulization. Thus, without more ado,

DSyn23.   ⌜*p* Fmla *a*⌝ may abbreviate ⌜(E*b*)(*p* FrIng *ab* . (*c*)(*p* FrIng *cb* ⊃ (*p* AtFmla *c* ∨ (E*d*)(E*e*)(E*e′*)(*p* Pr *dcb* . *p* Pr *ecb* . *p* Pr *e′cb* . (*p* Neg *cd* ∨ *p* Disj *cde* ∨ *p* Gen *cd* ∨ *p* Abst *cd* ∨ (E*a′*)(E*b′*)(E*c′*)*p* QuasiAtFmla *cdee′a′b′c′*)))))⌝.

This definition provides for one of the fundamental notions of syntax.

It was remarked earlier that expressions of the form ⌜(*x*1*A*)⌝ were not yet officially regarded as terms. Now that the notion 'Fmla' is available, this may be rectified as follows.

DSyn24.   ⌜*p* Trm′ *a*⌝ abbreviates ⌜(*p* Trm *a* ∨ (E*b*)(E*c*)(*p* Vbl *b* . *p* Fmla *c* . *p* (LP⌢*b*⌢One⌢*c*⌢RP) *a*))⌝.

A Trm′ then is either a term or an expression of the form ⌜(*x*1*A*)⌝.

F. 'SENTENCE'

With the notion 'Fmla' available, that of being a sentence is not far off, sentences after all being formulae containing no free variables.

The notion that *p* takes *a* to be a *free variable* of *b* may be defined by framed ingredients as follows.

DSyn25.   ⌜*p* FrVbl *ab*⌝ abbreviates ⌜(*p* Vbl *a* . (E*c*)(*p* FrIng *bc* . (*d*)(*p* FrIng *dc* ⊃ (*p* (Quew⌢*a*) *d* ∨ (E*e*)(*p* Trm *e* . (*p* (Quew⌢Ac⌢*a*⌢*e*) *d* ∨ *p* (Quew⌢Ac⌢

$e⌒a$) d)) ∨ (Ee)(p Trm e . (p ($a⌒$Id$⌒e$) d ∨ p ($e⌒$
Id$⌒a$) d)) ∨ (Ee)(p Trm e . (p (Pee$⌒a⌒e$) d ∨ p
(Pee$⌒e⌒a$) d)) ∨ (Ee)(p Trm e . (p (Bee$⌒a⌒e$) d ∨
p (Bee$⌒e⌒a$) d)) ∨ (Ee)(Ea')(p Vbl e . p Fmla a' .
(p (LB$⌒e⌒$Invep$⌒a'⌒$RB$⌒a$) d ∨ (Ee)(p Trm e .
(p (LHD$⌒e⌒$RHD$⌒a$) d ∨ p (LHD$⌒a⌒$RHD$⌒e$) d)) ∨
(Ee)(p Trm e . (p (LHD$⌒e⌒$Quew$⌒$RHD$⌒a$) d ∨
p (LHD$⌒a⌒$Quew$⌒$RHD$⌒e$) d)) ∨ (Ee)(Ee')(p Trm e .
p Trm e' . (p (LHD$⌒e⌒$Quew$⌒$Ac$⌒e'⌒$RHD$⌒a$) d ∨
p (LHD$⌒a⌒$Quew$⌒$Ac$⌒e⌒$RHD$⌒e'$) d ∨ p (LHD$⌒e⌒$
Quew$⌒$Ac$⌒a⌒$RHD$⌒e'$) d)) ∨ (Ee)(Ea')(Ea'')(e Pr dc .
a' Pr dc . a'' Pr dc . (p Neg de ∨ p Disj dea' ∨ (Eb')
(p Vbl b' . ∼ p Like ab' . p (LP$⌒b'⌒$RP$⌒e$) d) ∨
(Eb')(Ec')(p Vbl b' . ∼ p Like ab' . p Trm c' . p (LB$⌒$
$b'⌒$Invep$⌒e⌒$RB$⌒c'$) d) ∨ (Eb')(Ec')(Ed')(Ea')(Ea'')
(∼ p Like ab' . ∼ p like ac' . ∼ p Like ad' . p
QuasiAtFmla $dea'a''b'c'd'$))))))))⌐.[4]

Although the definiens here is somewhat long, observe that it
proceeds first by enumeration of the cases wherein a is taken to
be a free variable of an atomic formula b, and then by framed
ingredients to provide for more complicated cases by recursion.

A *sentence* now is an expression taken by p as a formula
containing no free variables.

DSyn26.   ⌐p Sent a⌐   abbreviates   ⌐(p Fmla a . ∼
(Eb) p FrVbl ba)⌐.

The notion of being a *primitive* predicate constant was
defined by *DSyn8* above. That of being a *one-place* primitive *or
defined* predicate constant may be introduced as follows.

DSyn27.   ⌐p PredConOne a⌐   abbreviates   ⌐(p Quew
a ∨ (Eb)(Ec)(p Vbl b . p Fmla c . p (LB$⌒b⌒$Invep$⌒$
$c⌒$RB) a . (d)(p FrVbl dc ⊃ p Like db)))⌐.

Recall that 'Q' was taken as the only one-place primitive predicate. All defined predicates may be introduced as shorthand for

---

4. In this definiens please read 'p Pr edc . p Pr $a'dc$. p Pr $a''dc$' for
'e Pr dc . a' Pr dc . a'' Pr dc'.

one-place abstracts containing no free variables. Hence such abstracts may as well be referred to as one-place predicate constants.

The notion of being taken as a *sentential form of just one variable* may be defined as follows.

DSyn28. ⌜*p* SentFormOne *ab*⌝ abbreviates
⌜(*p* Fmla *a* . *p* FrVbl *ba* . (*c*)(*p* FrVbl *ca* ⊃ *p* Like *cb*))⌝.

A sentential form *a* of the one variable *b* is any expression *a* taken by *p* to be a formula where *b* is taken to be a free variable of *a* and all expressions taken by *p* to be free variables of *a* are taken to be like *b*.

G. 'THEOREM'

The list of definitions of the fundamental notions of syntax is not complete without one for the notion 'theorem'. This in turn depends upon the notions 'axiom' and 'is a logical consequence of'.

The only primitive rules of inference admitted, it will be recalled, are *MP* and *Gen*. The notion of being an *immediate consequence of* is thus definable in terms of them. First,

DSyn29. ⌜*p* MP *abc*⌝ may abbreviate ⌜(E*d*)(*p* Neg *db* . *p* Disj *adc*)⌝.

p takes *a* to be obtainable from *b* and *c* by *MP* provided he takes some *d* to be a negation of *b* and *a* to be a disjunction of *d* and *c*. Then

DSyn30. ⌜*p* IC *abc*⌝ abbreviates ⌜(*p* MP *abc* ∨ *p* Gen *ab*)⌝,

so that *p* takes *a* to be an immediate consequence of *b* and *c* where he takes *a* to be obtainable from *b* and *c* by *MP* or from *b* by *Gen*.

The notion of being taken as an axiom can be spelled out by an enumeration of the various kinds admitted. Thus *p* takes *a* to be an axiom of the kind spelled out by *R1* provided he takes *a* to be of the proper shape. Similarly for *R2*, and so on. Thus

    DSyn31a.   ⌜*p* R1Ax *a*⌝ abbreviates ⌜(E*b*)(*p* Fmla
b . *p* (LP⌢Tilde⌢LP⌢*b*⌢Vee⌢*b*⌢RP⌢Vee⌢*b*⌢RP) *a*)⌝,

    DSyn31b.   ⌜*p* R2Ax *a*⌝ abbreviates ⌜(E*b*)(E*c*)
(*p* Fmla *b* . *p* Fmla *c* . *p* (LP⌢Tilde⌢*b*⌢Vee⌢LP⌢*b*⌢
Vee⌢*c*⌢RP⌢RP) *a*)⌝,

and similarly for 'R3Ax' and 'R4Ax'.

The spelling out of forms for *R5* is considerably more complicated, because of the proviso concerning occurrences of a free
variable or term in a formula wherever there are free occurrences
of a given variable in another. It should be recalled that such a
proviso is put on *A* and *B* in *R5*. This notion may be defined by
a kind of double or simultaneous induction accommodated by
the following definitions.

First, *p* may be said to take the pair *ab* as a framed ingredient
of *c* under the circumstances that he takes (*a*⌢Vee⌢Vee⌢*b*) to
be a framed ingredient of *c* provided nothing like *a* or *b* separately
is taken as a framed ingredient of *c*, and provided nothing having
the shape (Vee⌢Vee) is taken to be a segment of *a* or *b*.

    DSyn32.   ⌜*p* FrIng *ab,c*⌝ abbreviates ⌜(E*d*)(*p* (*a*⌢
Vee⌢Vee⌢*b*) *d* . *p* FrIng *dc* . ~ (E*d'*)((*p* Like *d'a* ∨
p Like *d'b*) . *p* FrIng *d'c*) . ~ (E*d'*)(*p* (Vee⌢Vee) *d'* .
(*p* Seg *d'a* ∨ *p* Seg *d'b*)))⌝.

Somewhat analogously, the pair *ab* may be said to be taken
by *p* as *prior* to the pair *cd* in *e* under suitable conditions as
follows.

    DSyn33.   ⌜*p* Pr *ab,cd,e*⌝ abbreviates ⌜(E*a'*)(*p* Bgn
a'e . *p* FrIng *ab,a'* . *p* FrIng *ab,e* . *p* FrIng *cd,e* . ~
p FrIng *cd,a'*))⌝.

Note that in the proviso on *R5*, *occurrences* of variables are
referred to, not just variables. Recall that officially the variables
are '*x*', '*x''*', and so on. Suppose '*x'''*' is taken to occur in some
formula. One would not wish to say also that the occurrence of
'*x''*' in '*x'''*' is an occurrence of '*x''*' in that formula. Hence the
definition as follows of the locution '*p* takes the variable *a* to
occur in *b*'.

DSyn34. ⌜*p* OccVbl *ab*⌝ abbreviates ⌜(*p* Vbl *a* . (E*c*)(*p* Bgn *cb* . *p* Ends *ac* . ~ (E*d*)(E*e*)(*p* Ac *d* . *p* C *ead* . *p* Ends *ec*)))⌝.

Then *p* may be said to take *a* as a *bound variable occuring in b* as follows.

DSyn35. ⌜*p* BdVbl *ab*⌝ abbreviates ⌜(*p* OccVbl *ab* . *p* FrVbl *ab*)⌝.

The definiendum of the following definition is to express that *p* takes *a* to differ from *d* only in containing free occurrences of a Trm' *b* in place of one or more free occurrences of the variable *c* in *d*.

DSyn36. ⌜*p* SF?$_c^b$ *ad*⌝ abbreviates ⌜(*p* Vbl *c* . (*p* Trm' *b* . (*e*)(*e'*)(*a'*)((*p* Vbl *e* . *p* Fmla *e'* . *p* (LP⌢*e*⌢ One⌢*e'*⌢RP) *b* . *p* FrVbl *a'e'* . ~ *p* Like *a'e*) ⊃ *p* FrVbl *a'a*)) . ((~ *p* FrVbl *cd* . *p* Like *ad*) ∨ (E*e*)(*p* FrIng *ad,e* . (*a'*)(*b'*)(*p* FrIng *a'b',e* ⊃ ((*p* (Quew⌢*c*) *b'* . *p* (Quew⌢*b*) *a'*) ∨ (E*a''*)(*p* Trm' *a''* . ((*p* (Quew⌢Ac⌢*c*⌢ *a''*) *b'* . *p* (Quew⌢Ac⌢*b*⌢*a''*) *a'*) ∨ (*p* (Quew⌢Ac⌢ *a''*⌢*c*) *b'* . *p* (Quew⌢Ac⌢*a''*⌢*b*) *a'*))) ∨ (E*a''*)(*p* Trm' *a''* . ((*p* (Pee⌢*c*⌢*a''*) *b'* . *p* (Pee⌢*b*⌢*a''*) *a'*) ∨ (*p* (Bee⌢ *c*⌢*a''*) *b'* . *p* (Pee⌢*b*⌢*a''*) *a'*) ∨ (*p* (*c*⌢Id⌢*a''*) *b'* . *p* (*b*⌢ Id⌢*a''*) *a'*) ∨ (*p* (*a''*⌢Id⌢*c*) *b'* . *p* (*a''*⌢Id⌢*b*) *a'*))) ∨ (E*a''*)(*p* Trm' *a''* . ((*p* (LHD⌢*a''*⌢RHD⌢*c*) *b'* . *p* (LHD⌢*a''*⌢RHD⌢*b*) *a'*) ∨ (*p* (LHD⌢*c*⌢RHD⌢*a''*) *b'* . *p* (LHD⌢*b*⌢RHD⌢*a''*) *a'*) ∨ (*p* (LHD⌢*a''*⌢Quew⌢ RHD⌢*c*) *b'* . *p* (LHD⌢*a''*⌢Quew⌢RHD⌢*b*) *a'*)) ∨ (*p* (LHD⌢*c*⌢Quew⌢RHD⌢*a''*) *b'* . *p* (LHD⌢*b*⌢Quew⌢ RHD⌢*a''*) *a'*))) ∨ (E*a''*)(E*b''*)(*p* Trm' *a''* . *p* Trm' *b''* . ((*p* (LHD⌢*a''*⌢Quew⌢Ac⌢*b''*⌢RHD⌢*c*) *b'* . *p* (LHD⌢ *a''*⌢Quew⌢Ac⌢*b''*⌢RHD⌢*b*) *a'*) ∨ (*p* (LHD⌢*a''*⌢ Quew⌢Ac⌢*c*⌢RHD⌢*b''*) *b'* . *p* (LHD⌢*a''*⌢Quew⌢Ac⌢ *b*⌢RHD⌢*b''*) *a'*) ∨ (*p* (LHD⌢*c*⌢Quew⌢Ac⌢*b''*⌢RHD⌢ *a''*) *b'* . *p* (LHD⌢*b*⌢Quew⌢Ac⌢*b''*⌢RHD⌢*a''*) *a'*))) ∨ (E*c'*)(E*d'*)(*p* Vbl *c'* . *p* Fmla *d'* . *p* (LB⌢*c'*⌢Invep⌢*d'*⌢ RB⌢*c*) *b'* . *p* (LB⌢*c'*⌢Invep⌢*d'*⌢RB⌢*b*) *a'*) ∨ (E*c'*) (E*d'*)(E*a''*)(E*b''*)(*p* Pr *c'd',a'b',e* . *p* Pr *a''b'',a'b',e* . ((*p*

Neg $a'c'$. p Neg $b'd'$) ∨ (p Disj $a'c'a''$. p Disj $b'd'b''$)
∨ (Ee')(Ed'')(p Vbl e' . p Trm' d'' . ∼ p Like $e'c$.
(c'')(d')((p Seg $c''b$. p FrVbl $d''c''$) ⊃ ∼ p Like $d''e'$) .
((p (LP⌢e'⌢RP⌢d') b' . p (LP⌢e'⌢RP⌢c') a') ∨ (p
(LB⌢c''⌢Invep⌢c'⌢RB⌢d'') a' . p (LB⌢c''⌢Invep⌢d'⌢
RB⌢d'') b') ∨ (p (LB⌢c''⌢Invep⌢c'⌢b) a' . p (LB⌢
c''⌢Invep⌢d'⌢c) b'))))))))))⌐.

Although the definiens here looks very long and cumbrous,
note that it proceeds by enumeration and double induction very
much as in other definitions above.

Given the notion just defined, it is easy enough to define now
the locution 'p takes a to differ from d only in containing free
occurrences of b wherever there are free occurrences of the
variable c in d'.

DSyn37.   ⌐p SF$_c^b$ ad⌐ abbreviates ⌐(p SF?$_c^b$ ad .
(p FrVbl ca ⊃ p Like bc))⌐.

It is after all this locution that is needed now in the definition
of being taken as an *R5*-axiom. Thus

DSyn38a.   ⌐p R5Ax a⌐ abbreviates ⌐(Eb)(Ec)(Ed)(Ee)
(p Fmla d . p SF$_b^e$ dc . p (LP⌢Tilde⌢LP⌢b⌢RP⌢c⌢
Vee⌢d⌢RP) a)⌐.

And also

DSyn38b.   ⌐p R6Ax a⌐ abbreviates ⌐(Eb)(Ec)(Ed)(p
Vbl b . p Fmla c . p Fmla d . ∼ (Eb'')(p Like $b''b$.
p FrOcc $b''c$) . p (LP⌢Tilde⌢LP⌢b⌢RP⌢LP⌢c⌢Vee⌢
d⌢RP⌢Vee⌢LP⌢c⌢Vee⌢LP⌢b⌢RP⌢d⌢RP⌢RP) a)⌐.

In a similar fashion, now

'p IdAx1 a',
'p IdAx2 a',
'p AbstAx a',

and so on, may be defined. Then

'p Ax a'

may be defined to express that *p* takes *a* as an axiom. These definitions are *D38c*, *D38d*, and so on, and *D39* respectively.

Finally now the notion of being taken as a *theorem* is definable by framed ingredients in familiar fashion.

D40. ⌜*p* Thm *a*⌝ abbreviates ⌜(E*b*)(*p* FrIng *ab* .
(*c*)(*p* FrIng *cb* ⊃ (*p* Ax *c* ∨ (E*d*)(E*e*)(*p* Pr *dcb* .
p Pr *ecb* . (*p* MP *cde* ∨ *p* Gen *cd*)))))⌝.

D40 introduces the notion of being a theorem only as based on *R1–R6*, *IdR1–IdR2*, *Abst*, *IndR1–IndR8*, *EvId1–EvId2e*, and *EvR1–EvR19*, together of course with *MP* and *Gen*. This is a notion of theorem in a narrow sense, the notion of *theorem of event logic*. When nonlogical axioms, characterizing the nonlogical primitive predicates and individual constants, are taken into account, a wider notion of theorem is of course forthcoming.

H. SOME FURTHER NOTIONS AND PRINCIPLES

A few additional syntactical principles are as follows.

TSyn15. ⊢ (*p* AcStr *a* . *p* AcStr *b* . (E*c*)(E*d*)(E*a*′)
(E*b*′)(*p* Ac *a*′ . *p* C *caa*′ . *p* Ac *b*′ . *p* C *dbb*′ .
p EqLng *cd*)) ⊃ *p* EqLng *ab*.

TSyn16. ⊢ ((*a*)(*p* Ac *a* ⊃ *Fa*) . (*a*)(*b*)(*c*)((*p*
AcStr *a* . *p* Ac *b* . *Fa* . *p* C *cab*) ⊃ *Fc*)) ⊃ (*a*)(*p*
AcStr *a* ⊃ *Fa*).

TSyn17a. ⊢ (*p* Fmla *a* . *p* (Tilde⌢*a*) *b*) ⊃ *p* Fmla *b*,

TSyn17b. ⊢ (*p* Fmla *a* . *p* Fmla *b* . *p* (LP⌢*a*⌢Vee⌢
b⌢RP) *c*) ⊃ *p* Fmla *c*,

TSyn17c. ⊢ (*p* Fmla *a* . *p* Vbl *b* . *p* (LP⌢*b*⌢RP⌢*a*)
c) ⊃ *p* Fmla *c*,

and so on.

TSyn18a. ⊢ *p* R1Ax *a* ≡ (E*b*)(E*c*)(E*d*)(E*e*)(E*e*′)
(*p* Fmla *b* . *p* Like *cb* . *p* Like *db* . *p* Disj *ebc* . *p*
Neg *e*′*e* . *p* Disj *ae*′*d*),

TSyn18b. ⊢ *p* R2Ax *a* ≡ (E*b*)(E*c*)(E*d*)(E*e*)(E*e'*)
(*p* Fmla *b* . *p* Fmla *d* . *p* Like *cb* . *p* Neg *eb* . *p*
Disj *e'cd* . *p* Disj *aee'*),

and similarly for 'R3Ax' and 'R4Ax'.

TSyn19. ⊢ *p* Thm *a* ⊃ *p* Fmla *a*.
TSyn20a. ⊢ (*p* Thm *a* . *p* Thm *b* . *p* MC *cab*) ⊃
p Thm *c*.
TSyn20b. ⊢ (*p* Thm *a* . *p* Gen *ba*) ⊃ *p* Thm *b*.

The notion of being a theorem has been formally introduced, but not that of being a *proof*. Let

DSyn41. ⌜*p* Proof *ab*⌝ abbreviate ⌜(*p* FrIng *ba* .
(*d*)(*p* FrIng *da* ⊃ (*p* Ax *d* ∨ (E*e*)(E*e'*)(*p* Pr *eda* .
p Pr *e'da* . (*p* MP *dee'* ∨ *p* Gen *d*)))))⌝.

User *p* takes *a* as a proof of *b*, then, if *p* takes *b* as a certain expression one of whose framed ingredients he takes as *b*. Clearly then,

TSyn21. ⊢ *p* Thm *a* ≡ (E*b*)*p* Proof *ba*.

It is often useful to distinguish between proofs and *derivations* from a given virtual class of formulae taken as premisses. Thus,

DSyn42. ⌜*p* Drv *aF*⌝ abbreviates ⌜((*b*)(*Fb* ⊃
p Fmla *b*) . (E*c*)(*p* FrIng *ac* . (*d*)(*p* FrIng *dc* ⊃ (*Fd* ∨
p Ax *d* ∨ (E*e*)(E*e'*)(*p* Pr *edc* . *p* Pr *e'dc* . (*p* MP *dee'*
∨ *p* Gen *de*))))))⌝.

Clearly then

TSyn22. ⊢ *p* Thm *a* ≡ *p* Drv *a*Λ.

A virtual class of formulae is said to be taken as *consistent* provided no two formulae, one of which is taken to be a negative of the other, are derivable from it.

DSyn42. ⌜*p* Cnst *F*⌝ abbreviates ⌜((*a*)(*Fa* ⊃
p Fmla *a*) . (*a*)(*b*)((*Fa* . *Fb* . *p* (Tilde⌢*a*) *b* . *p* Drv *aF*)
⊃ ∼ *p* Drv *bF*))⌝.

Also a virtual class of formulae F is said to be *complete* provided the class consisting of F together with the class whose only member is some formula not in F, is not consistent.

DSyn43. $\ulcorner p$ Cmplt $F \urcorner$ abbreviates $\ulcorner ((a)(Fa \supset p$ Fmla $a)$. $(a)((p$ Fmla a . $\sim Fa) \supset \sim p$ Cnst $(F \cup \{a\}))\urcorner$.

Clearly then

TSyn23. $\vdash ((a)(Fa \supset p$ Fmla $a)$. $\sim p$ Cnst $F) \supset p$ Cmplt F.

Another interesting syntactical notion is a quasimodal notion of logical *necessity*. Formulae are here regarded as necessary only *relative* to a virtual class of formulae, not absolutely. In fact

DSyn44. $\ulcorner p$ Nec $aF \urcorner$ is merely another notation for $\ulcorner p$ Drv $aF \urcorner$.

Then other modal notions may be introduced as follows, notions of logical *impossibility*, *possibility*, and *contingency*.

D45a. $\ulcorner p$ Impsbl $aF \urcorner$ abbreviates $\ulcorner (Ec)(p$ (Tilde$^\frown a)$ c . p Nec $cF)\urcorner$.

D45b. $\ulcorner p$ Psbl $aF \urcorner$ abbreviates $\ulcorner (Ec)(p$ (Tilde$^\frown a)$ c . $\sim p$ Nec cF . $(b)(Fb \supset p$ Fmla $b))\urcorner$,

D45c. $\ulcorner p$ Cntgt $aF \urcorner$ abbreviates $\ulcorner (Ec)(p$ (Tilde$^\frown a)$ c . $\sim p$ Nec aF . $\sim p$ Nec cF . $(b)(Fb \supset p$ Fmla $b))\urcorner$.

On the basis of these definitions a kind of modal logic emerges within the syntax here.

Although quite narrow as to modes of expression, the syntax here is seen to be a very powerful tool for logico-philosophical analysis. Even so, much is left out, and it is to what is left out that attention must be turned in the next chapter.

I. CONCEPTUALISM

It should be noted that the foregoing syntactical notions and principles have all been relativized to the user in the sense that a parameter 'p' for the user occurs in them fundamentally. The result is of course a pragmatized syntax. No allowance has been made for any aberration on the part of the individual user, the definitions and principles being in effect those of correct use or ideal usage. What is perhaps not so evident, however, is that the foregoing may also be regarded as a *conceptualistic* syntax, neither nominalist nor platonic but in some sense partaking of both.

The theory here is of course nominalistic in the sense that events and events only are taken as values for variables, with virtual classes and relations, not real ones. It goes far beyond nominalism, however, in allowing the individual user to take whatever he wishes as a sign event. Strictly, in nominalistic syntax as usually formulated, the sign events are spread out in advance, so to speak, and the user has no choice whatever with regard to them. In conceptualistic syntax there is considerable latitude, in effect allowing for what might be referred to as *concepts*.

Consider again the form

$$\text{`}p \ C \ abc\text{'},$$

expressing that the user p takes a to be the concatenate of b with c. Although a, b, and c here are all events, nothing requires that they be actually exhibited in nature as ink or chalk marks or something of the kind. All that is required is that p regards some entity a as though it were the concatenate of b with c. It might be said here that p has a concept of a as the concatenate of b with c. No additional realm of concepts is introduced, however, with this mode of speaking, no new variables or anything of the kind. Concepts are spoken of only in restricted contexts and are given in effect a very exact characterization by the definitions and principles.

It is of particular interest in this context to reflect upon the Principle of Concatenational Existence *SynR9*, to the effect that given any entities a and b taken by p as sign events, there is some entity c taken by p as the concatenate of them. It might obtain that a and b as exhibited entities would be so long that a and b run end to end could not fit into the physical cosmos.

The user p, however, can still regard something c as their concatenate. In fact he can take c as anything he wants, the only constraint being that he should use it throughout as the concatenate of a with b in accord with the definitions and principles.

The definitions and principles given characterize ideal linguistic usage. The actual usage of some individual p may or may not accord with this in practice. If it does, all well and good. If not, *tant pis* for p's linguistic behavior regarded as correct. Such aberrations abound in practice and few of us can boast of perfect usage at all times.

Very little has been said thus far about a canonical notation. Of course some such notation is usually used in practice and can be fixed or determined by fiat outside the system, so to speak. Another way of doing this, within the system, is to pick out an ideal user and to take his choice of notation as canonical. Let 'WVQ' be the proper name of such a person. Then

$$\ulcorner LP\ a \urcorner \quad \text{may abbreviate} \quad \ulcorner WVQ\ LP\ a \urcorner,$$

so that a is a canonical left parenthesis if it is taken by the ideal user WVQ to be a left parenthesis. And similarly for other notions of syntax.

CHAPTER VI

REFERENCE AND ACCEPTANCE

Let 'reference' be construed here in
the widest sense in accord with which human persons use whatever they take as sign events to refer to the entities of their
experience in the cosmos. The notion of reference is usually
left rather vague in philosophical discussion and hence it will
be of interest to attempt to formulate a precise theory. If it is
asked, What is it that refers to what? the answer is that human
persons take sign events, usually as embedded in certain linguistic contexts, to refer to entities on certain occasions. Sign events
so used are in effect the words and phrases of his language.
Clearly different persons use the same or similar words to refer
to distinct entities, and different words on different occasions
of use to refer to the same entity. Also the same person may
use different words on different occasions to refer to the same
object. Thus in the theory of reference at least five factors
should be recognized: the person, the sign event, the entity, the
linguistic context, and the occasion of use.[1]

1. For further preliminary discussion, see "On Truth, Reference, and Acts
of Utterance," in *Events Etc.*

We could let

'p Ref axb'

express primitively that person p uses the sign event a as occurring in the sentence b to refer to the entity x. Then

'$\langle p, \text{Ref}, a, x, b \rangle e$'

would express that e is an occasion or act of p's using a in b to refer to x. Thus the relation of reference might be taken as a quadratic relation, a notation for the occasion of use being forthcoming in event logic.

Another approach is to take

'p Ref ax'

as the primitive sentential form, with the linguistic context dropped. The quadratic form is then immediately forthcoming, however, for

'p Ref axb'

then holds just where p Ref ax, p takes a to be of a proper form and as a segment of b, and p takes b as a sentence. And then of course both

'$\langle p, \text{Ref}, a, x \rangle e$'

and

'$\langle p, \text{Ref}, a, x, b \rangle e$'

are forthcoming as above. This second approach will be followed in the sequel.

A.   PERSONAL PRONOUNS AND DEMONSTRATIVES

The only expressions taken to refer that have been introduced thus far are the primitive or defined individual constants, expressions of the form $\ulcorner (x 1 A) \urcorner$ (where A contains no free variables other than x), and primitive or defined one-place predicates (containing no free variables). There are other types of expressions that may be regarded as referential, however, in particular, the personal pronouns and demonstrative phrases of the form 'that F' or 'those F'.

Let 'I', 'you$_s$', 'he', 'she', 'it', 'we', 'you$_p$', 'they' now be regarded as additional primitive expressions. Thus 'Q I' expresses now that I am a member of the virtual class Q, 'Q you$_s$' that you (in the singular—hence the subscript 's') are in Q, and so on. Similarly let '(that F)' and '(those F)', for all virtual class expressions F, be primitively significant, so that

$$\text{'Q(that } F)\text{'}$$

expresses that that F is in Q and

$$\text{'Q(those } F)\text{'}$$

that those F are in Q. 'I', 'you$_s$', and so on, and '(this F)' and '(those F)' are to be regarded as referential phrases, and rules of correct reference concerning them will be laid down. In addition of course rules concerning the other kinds of referential expressions will also be given.

The object language is now to be presumed augmented with the addition of the personal pronouns and demonstratives regarded as a new kind of term for individuals. Note that the plural terms afford no difficulty, for 'we' can be accommodated in terms of a sum of several persons, '(those F)' in terms of the fusion of the individuals in F. The material of the preceding chapters is now to be extended so as to include these new expressions.

It is interesting to note that no object-language axioms are laid down concerning the personal pronouns and the demonstratives. The reason is that their reference may vary with different occasions of use and from user to user. On the other hand, object-language axioms are presumed laid down for the primitive InCon's and PredCon's, for these are always used with the same reference by all persons who follow the rules of the language. But all referential phrases are of course subject to the semantical rules of reference, to be given in a moment.

In the syntactical metalanguage additional shape-descriptive predicates are needed now to express that person p takes a given sign event as an 'I'-expression, a 'you'-expression, and so on. Thus 'p I a', 'p You$_s$ a', and so on, are additional sentential functions of syntax expressing respectively that p takes a as a sign event of the shape 'I', that p takes a as a sign event of the shape 'you$_s$', and so on.

The following two additional syntactical predicates are now useful.

DSyn46.   ⌜p PerPrn a⌝   abbreviates   ⌜(p I a ∨ ... ∨ p They a)⌝

and

DSyn47.   ⌜p Dmtv a⌝   abbreviates   ⌜(Eb)(p PredConOne b . (p (LP⌢That⌢b⌢RP) a ∨ p (LP⌢ Those⌢b⌢RP) a))⌝.

Note that with the addition of the shape-descriptive predicates for PerPrn's and Dmtv's, the syntactical rules and some definitions must now be extended in obvious ways. Thus *SynR1* is now extended as follows.

SynR1'.   ⊢ ((p LP a . p RP b) ∨ ... ∨ (p LP a . p I a) ∨ ... ∨ (p That a . p Those a)) ⊃ Dab.

And similarly for the other rules where needed. And of course 'Char', 'SgnEv', and so on, are now broadened accordingly.

A predicate for 'is a human person' has not yet been formally introduced. Human persons are though *par excellence* to be the users of language, more particularly, the users of language in a referential way. Computers and the like may well "use" language in some sense or other, but they do not use language with referential intent. In any case we let

DRef1.   'Per' abbreviate 'D'Ref',

so that persons are taken to be just those entities who use some sign events to refer to something or other. Man is above all a referring animal.

The following is in effect an additional rule of syntax.

SynR16.   ⊢ p SgnEv a ⊃ Per p.

B.   PRINCIPLES OF CORRECT REFERENCE

In the next chapter, on the foundations of mathematics, an additional kind of phrase will be regarded as referential, namely, AcStr's. In order to accommodate numbers, AcStr's will be introduced as counters. This use must be taken account of now in stating one of the Rules of Reference. Later suitable rules concerning the arithmetical use of them will of course be given. The interesting circumstance will emerge for the philosophy of mathematics that arithmetic turns out merely as a branch of the theory of reference. But this is anticipating.

Let any expression of the form $\ulcorner(x1A)\urcorner$, where A is taken as a sentential form of the one variable x, be regarded as an *atomic-summation term*. Thus

DSyn48. $\ulcorner p$ AtSumTrm $a\urcorner$ abbreviates $\ulcorner(\mathrm{E}b)(\mathrm{E}c)$ (p SentFormOne bc . p (LP⁀c⁀One⁀b⁀RP) $a)\urcorner$.

The first Rule of Reference is a *Principle of Limitation*, to the effect that only certain kinds of expressions are taken as referential.

RefR1.   ⊢ p Ref ax ⊃ (E! p . (p InCon a ∨ p AtSumTrm a ∨ p PredConOne a ∨ p PerPrn a ∨ p Dmtv a ∨ p AcStr a)).

Clearly the kinds of referential expressions, according to this rule, are InCon's or AtSumTrm's or PredConOne's or PerPrn's or Dmtv's or AcStr's, nothing else. Also where p Ref ax, p must be non-null.

The *Principle of Uniqueness for Primitive Individual Constants* is to the effect that the user uses an InCon to refer to at most one entity.

RefR2.   ⊢ (p InCon a . p Ref ax . p Ref ay) ⊃ $x = y$.

And similarly there is the *Principle of Uniqueness for Atomic-Summation Terms*.

RefR3.   ⊢ (p AtSumTrm a . p Ref ax . p Ref ay) ⊃ $x = y$.

Recall *DSyn7* above in (VII,C), which introduced the defined shape-descriptive predicates, or as one might say, concatenates of the primitive ones. In general now, if

$$\ulcorner p \ (S_1 \frown \ldots \frown S_n) \ a \urcorner$$

holds in a special instance, that is, for a particular person p and a particular sign event a, then $\ulcorner (S_1 \frown \ldots \frown S_n) \urcorner$ will be said to be the *shape-descriptive predicate* or the *shape description of* the sign event a. Thus if p (Ex⌢Ac) a, then '(Ex⌢Ac)' is the shape-descriptive predicate of a. If

$$p \ (LB \frown Ex \frown Invep \frown Pee \frown Ex \frown Ex \frown RB) \ a,$$

then '(LB⌢Ex⌢Invep⌢Pee⌢Ex⌢Ex⌢RB)' is taken to be the shape-descriptive predicate of a.

Next come the *Shape-Descriptive Principles* concerning In-Con's, AtSumTrm's, and PredConOne's respectively.

RefR4.   ⊢ $(p \ S \ a \ . \ p \ \text{Ref} \ ax) \supset x = y$, where y is an object-language individual constant whose shape-description is S.

RefR5.   ⊢ $(p \ S \ a \ . \ p \ \text{Ref} \ ax) \supset x = y$, where y is an atomic-summation term whose shape-description is S.

RefR6.   ⊢ $(p \ S \ a \ . \ p \ \text{Ref} \ ay) \supset (p \ \text{Ref} \ ax \equiv$ $\ldots x \ldots)$, where (i) $\ulcorner \ldots x \ldots \urcorner$ is a sentential form containing x as its only free variable (if any) and S is the shape-description of the abstract $\ulcorner \{x3 \ldots x \ldots\} \urcorner$ or (ii) $\ulcorner \ldots x \ldots \urcorner$ consists of a one-place primitive predicate constant followed by the variable x and S is the shape-description of that constant.

These three principles are crucial in laying down the correct reference for InCon's, AtSumTrm's, and PredConOne's.

C.   PRONOMIAL PRINCIPLES

The rules of reference required for the personal pronouns will now be considered.

RefR7 is the *Principle of Unique Self-Referentiality for 'I'*.

RefR7.   ⊢ $(p \ I \ a \ . \ p \ \text{Ref} \ ax) \supset x = p$.

Clearly if p takes a as an 'I' and uses it to refer at all, he then uses it correctly to refer to himself and to nothing else.

RefR8 is the *Principle of Multiple Self-Referentiality for 'we'*.

RefR8. $\vdash (p \text{ We } a \;.\; p \text{ Ref } ax) \supset (p \text{ Ref } ap \;.\; (\mathrm{E}y)$ $(\sim y = p \;.\; \text{Per } y \;.\; p \text{ Ref } ay))$.

If p takes a to be a 'we' and uses a to refer at all then p uses it to refer to himself as well as to some other person.

Similarly we have a *Principle of Unique Referentiality for 'you$_s$'* and a *Principle of Multiple Referentiality for 'you$_p$'*.

RefR9. $\vdash (p \text{ You}_s a \;.\; p \text{ Ref } ax) \supset (\text{Per } x \;.\; (y)(p$ $\text{Ref } ay \supset y = x))$.

RefR10. $\vdash (p \text{ You}_p a \;.\; p \text{ Ref } ax) \supset (\text{Per } x \;.\; (\mathrm{E}y)$ $(\text{Per } y \;.\; \sim y = x \;.\; p \text{ Ref } ay))$.

Also *Principles of Unique Referentiality* are needed *for 'he'*, *'she'*, and *'it'*. Let now 'Mp' express primitively that p is a male. 'Fem p' may then obviously express that p is a female.

⌜Fem p⌝   may abbreviate   ⌜(Per p . $\sim$ Mp)⌝.

Clearly means must be at hand for distinguishing the masculine, feminine, and neuter genders. 'M' may be understood as one of the nonlogical primitive PredConOne's. It is assumed that

$$\vdash \text{M}p \supset \text{Per } p.$$

The following principles then obtain.

RefR11a. $\vdash (p \text{ He } a \;.\; p \text{ Ref } ax) \supset (\text{M}x \;.\; (y)(p$ $\text{Ref } ay \supset y = x))$.

RefR11b. $\vdash (p \text{ She } a \;.\; p \text{ Ref } ax) \supset (\text{Fem } x \;.\; (y)(p$ $\text{Ref } ay \supset y = x))$.

Ref R11c. $\vdash (p \text{ It } a \;.\; p \text{ Ref } ax) \supset (\sim \text{M}x \;.\; \sim$ $\text{Fem } x \;.\; (y)(p \text{ Ref } ay \supset y = x))$.

It might be objected that these rules, *RefR8–RefR11c*, are too restrictive. The words 'we', 'you$_s$', 'you$_p$', 'he', and 'she' may on occasion be used correctly to refer to entities other than persons, for example, to animals, and the word 'it' may be used to refer to persons. Obviously the rules here are concerned only with the *interpersonal* referential uses of these words (except 'it'), by far the most important. The rules may readily be generalized to other uses.

Next there is the *Principle of Multiple Referentiality for 'they'*.

Ref R12.   ⊢ (*p* They *a* . *p* Ref *ax*) ⊃ (E*y*)(∼ *y* = *x* . *p* Ref *ay*).

If *p* uses a 'they' expression to refer correctly to an entity *x* he also is using it to refer correctly to some entity other than *x*.

It was mentioned above that the plural pronouns in their collective use may be handled in terms of logical sums of individuals. Thus an inscription of the form 'we' in a given context may be regarded in effect as short for 'Fu'*F*' where *F* is the virtual class of persons referred to in that context. And similarly for the others. And similarly no doubt for plural nouns or phrases taken in the collective sense. Several examples of these will be given below.

D.   DEMONSTRATIVE PRINCIPLES

Note that the Rules of Reference conveniently divide into just six kinds. The first kind has only one rule, the *Rule of Limitation (Ref R1)*, stating that only sign events of just six kinds may be used to refer. There are then Rules for each of these kinds. *Ref R2* and *Ref R4* are rules concerning the individual constants, *Ref R3* and *Ref R5* concern the AtSumTrm's, and *Ref R6* concerns one-place predicate constants. *Ref R7–Ref R12* concern the personal pronouns. The rules governing the demonstratives 'that' and 'those' will now be given. In the next chapter various Rules of Reference covering the quasi-numerical strings of accents will be considered.

First there is the *Principle of Unique Referentiality for 'that'*.

Ref R13.   ⊢ (E*b*)(*p* PredConOne *b* . *p* (LP⌢That⌢*b*⌢ RP) *a* . *p* Ref *ax*) ⊃ (*y*)(*p* Ref *ay* ⊃ *y* = *x*),

and the *Principle of Multiple Referentiality for 'those'*.

Ref R14.   ⊢ (E*b*)(*p* PredConOne *b* . *p* (LP⌢Those⌢ *b*⌢RP) *a* . *p* Ref *ax*) ⊃ (E*y*)(∼ *y* = *x* . *p* Ref *ay*).

Also there is a common *Shape-Descriptive Principle for 'that' and 'those'*.

RefR15. ⊢ ((*p* That *a* ∨ *p* Those *a*) . (E*b*)(E*c*)(*p* (LP⁀*a*⁀*b*⁀RP) *c* . *p* **S** *b* . *p* Ref *cx*)) ⊃ *Fx*, where *F* is a PredConOne whose shape-description is **S**.

This rule is to the effect that whenever a person uses correctly a phrase of the kind '(that *F*)' or '(those *F*)' in sentence *d* to refer, the entity or entities to which he refers are in the virtual class *F*.

Two further rules of reference, one for 'that' and one for 'those', will be given later.

Two additional principles of a restrictive character are required. It is to be understood of course that correct reference does not extend to entities taken as sign events. In other words, the sign events of the object language are never correctly referred to within the semantical metalanguage, but only within a metalanguage of higher order. Thus the *Principle of Self-Referentiality Exclusion* is needed.

RefR16. ⊢ *p* Ref *ax* ⊃ ∼ *p* SgnEv *x*.

Also no person is to be taken as a sign event. Thus the *Principle of Person Exclusion*:

RefR17. ⊢ Per *q* ⊃ ∼ *p* SgnEv *q*.

To assure consistent referential behavior on the part of *p*, a *Principle of Likeness* is needed.

Ref R18. ⊢ (*p* Ref *ax* . *p* Like *a'a* . ∼ *p* PerPrn *a* . ∼ *p* Dmtv *a*) ⊃ *p* Ref *a'x*.

Clearly now

TRef1. ⊢ *p* Ref *ax* ⊃ (Per *p* . *p* SgnEv *a*).
TRef2. ⊢ ∼ (E*x*)*p* Ref *xx*.

E. DESIGNATION, DENOTATION, SATISFACTION, DETERMINATION

A very broad relation of reference has been taken here as the fundamental relation of semantics. Narrower relations are immediately definable, some of which have played an important role in the literature.

Consider first the relation of *designation*, taken as a relation between individual constants or atomic-summation terms and the entities for which they are supposed to stand. This relation may be introduced as follows.

DRef2.   ⌜*p* Des$_{In}$ *ax*⌝ abbreviates ⌜((*p* InCon *a* ∨ *p* AtSumTrm *a*) . *p* Ref *ax*)⌝.

Thus *p* may be said to use *a* to designate the individual *x* provided he takes *a* as an InCon or an AtSumTrm and uses it to refer to *x*.

The following three basic *Principles of Designation* are provable. The first is the *Uniqueness Principle for Designation*.

Des$_{In}$R1.   ⊢ (*p* Des$_{In}$ *ax* . *p* Des$_{In}$ *ay*) ⊃ *x* = *y*.

The second is the *Shape-Descriptive Principle for Designation*.

Des$_{In}$R2.   ⊢ (*p* S *a* . *p* Des$_{In}$ *ax*) ⊃ *x* = *y*, where *y* is an individual constant or atomic-summation term whose shape description is *S*.

The third is the *Principle of Limitation for Designation*.

Des$_{In}$R3.   ⊢ *p* Des$_{In}$ *ax* ⊃ (*p* InCon *a* ∨ *p* AtSumTrm *a*).

Denotation is traditionally taken in the sense in which one-place predicates may be said to apply to their object. Thus here one may let

DRef3.   ⌜*p* Den *ax*⌝ abbreviate ⌜(*p* PredConOne *a* . *p* Ref *ax*)⌝.

Immediately then the two *Principles of Denotation* are provable. *DenR1* is the *Shape-Descriptive Principle* and *DenR2* the *Principle of Limitation*.

DenR1.   ⊢ (*p* S *a* . *p* Ref *ay*) ⊃ (*p* Den *ax* ≡ . . .*x*. . .), if (as in *Ref R6*).

DenR2.   ⊢ *p* Den *ax* ⊃ *p* PredConOne *a*.

In terms of denotation the relation of *virtual-class designation* is definable, as follows.

DRef4. $\ulcorner p$ Des$_{VC}$ $aF \urcorner$ abbreviates $\ulcorner (p$ PredConOne a . $(x)(p$ Den $ax \equiv Fx))\urcorner$, where F is a PredConOne.

The following principles then obtain.

Des$_{VC}$R1. $\vdash (p$ Des$_{VC}$ aF . p Des$_{VC}$ $aG) \supset F = G$.

Des$_{VC}$R2. $\vdash (p$ S a . p Des$_{VC}$ $aF) \supset F = G$, where G is a PredConOne whose shape description is S.

Des$_{VC}$R3. $\vdash p$ Des$_{VC}$ $aF \supset p$ PredConOne a.

The relation of *satisfaction* is taken here as a relation between an entity and a sentential form of one variable. It may be defined in terms of 'Ref' as follows.

DRef5. $\ulcorner p$ Sat $xa \urcorner$ abbreviates $\ulcorner (Ec)(Ed)(p$ SentFormOne ac . p (LB$^\frown c^\frown$Invep$^\frown a^\frown$RB) d . p Ref $dx)\urcorner$.

Here again the two fundamental principles concerning satisfaction, the *Shape-Descriptive Principle* and the *Principle of Limitation*, are provable.

SatR1. $\vdash (p$ S a . p Sat $ya) \supset (p$ Sat $xa \equiv$ . . .x. . .), if $\ulcorner$. . .x. . .$\urcorner$ is a sentential form of the one variable x whose shape description is S.

SatR2. $\vdash p$ Sat $xa \supset (Ec)p$ SentFormOne ac.

A fifth interesting semantical relation is that of *determination*, according to which a sentential form of one variable is taken to determine a virtual class. More particularly, one may let

DRef6. $\ulcorner p$ Det $aF \urcorner$ abbreviate $\ulcorner ((Ec)p$ SentFormOne ac . $(x)(p$ Sat $xa \equiv Fx))\urcorner$, where F is a PredConOne.

As *Rules of Determination* there are, again, a *Uniqueness Principle*, a *Shape-Descriptive Principle*, and a *Principle of Limitation*.

DetR1.   ⊢ (*p* Det *aF* . *p* Det *aG*) ⊃ *F* = *G*.

DetR2.   ⊢ (*p* **S** *a* . *p* Det *aF*) ⊃ *p* Det *a*{*x*3
. . .*x*. . .}, where **S** is the shape-description of ⌜. . .*x*. . .⌝, this
latter being a sentential form of the one variable *x*.

DetR3.   ⊢ *p* Det *aF* ⊃ (E*c*)*p* SentFormOne *ac*.

Another way of providing for these five semantical relations
is to bring in the canonical notation and the ideal user WVQ.
Then, for denotation,

⌜*a* Den *x*⌝   may abbreviate   ⌜(WVQ PredConOne *a* .
WVQ Ref *ax*)⌝.

An expression is then said to denote entity *x* provided WVQ
takes it as a canonical PredConOne and uses it to refer to *x*. And
similarly for the other semantical relations.

Recall that Ref is a relation of correct reference. Of course
person *p* may use some expression with the *intent* to refer to
something by means of it, but this of course is a very different
matter. The relation of *intending to refer* is an intentional
relation to be handled in terms of 'Intd' for the general relation
of intending to do. More will be said about this relation later.

Of course, should it happen that all users of the language agree
that *a*, say, is a PredConOne, then we could also define

⌜*a* Den *x*⌝   as   ⌜(*p*)(Per *p* ⊃ (*p* PredConOne *a* .
p Ref *ax*))⌝   or even as   ⌜((*p*)(Per *p* ⊃ *p* PredConOne *a*)
. (E*p*)*p* Ref *ax*)⌝.

However, no harm can arise from retaining the parameter '*p*'
throughout even though it may not always strictly be needed.
But of course it is strictly needed in the underlying syntax
because of its pragmatized character, and also in those parts of
semantics concerned with personal pronouns, demonstratives,
and the like.

F.   TRUTHS FOR ETERNAL SENTENCES

Following Quine in essentials, let an *eternal* sentence be one
containing neither personal pronouns nor demonstratives, an

occasion sentence containing at least one such.[2] Thus

> *DSyn49.* $\ulcorner p$ EtSent $a\urcorner$ abbreviates $\ulcorner(p$ Sent a . $\sim$ $(Eb)(p$ Seg ba . $(p$ PerPrn b $\vee$ p Dmtv $b)))\urcorner$,
> *DSyn50.* $\ulcorner p$ OccSent $a\urcorner$ abbreviates $\ulcorner(p$ Sent a . $\sim$ p EtSent $a)\urcorner$.

Two truth predicates must be introduced, one for eternal sentences, and one for occasion sentences. For the present, only eternal sentences are considered, occasion sentences being introduced below.

Consider an eternal sentence a of the object language, say '(-----)'. Being a sentence of course it contains no free variables. Consider the abstract $\ulcorner\{x3(\text{-----})\}\urcorner$ where x is any variable. Suppose an abstract of this form is taken by p to refer to all entities whatsoever. Then and only then is a regarded as a true eternal sentence.[3] Thus one may let

> *DRef7.* $\ulcorner p$ TrEtSent $a\urcorner$ abbreviate $\ulcorner(p$ EtSent a . $(Eb)(Ec)(p$ Vbl b . p $(\text{LB}^\frown b^\frown \text{Invep}^\frown a^\frown \text{RB})$ c . $(x)p$ Den $cx))\urcorner$.

The fundamental principle governing the truth of eternal sentences is the *Principle of Adequacy.*

> *Adeq.* $\vdash$ $(p$ S a . $(Eb)(Ec)(Ex)(p$ Vbl b . p $(\text{LB}^\frown b^\frown \text{Invep}^\frown a^\frown \text{RB})$ c . p Ref $cx))$ $\supset$ $(p$ TrEtSent a $\equiv$ $A)$,

where A is any eternal sentence whose shape-description is S.

Some additional principles concerning the relation TrEtSent are as follows.

> *TTr1.* $\vdash$ $(p$ EtSent a . p $(\text{Tilde}^\frown a)$ $b)$ $\supset$ $(p$ TrEtSent a $\equiv$ $\sim$ p TrEtSent $b)$.
> *TTr2.* $\vdash$ $(p$ EtSent a . $(Eb)(Ec)(p$ EtSent b . p EtSent c . p $(\text{LP}^\frown b^\frown \text{Vee}^\frown c^\frown \text{RP})$ $a))$ $\supset$ $(p$ TrEtSent a $\equiv$ $(p$ TrEtSent b $\vee$ p TrEtSent $c))$.

---

2. W. V. Quine, *Word and Object* (Cambridge: The Technology Press of the Massachusetts Institute of Technology and New York and London: John Wiley and Sons, 1960), p. 12, pp. 35 ff., and *passim.*
3. Cf. *Truth and Denotation*, p. 119.

TTr3. ⊢ (*p* TrEtSent *a* . (E*b*)(E*c*)(E*e*)(*p* SentFormOne *bc* . *p* (LP⌒*c*⌒RP⌒*b*) *a* . *p* SF$_c^e$ *db* . (*p* InCon *e* ∨ *p* AtSumTrm *e*))) ⊃ *p* TrEtSent *d*.

TTr4. ⊢ (*p* Thm *a* . *p* EtSent *a*) ⊃ *p* TrEtSent *a*.

TTr5. ⊢ (*p* EtSent *a* . *p* (Tilde⌒*a*) *b*) ⊃ ∼ (*p* TrEtSent *a* . *p* TrEtSent *b*).

TTr6. ⊢ (*p* EtSent *a* . *p* (Tilde⌒*a*) *b*) ⊃ ∼ (*p* Thm *a* . *p* Thm *b*).

With 'TrEtSent' or 'Den' now available, an additional Principle of Reference concerning 'that' may be given as follows, to the effect that when *p* uses a '(that *F*)' to refer to *x*, he takes *x* to be the one and only entity in *F* and also in some (perhaps other) virtual class *G*, in other words, that *x* is the one and only member of {*y*3(*Fy* . *Gy*)}. Thus

RefR19. ⊢ (*p* PredConOne *a* . *p* (LP⌒That⌒*a*⌒RP) *b* . *p* Ref *bx*) ⊃ (E*c*)(E*d*)(*p* PredConOne *c* . *p* Den *dx* . *p* (LB⌒Ex⌒Invep⌒Tilde⌒LP⌒Ex⌒Ac⌒RP⌒LP⌒LP⌒LP⌒ Tilde⌒*a*⌒Ex⌒Ac⌒Vee⌒Tilde⌒*c*⌒Ex⌒Ac⌒RP⌒Vee⌒ Tilde⌒Ex⌒Id⌒Ex⌒Ac⌒RP⌒Vee⌒Tilde⌒LP⌒Ex⌒Ac⌒ Ac⌒RP⌒LP⌒LP⌒Tilde⌒*a*⌒Ex⌒Ac⌒Ac⌒Vee⌒Tilde⌒*c*⌒ Ex⌒Ac⌒Ac⌒RP⌒Vee⌒Ex⌒Ac⌒Ac⌒Id⌒Ex⌒Ac⌒RP⌒ RP⌒RB) *d*).

Observe here that *d* is taken in effect to be of the form

'{*x*3∼ (*x*′)(((∼ *Fx*′ ∨ ∼ *Gx*′) ∨ ∼ *x* = *x*′) ∨ ∼ (*x*″)((∼ *Fx*″ ∨ ∼ *Gx*″) ∨ *x*″ = *x*′))}',

where *a* stands for *F* and *c* for *G*, this being merely the primitive expansion of the appropriate abstract for the virtual class whose only member is the one entity in both *F* and *G*.

There is an analogous principle concerning 'those', to the effect that when *p* uses '(those *F*)' to refer to *x*, he takes *x* to be one of the entities in *F* and also in some (perhaps other) virtual class *G* as well, in other words, that *x* is any selected member of '{*y*3(*Fy* . *Gy*)}'. Thus

RefR20. ⊢ (*p* PredConOne *a* . *p* (LP⌒Those⌒*a*⌒RP) *b* . *p* Ref *bx*) ⊃ (E*c*)(E*d*)(*p* PredConOne *c* . *p* Den *dx* . *p* (LB⌒Ex⌒Invep⌒Tilde⌒LP⌒Tilde⌒*a*⌒Ex⌒Vee⌒Tilde⌒ *c*⌒Ex⌒RP⌒RB) *d* . ∼ (*x*)(*p* Den *cx* ≡ *x* = *x*)).

The point of introducing an expression for the additional virtual class G, in *RefR19*, is to assure that '$(F \cap G)$' have a unique referent even if 'F' does not. The user may correctly use '(that F)', but only where '$(F \cap G)$' for a suitable 'G' denotes uniquely. And similarly, '(those F)' may be correctly used where '(those $(F \cap G)$)' would be more accurate. (Note that an analogous law is not needed for '$(\imath F)$', this phrase correctly referring to one and only one F if it refers at all.)

Up to this point there has been no need to bring in formally the linguistic context of reference, as mentioned above. Now, however, we may let

DRef 8.   ⌜p Ref axb⌝ abbreviate ⌜$(p$ Ref ax . p Seg ab . p Sent $b)$⌝.

Here the context of reference is made explicit.

Let us now glance very briefly, in the remainder of this chapter, at some further relations of pragmatics that cry out for a deeper and fuller characterization than can be given here.

G.   UTTERANCE, APPREHENSION, ACCEPTANCE, ASSERTION

Three new pragmatical primitives may now be introduced. Let

'p Utt aq'

express that person p *utters* sign event a to person q in some suitable behavioral sense. He may make certain sounds in q's presence suitably correlated with a, he may exhibit a to q in some appropriate way, he may point to a, and so on, depending upon just what kind of an entity a is.

Similarly let

'p Apprh a'

express primitively that that person p *apprehends* sign event a in the sense that he grasps whatever it is that a is supposed to say or mean or communicate.

Finally let

'p Acpt a'

express that person p *accepts* sign event a in the sense either of taking it as true or as a likely hypothesis or as being worthy to be acted upon, or as having suitable evidential support in its favor, or the like.[4]

Concerning these three notions the following principles are assumed. The first is a *Limitation Principle for Utterance*, that only sentences are uttered to persons.

RefR21.   ⊢ p Utt aq ⊃ (p Sent a . Per q).

The next is the *Segmental Principle for Utterance.*

RefR22.   ⊢ (p Utt aq . p Seg ba . p Sent b) ⊃ p Utt bq.

According to this, p utters all sentential segments of sentences he utters. Also, more strictly, it is required that the order of utterance follow the concatenational order. Because '∨' is a primitive sentential connective, the following rule is also needed.

RefR23.   ⊢ ($\langle p,\text{Utt},c,q\rangle e$. p Sent a . p Sent b . p (LP⌢a⌢Vee⌢b⌢RP) c) ⊃ (Ee_1)(Ee_2)(B$e_1 e_2$. $\langle p,\text{Utt},a,q\rangle e_1$. $\langle p,\text{Utt},b,q\rangle e_2$. P$e_1 e$. P$e_2 e$).

Concerning Apprh and Acpt, the following principles are needed. The first is the *Principle of Limitation for Apprh*, that only sentences are apprehended.

RefR24.   ⊢ p Apprh a ⊃ p Sent a.

The *Acpt-Apprh Rule* is that whatever is accepted is apprehended.

RefR25.   ⊢ p Acpt a ⊃ p Apprh a.

There is also a *Segmental Principle for Apprh*

RefR26.   ⊢ (p Apprh a . p Seg ba . p Sent b) ⊃ p Apprh b.

---

4. See Frege's famous paper "Der Gedanke" (translated in *Mind* 65 (1956): 289–311). Cf. the author's "Frege's Pragmatic Concerns," in *Peirce's Logic of Relations and Other Studies* (*Studies in Semiotics*, Vol. 12, ed. by T. Sebeok; Lisse, Netherlands: Peter de Ridder Press, 1978).

The *Principle of Limitation for Acpt* is of course provable.

TRef3.   ⊢ p Acpt a ⊃ p Sent a.

Another important pragmatical predicate is that for *assertion*. A new primitive is not needed for assertion seems to be merely simultaneous acceptance and utterance. Thus

DRef9.   ⌜p Assrt aq⌝ abbreviates ⌜(Ee)(⟨p,Acpt,a⟩e . ⟨p,Utt,a,q⟩e)⌝.

Thus p may be said to assert a to q provided there is an e that is both an act or state of acceptance on p's part of a and also an act of uttering it to q. Person p might utter a to q but not accept it at the same time, or he might accept it but not utter it, in which cases one would not say that he was asserting it to q. Assertion seems to require simultaneous acceptance and utterance in some one complex act.

H.   UNDERSTANDING, BELIEF, AND KNOWLEDGE

Some *epistemic* relations may be introduced by definition.

Person p may be said to *understand* entity x as characterized by the predicate a provided a is taken as a PredConOne and p uses some b to refer to x and *apprehends* that a applies to x. Thus

DRef10.   ⌜p Unds xa⌝ abbreviates ⌜(p PredConOne a . (Eb)(Ec)(p Ref bxc . p ($a⌒b$) c . p Apprh c))⌝.

Similarly person p may be said to *believe of* entity x that it is characterized by the predicate a provided a is taken as a PredConOne and p uses some b to refer to x and he *accepts* that a applies to x.

DRef11.   ⌜p Blv xa⌝ abbreviates ⌜(p PredConOne a . (Eb)(Ec)(p Ref bxc . p ($a⌒b$) c . p Acpt c))⌝.

Finally, person p may be said to *know-eternally* of entity x that it is characterized by the PredConOne a provided p takes as *true* some eternal sentence to the effect that a applies to x.

DRef12.   ⌜p KnEt xa⌝ abbreviates ⌜(p PredConOne a . (Eb)(Ec)(p Ref bxc . p ($a⌒b$) c . p TrEtSent c))⌝.

Another notion of knowing, for occasion sentences, will be discussed below.

Corresponding notions may also be introduced for two-place predicates, and so on, so that ⌜p Unds xya⌝, ⌜p Blv xya⌝, and ⌜p KnEt xya⌝, and so on, may also be presumed defined.

These definitions merely serve to reduce these epistemic notions to prior, Fregean, pragmatic ones, including truth for eternal sentences. A few principles concerning Apprh and Acpt have been given, but more are needed of course for a full account. Perhaps these latter may themselves be defined in terms of more basic notions, psycho- and socio-linguistic ones no doubt, but this seems not to have been done to date. Further, these definitions introduce only very restricted notions, capturing only some of their ordinary uses.

I. QUESTIONS, COMMANDS, EXCLAMATIONS, SUBJUNCTIVES

Some further pragmatic primitives may be introduced as follows.

Let

$$'p \text{ Qstn } aq'$$

express that p *questions* a of q. Questioning, like utterance and assertion, are person directed, and hence the presence here of the parameter 'q' for a person. All questions are apprehended by the user. Thus

Ref R27.   ⊢ p Qstn aq ⊃ p Apprh a.

In similar vein let

$$'p \text{ Cmnd } aq'$$

and

$$'p \text{ Excl } aq'$$

express that p *commands* a of q and that p *exclaims* a to q.

Also let

$$\text{'}p \text{ Subj } aq\text{'}$$

express that p entertains a in the *subjunctive* mood and makes it known to q. Here also

Ref R28. $\vdash (p \text{ Cmnd } \textbf{\textit{aq}} \lor p \text{ Excl } \textbf{\textit{aq}} \lor p \text{ Subj } \textbf{\textit{aq}})$ $\supset p \text{ Apprh } \textbf{\textit{a}}.$

These pragmatical relations are intended to provide for the handling of the various sentential moods, just as 'Assrt' is for assertion. In the theory it is assumed of course that the moods are all distinct, in the sense that no assertoric act is an interrogative one, and so on. Thus

Ref R29. $\vdash (e)(\langle p,\text{Assrt},\textbf{\textit{a}},\textbf{\textit{q}}\rangle e \supset \sim \langle p,\text{Qstn},\textbf{\textit{a}},\textbf{\textit{q}}\rangle e)$. $(e)(\langle p,\text{Assrt},\textbf{\textit{a}},\textbf{\textit{q}}\rangle e \supset \sim \langle p,\text{Cmnd},\textbf{\textit{a}},\textbf{\textit{q}}\rangle e)$. $(e)(\langle p,\text{Assrt},\textbf{\textit{a}},\textbf{\textit{q}}\rangle e$ $\supset \sim \langle p,\text{Excl},\textbf{\textit{a}},\textbf{\textit{q}}\rangle e)$. $(e)(\langle p,\text{Assrt},\textbf{\textit{a}},\textbf{\textit{q}}\rangle e \supset$ $\sim \langle p,\text{Subj},\textbf{\textit{a}},\textbf{\textit{q}}\rangle e)$. $(e)(\langle p,\text{Qstn},\textbf{\textit{a}},\textbf{\textit{q}}\rangle e \supset \sim \langle p,\text{Cmnd},\textbf{\textit{a}},\textbf{\textit{q}}\rangle e$. $\ldots . (e)(\langle p,\text{Excl},\textbf{\textit{a}},\textbf{\textit{q}}\rangle e \supset \sim \langle p,\text{Subj},\textbf{\textit{a}},\textbf{\textit{q}}\rangle e).$

Of course one and the same a, or at least similar ones, may be asserted, commanded, and so on, on different occasions or in different acts, but not in one and the same act.

Also it seems clear that any sentence taken as true is not simultaneously questioned, commanded, or subjunctivized. Thus

Ref R30. $\vdash (e)(\langle p,\text{TrEtSent},\textbf{\textit{a}}\rangle e \supset \sim (\langle p,\text{Qstn},\textbf{\textit{a}},\textbf{\textit{q}}\rangle e$ $\lor \langle p,\text{Cmnd},\textbf{\textit{a}},\textbf{\textit{q}}\rangle e \lor \langle p,\text{Subj},\textbf{\textit{a}},\textbf{\textit{q}}\rangle e)).$

Now that the various moods are accommodated, an additional principle is needed to assure that reference takes place not *in vacuo* but in the context of a sentence entertained in one or other of the moods of usage. This is the *Principle of Referential Context* as follows.

Ref R31. $\vdash \langle p,\text{Ref},\textbf{\textit{a}},\textbf{\textit{x}},\textbf{\textit{b}}\rangle e \supset (E\textbf{\textit{e}}')(E\textbf{\textit{q}})(\langle p,\text{Utt},\textbf{\textit{b}},\textbf{\textit{q}}\rangle e \lor$ $\langle p,\text{Apprh},\textbf{\textit{b}}\rangle e \lor \langle p,\text{Acpt},\textbf{\textit{b}}\rangle e \lor \langle p,\text{Assrt},\textbf{\textit{b}},\textbf{\textit{q}}\rangle e \lor$ $\langle p,\text{Qstn},\textbf{\textit{b}},\textbf{\textit{q}}\rangle e \lor \langle p,\text{Cmnd},\textbf{\textit{b}},\textbf{\textit{q}}\rangle e \lor \langle p,\text{Excl},\textbf{\textit{b}},\textbf{\textit{q}}\rangle e \lor$ $\langle p,\text{Subj},\textbf{\textit{b}},\textbf{\textit{q}}\rangle e).$

The moods discussed and the rules concerning them provide a novel approach to the study of the different moods of speech in a natural language. No separate "logics" for the separate moods are needed, all of them being incorporated here within a unified theory. Of course new primitives are needed, but such are needed in some shape or form no matter what. The unified, pragmatic approach here holds promise of providing a theory of moods of sufficient breadth and flexibility, so as to help accommodate sentences no matter how complex of a natural language.[5]

J. TRUTH FOR OCCASION SENTENCES

Let us reflect now upon truth for occasion sentences, and consider first occassion sentences containing just one personal pronoun or demonstrative phrase. Let

$$\text{'}p \text{ SF}'^d_b \text{ } ca\text{'}$$

be defined to express that p takes c to differ from a only in containing occurrences of a variable d, not occurring in a, wherever the personal pronoun or demonstrative phrase b occurs in a. The definiens is very much like that of $DSyn36$ above and need not be given here. The definition of the truth predicate for occasion sentences may now be given as follows.

$DRef13.$ ⌜p TrOccSent axq⌝ abbreviates
⌜(p OccSent a . (Eb)(Ec)(Ed)(Ea')(Eq')((p PerPrn b ∨
p Dmtv b) . p Seg ba . ~ (Ec')((p PerPrn c' ∨
p Dmtv c') . p Seg $c'a$. ~ p Like bc') . p SF$'^d_b$ ca .
p (LB⁀d⁀Invep⁀c⁀RB) a' . p Den $a'x$. (q Utt aq' ∨
q Acpt a ∨ q Apprh a ∨ q Assrt aq')))⌝.

Let ⌜---a---⌝ be an occasion sentence a containing a as its only personal pronoun or demonstrative. This sentence a is taken

---

5. For some incisive comments on commands, see Nicholas J. Moutafakis, *Imperatives and Their Logics* (New Delhi: Sterling Publishers, 1975).

by p to be *true of* x and q provided p takes some abstract of the form '$\{y3\text{---}y\text{---}\}$' to denote x, where q utters a or accepts it or whatever.

This definition may be generalized in a straightforward way as follows. First let

$DSyn51.$ ⌜p SentFormTwo abc⌝ abbreviate
⌜(p Fmla a . p Vbl b . p Vbl c . $\sim p$ Like bc .
p FrVbl ba . p FrVbl ca . $\sim$ (Ed)(p Vbl d . p FrVbl da .
$\sim$ (p Like db $\vee$ p Like dc)))⌝.

Person p takes a as a sentential form of just the two variables b and c just where p takes a as a formula containing b and c as free variables but not containing any free variables unlike them. (The three 'Vbl'-clauses here are not needed.)

Also a subsidiary definition is needed for *two-place denotation*.

$DRef14.$ ⌜p Den axy⌝ abbreviates
⌜(Eb)(Ec)(Ed)(Ea')(p Des$_{\text{In}}$ by . p SentFormTwo $a'cd$.
p (LB⌢c⌢Invep⌢LB⌢d⌢a ⌢RB⌢b⌢RB) a . p Den ax)⌝.

Thus p takes an abstract a to denote x and y in this order provided a is of a certain form and is taken to denote x. Then

$DRef15.$ ⌜p TrOccSent $axyq$⌝ abbreviates ⌜(p
OccSent a . (Eb)(Ec)(Ed)(Ea')(Ec')(Ed')(Ea'')(Eq)(Eq')((p
PerPrn b $\vee$ p Dmtv b) . (p PerPrn c $\vee$ p Dmtv c) .
p Seg ba . p Seg ca . $\sim$ (Eb'')((p PerPrn b'' $\vee$
p Dmtv b'') . p Seg $b''a$. $\sim$ (p Like $b''b$ $\vee$ p
Like $b''c$)) . p SF$'^d_b$ $a'a$. p SF$'^d_c$ $a''a'$. p Ref $c'y$.
p SentFuncTwo $a''dd'$. p (LB⌢d⌢Invep⌢LB⌢d'⌢a''⌢
RB⌢c'⌢RB) a'' . p Den $a''xy$. (q Utt aq' $\vee$
q Assrt aq' $\vee$ q Apprh a $\vee$ q Acpt a)))⌝.

A completely general definition of the truth predicate for occasion sentences may be given, a straightforward generalization of the preceding, by defining

$$⌜p \text{ TrOccSent } ax_1\ldots x_nq⌝.$$

For this definitions of

$$\ulcorner p \ \text{SentForm}_n \ ab_1 \ldots b_n \urcorner$$

and

$$\ulcorner p \ \text{Den} \ ax_1 \ldots x_n b \urcorner$$

are presupposed.

There are not only true eternal sentences and true occasion sentences, there are also true utterances of either eternal or occasion sentences, true apprehensions of either, true acceptances, and true assertions. Appropriate predicates for each of them may readily be defined in context as follows:

$$\ulcorner p \ \text{TrEtSentUtt} \ aq \urcorner,$$

$$\ulcorner p \ \text{TrOccSentUtt} \ ax_1 \ldots x_n qq' \urcorner,$$

$$\ulcorner p \ \text{TrEtSentApprh} \ a \urcorner,$$

$$\ulcorner p \ \text{TrOccSentApprh} \ ax_1 \ldots x_n q \urcorner,$$

and so on. These definitions are *DRef16a*, *DRef16b*, and so on.

Also, as remarked above, there is knowledge of entities as talked about in occasion sentences. Thus

DRef17. $\ulcorner p \ \text{KnOcc} \ x_1 \ldots x_n aq \urcorner$ abbreviates $\ulcorner (p \ \text{PredCon}_n \ a \ . \ (Eb_1) \ldots (Eb_n)(Ec)(p \ \text{Ref} \ b_1x_1c \ldots . \ p \ \text{Ref} \ b_nx_nc \ . \ p \ (a\frown b_1\frown \ldots \frown b_n) \ c \ . \ p \ \text{TrOccSent} \ cx_1 \ldots x_n q)) \urcorner.$

Note that in *DRef17* as in *DRef15*, two parameters occur for the human person. In the case of true occasion sentences, for example, p is said to take q's utterance or assertion or whatever of a sentence as true of the appropriate objects. In a special case of course p and q may be the same, but for the general case, the two parameters are needed. (Note that a definition of $\ulcorner \text{PredCon}_n \urcorner$ is presupposed here.)

There has been a good deal of talk in the recent philosophical literature concerning truth for occasion sentences, but apparently no one has heretofore formulated an exact definition. Although not especially difficult, the definitions here do presuppose a very considerable extension of semantics as usually conceived.

K. PARAPHRASE AND SYNONYMY

Without going too deeply into the matter, let us introduce one more primitive for *paraphrase*. Let

$$\text{'}p \text{ Prphs } ab\text{'}$$

express that *p paraphrases a* as *b* if and when he wishes to. In other words, *p* paraphrases *a* into *b* just when he regards *b* as merely another way of expressing what he wishes *a* to express.[6]

Immediately some *Principles of Paraphrase* are in order. The first is the *Limitation Principle*.

RefR32. $\vdash$ *p* Prphs *ab* $\supset$ (*p* Sent *a* . *p* Sent *b*).

The next are the *Principle of Symmetry*,

RefR33. $\vdash$ *p* Prphs *ab* $\supset$ *p* Prphs *ba*,

and the *Principle of Transitivity*,

RefR34. $\vdash$ (*p* Prphs *ab* . *p* Prphs *bc*) $\supset$ *p* Prphs *ac*.

There is also a *Principle of Likeness*,

RefR35. $\vdash$ (*p* Like *ab* . *p* Sent *a*) $\supset$ *p* Prphs *ab*.

From this it follows that

TRef4. $\vdash$ *p* Sent *a* $\supset$ *p* Prphs *aa*.

The following *Principle of the Common Referent* seems less certain, but nonetheless suitable to assume.

RefR36. $\vdash$ (*p* Prphs *ab* . *p* Ref *cxa*) $\supset$ (E*d*)*p* Ref *dxb*.

If a person paraphrases *a* as *b* and refers in *a* to *x* by means of *c*, he then refers to *x* also in *b* by some expression or other,

---

6. See H. Hiż, "The Role of Paraphrase in Grammar," in *Monograph Series on Language and Linguistics* (April, 1964) and "Congrammaticality, Batteries of Transformations, and Grammatical Categories," in *Structure of Language and Its Mathematical Aspects, Proceedings of Symposia in Applied Mathematics*, The American Mathematical Society, 12 (1961): 43–50. Cf. also Richard M. Smaby, *Paraphrase Grammars* (Dordrecht: Reidel, 1971), pp. 137–165.

not of course necessarily by c. In other words, whatever individuals are referred to by p in a sentence are referred to in all his paraphrases of it.

In terms of paraphrase various notions of synonymy are immediately definable.[7]

Closely related with paraphrase is the Fregean notion of the *Art des Gegebenseins* or mode of linguistic description under which an individual or event or person or virtual class or relation may be taken.[8] An entity so taken is in essentials a *concept* of that entity, in the objective, semantical sense, and entities taken under paraphrastic descriptions constitute the same concept. The *Art des Gegebenseins* will be discussed at the relevant places below.

The various rules and definitions given in this chapter, as well as those to be given in the next, are somewhat tentative. Some of them may require a more careful formulation, and additional ones no doubt are needed. Even so, the list here may be useful as providing first steps towards delineating an exact theory.

7. See, for example, *Belief, Existence, and Meaning*, Chapter VII.

8. See Frege's "On Sense and Reference," second paragraph, and *Begriffsschrift*, §8, in *Translations from the Philosophical Writings of Gottlob Frege*, ed. by P. Geach and M. Black (Oxford: Basil Blackwell, 1952).

PROLEGOMENA TO MATHEMATICS

The foundations of mathematics may now be approached on the basis of the foregoing. There need be no abrupt transition, for mathematics is here conceived as merely a continuation of pragmatics. In particular the *arithmetic of the positive integers* is regarded as merely a branch of the theory of reference. *Geometry* and the theory of *real numbers* emerge in terms of a suitable method of handling theoretical constructs, as in any theoretical science. These theories constitute prolegomena to mathematics, mathematics proper being merely in turn a continuation of these. These prolegomena, with the theory of virtual classes and relations, may be made so powerful in fact as to go a long way towards providing adequate foundations for mathematics.[1]

A. CARDINATION

It has already been remarked that the procedure of counting may be regarded as one more species of reference, more particularly, as reference by means of AcStr's. Such reference is here

1. Again, for further preliminary discussion, see "The Pragmatics of Counting," in *Events Etc.*

called '*cardination*'. Counting or cardination, however, is always with respect to membership in a given virtual class.

First, one may let

DArith1. $\ulcorner p$ Card $axF\urcorner$ abbreviate $\ulcorner(p$ AcStr a . p Ref ax . $((Fx$. $\sim (Ey)(PPyx$. $Fy)) \lor (\sim Fx$. $(Ey)(PPyx$. $Fy)$. $(y)(z)((\sim y = z$. $PPyx$. $PPzx$. Fy . $Fz) \supset Dyz))))\urcorner$.

Thus p cardinates the AcStr a to x with respect to F where p refers to x by means of a and either x is a member of F and no proper part of x is, or x is not a member of F but some proper part is in which case any two proper parts of x in F are discrete. (The point of this proviso concerning F will become clear as soon as particular integers are considered.)

To characterize cardination, an additional Rule of Reference is required, the *Principle of Shape-Descriptions for AcStr's.*

RefR37. $\vdash (Eb_n)$...$(Eb_n)(p$ Ac b_1 . p Ac b_2 . . . . . p Ac b_n . p C ab_1...b_n . p Card $axF) \supset (Ex_1)$...(Ex_n) $(x = (Fu`\{x_1, \ldots ,x_n\})$. Dx_1x_2 . Dx_1x_3 . . . . . $Dx_{n-1}x_n$. Fx_1 . . . . . Fx_n . $(y)((Fy$. $PPyx) \supset (y = x_1 \lor \ldots \lor y = x_n)))$, for $n = 1,2,\ldots$.

The *Principle of Limitation for AcStr's* follows immediately from the definition.

TArith1. $\vdash p$ Card $axF \supset p$ AcStr a.

The point of *RefR37* is to the effect that if p cardinates an AcStr consisting of just n accents to an entity x with respect to a virtual class F, then F must contain just n discrete proper parts each of which is a member of F where nothing else is.

Consider now expressions for the numerals '1', '2', and so on. One may let

DArith2a. $\ulcorner p$ Card $1xF\urcorner$ abbreviate $\ulcorner(Ea)(p$ Ac a . p Card $axF)\urcorner$,

DArith2b. $\ulcorner p$ Card $2xF\urcorner$ abbreviate $\ulcorner(Ea)(p$ $(Ac\frown Ac)$ a . p Card $axF)\urcorner$,

and so on. Then clearly the fundamental *Principles of Counting* for the particular positive integers are provable as follows.

TArith2a.   ⊢ *p* Card 1*xF* ⊃ (*Fx* . ∼ (E*y*)(PP*yx*. *Fy*)),

TArith2b.   ⊢ *p* Card 2*xF* ⊃ (∼*Fx* . (E*y*)(E*z*)(*Fy* . *Fz* . D*yz* . *x* = (Fu'{*y*,*z*}))),

and so on. In this way each finite integer is shown to play its proper role in the theory of counting, in accord with *Ref R37*.

What happens now with the principles of arithmetic within the present setting? What happens to Peano's Postulates? How may addition and multiplication be introduced? Let this last question be considered first.

One may right off let

DArith3.   ⌜*p* Card (*a* + *b*)*xF*⌝ abbreviate ⌜(*p* AcStr *a* . *p* AcStr *b* . (E*c*)(*p* C *cab* . *p* Card *cxF*))⌝,

so that *p* cardinates the "sum" *c* of AcStr's *a* and *b* to *x* with respect to the virtual class *F* just where *p* C *cab*. The sum of two integers is thus in effect merely the concatenate of their respective AcStr's. Clearly now

TArith3.   ⊢ *p* Card (*a* + *b*)*xF* ≡ *p* Card (*b* + *a*)*xF*,

TArith4.   ⊢ *p* Card ((*a* + *b*) + *c*)*xF* ≡ *p* Card (*a* + (*b* + *c*))*xF*,

and so on.

The introduction of multiplication is a little more difficult. However, this may be accomplished with one key preliminary definition. Let

$$\text{'}p \; S_{Ac}^{AcStr} \; cab\text{'}$$

be defined to express that *p* takes *c* to be an AcStr differing from the AcStr *b* only in containing some AcStr equally long with *a* in place of each Ac of *b*. Where this holds *p* takes *c* to be an AcStr such as:

$$\underbrace{\underbrace{''...'}_{a \text{ times}} \; \underbrace{''...'}_{a \text{ times}} \; \cdots \; \underbrace{''...'}_{a \text{ times}}}_{b \text{ times}}$$

More specifically one may let

DArith4. $\ulcorner p\ S_{Ac}^{AcStr}\ cab\urcorner$ abbreviate $\ulcorner(p\ \text{AcStr}\ a\ .\ p$
AcStr b . p AcStr c . $((p\ \text{Ac}\ b\ .\ p\ \text{EqLng}\ ca)\ \vee\ (\text{E}d)$
$(p\ \text{FrIng}\ ab,d\ .\ (e)(e')(p\ \text{FrIng}\ ee',d\ \supset\ (\text{E}a')(\text{E}b')$
$(p\ \text{Pr}\ a'b',ee',d\ .\ p\ (b'^\frown\text{Ac})\ e'\ .\ p\ (a'^\frown a)\ e))))\urcorner$.

With this key definition in mind, one may now let

DArith5. $\ulcorner p\ \text{Card}\ (a\ \times\ b)xF\urcorner$ abbreviate
$\ulcorner(\text{E}c)(p\ S_{Ac}^{AcStr}\ cab\ .\ p\ \text{Card}\ cxF)\urcorner$.

Here also the fundamental laws concerning the multiplication
of integers are immediately forthcoming from corresponding
laws concerning the syntax of AcStr's. Thus

TArith5. $\vdash\ p\ \text{Card}\ (a\ \times\ b)xF\ \equiv\ p\ \text{Card}\ (b\ \times\ a)xF$,
TArith6. $\vdash\ p\ \text{Card}\ (a\ \times\ (b\ \times\ c))xF\ \equiv\ p\ \text{Card}$
$((a\ \times\ b)\ \times\ c)xF$,
TArith7. $\vdash\ p\ \text{Card}\ (a\ \times\ (b\ +\ c))xF\ \equiv\ p\ \text{Card}$
$((a\ \times\ b)\ +\ (a\ \times\ c))xF$,
TArith8. $\vdash\ p\ \text{Ac}\ b\ \supset\ (p\ \text{Card}\ (a\ \times\ b)xF\ \equiv\ p$
Card axF),
TArith9. $\vdash\ p\ (\text{Ac}^\frown\text{Ac})\ b\ \supset\ (p\ \text{Card}\ (a\ \times\ b)xF\ \equiv$
$p\ \text{Card}\ (a\ \times\ a)xF$),

and so on.

B.   ARITHMETIC PRINCIPLES

Up to this point arithmetic has been confined to person
p–intrapersonal arithmetic, as it were. It is of interest to consider also the more usual *inter*personal arithmetic without such
restriction. Peano's Postulates after all make no reference to
the person.

First one should ask the question: what is an integer, inter-
personally regarded, on the present account? Merely an AcStr
taken by someone as a basis for someone to cardinate to some
entity with respect to some virtual class. Thus one might let

$$`p\ \text{Int}_F\ a`$$

be defined to express that a is AcStr taken by p to correlate to something with respect to F. But this would clearly be too narrow a definition, for according to it the integers are always relativized to given virtual classes. Clearly, however, one may take F as V, and thus let

DArith6. $\ulcorner p$ Int $a\urcorner$ abbreviate $\ulcorner(Ex)p$ Card $axV\urcorner$.

In the present notation, two of Peano's Postulates may read as follows.

P1.   ⊢ $(Ea)(Ep)(p$ Ac a . p Int $a)$.

P2.   ⊢ $(p)(a)(p$ Int a ⊃ $(Eb)(Ec)(p$ Ac b . p C cab . p Int $c))$.

The question arises as to what is meant by the *identity* of integers. Clearly one may let

DArith7. $\ulcorner a \approx_p b\urcorner$ abbreviate $\ulcorner(p$ Int a . p Int b . p EqLng $ab)\urcorner$,

so that identical integers are AcStr's correctly taken to be equally long. Two more of Peano's Postulates are then as follows.

P3.   ⊢ $(p)(a)((p$ Ac a . p Int $a)$ ⊃ ~ $(Eb)(p$ $(Ac\frown Ac)$ b . $a \approx_p b))$.

P4.   ⊢ $(p)(a)(b)((p$ Int a . p Int b . $(Ec)(Ed)(p$ $(a\frown Ac)$ c . p $(b\frown Ac)$ d . $c \approx_p d))$ ⊃ $a \approx_p b)$.

Finally there is the *Induction Schema.*

P5.   ⊢ $(p)(((a)((p$ Ac a . p Int $a)$ ⊃ $Fa)$. $(a)(b)((p$ Int a . Fa . p $(a\frown Ac)$ b . p Int $b)$ ⊃ $Fb))$ ⊃ (a) $(p$ Int a ⊃ $Fa))$.

Of these *P1* is clearly an empirical assumption concerning actual behavior. *P3* follows from the syntactical principle *TSyn13* by noting that

⊢ $(p$ Ac a . p $(Ac\frown Ac)$ $b)$ ⊃ ~ p EqLng ab.

P4 likewise is provable, from the syntactical principle *TSyn15*, and the Induction Schema is provable from the principle *TSyn16*.

It should be noted that *P2* is in effect an *Axiom of Infinity*. Here it is rather a *Principle of Perpetuity*. It is the principle that *vita brevis, arithmetica longa*. It requires that if *p* Int *a*, even if *a* is so long as to exhaust all actually exhibited AcStr's, still *p* can at least imagine a longer one and use it in a counting *Gedankenexperiment*. *P2* is not provable, but, as with Russell's handling of the Axiom of Infinity, may be taken as hypothesis where needed. Note that from the Principle of Concatenational Existence, *SynR9*, the existence of a longer AcStr is always assured, but it need not be used as a basis for cardination.

C. ORDINATION

Another approach to the foundations of arithmetic is by means of the finite *ordinal* numbers. These correspond roughly with the English words 'first', 'second', and so on, rather than with 'one', 'two', and so on. In place of cardination a relation of *ordination* is now to be introduced. By means of ordination an ordering of the entities considered may be given, no such ordering being present in mere counting or cardination.[2]

Let now

DArith8.   ⌜*p* Ord *axFe*⌝ abbreviate   ⌜(*Fx* . *p* AcStr
a . (E*e′*)(⟨*p*,Ref,*a*,*x*⟩*e′* . P*e′e*) . (*y*)(*Fy* ⊃ (E*e′*)
(⟨*p*,Ref,*b*,*y*⟩*e′* . P*e′e*)) . (*e′*)(*b*)(*y*)((⟨*p*,Ref,*b*,*y*⟩*e′* . P*e′e*) ⊃
(*Fy* . *p* AcStr *b*)))⌝,

so that *p* ordinates an AcStr *a* with *x* where *x* is a member of *F* in the "system" *e* provided *p* refers to *x* by means of *a* in some act that is a part of *e*.

As Rules of Reference governing ordination, there are now the following.

RefR38.   ⊢ (*p* Ord *axFe* . *p* Ord *ayFe*) ⊃ *x* = *y*.

RefR39.   ⊢ (*p* Ord *axFe* . *p* Ord *bxFe*) ⊃ *a* = *b*.

---

2. The author is indebted to the late Aron Gurwitsch for some insights concerning the material of this section.

RefR40.   ⊢ (*p* Ord *axFe* . *p* Ord *axGe*) ⊃ **F** = **G**.

Ref R41.   ⊢ (*p* Ord *axFe* . ~ *p* Ac *a*) ⊃ (E*b*)(E*y*)
(*p* Lngr *ab* . *p* Ord *byFe* . D*xy*).

RefR38–RefR40 are *Principles of Uniqueness for Ordination*, and *RefR41* is the *Principle of Predecessors*. The last is aptly named, for it requires that if *p* ordinates something that is not an Ac to *x* with respect to *F* in *e*, then there is some predecessor in the ordering, discrete from *x*, to which *p* ordinates a shorter AcStr.

Also the following *Principle of Ordinal Systems* is required,

RefR42.   ⊢ *p* Ord *axFe* ⊃ (*e'*)((At *e'* . P*e'e*) ⊃ (E*b*)(E*y*)(E*e''*)(P*e'e''* . ⟨*p*,Ord,*b*,*y*,*F*,*e*⟩*e''*)),

to the effect that if *p* Ord *axFe*, every atomic part of *e* is a part of some act or state of *p*'s ordinating in *e* some AcStr with some member of *F*.

Ordination is always relative to a system, whereas cardination is not. In ordination assignment of AcStr's may take place in several ways and *x* may be assigned one ordinal in one system and quite another one in another. Hence relativization to the system is needed. Note that where *p* Card *axF* the *x* is cumulative in the sense of being the sum of the individuals that are members of *F*. Where *p* Ord *axFe*, however, the *x* is not cumulative in this way. The Principle of Systems requires that where *p* Ord *axFe* then *e* is a system of *p*'s ordinations of members of *F*, one perhaps out of many. Note also that if *p* Ord *axFe* and *p* Ord *axFe'*, it need not follow that *e* = *e'*, for the order of the successive acts or states constituting *e* and *e'* may differ.

The *finite ordinal numerals* may now be introduced definitionally as follows.

DArith9a.   ⌜*p* Ord (1st)*xFe*⌝ abbreviates ⌜(E*a*)(*p* Ac *a* . *p* Ord *axFe*)⌝,

DArith9b.   ⌜*p* Ord (2nd)*xFe*⌝ abbreviates ⌜(E*a*)(*p* (Ac⌢Ac) *a* . *p* Ord *axFe*)⌝,

and so on.

Clearly the following principles hold concerning the finite ordinals.

TArith10a.   ⊢ *p* Ord (1st)*xFe* ⊃ *Fx*,
TArith10b.   ⊢ *p* Ord (2nd)*xFe* ⊃ ((E*y*)(D*yx* .
p Ord (1st)*yF* . *Fy*) . *Fx*),

and so on.

The addition of finite ordinals may be introduced, but it is merely cardinal addition over again. One may let

DArith9.   ⌜*p* Ord ((*a*th) + (*b*th))*xFe*⌝   abbreviate ⌜*p* Ord ((*a* + *b*)th)*xFe*⌝,

and also

DArith10.   ⌜*p* Ord ((*a*th) × (*b*th))*xFe*⌝   abbreviates ⌜*p* Ord ((*a* × *b*)th)*xFe*⌝.

Nothing essentially new is achieved by these definitions, and the arithmetic principles concerning finite ordinal addition and multiplication are essentially the same as the corresponding ones concerning the finite cardinals.

How are ordination and cardination related philosophically, then? The following principle would seem to obtain concerning their interrelation.

RefR43.   ⊢ (*x* = (Fu'{*y*3(E*b*)*p* Ord *byFe*}) .
(*y*)(*Fy* ⊃ (E*b*)*p* Ord *byFe*) . *e* = (Fu'{*e'*3(E*b*)(E*y*)(*Fy* .
P*yx* . ⟨*p*,Ref,*b*,*y*⟩*e'* . *p* AcStr *b*)})) ⊃ (*p* Card *a*,*x*,*F* ≡
(E*z*)(P*zx* . *p* Ord *azFe* . (*w*)((P*wx* . *p* Ord *awFe*) ⊃
w = *z*) . (*b*)(*y*)((*p* Ord *b*,*y*,*F*,*e* . P*yx* . ~ *y* = *z*) ⊃
a Lngr *b*))).

In other words, *p* cardinates *a* with *x* with respect to *F* just where *p* ordinates the *a*-th *F*-part of *x*, *x* being the sum of all the *F*-parts of *x* ordinated by AcStr's shorter than *a*.

These various suggestions concerning cardination and ordination may be of interest in laying foundations for the study of the complex acts of counting, and hence of measurement, that play so important a role in science and also in daily life. Such acts seem never to have been studied with any care.

D.   SOME GEOMETRIC NOTIONS

The concern above has been with the ontology of arithmetic proper, with principles, in other words, that fix or determine that ontology. Such a principle is *RefR37*. But such considerations flow directly into arithmetic proper by means of the definitions. So here, the concern is primarily with fixing the ontology of geometry in general, but will quickly flow into the special geometries by means of definitions and special assumptions.

The key definition to be provided for is the general notion of a *point* common to all special geometries. Of any atomic individual *x* there are no proper parts other than N. Such parts, however, can be imagined or conceived or hypothecated, or something of the kind. In particular the geometer *subjunctivizes* that there are points and carries out his official work on the basis of this. Geometry is thus to be thought of as carried out in the subjunctive mood, the foundations of geometry becoming therewith a branch of the logic of subjunctives.

First, two useful abbreviations are in order, of a purely syntactical kind.

DSyn52. $\ulcorner p \, (a \frown \text{Dot} \frown b) \, c \urcorner$ abbreviates $\ulcorner p \, (\text{Tilde} \frown$
LP$\frown$Tilde$\frown a \frown$Vee$\frown$Tilde$\frown b \frown$RP) $c \urcorner$,

and

DSyn53. $\ulcorner p \, (\text{PP} \frown a \frown b) \, c \urcorner$ abbreviates $\ulcorner p \, (\text{Tilde} \frown$
LP$\frown$Tilde$\frown$Pee$\frown a \frown b \frown$Vee$\frown$Pee$\frown b \frown a \frown$RP) $c \urcorner$.

Note that 'Dot' functions as though it were the shape description of '.' and 'PP' autonymously as the shape description of the 'PP' for the relation of being a proper part of.

Person *p* may be said to subjunctivize the *existence* of *a* provided he subjunctivizes a statement to the effect that what *a* refers to exists.

DGeom1. $\ulcorner p \, \text{SubjExis} \, a \urcorner$ abbreviates $\ulcorner (Eb)(Eq)(p$
(Tilde$\frown a \frown$Id$\frown$LP$\frown$Ex$\frown$One$\frown$Tilde$\frown$Ex$\frown$Id$\frown$Ex$\frown$RP) b .
p Subj $bq) \urcorner$.

Person p may then be said to take or to subjunctivize e_1 as a *point* of e_2 provided e_2 is an atom and p subjunctivizes that e_1 is a proper part of e_2 itself containing no proper parts. Thus

DGeom2. $\ulcorner p$ Pt $e_1 e_2 \urcorner$ abbreviates $\ulcorner$(At e_2 . (Ea)(Eb)(Ec)(Ed)(Ea')(Eq)(p Ref ae_1a' . (p Ref be_2a' . p SubjExis a . p (PP⌢a⌢b) c . p (LP⌢Ex⌢RP⌢Tilde⌢ PP⌢Ex⌢a) d . p (c⌢Dot⌢d) a' . p Subj $a'q$))$\urcorner$.

Person p takes e as a "point" if he takes e as a point contained in some atom.

DGeom3. $\ulcorner p$ Pt $e \urcorner$ abbreviates $\ulcorner$(Ee')p Pt $ee' \urcorner$.

Person p may be said to take e_1 and e_2 as identical as follows.

DGeom4. $\ulcorner e_1 =_p e_2 \urcorner$ abbreviates $\ulcorner$(Ea)(Eb)(Ec)(Eq) (p Ref ae_1c . p Ref be_2c . p (a⌢Id⌢b) c . p Subj cq)$\urcorner$.

And p is said to take e_1 as a proper part of e_2 as follows.

DGeom5. $\ulcorner$PP$_p e_1 e_2 \urcorner$ abbreviates $\ulcorner$(Ea)(Eb)(Ec)(Eq) (p Ref ae_1c . p Ref be_2c . p (PP⌢a⌢b) c . p Subj cq)$\urcorner$.

Next, p may be said to take "point" e_2 as *between* "points" e_1 and e_3 as follows.

DGeom6. $\ulcorner p$ Bet $e_1 e_2 e_3 \urcorner$ abbreviates $\ulcorner$(p Pt e_1 . p Pt e_2 . p Pt e_3 . $\sim e_1 =_p e_2$. $\sim e_1 =_p e_3$. $\sim e_2 =_p e_3$. (Ea)(Eb)(Ec)(Ed)(Ea')(Eb')(Ea'')(Eb'')(Ec')(p Ref ae_1c' . p Ref be_2c' . p Ref ce_3c' . p (Bee⌢a⌢b) a' . p (Bee⌢b⌢c) b' . p (Bee⌢c⌢b) a'' . p (Bee⌢b⌢a) b'' . p (a'⌢Dot⌢b') d . p (a''⌢Dot⌢b'') a' . p (LP⌢d⌢Vee⌢ a'⌢RP) c' . p Subj c'))$\urcorner$.

Here again p is merely taking the "points" under the subjunctive mood in a certain order as provided by B.

Person p may be said to take e as a *segment* determined by e_1 and e_2 as follows.

DGeom7. $\ulcorner p$ Seg $ee_1 e_2 \urcorner$ abbreviates $\ulcorner$(p Pt e_1 . p Pt e_2 . $\sim e_1 =_p e_2$. (e')(p Pt $e' \supset$ (PP$_p e'e \equiv$ ($e' =_p e_1 \lor e' =_p e_2 \lor p$ Bet $e_1 e' e_2$))))$\urcorner$.

And p may be said to take e as a *line* determined by e_1 and e_2 as follows.

DGeom8. $\ulcorner p$ Ln $ee_1e_2\urcorner$ abbreviates $\ulcorner(p$ Pt e_1 . p Pt e_2 . $\sim e_1 =_p e_2$. $(e')(p$ Pt $e' \supset (\text{PP}_p e'e \equiv (e' =_p e_1 \lor e' =_p e_2 \lor p$ Bet $e_1e'e_2 \lor p$ Bet $e_1e_2e' \lor p$ Bet $e'e_1e_2))))\urcorner$.

And that p takes e as a line *simpliciter* as follows.

DGeom9. $\ulcorner p$ Ln $e\urcorner$ abbreviates $\ulcorner(Ee_1)(Ee_2)p$ Ln $ee_1e_2\urcorner$.

One more definition will be useful, that of *lying on*. But clearly

DGeom10. $\ulcorner p$ On $e_1e_2\urcorner$ may abbreviate merely $\ulcorner\text{PP}_p e_1e_2\urcorner$,

so that one geometric element may be said to be taken by p to lie on another if and only if it is taken by him to be a proper part of the other.

Some logical consequences are as follows.

TGeom1. $\vdash p$ Bet $e_1e_2e_3 \supset (p$ Pt e_1 . p Pt e_2 . p Pt e_2 . $\sim e_1 =_p e_2$. $\sim e_1 =_p e_2$. $\sim e_2 =_p e_3)$.
TGeom2. $\vdash (p$ Pt e_1e_2 . p Pt e_1e_3 . $(a)(b)(c)((p$ Sent a . p IC abc . p Subj b . p Subj $c) \supset p$ Subj $a)$. $(a)((p$ Thm a . $_p$ Sent $a) \supset p$ Subj $a)) \supset e_2 =_p e_3$.

The two hypotheses containing 'Subj' in *TGeom2* are important enough to justify a separate notation. Let them be abbreviated respectively as

'ICSubj p'

and

'ThmSubj p',

reading respectively 'p subjunctivizes all immediate consequences of sentences he subjunctivizes' and 'p subjunctivizes all theorems he takes to be sentences'.

E.   EUCLIDEAN PRINCIPLES

With the notions 'Pt', 'Ln', 'Seg', and 'Bet' available, one can proceed at once to enunciate geometric principles. Almost immediately, however, a choice must be made as to the kind of geometry to be considered. There is enormous latitude here of course, and one's choice will depend upon the special purpose at hand. For the present let attention be confined to just Euclidean geometry, and more particularly to the theory of order governing 'Bet'.

The following principles may be taken as basic.

GeomR1. $\vdash$ (p On e_1e_3 . p On e_2e_3 . p Ln $e_3e_4e_5$. p Ln $e_6e_1e_2$) $\supset$ p On e_4e_6.

GeomR2. $\vdash$ (p Pt e_1 . p Pt e_2 . $\sim$ $e_1 =_p e_2$) $\supset$ (Ee_3) p Bet $e_1e_3e_2$.

GeomR3. $\vdash$ (p Pt e_1 . p Pt e_2 . p Pt e_3 . $\sim$ $e_1 =_p e_2$. $\sim$ $e_2 =_p e_3$. $\sim$ $e_1 =_p e_3$. $\sim$ (Ee)(p On e_1e . p On e_2e . p On e_3e) . p Bet $e_2e_3e_4$. p Bet $e_3e_5e_1$) $\supset$ (Ee)(p Bet e_1ee_2 . (Ee')(p On e_4e' . p On e_5e' . p On ee')).

GeomR4. $\vdash$ (Ee_1)(Ee_2)(Ee_3)(p Pt e_1 . p Pt e_2 . p Pt e_3 . $\sim$ $e_1 =_p e_2$. $\sim$ $e_2 =_p e_3$. $\sim$ $e_1 =_p e_3$. $\sim$ p Bet $e_1e_2e_3$. $\sim$ p Bet $e_2e_3e_1$. $\sim$ p *Bet* $e_3e_1e_2$).

A few logical consequences are as follows.

TGeom3. $\vdash$ (ICSubj p . ThmSubj p . p Bet $e_1e_2e_3$) $\supset$ (p Bet $e_3e_2e_1$. $\sim$ p Bet $e_3e_1e_2$. $\sim$ p Bet $e_2e_1e_3$. $\sim$ p Bet $e_1e_3e_2$. $\sim$ p Bet $e_2e_3e_1$).

TGeom4. $\vdash$ (ICSubj p . ThmSubj p . p Ln ee_1e_2) $\supset$ p Ln ee_2e_1.

TGeom5. $\vdash$ (ICSubj p . ThmSubj p . p Seg ee_1e_2) $\supset$ p Seg ee_2e_1.

TGeom6. $\vdash$ (p Bet $e_1e_2e_3$. p Ln $e_4e_1e_2$. p Ln $e_5e_2e_3$. p Ln $e_6e_3e_1$) $\supset$ (p On e_1e_4 . p On e_2e_4 . p On

e_3e_4 . p On e_1e_5 . p On e_2e_5 . p On e_3e_5 . p On e_3e_6 .
p On e_4e_6 . p On e_5e_6).
  TGeom7. $\vdash$ (p Pt e_1 . p Pt e_2 . $\sim e_1 =_p e_2$) $\supset$
$(Ee)(p$ Ln ee_1e_2 . p On e_1e . p On e_2e . $(e')((p$ Ln
$e'e_1e_2$. p On e_1e' . p On $e_2e') \supset e' =_p e))$.

This is not the occasion to develop any special branch of
geometry further. Nor was it the occasion above to develop
further the arithmetic of integers. In both cases, however,
enough has been shown to see how this may be done. For the
development of Euclidean geometry additional assumptions
are of course needed, and for the development of alternative
geometries, alternative assumptions.

It might be thought that for any further development the use
of quantifiers over sets or relations would be essential. Note
that for arithmetic as developed above this was not the case.
Of course there are theorems of arithmetic that require quantification over sets of or relations between or among integers in
their proofs, theorems of analytic number theory so called. But
for many such theorems proofs have been devised without using
such quantifiers and it is thought a considerable mathematical
victory when this is done. From the point of view of the philosophy of arithmetic taken here, those theorems are to be rejected
that are not provable by purely elementary procedures.

A similar situation arises in the development of geometry. It
is required from the point of view of the philosophy of geometry
taken here, that all geometric notions be definable in terms of the
notions provided without quantifiers over sets of or relations
between or among the various geometrical entities. It might be
thought that this restriction is too severe. However, all manner
of virtual classes and relations are available, as well as the notion
of fusion from the calculus of individuals. A segment, for
example, is sometimes said to be the set of points between and
including its end points. Above, however, a segment was taken
in effect as the fusion of all such points. For many purposes in
geometry, virtual sets and relations and fusions of virtual sets
of geometric entities can be made to suffice. (Precisely what
areas of geometry can be provided in this way is a matter for

further research to decide.) Elementary geometry, in the technical sense of first-order geometry, must of course be developed without quantifiers over sets or relations, and it is only this that is under consideration here.

F. REAL ANALYSIS

In the preceding section a method of treating geometric entities as idealized or fictional constructs was outlined. The method bears some family resemblance to Whitehead's use of coordinate divisions.[3] It consists in essentials of a method of *extrapolation* in which geometric points are built up in terms of atomic events. In terms of the foregoing the *theory of real numbers* may now be formulated.

The theory of a one-dimensional continuum of points on a line is needed before the complexities required for a full axiomatization of some special geometry, Euclidean, Riemanian, or whatever, are brought in. The leading idea now is to allow the geometer or person p to identify a point with a real number, different ones with different ones, in such a way that all talk of real numbers becomes merely a certain way of talking about points. To see this, let us consider at once the vocabulary and principles required.[4]

First, the person p is supposed to pick out some one line as the *real-number axis*. Thus

$$\text{`} p \text{ Axis } e \text{'}$$

is to express primitively that p takes e as the axis. Clearly then

NRR1. $\vdash p \text{ Axis } e \supset p \text{ Ln } e,$

and

NRR2. $\vdash (Ee)(p \text{ Axis } e \, . \, (e')(p \text{ Axis } e' \supset e =_p e')).$

---

3. See the author's "On Coordinate Divisions in the Theory of Extensive Connection" in *Whitehead's Categoreal Scheme and Other Papers*.

4. See also "On Mathematics and the Good," in *Whitehead's Categoreal Scheme Etc.*

Thus there is one and only one entity that p takes as axis, and that is taken by him to be a line. *NRR1* is the *Ontological Principle of the Axis*, and *NRR2*, the *Principle of the Unique Existence of the Axis*.

What now is a real number? Simply a point on the line taken as axis. Thus

DNR1. ⌜p NR e⌝ abbreviates ⌜(p Pt e . $\{e'3p$ On $ee'\}(\imath\{e'3p$ Axis $e'\}))$⌝.

Let now

'p Zero e'

and

'p One e'

express primitively that p takes e to be the real numbers 0 or 1 respectively. Here likewise

NRR3. ⊢ p Zero e ⊃ p NR e,

and

NRR4. ⊢ (Ee)(p Zero e . (e')(p Zero e' ⊃ e =$_p$ e')).

These are respectively the *Ontological Principle for O* and the *Principle of the Unique Existence of O*. And similarly for 'One'.

NRR5. ⊢ p One e ⊃ p NR e,

and

NRR6. ⊢ (Ee)(p One e . (e')(p One e' ⊃ e =$_p$ e')).

And also of course, 0 and 1 are taken as distinct points, via the *Principle of Distinctness of 0 and 1*.

NRR7. ⊢ (p Zero e . p One e') ⊃ ∼ e =$_p$ e'.

Next let

'e_1 < e_2'

express primitively that p takes the "real number" e_1 to be *less than* the "real number" e_2. Clearly then

NRR8. $\vdash e_1 <_p e_2 \supset (p$ NR e_1 . p NR e_2 . $\sim$ $e_1 =_p e_2$. $(Ee)p$ Bet $e_1ee_2)$.

In terms of '$<_p$' suitable *Principles of Order* may be given. In particular the following are assumed.

NRR9. $\vdash (p$ NR e_1 . p NR $e_2) \supset (e_1 =_p e_2 \vee$ $e_1 <_p e_2 \vee e_2 <_p e_1)$.

NRR10. $\vdash e_1 <_p e_2 \supset \sim e_2 <_p e_1$.

NRR11. $\vdash (e_1 <_p e_2$. $e_2 <_p e_3) \supset e_1 <_p e_3$.

Let now

$$'(e_1 + e_2)_p e'$$

and

$$'(e_1 \times e_2)_p e'$$

express primitively that person p takes e to be the *sum* or *product* respectively of the real numbers e_1 and e_2. Clearly

NRR12. $\vdash ((e_1 + e_2)_p e \vee (e_1 \times e_2)_p e) \supset (p$ NR e_1 . p NR e_2 . p NR $e)$.

The foregoing foundational principles are concerned mainly with fixing the ontology of real-number theory and with other elementary matters. The following principles are of a more mathematical nature and lead at once into real-number theory proper. It is well known in fact that with '0', '1', '$<$', '$+$', and '$\times$' available as primitives (for the numbers 0,1, the relation between reals of being less than, and the operations of real addition and multiplication respectively), the whole real-number system may be axiomatized upon the basis of standard first-order logic. In particular then the following principles are needed.

First, the *Principle of the Unique Existence of the Sum* of any two reals is assumed.

NRR13. $\vdash (p\ NR\ e_1 \cdot p\ NR\ e_2) \supset (Ee)(p\ NR\ e\ .$
$(e_1 + e_2)_p e \cdot (e')((e_1 + e_2)_p e' \supset e =_p e'))$.

Any real number added to 0 is merely that real number, the
Principle of Addition by 0.

NRR14. $\vdash ((e_1 + e_2)_p e \cdot p\ Zero\ e_2) \supset e =_p e_1$.

Also there are the *Commutative and Associative Laws for
Addition.*

NRR15. $\vdash ((e_1 + e_2)_p e \cdot (e_2 + e_1)_p e') \supset e =_p e'$.

NRR16. $\vdash ((e_2 + e_3)_p e \cdot (e_1 + e)_p e' \cdot (e_1 + e_2)_p e''$
$(e'' + e_3)_p e''') \supset e' =_p e'''$.

NRR17 is the *Principle of Monotony for Addition.*

NRR17. $\vdash (e_1 <_p e_2 \cdot (e_3 + e_1)_p e \cdot (e_3 + e_2)_p e') \supset$
$e <_p e'$.

Next there are several principles concerning multiplication.

NRR18. $\vdash (p\ NR\ e_1 \cdot p\ NR\ e_2) \supset (Ee)(p\ NR\ e\ .$
$(e_1 \times e_2)_p e \cdot (e')((e_1 \times e_2)_p e' \supset e =_p e'))$.

NRR19. $\vdash ((e_1 \times e_2)_p e \cdot p\ One\ e_2) \supset e =_p e_1$.

NRR20. $\vdash ((e_1 \times e_2)_p e \cdot (e_2 \times e_1)_p e') \supset e =_p e'$.

NRR21. $\vdash ((e_2 \times e_3)_p e \cdot (e_1 \times e)_p e' \cdot (e_1 \times e_2)_p e''$
$(e'' \times e_3)_p e''') \supset e' =_p e'''$.

NRR22. $\vdash (p\ Zero\ e_1 \cdot e_1 <_p e_2 \cdot e_3 <_p e_4\ .$
$(e_2 \times e_3)_p e \cdot (e_2 \times e_4)_p e') \supset e <_p e'$.

NRR18 is the *Principle of the Unique Existence of the Product*
of any two reals. *NRR19* is the *Principle of Multiplication by 1,*
and *NRR20* and *NRR21* are respectively *Commutative* and
Associative Principles for Products. *NRR22* is the *Principle of
Monotony for Products*. Also there is the *Distributive Law* as
follows.

NRR23. $\vdash ((e_2 + e_3)_p e \cdot (e_1 \times e)_p e' \cdot (e_1 \times e_2)_p e''$
$\cdot (e_1 \times e_3)_p e''' \cdot (e'' + e''')_p e'''') \supset e' =_p e''''$.

The next two principles are respectively the *Principles of Existence for the Difference and for the Quotient* of any two reals.

NRR24. $\vdash (Ee_3)(e_2 + e_3)_p e_1.$

NRR25. $\vdash \sim p$ Zero $e_2 \supset (Ee_3)(e_2 \times e_3)_p e_1.$

Finally there is the *Dedekindian Principle* as follows.

NRR26. $\vdash (\sim F = \Lambda \,\, . \,\, \sim G = \Lambda \,\, . \,\, (e)(Fe \supset$
p NR $e) \,\, . \,\, (e)(Ge \supset p$ NR $e) \,\, . \,\, (e_1)(e_2)((Fe_1 \,\, . \,\, Ge_2) \supset$
$e_1 <_p e_2)) \supset (Ee_3)(e_1)(e_2)((Fe_1 \,\, . \,\, Ge_2 \,\, . \,\, \sim e_3 =_p e_1 \,\, .$
$\sim e_3 =_p e_2) \supset (e_1 <_p e_3 \,\, . \,\, e_3 <_p e_2)).$

It can easily be verified that these principles, plus such principles of geometry as are needed, provide for the full theory of the first-order arithmetic of real numbers. The second-order arithmetic of real numbers admits also variables and quantifiers over sets and functions of real numbers, but these are not provided for here. This limitation is not so very serious, however, for the first-order theory presumably suffices for most of the needs of the physical sciences, in particular for the purposes of measurement, which will be considered in the next section.

The philosophy of real arithmetic that emerges from the foregoing has the following features. Real numbers are regarded as subjective or "mental" entities, not as real abstract objects in the objective world. The only ontology admitted is that required above, in particular, some one "line" picked out as the real-number axis. The primitives required are of a pragmatic kind, a parameter for the "user" p occurring in all the atomic sentential forms. The entire theory is couched within event logic as extended with the new primitives. Unrestricted quantifiers over the reals are admitted. The method here contrasts sharply with other ways of handling the reals; the real numbers are not regarded as sets or classes of rationals (as in set-theoretic accounts) nor are they taken as values for a special kind of variable. The theory here is "constructivistic" in a kind of Kantian sense, but not in the sense that the reals are constructed or built out of some prior kind of number (rational or integral). Strictly, here there are no such things as real numbers—they are mere fictions or hypothetical or subjunctive constructs, in no way entities in their own right. Nonetheless, the uses to which real numbers are ordinarily put in science may be provided for here without difficulty. The view is thus a kind of pragmatic, instrumentalist fictionalism, provided for within the confines of event logic.[5]

G. MEASUREMENT

The real numbers are of interest beyond the confines of mathematics mainly because of their role in measurement as required in the sciences. Just as integers of interest primarily for the purposes of counting, so are the reals of interest primarily for measurement. Just as counting is handled by correlating integers with entities in a certain way, so measurement is a matter of assigning real numbers to certain physical or other entities in certain ways. A complete theory of measurement cannot be put forward here, but merely a hint or so as to how this may be done in the case of distance.

Let

$$\text{'}p \text{ Dist } ee_1e_2\text{'}$$

be regarded as a primitive expressing that person or physicist p assigns the real number e to the segment determined by points e_1 and e_2. By means of such an atomic sentential function the measurement of distance is handled as a certain kind of scientific activity. Physicists assign real numbers to certain phenomena or entities or processes or whatever in certain ways. The notion of distance is not some Platonic essence but a human artifact or construct needed in science. For 'Dist' to perform what is expected of it, certain assumptions must be made. Among these are the following basic ones.

First there is, as usual, a *Principle of Limitation*.

DistR1.   ⊢ p Dist ee_1e_2 ⊃ (Per p . p NR e . p Pt e_1 . p Pt e_2).

---

5. For some alternative philosophies of mathematics, particularly of set theory, see "On Common Natures and Mathematical Scotism" and "Set Theory and Royce's Modes of Action," in *Peirce's Logic of Relations and Other Studies*.

Then there is a *Principle of the Existence and Uniqueness of the Distance Measure.*

DistR2.   ⊢ p Seg ee_1e_2 ⊃ (Ee)(p NR e . p Dist ee_1e_2 . (e')((p NR e' . p Dist $e'e_1e_2$) ⊃ $e =_p e'$)).

The *Principle of Zero Distance* is as follows.

DistR3.   ⊢ p Dist ee_1e_2 ⊃ (p Zero e ≡ $e_1 =_p e_2$).

The *Principle of Additivity* is as follows.

DistR4.   ⊢ (p Dist ee_1e_2 . p Dist $e'e_1e_3$. p Dist $e''e_2e_3$. p Bet $e_1e_2e_3$) ⊃ ($e' + e''$)$_p e$.

Needed also is the *Principle of the Unit Distance.* Let E_1 and E_2 be fixed endpoints of, say, the International Prototype Meter in Paris. Then

DistR5.   ⊢ p Dist eE_1E_2 ⊃ p One e.

The notion of *congruence* has not yet been mentioned. For some purposes it would be best to regard an expression for it as undefined, but for the present it may be defined in terms of 'Dist' as follows.

DGeom11.   ⌜p Cong $e_1e_2e_3e_4$⌝ abbreviates ⌜(Ee)(p Dist ee_1e_2 . p Dist ee_3e_4)⌝.

The *Principle of Congruent Distances* is then immediate.

DistR6.   ⊢ (p Dist ee_1e_2 . p Dist $e'e_3e_4$) ⊃ (p Cong $e_1e_2e_3e_4$ ≡ $e =_p e'$).

The measurement of mass may be handled roughly as follows. Let

'Obj x'

express that x is a physical object, and

'p Mass ex'

express that p assigns e to x as a measure of its mass. The following principles are then assumed.

MassR1.   ⊢ p Mass ex ⊃ (Per p . p NR e . Obj x).

MassR2.   ⊢ $(x)(\mathrm{E}e)(p$ Mass *ex* . $(e')(p$ Mass $e'x \supset$
$e' =_p e)$).

MassR3.   ⊢ p Mass *ex* $\supset$ (p Zero $e \equiv x = $ N).

MassR4.   ⊢ (p Mass *ex* . $x = (y \cup z)$. $\sim$ O*yz* .
p Mass e_1y . p Mass e_2z) $\supset (e_1 + e_2)_p e$.

And finally, where X is the International Prototype Kilogram, or whatever,

MassR5.   ⊢ p Mass eX $\supset$ p One e.

These rules are somewhat oversimplified, but they suffice to show that a theory of the measurement of distance may be incorporated within the theory here. The measurement of other magnitudes may be introduced similarly by other appropriate extensions.

Further study is needed to explore the role of cardination and ordination in the theory of measurement. Unfortunately, studies of this latter have not yet been pressed sufficiently deep to bring out this important interconnection.

PART B

LINGUISTIC STRUCTURE

CHAPTER VIII

HARRIS'S SYSTEMS
OF REPORT AND
PARAPHRASE

The study of natural language has been relegated to the background in the foregoing. Various logico-philosophical principles have been exhibited and occasionally an example from natural language has been given. Also occasionally a definiendum has been given a "reading" in natural language. As a matter of fact, however, the foregoing event logic provides in essentials the foundations for a rather far-reaching theory of logical form for English sentences. This has already been shown to some extent in *Events, Reference, and Logical Form*. Rather than merely repeat or amplify, let us go on, in this chapter and the following ones, to relate the foregoing material to the concrete practice of contemporary linguists.

In Part B of this book, therefore, the concern is almost exclusively with exhibiting specific logical forms for specific English sentences, rather than with general principles concerning particular words, or kinds of words, parts of speech, kinds of clauses, and so on. This concern for form and not for principles seems appropriate at the present stage of research, in which little about logical form is known with any certainty. In fact, many of the sentences to be considered have not heretofore been given any logical forms at all, let alone within the context of a well-articulated system such as the foregoing. Thus with each sentence, some little victory is achieved whenever some semblance of a suitable form is given, especially if the sentence is one that has raised some difficulties or problems among linguists and philosophers of language. Also we must be careful not to generalize too hastily from one sentence to others like it. As will be seen from examples, a slight change in word order or an insertion of a word here or there may alter fundamentally the logical form of the original. Thus for the present all manner of sentences are to be examined *seriatim*, with the hope of course that a form given for one will be essentially the same as that given for another of the same kind. In any case, the piecemeal, *seriatim* method seems the most suitable one to use at the present stage of research. Part B is thus more like a voyage of discovery than a description of well-charted seas.

In citing a logical form of a sentence, we should try to capture as well as we can whatever it is that that sentence is supposed to convey. And, secondly, we should try to capture the logical consequences of the sentences, whatever these consequences are felt to be. Perhaps these two tasks reduce to one and the same; for if the latter is achieved, the other comes tumbling after. Of course in practise it is often difficult to be sure just what logical consequences a sentence is supposed to have, even after "disambiguation." This may well vary somewhat from speaker to speaker. Even so, there seems to be a minimum core of consequences that each sentence has, and the aim is primarily to capture at least that much.

Although the technical development of Part A above is in general presupposed, it need not be strictly adhered to in all detail. The notation may be varied in minor respects and other small departures allowed. Nonlogical constants, as is customary in writings on the logical forms of English sentences, are formed by capitalizing the appropriate English word. All other innovations will be explained in the appropriate contexts. These will for the most part be motivated by the desire to bring the logical notation into closer conformity with English word order. There will be progress in this and other respects as we go on from chapter to chapter.

In his remarkable monograph "The Two Systems of Grammar: Report and Paraphrase"[1], the eminent linguist Zellig Harris makes a number of timely observations concerning logical form or structure. "From an attempt to isolate the independent elements of sentence construction," he notes (p. 613), "we arrive at two different and separately acting grammatical systems. . . : a system of predicates. . . and a system which can be considered an extension of morphophonemics. . . . The predicate system carries all the objective information in the sentence, and the most natural interpretation of its structure is that of giving a report. The morphophonemic system is interpretable as being paraphrastic, and changes at most the speaker's or hearer's relation to the report. The grammar of the language as a whole is simply the resultant of these two systems."

The "predicate" system may perhaps be thought of as providing deep structures or logical forms. The morphophonemic system may then be thought of as an extension of the predicate system, arising from the latter by the addition of suitable rules of paraphrase. The present chapter will be concerned primarily with the predicate system, for it is only after we have a quite clear idea as to what this is that we can even formulate rules of paraphrase and hence get at "the grammar of the language as a whole."

It is perhaps not quite Harris's intent to identify the predicate system with a system of logical structure. Much of what he says of the one, however, is readily applicable to the other. The predicate system is a "sublanguage" of the system of the whole, he writes, and (p. 614) "carries all the objective information, or report, which is carried in the language, and can be used without the rest of the language." Similarly, surely, for a logical system of deep structures. "Indeed," Harris continues, "every sentence of the language can be decomposed (by an algorithm) into a sentence of the report-sublanguage (containing all that is reported in the original sentence) plus various paraphrastic transformations." Similarly of course for the logical form,

1. In *Papers in Structural and Transformational Linguistics* (Dordrecht: Reidel, 1972). Cf. also his "On a Theory of Language," *The Journal of Philosophy* 73(1976): 253–276.

although the algorithms needed must surely be spelled out, no easy matter. "A discourse [consisting of many sentences *seriatim*] can be reduced to one in the sublanguage by reducing each sentence to its source in this sublanguage." Similarly for logical forms regarded as the "sources." "Many sentences . . . are grammatically ambiguous, i.e. have more than one source from which they could be transformationally derived." Similarly if the source is regarded as a logical form. "In the sublanguage the connection between the simple syntactic relations in it and the meaning of words and classes [sic!] becomes much sharper than in the language as a whole." One of the great advantages of using logical forms at all is of course just that their syntax can be made pellucid and the meanings of their constituent words and phrases subject to exact semantical rule. Likewise "investigation of what kind of information can be borne in language, and how language can be modified to carry other kinds of information, is made possible by analysis of the structure of this report-sublanguage, in which every item of structure is relevant to the informational burden that language carries." The word 'information' is presumably being used here somewhat non-technically, but the foregoing observation surely holds on more technical meanings, as the work of Carnap, Bar-Hillel, and others has shown.[2]

Harris contends—and here we must merely bow to his authority and hope that he is right—that (p. 615) "the whole of the rest of language can be derived out of this sublanguage, as source, by a system of paraphrastic transformations. . . , which themselves have a particular grammatical structure, and a subjective (or purely paraphrastic) semantic character. They bring no new independent words (or new report) into the sentence, but are especially useful for abbreviation." This fascinating observation puts the study of logical form, of the report sublanguage, at the very center of linguistics, giving it a role much more important than seems heretofore to have been

2. See especially Y. Bar-Hillel, *Language and Information* (Reading, Mass., Palo Alto, and London: Addison-Wesley, Jerusalem: The Jerusalem Academic Press, 1964).

recognized. In fact, according to it, we can scarcely being the enterprise of modern structural lingusitics without a prior delineation of the report system. Adequate rules of paraphrase cannot even be formulated without going back ultimately to the source forms. (Of course limited rules of paraphrase as between derived forms can be given, but these would not be ultimately satisfactory and would leave the characterization of structure hanging in mid-air.) Thus modern logic is seen to be at the very center of structural linguistics, and the sentences of ordinary language may be regarded merely as "abbreviations" for their "prior" sources, which are usually longer and seemingly more complicated.

"One can," Harris notes (p. 615) in concluding his introductory remarks, "make a description of the whole language, but it is now possible to see that there is no coherent structure in the grammar of a whole language. The whole grammar is a resultant of two quite different structures, the second operating on the prior one. Each system is coherent, as being derivable from a tightly interrelated set of primitives, in a way that the whole grammar is not; and each has a natural interpretation. Together they account for the forms and the interpretation (meaning) of the whole language." Coherency of structure here is presumably just that of a logical system, even rules of paraphrase eventually to be couched in terms of such. Harris cites no reason why "there is no coherent structure in the grammar of a whole language." Perhaps it is that "every language contains metalinguistic sentences" and thus (pp. 608–9) that "the metalanguage of a language is itself a set of sentences and a subset of the whole language." And similarly no doubt for the metalanguage, and so on. The hierarchy of languages is thus perhaps to be built fundamentally into the system of report, and coherency of structure is achieved only by lopping off the hierarchy at some finite point. In this way a limited report sublanguage is formulated, generating by rules of paraphrase a limited morphophonemic system. And this is about the best we can do, Harris seems to say. Coherency of structure can be achieved at any finite stage, but not for the whole language whose report-source would have to be a metalanguage exceeding finite bounds.

Harris devotes a great deal more attention to the derived system than he does to the source system, and in fact the character of this latter never emerges too clearly. Let us attempt to characterize it here in terms of the event logic discussed above. It is hoped that kind of system Harris needs will be supplied in this way. Let us plunge into the middle by providing logical forms for most of the kinds of sentences he considers, following him more or less page by page.

Sentences such as

'The ball rolls slowly'

and its paraphrastic transformation

'The ball's rolling is slow',

if for the moment we disregard tense, are "derivable" from the source form

'$(Ee)(\langle(\text{the Ball}),\text{Rolls}\rangle e$. e Low_{sp} Slower-Than,'$\{e'3$ $(Ex)(\text{Ball } x$. $\langle x,\text{Rolls}\rangle e')\}$'$)$',

to the effect that there is an e, an event or process describable as a rolling of the ball, that is low in the speaker's slower-than scale—sp is the speaker—relative to the reference predicate (or virtual-class expression) 'rollings of balls'. This and allied forms have been studied to some extent elsewhere.[3]

The novelty here is to construe what previously were regarded as reference classes as now reference *predicates*. In this way adverbs—and indeed adjectives likewise—are handled intentionally. Thus to say that e, a rolling of the ball, is slow is to say that e is regarded by the speaker as low in his slower-than scale as confined to objects to which he is willing to apply a predicate of the form '$\{e'3(Ex)(\text{Ball } x$. $\langle x,\text{Rolls}\rangle e')\}$'.

The form

'e Low_{sp} Slower-Than, 'F''

---

3. See especially "On How Some Adverbs Work," in *Events, Reference, and Logical Form*, and "On Adverbs and Intentionality," presented at the First Congress of the International Association for Semiotical Studies, Milan, June, 1974.

requires comment. It expresses that the speaker places e low in a rough-and-ready scale, starting with the lowest at the bottom to the highest at its top, confined to entities to which he thinks the predicate 'F' applies, with respect to their slowness. Similarly

$$\text{'}e \text{ Mid}_{sp} \text{ Slower-Than, 'F''} \quad \text{and} \quad \text{'}e \text{ High}_{sp} \text{ Slower-Than, 'F''}$$

express that the speaker places e somewhere in the middle or high on the same scale. Nothing too exact is expressed by these forms, and a great deal of slack is allowed. Presumably the three forms are mutually exclusive for one and the same speaker, but not necessarily otherwise. Also there is often considerable choice as to the most appropriate reference predicate. Perhaps a clause should be added, in the reference predicate in the example above, to the effect that the ball x is *like* or *similar* to (the Ball).

It should be observed that in the form

$$\text{'}e \text{ Low}_{sp} \text{ Slower-Than, 'F'',}$$

the 'F' is a shape or sign-design, single quotes are being used in their ordinary sense.

If the underlying syntax is based on sign events as above, however, this form is not appropriate. We may remedy this seeming defect as follows. Let

$$\text{''F'}a\text{'}$$

express that a is a sign event of the shape 'F'. Our form may then be regarded as short for

$$\text{'}(Ea)(e \text{ Low}_{sp} \text{ Slower-Than, } a \ . \ \text{'F'}a)\text{'}$$

without more ado. And similarly for other forms subsequently to be introduced.

We cannot of course, at the present stage of research, spell out all the shape-descriptive predicates needed for a natural language. Hence here in Part B single-quoted material is used in formulae, rather than shape-descriptive predicates as in Part A.

In the sources one wants forms as "unrestricted" or general as possible. "The whole work of distributional linguistics [p. 619] has been to replace restricted elements by less restricted ones."

In a similar vein one wants forms as concrete as possible, not only concrete words or phrases but a minimum of logical apparatus in any way transcending the concrete. Thus abstract nouns are to be "derived" from more concrete ones in the source forms, and the latter themselves are to contain no logical words other than those provided by the resources of first-order event logic. Thus the source forms contain no variables for sets or objects of higher logical type. Although Harris makes neither of these points explicitly, they are both surely consonant with his point of view. Set theory, or any variant thereof, is scarcely mentioned and no fundamental or uneliminable use of it seems to be made. And similarly concrete nonlogical words and phrases seem always preferred to abstract ones.

Consider now

'I am writing poetry',

'I write poetry',

'I am in process of writing poetry',

and

'My writing of poetry is in process'.

Poetry-writing is a special kind of writing and is not merely the writing of poems. One may poetry-write and never succeed in writing a poem. Thus the source form here is

$$\text{'}(Ee)\langle I, \text{Poetry-Write}\rangle e\text{'}.$$

And where 'now_{sp}' is a demonstrative word referring to whatever—to within of course suitable constraints—the speaker takes as the present time, 'e During now_{sp}' may express that e takes place during the present. To provide for the present active tense, we have here then

$$\text{'}(Ee)(\langle I, \text{Poetry-Write}\rangle e \; . \; e \text{ During } now_{sp})\text{'}$$

as the source form.

On the other hand

'I am writing a poem'

or

'I am in process of writing a poem',

concrete forms not considered by Harris, are very closely related to the foregoing. Somehow, it would seem, 'poetry-writes' ought to be definable in terms of 'writes a poem'. Note that

$$\text{'(E}e)(\text{E}a)(\text{E}x)(\langle I,\text{Write},x,a\rangle e \ . \ \text{'}\{y3(\text{E}z)(\text{Poem } z \ .$$
$$y \text{ P } z)\}\text{'}a \ . \ e \text{ During } now_{sp})\text{'}$$

expresses that there is some present process or event of my writing something under the linguistic description that it is a part of some poem. 'y P z' is written here in place of 'Pyz', being more suggestive of English word order. In this way I can be said to be writing a poem even if no poem gets written, for I am said only to be writing something x under the given description. If I am doing no writing at all, both of these forms are false. Likewise if I am writing something other than a part of a poem. It seems likely in fact these two forms should be regarded as equivalent.·

Consider now 'finally' or 'at last' in

'I am finally owning a car'

or

'My owning a car is finally in process'.

Let 'e B e''' express, essentially as in IV above, that e takes place wholly before e' in a suitable temporal ordering (that e.g. of Greenwich meridian time). Also let

'e Final B,F'

express that event e is the final or last process or event in the series of events ordered by B as confined to events in the virtual class F. The relevant F here will be

$$\{e'3(\sim \ (\text{E}x)(\text{Car } x \ . \ \langle I,\text{Own},x\rangle e' \ . \ e' \text{ B } e \ . \ \sim(\text{E}e'')(\text{E}y)$$
$$(\text{Car } y \ . \ \langle I,\text{Own},y\rangle e'' \ . \ e' \text{ B } e'' \ . \ e'' \text{ B } e)) \ \vee \ e' = e)\},$$

the (virtual) class of all states e' of my not owning a car prior to e where there is no state between e' and e of my owning car, together with e itself. The entire source form for

'I am (now) finally owning a car'

is then

'$(Ee)(Ex)(\text{Car } x$. $\langle I, \text{Own}, x\rangle e$. e During now_{sp} . e Final B,F)'.

A closely related sentence, due to Henry Hiż, is

'John in his late childhood had an incurable illness'.

There are two interesting problems in handling this sentence, how to accommodate 'in his late childhood' and the '-able' of 'incurable'. Let

'p Able$_{sp}$ e,'F'',   defined as   '$(Ea)(p$ Able$_{sp}$ e,a . 'F'$a)$',

express that speaker takes person p to be able or capable of doing e or of being in state or process e as described by a predicate of the form 'F'. And let

'e Late$_{sp}$ B,'F''

express that e is late in the speaker's scale of events ordered by B as confined to a predicate of the form 'F'. Our sentence may then be given the source form

'$(Ee)(e$ Late$_{sp}$ B,'$\{e'3(Ee'')(\langle \text{John,Child}\rangle e''$. e' During $e'')\}$' . e B now_{sp} . $\langle \text{John,Ill}\rangle e$. $\sim (Ep)(Ee')(Ea)(Eb)$ (Per p . a Des p . b Des e . p Able$_{sp}$ $e',\ulcorner\{e''3\langle a,\text{Cure},b\rangle e''\}\urcorner))$'.[4]

The '$\langle \text{John,Child}\rangle e''$' here expresses that e'' is a state of John's being a child, and '$\langle \text{John,Ill}\rangle e$' that e is a state of his being ill.

A closely related, but somewhat simpler, example, also due to Hiż, is

'We will leave late in the evening',

---

4. Note the formal need here of Quine's quasi-quotes or corners. Note also that 'Des' here, as indeed hereafter, is taken in the sense of a canonical 'Des$_{In}$'.

which may be given the source form

'(Ee)($\langle we$,Leave$\rangle e$. now_{sp} B e . e Late$_{sp}$ B,'{$e'3e'$ During (the Evening)}')'.

Note that several of the foregoing source forms are metalinguistic. That this is the case is harmless enough, the source system being a metalanguage containing both a syntax and semantics of a part of itself. Note also that '(the Evening)' and similar phrases are handled as (usually anaphoric but occasionally epiphoric) Russellian descriptions.

Let us return now to Harris's examples,

'My writing is regrettable',

'My writing being still only in process is regrettable',

and

'That I am still only writing is regrettable'.

The word 'regrettable' here may perhaps be intended to be a moral word in the sense of 'should be regretted'. If so, the (tenseless) source form could be

'(Ee)I Oblg$_{sp}$ e,'{$e'3\langle I$,Regret,(my Writing)$\rangle e'$}'",

to the effect that I am obliged to do e under the description of its being a regretting by me of my writing. If the 'regrettable' is taken rather in the sense of 'is possible to be regretted', the form is rather

'(Ee)I Psbl$_{sp}$ e,'{$e'3\langle I$,Regret,(my Writing)$\rangle e'$}'".

The key form for possibility (as *mut. mat.* for ability and for capability) is

'p Psbl$_{sp}$ e,'F'",

expressing that the speaker takes it as possible for person p to do or to be in the state e as described by a predicate of the form 'F'. (Recall the corresponding syntactical notion in (V,G) above.)

In connection with

'My writing is regrettable'

the question 'Regrettable to whom?' arises. The examples given assume it is only the speaker. 'My writing is regrettable to you' becomes, however,

'(Ee)*You* Psbl$_{sp}$ e,'{e'3$\langle$ *you*,Regret,(my Writing)$\rangle e'$}'",

and so on. Some further examples concerning possibility and the like will be given below.

Bringing in 'still' and 'only' now, we need some additional construction. To be only writing is to be writing and not doing something else. And to be still writing is to be writing now where there was at least one, possibly many, writings going on before now. Incorporating these addenda, we see that

'My writing still being only in process is regrettable (to me)'

or its paraphrase

'That I am still only writing is regrettable to me'

may have as their source form

'(Ee)(Ea)(PredConOne a . $\sim$ 'Writes' a . I Psbl$_{sp}$ e,$^{\ulcorner}${e'3(Ee'')($\langle I$,Regret,$e''\rangle e'$. $\langle I$,Write$\rangle e''$. $\sim$ $\langle I,a\rangle e''$. e'' During *now*$_{sp}$. (Ee_1)(e_1 B e'' . $\langle I$,Write$\rangle e_1$. $\sim$ (Ee_2)(Ee_3)(e_1 B e_2 . e_2 B e'' . e_3 During e_2 . $\sim$ $\langle I$,Write$\rangle e_3$)))}$^{\urcorner}$)'.

'PredConOne a' here expresses of course that a is a canonical one-place predicate constant.

No doubt 'regrets' itself should also be handled intentionally, so that

'p Rgrt$_{sp}$ e,'F'", defined as   '(Ea)(p Rgrt$_{sp}$ e,a . 'F'a)',

is the desired form. In the foregoing two forms 'regrets' is already in the description, so to speak, so that intentionality is to some extent already provided for.

'I regret my (activity of) writing'

would, however, have as its source

'(Ee)I Rgrt$_{sp}$ e,'{e'3$\langle I$,Write$\rangle e'$}'".

The adverb 'very' and its free variant 'to a great extent' may be handled somewhat as follows.

'He favors it (now) to a great extent',

'He is (now) favorable to it to a great extent',

or

'He (now) favors it highly'

become

'$(Ee)(\langle he,\text{Favor},it\rangle e$. e During now_{sp} . e High$_{sp}$ Less-Extended-Than, '$\{e'3(Ep)(\text{Per } p$. $\langle p,\text{Favor},it\rangle e')\}$')'.

The notion of the extent of his favoring it is handled by means of the comparative relation Less-extended-than as confined intentionally, relative to the speaker sp, to human favorings of it.

Let

'e Very$_{sp}$ e',Less-Extended-Than,'F''

express that the speaker takes e as *very much* below e' in his scale for Less-extended-than relative to a predicate of the form 'F'. Then

'e VeryHigh$_{sp}$ Less-Extended-Than,'F''   may abbreviate

'$(Ee')(e'$ High$_{sp}$ Less-Extended-Than,'F' . e' Very$_{sp}$ e,Less-Extended-Than,'F')'.

In this way 'VeryHigh' is definable in terms of 'Very' and 'High', as it should be. And similarly for 'VeryVeryHigh', 'VeryLow', and so on.

The sentence

'He favors it very highly'

would then have a form similar to the above but with 'VeryHigh' replacing 'High'. And similarly for

'He is very favorable to it'

or

'He favors it very much',

which presumably are mere paraphrases of it.

The phrase 'to a great extent' invites comparison with 'to a certain extent', 'to some extent', 'to a little extent', and so on. Presumably all of these may be handled by replacing 'High' by 'Low' or 'Mod', or some other, in the relevant clause. Thus

> 'He (now) favors it to a little extent'

or

> 'He (now) favors it a little'

become

> '(Ee)($\langle he$,Favor,$it\rangle e$. e During now_{sp} . e Low$_{sp}$ Less-Extended-Than,'$\{e'$3(Ep)(Per p . $\langle p$,Favor,$it\rangle e')\}'$)'.

> 'He favors it just a little'

or

> 'He favors it very little'

would have a similar form with 'VeryLow' in place of 'Low'. Some sentences will require introducing numbers as measures of extent, as we shall see in a moment, but such an introduction is not needed here.

In some of the forms here the choice of a reference predicate may appear somewhat arbitrary. There is often considerable latitude of choice and different readings result. Whether there is one best choice is a matter that is left open for the present.

Compare now the adverbs of manner in

> 'His (present) driving of the car is quite slow'

and in

> 'His driving of the car is quite frequent'.

(The word 'quite' differs from 'very' in indicating less extent, as it were. Perhaps we may let

> 'e QuiteLow$_{sp}$ Slower-Than,'F'' abbreviate 'e Low$_{sp}$ Slower-Than,'$\{e'$3e' Low$_{sp}$ Slower-Than,'F'$\}$'',

so that e is taken as quite slow just where it is taken as slow amongst the slow.) The first may then be handled essentially as above, with 'QuiteLow' indicating the place on the speaker's scale for Slower-than, resulting in

'(Ee)($\langle he$,Drive,(the Car)$\rangle e$. e During now_{sp} . e QuiteLow$_{sp}$ Slower-Than,'$\{e'3(Ep)(Ex)($Per p . Car x . $\langle p$,Drive,$x \rangle e')\}$'')'.

On the other hand 'frequent' is like a numerical word in being characteristic of a (virtual) class of entities. It is not any single driving by him of the car that is frequent, but rather the (virtual) class of all his drivings of the (one and the same) car. Also the word is taken intentionally as relativized to a given predicate. Thus

'F Frequent$_{sp}$ 'G''

may express that the speaker takes the members of F to be frequent in the sense of 'frequent' he takes appropriate for entities denoted by 'G'. In a similar way

'F Many$_{sp}$ 'G'' and 'F Few$_{sp}$ 'G''

express that the members of F are taken to be many or few (in number) relative to 'G'. 'Frequent' is thus applicable to classes of events or processes in essentially the same way that 'Many' and 'Few' are applicable to classes of individuals.

'His driving of the car is frequent'

thus has as its source form

'$\{e3\langle he$,Drive,(the Car)$\rangle e\}$ Frequent$_{sp}$ '$\{e3(Ex)(Ep)($Per p . TypDr p . Car x . $\langle p$,Drive,$x \rangle e)\}$'')',

where 'TypDr p' expresses that p is a typical driver in some suitable sense. Note that 'frequent' is construed here both pragmatically and intentionally, being always relativized to the speaker and to a given reference predicate.

How now are we to handle 'quite frequent' in

'His driving of the car is quite frequent'

or 'quite frequently' in

'He drives the car quite frequently'?

Let

$$\text{'}e \text{ Less-Frequent-Than } e\text{'},\text{'F''}$$

express that e and e' are sums of individuals that are members of F and that the parts of e that are members of F are less frequent than the parts of e' that are members of F. In terms of this relation we have also the forms

$$\text{'}e \text{ Low}_{sp} \text{ Less-Frequent-Than,'F''},$$

and so on, as for Slower-than and other comparative relations. And then also

'F QuiteFrequent$_{sp}$ 'G'' may abbreviate '(Fu'F) High$_{sp}$ Less-Frequent-Than,'$\{e'3e'$ Mid$_{sp}$ Less-Frequent-Than,'G'$\}$'.

'His driving of the car is quite frequent'

then has the source form

'$\{e3\langle he,$Drive,(the Car)$\rangle e\}$ QuiteFrequent$_{sp}$
'$\{e3(Ep)(Ex)($Per p . TypDr p . Car x . $\langle p,$Drive,$x\rangle e)\}$'''.

Note incidentally that

'F Frequent$_{sp}$ 'G'' may perhaps be defined as '(Fu'F) High$_{sp}$ Less-Frequent-Than,'G''.

And similarly perhaps

'F Many$_{sp}$ 'G'' may abbreviate '(Fu'F) High$_{sp}$ Less-Numerous-Than, 'G'',

where 'Less-Numerous-Than' is taken as a pragmatical, intentional primitive. And with 'Very' available in the appropriate contexts, perhaps

'F Few$_{sp}$ 'G'' may be taken to abbreviate '(Fu'F) VeryLow$_{sp}$ Less-Numerous-Than,'G''.

However, these are systematic matters that need not concern us further for the moment. They require careful delineation on the basis of the material of VII above.

Many adverbs of manner may be expressed by means of a form 'in such and such a manner'.

'He pronounced my name unexpectedly'

and

'He pronounced my name in an unexpected manner'

are paraphrases on one reading of the first. However, the first is ambiguous, another reading of it being

'I did not expect him to pronounce my name',

with the source form

$(Ee)(Ee')(\sim \ \langle I,$Expct$,e,$'$\{e'3\langle he,$Pronounce,(my Name)$\rangle e'\}$'$\rangle e_1 \ . \ e_1$ B $now_{sp})$'.

The other reading has as its source

'$(Ee)(\langle he,$Pronounce,(my Name)$\rangle e \ . \ e$ B $now_{sp} \ . \ e$ Low$_{sp}$ Less-Extended-Than,'$\{e'$3$(Ee'')(Ep)($Per $p \ . \ \langle p,$Expct$,e'',$'$\{e'''$3$(Eq)($Per $q \ . \ \langle q,$Pronounce,(my Name)$\rangle e'''$)$\}$'$\rangle e'$)$\}$'$)$'.

Of course 'in an unexpected manner' contains both 'in' and 'manner', words not being "represented" in the source. However, 'in' in the sense of 'in such and such a manner' may be represented by the relational expression 'In$_{\text{Manner}}$'. Then

$$`e \ \text{In}_{\text{Manner}} \ \text{F}'$$

expresses that e takes place in the manner of entities in F. And concerning this, we have the meaning postulate that

$\vdash \ e \ \text{In}_{\text{Manner}} \ \{e'3e' \ Low_{sp}$ Less-Extended-Than,'G' $\} \ \equiv \ e' \ Low_{sp}$ Less-Extended-Than,'G',

and hence the above form for 'He pronounced my name in an unexpected manner' is equivalent to

'$(Ee)\langle he,$Pronounce,(my Name)$\rangle e \ . \ e$ B $now_{sp} \ . \ e$ In$_{\text{Manner}}$ $\{e'$3$e' \ Low_{sp}$ Less-Extended-Than,'G'$\}$),

for the appropriate 'G'.

'Unexpected' has been taken here in the sense of 'unexpected by me'. Variants are of course 'unexpected by you', 'unexpected by us', 'unexpected by him', and so on. These may all be handled in terms of the predicate 'Expct' by varying the first argument, for the first form. Thus

'He pronounced my name unexpectedly to us'

becomes, on the first reading,

'(Ee)(Ee_1)($\sim$ $\langle we$,Expct,e,'$\{e'3\langle he$,Pronounce,(my Name)$\rangle e'\}$'$\rangle e_1$. e_1 B now_{sp})'.

And the desired variations in the second form may be gotten by putting some pronoun or proper name in place of the subscript 'sp'. Thus

'He pronounced my name in a manner unexpected by us'

becomes

'(Ee)($\langle he$,Pronounce,(my Name)$\rangle e$. e B now_{sp} . e In$_{\text{Manner}}$ $\{e'3e'$ Low$_{we}$ Less-Extended-Than,'G')$\}$)',

for the appropriate 'G'.

Consider now the subjunctives in contexts such as

'I request that he go there'

and

'I won't go for fear [or lest] he go there'.

For these we can find free variants, Harris contends, without the subjunctives,

'I request his going there'

and

'My not going is for fear of his going there'.

This latter is "no different from" (Harris's phrase)

'My not going is because of his going there'.

But is it no different? For the first, we have

'(Ee)(I Rqst e,'$\{e'3\langle he$,Go$\rangle e'$. e' To $there_{sp}$)$\}$'$)$',

where To is a suitable prepositional relation and '$there_{sp}$' a demonstrative or egocentric word like 'now_{sp}'. For the second a causal form is needed. Causation seems best treated as a quadratic relation as between events under given descriptions.[5] Let

$$\text{'}(e,a) \text{ Cause } (e',b)\text{'}$$

express that e under the (predicate) description a causes e' under the (predicate) description b. Then

'My not going is because of his going there'

has then as a reasonable source.

$\text{'}(Ee)(Ee')(Ea)(Eb)(\text{'}\{e''3(\langle he,Go\rangle e'' \ . \ e'' \text{ To } there_{sp})\}\text{'}a \ .$
$\text{'}\{e''3 \sim \langle I,Go\rangle e''\}\text{'}b \ . \ \sim \langle I,Go\rangle e \ . \ \langle he,Go\rangle e' \ . \ e' \text{ To }$
$there_{sp} \ . \ (e',a) \text{ Cause } (e,b))\text{'}.$

Note that this source has as a logical consequence both that I go and that he does not go there, as it should. The variants

'My not going is for fear of his going there'

or

'My not going is because of my fear of his going there'

have as a consequence that I go but not that he goes there. These therefore seem to require a more complicated source involving a construction with 'fear'. Also they have the consequence that I fear of his going there, which must somehow be provided for. For these, then, the following quite different form seems appropriate.

$\text{'}(Ee)(Ee')(Ee'')(Ea)(Eb)(\sim \langle I,Go\rangle e \ .$
$\langle I,Fear,e',\text{'}\{e'''3(\langle he,Go\rangle e''' \ . \ e''' \text{ To } there_{sp})\}\text{'}\rangle e'' \ .$
$\text{'}\{e'''3(Ee')\langle I,Fear,e',\text{'}\{e''''3(Ee')\langle I,Fear,e',\text{'}\{e''''3(\langle he,Go\rangle e'''' \ .$
$e'''' \text{ To } there_{sp})\}\text{'}\rangle e'''\}\text{'}a \ . \ \text{'}\{e''' \sim \langle I,Go\rangle e'''\}\text{'}b \ .$
$(e'',a) \text{ Cause } (e,b))\text{'}.$

This form has the consequences presumably desired of the original sentence.

5. Cf. the suggestions concerning causality in the author's "On Stevenson's If-iculties," *Philosophy of Science* 39 (1972): 515–521 and D. Davidson, "Causal Relations," *The Journal of Philosophy* 64 (1967): 691–703.

We may now bring in some time-location adverbs such as 'yesterday', 'today', and 'tomorrow'.

'I denied yesterday that he went the day before yesterday',

for example, becomes

'$(Ee)(Ee')(e'$ During $yesterday_{sp}$.
$\langle I,Deny,e,'\{e''3(\langle he,Go\rangle e''$. e'' During $(\imath e_1$. (Day e_1 .
e_1 B $yesterday_{sp}$. $\sim (Ee_2)(Day\ e_2$. e_1 B e_2 . e_2 B
$yesterday_{sp})))\}'\rangle e')$'.

And similarly for

'I denied yesterday that he will go tomorrow',

'I requested the day before yesterday that he go yesterday',

'I went yesterday because he went the day before yesterday',

and so on.

The various time-conjunctions 'before', 'after', 'until', 'since', 'while', and the like, may all presumably be handled in terms of the before-than relation B together with During. (See XIII below.)

'He returned (yesterday) before she arrived (yesterday)',

for example, has as its source

'$(Ee)(Ee')(\langle he,Return\rangle e$. e During $yesterday_{sp}$. $\langle she,$
Arrive$\rangle e'$. e B e' . e' During $yesterday_{sp})$'.

And similarly no doubt for allied examples.

On the other hand,

'Gödel's backward-running time could make one's return tomorrow be before one's arrival today'

raises additional intriguing problems. As a rough approximation, and for shear philosphical sport, let us consider the following. It is assumed, to oversimplify, that there is a relation B' in terms of which the backward-running time theory is formulated. Such a time is at least conceived, but it may not be actual. Let

$$\text{'}p \text{ Cncv } e,\text{'F'',}$$

express that person p has a conception of e under the predicate description 'F'. Let 'Mom e' express that e is a momentary time. Consider then the form

'(Ee)(Ee')(Gödel Cncv e,'$\{e''$3e'' = (Fu'$\{e_2$3$((Ee_3)(e_2$ B' $e_3 \lor e_3$ B' $e_2)$. $(e_1)(e_2)((\text{Mom } e_1$. Mom e_2 . $\sim e_1 =$ $e_2) \supset (e_1$ B $e_2 \equiv e_2$ B' $e_1)))\}$)$\}$' . e Psbl$_{sp}$ e','$\{e_4$3(Ee_1) $(Ee_2)(Ee_3)(Ep)(e_4$ Makes e_3 . Per p . $\langle p,\text{Return}\rangle e_1$. e_1 During $tomorrow_{sp}$. $\langle p,\text{Arrive}\rangle e_2$. e_2 During $yesterday_{sp}$. $\langle e_1, \text{B}, e_2 \rangle e_3)\}$')'.

The clause concerning Gödel's conception has as its constituent predicate description one describing the fusion of the field (or campus) of the relation B' where of any two moments, B holds between them if and only if B' does in the opposite order. And it is possible for this conception e to make a state e_3 of some person's returning tomorrow be before his arrival today (on the normal meanings of 'today' and 'tomorrow' as based on B). This form is perhaps acceptable as a first somewhat over-simplified approximation. (Perhaps 'Makes' here should be construed in terms of 'Cause'.)

Let us turn now to a few comparative sentences (p. 632 in Harris) such as

'More men read books than women (read) magazines',

'Men read more books than are worthwhile',

and the like. Construing numbers as counters assigned to virtual classes giving their numerosity, we may let

$$\text{'}a \text{ Num F'}$$

express that the expression a is the number of members of the virtual class F. The notion of being the number of a class may easily be introduced in terms of the material of (VII,C) above. We may in fact let

'a Num F'   abbreviate   '$((Ep)p$ AcStr a . $(p)(x)(b)((p$ Card bxF . $x = (\text{Fu'F})) \supset a$ EqLng $b))$'.

The first sentence above then becomes

'(Ea)(Eb)(a Num {p3(Ex)(Book x . Man p . p Read x)} . b Num {p3(Ex)(Mag x . Woman p . p Read x)}. $a > b$)',

and the second

'(Ea)(Eb)(a Num {p3(Ex)(Book x . Man p . p Read x)} . b Num {x3(Book x . x High$_{sp}$ Less-Extended-Than,'{y3(Book y . Worthwhile y)}')} . $a > b$)'.

'He is (now) richer than she'

can be handled in terms of a comparative relation *more rich than*, or in terms of the scale of less-valuable-than as confined to a predicate taken to denote entities owned by persons. Thus we have either

'(Ee)((⟨*He*,Richer-Than,*she*⟩e . e During *now*$_{sp}$)'

or

'(Ee)(Ee')(e = (Fu'{x3(Ee'')(⟨*he*,Own,x⟩e'' . e'' During *now*$_{sp}$)}) . e' = (Fu'{x3(Ee'')(⟨*she*,Own,x⟩e'' . e'' During *now*$_{sp}$)}) . e' Less-Valuable-Than$_{sp}$ e,'{x3(Ep)(Per p . p Own x)}'))'.

This last clause expresses that e' is less-valuable-than e in the speaker's less-valuable-than scale as confined to entities describable as humanly possessed. This last clause may also be expressed in terms of the relation Less-Extended-Than, as

'e Less-Extended-Than$_{sp}$ e','{x3(Ep)(Per p . p Own x . p Value x)}')'.

Of course 'Value' here is ambiguous, just as 'Richer-Than' is. But whatever 'Richer-Than' is taken to mean, richer in property, in money, in friends, and so on, so 'Value' is taken to mean here.

Consider next (p. 633)

'He is too ill for you to leave now'

or

'He is so ill that you should not leave now'.

"These are derivable from morphophonemic replacements," Harris says, from

'He is more ill than is appropriate for your leaving now'

or

'The degree of his illness is more than the degree of his illness which is appropriate for your leaving now'.

'Degree' here is perhaps too exact; 'extent' is better. Note that two scales are involved, however, one as to the extent of his illness and the other as to the extent of the appropriateness of his leaving now. Hence the use of the Less-Extended-Than relation as confined to just one scale seems unsuitable. Thus we should now let

$$\text{'}(e,a)\ \text{Less-Extended-Than}_{sp}\ (e',a')\text{'}$$

express that the speaker takes e in his scale determined by a to be less extended than e' in his scale determined by a'. In this way items on two scales may be compared. How now is 'appropriate' to be handled? Again, as an intentional relation involving a mode of description. Let

'e Approp$_{sp}$ e','F'',   defined as   '(Ea)(a Approp$_{sp}$ e',a . 'F'a)',

express that the speaker takes it as appropriate for e to be in the state or process e' under the predicate description 'F'. Our structure then becomes

'(Ee)(Ee')(Ee'')(Ea)(Eb)($\langle he,$Ill$\rangle e$. e During now_{sp} . $\langle you,$ Approp$_{sp}$,e','$\{e_3 3(\langle you,$Leave$\rangle e_3$. e_3 During $now_{sp})\}$'$\rangle e''$. '$\{e_1 3(\langle he,$Ill$\rangle e_1$. e_1 During $now_{sp})\}$'a . '$\{e_1 3($E$e_2)$ ($\langle you,$Leave$\rangle e_2$. e_2 During now_{sp} . $\langle you,$Approp$_{sp}$,e_2, '$\{e_3 3(\langle you,$Leave$\rangle e_3$. e_3 During $now_{sp})\}$'$\rangle e_1\}$'b . (e'',b) Less-Extended-Than$_{sp}$ $(e,a))$'.

Note that this has as a consequence that he is now ill. It does not have as a consequence that you are now leaving, but only that there is some state of appropriateness with respect to your leaving. Note also that the structure is metametalinguistic, as two or three others above have been, b being a mode of description containing a mode of description.

Consider also

'It's solid enough (now) to break the wall'

or

'It is so solid (now) that it can break the wall'.

This may be rendered approximately as

'The state of its solidity (now) where it is capable of breaking the wall is greater than that of anything not capable of breaking the wall',

and thus as

'$(Ee)(Ee')(Ee'')(\langle it,\text{Solid}\rangle e$. e During now_{sp} . $\langle it,\text{Cpbl},e'$, '$\{e_1 3\langle it,\text{Break},(\text{the Wall})\rangle e_1\}$'$\rangle e''$. e'' During now_{sp} . $(e_1)(e_2)(x)(a)((\langle x,\text{Solid}\rangle e_1$. a Des x . $\sim x$ Cpbl e_2, $\ulcorner\{e_1 3\langle a,\text{Break},(\text{the Wall})\rangle e_1\}\urcorner) \supset e_1$ Less-Extended-Than$_{sp}$ e,'$\{e_1 3(Ey)\langle y,\text{Solid}\rangle e_1\}$')))'.

Or, better, essentially as with Harris,

'The amount [or extent] of its solidity equals the amount of solidity necessary (or appropriate) for it to break the wall',

and thus

'$(Ee)(Ee')(Ea)(Ea')(\langle it,\text{Solid}\rangle e$. e During now_{sp} . '$\{e_1 3 \langle it,\text{Solid}\rangle e_1\}$'$a$. '$\{e_2 3(Ee_3)(\langle it,\text{Solid}\rangle e_2$. e_2 Approp$_{sp}$ e_3, '$\{e_1 3\langle it,\text{Break},(\text{the Wall})\rangle e_1\}$')}'$a'$. (e,a) EqExt$_{sp}$ $(e',a'))$',

where 'EqExt$_{sp}$' stands for the relation of equal in extent. (Presumably

'(e,a) EqExt$_{sp}$ (e',a')'   may be taken as short for   '$(\sim (e,a)$ Less-Extended-Than$_{sp}$ (e',a') . $\sim (e',a')$ Less-Extended-Than$_{sp}$ $(e,a))$'.)

These forms are provided in terms of the comparative relation Less-Extended-Than relativized to the speaker and a given reference predicate. The next examples do seem to require fundamentally the introduction of numerical degrees of extent. Consider

'The bigger they are the harder they fall'.

Harris gives this the structure

'The excess of how (much) bigger they are is the excess of how (much) harder they fall'

or

'N_k which is the excess of how (much) bigger they are is as M_k which is the excess of how (much) harder they fall'.

Clearly a proportion is needed here, not a mere identity. Bigger-than being a comparative relation, a (zeroed) reference to those than whom they are bigger is needed in the source form. Thus the given sentence is a paraphrase of something like

'The bigger *they₁* are than *they₂*, the harder *they₁* fall than *they₂*'.

The pronouns '*they₁*' and '*they₂*' are used here referentially to stand for sums of persons (in the sense of the calculus of individuals). Let 'a ExtSize p' express that a is the numerical extent of p's size in the relevant social, economic, or political sense (p being a logical sum of persons), and 'a ExtFall e' that a is the extent of e as a falling, again in the relevant sense. These two sentential forms enable us to handle the requisite form of measurement here. The given sentence then has a source form something like

'$(p)(q)(a)(b)(a')(b')(e)(e')(($Per p . a ExtSize p . p P *they₁* . b ExtFall e . $\langle p,$Fall$\rangle e$. Per q . a' ExtSize q . q P *they₂* . b' ExtFall e' . $\langle q,$Fall$\rangle e'$. $\sim a' = 0$. $\sim b' = 0$. $a > a') \supset (a/a') = (b/b')))$'.

Consider now the dependent clause construction (p. 636) in

'He found the book which had disappeared'.

Doing a little editorial "which-hunting" here, we should distinguish this from

'He found the book that had disappeared'.[6]

This latter, in terms of a Russellian description, becomes (with some oversimplification perhaps in the handling of tense) something like

'$(Ee)(Ex)(x = (\imath y$. $(Ee')(e'$ B now_{sp} . Book y . $\langle y,$ Disappear$\rangle e'))$. $\langle he,$Find$,x\rangle e$. e B $now_{sp})$',

whereas the former becomes

'$(Ee)(Ee')(\langle he,$Find$,(\imath x$. Book $x)\rangle e$. e B now_{sp} . $\langle(\imath x$. Book $x),$Disappear$\rangle e'$. e' B $e)$'.

In both cases the descriptions are incomplete, either anaphoric or epiphoric.

The handling of '$they_1$' and '$they_2$' above utilizes the calculus of individuals, not mentioned or used by Harris. He remarks (p. 637) that his various claims are "not based on any general principle that everything can be said in a language." But surely we should aim to be able to say as much as possible, and where we fail, no doubt the inventory of our source forms is too narrow. "There are indeed," he continues, "things that cannot be precisely said: e.g. it is difficult to state a precise paraphrase of that which is intended in *They came in one after the other* (where the first person came in after no one)." But surely now the source form

'$(p)((\text{Per } p$. p P *they*$)$ $\supset$ $(Ee)(\langle p,$Come in$\rangle e$. e B $now_{sp}))$. $(Ep)(Eq)(\text{Per } p$. Per q . $\sim p = q$. p P *they* . q P *they*$)$. $(p)(q)(e')(e'')((\text{Per } p$. Per q . p P *they* . q P *they* . $\sim p = q$. $\langle p,$Come in$\rangle e$. e B now_{sp} . $\langle q,$Come in$\rangle e'$. e' B $now_{sp})$ $\supset$ $(e$ B e' $\vee$ e' B $e))$. $(Ep)(Ee)(\text{Per } p$. $\langle p,$Come in$\rangle e$. e B now_{sp} . $(q)(e')$ $((\text{Per } q$. q P *they* . $\sim p = q$. $\langle q,$Come in$\rangle e'$. e' B $now_{sp})$ $\supset$ e B $e'))$'

comes rather close to saying here precisely what is intended.

6. Cf. H. W. Fowler, *A Dictionary of Modern English Usage* (Clarendon Press, Oxford: 1927 ed.), pp. 709 ff.

The handling of plurals via the calculus of individuals seems attractive, especially for plurals in the collective use. The distributive use may often be handled by means of quantifiers in the more or less usual way.

'I need books'

is no doubt paraphrastic of

'I need two or more books'.

On the other hand

'Americans elected Nixon'

does not reduce to

'Some Americans elected Nixon'

or to

'All Americans elected Nixon',

for neither you nor I nor any single person did. The collective sense of 'Americans' is needed. Thus we have here

'$(Ee)(Ex)(x = (Fu'\{p3(Per \ p \ . \ American \ p)\}) \ . \ \langle x,Elect, n\rangle e \ . \ e \ B \ now_{sp})$'

as a possible source form, where the collective sense is construed as the fusion of all American persons.

It is interesting that in the discussion of tense (pp. 638 ff.) Harris comes down in favor of "untensed morphophonemic sources," for example, *He go* for handling 'He went', 'He will go', and 'He goes'. "Semantically, the time of such forms is indefinite or indeterminate," he notes, "rather than being some kind of generalized present." Harris's comments here seem in accord with the handling of tense in terms of 'B'. Harris considers only past, present, and future. Further tenses may, however, presumably be introduced in a somewhat Reichenbachian fashion.[7]

7. See H. Reichenbach, *Elements of Symbolic Logic*, Chapter VII and *Logic, Language, and Metaphysics*, pp. 112 ff. See also the author's "On Tense, Aspect, and Meaning," *Philosophica*, to appear, and "On Existence, Tense, and Logical Form." *American Philosophical Quarterly*, to appear.

All manner of words involving time must be suitably handled, not only 'before', 'now', 'today', 'yesterday', 'tomorrow', 'finally', and 'at last', but also 'then', 'soon', 'shortly', 'recently', 'subsequently', 'afterwards', 'punctually' or 'on time', and so on. An example involving two of these is (p. 642)

'His having arrived will spoil their leaving on time soon'.

Let 'F Few$_{sp}$ 'G'' as above express that the numerosity of F is taken by sp to be few relative to 'G'. Then a source form is

'$(Ee)(Ee')(Ee'')(\langle he,\text{Arrive}\rangle e$. e B now_{sp} . $\langle they,\text{Leave}\rangle e'$. $\{e_1 3(\text{Mom } e_1$. now_{sp} B e_1 . e_1 B $e')\}$ Few$_{sp}$ 'Mom' . e' High$_{sp}$ Less-Punctual-Than,'$\{e_1 3\langle they,\text{Leave}\rangle e_1\}$' . $\langle e,\text{Spoil},e'\rangle e''$. now_{sp} B $e'')$'.

'Soon' is handled by means of the clause concerning Few and 'on time' by that concerning Less-Punctual-Than.

> 'I request (now) that he go'

or

> 'I request (now) his going afterwards'

become

'$(Ee)(Ee')(\langle I,\text{Rqst},e,'\{e'' 3(\langle he,\text{Go}\rangle e''$. now_{sp} B $e'')\}'\rangle e'$. e' During $now_{sp})$'.

On the other hand, the 'afterwards' might be intended rather in the sense of 'after my request', in which case we have

'$(Ee)(Ee')(Ee'')(Ea)(\langle I,\text{Rqst},e,'\{e_1 3\langle he,\text{Go}\rangle e_1\}'\rangle e'$. e' During now_{sp} . a Des e' . I Rqst $e,\ulcorner\{e_1 3 a$ B $e_1\}\urcorner)$'.

Consider now (pp. 644 ff.)

> 'A met B and B met A'.

The relation *meets* is presumably symmetric, at least as confined to human beings, so that

$\vdash (x)(y)((\text{Per } x$. Per y . x Meet $y) \supset y$ Meet $x)$.

Meets contrasts with *sees* in that this latter is not symmetric in this sense. Thus 'A saw B' does not entail that B saw A, whereas

'A met B' does entail that B met A. Hence also 'A and B met' is a suitable paraphrase of 'A met B' but 'A and B saw' is not paraphrastic of 'A saw B'. Similarly for 'A and B are equal' but not 'A and B calumniate'. Harris' discussion therefore of reciprocal verbs seems best couched in terms of symmetrical relations.

Consider now the difference between

'They prevented his taking it'

and

'They prevented him from taking it'.

The former has as a form

'$(Ee)(Ee')(\langle they, \text{Prevent}, e, \text{'}\{e_1 3 \langle he, \text{Take}, it \rangle e_1\}\text{'} \rangle e'$. e' B $now_{sp})$',

and the latter

'$(Ee)(\langle they, \text{Prevent}, him, \text{'}\{p3(\text{Per } p \ . \ p \text{ Take } it)\}\text{'} \rangle e$. e B $now_{sp})$'.

In the former it is an act that is the object of the preventing, the latter a person. The latter perhaps entails the former, but not conversely. They could prevent his taking poison, say, by putting it beyond availability, but this would not prevent him from taking it if it were available or at some other time. For the latter, Harris suggests as an untensed source form

'$\text{prevent}(N, N_j, V(N_j, N))$'.

The forms used above, however, are more pliable and help to bring out the difference if any between these two sentences.

For 'undergoes' Harris suggests the form

'$\text{undergo}(N_j, V(N_j, N))$'.

But

'He underwent testing'

can be handled merely as

'$(Ee)(Ep)(Ee')(\text{Per } p \ . \ \langle he, \text{Undergo}, e \rangle e'$. $\langle p, \text{Test}, him \rangle e$. e' B $now_{sp})$'.

And similarly

'Everything he underwent was a testing'

or

'Everything that occurred (or happened) to him was a testing'

require forms for both 'undergo' and 'occurs'. The former thus,

'$(e)((Ee')(\langle he, \text{Undergo}, e \rangle e'$. e' B $now_{sp}) \supset (Ep)(\text{Per } p$. $\langle p, \text{Test}, him \rangle e$. e B $now_{sp}))$',

and the latter,

'$(e)((Ee')(\langle e, \text{Occur}, him \rangle e'$. e' B $now_{sp}) \supset (Ep)(\text{Per } p$. $\langle p, \text{Test}, him \rangle e$. e B $now_{sp}))$'.

Consider again 'A and B met'. One might be tempted to construe this as '$(A \cup B)$ met', where

$$(A \cup B) = (\text{Fu}`\{A, B\}).$$

This might be suitable in the case of a symmetric relation, but not otherwise. The idea of using logical sums of individuals to represent plural nouns or noun phrases taken collectively is, however, attractive, as some of the foregoing examples have shown. In some instances, moreover, the sum must be ordered, as in contexts involving asymmetric and nonsymmetric relations.

Not much has been said thus far about prepositional relations To, From, By, Out, Towards, and so on.[8] Consider (p. 652)

'They looked out the window',

'He looked up',

'They threw the food out',

and so on. The source forms for these require prepositional relations. Thus we have here something like

'$(Ee)(\langle they, \text{Look} \rangle e$. e B now_{sp} . e Out (the Window))',

'$(Ee)(\langle he, \text{Look} \rangle e$. e B now_{sp} . Upwards e)',

8. See Chapter X below.

'$(Ee)(\langle they,\text{Throw},(\text{the Food})\rangle e$. e B now_{sp} . Outwards $e)$',
and so on.

Three interesting further examples concerning ability, capability, and possibility (p. 655) are

'A boy can jump all day (and not get tired)',

'A boy can jump all day (and not get caught)',

and

'A boy can speak five languages (but it is rare)'.

In the first "the action is a capability," Harris says, but in the third "the occurrence of the action is". This way of stating the difference seems rather obscure. The difference seems rather to be that between a capability and an ability (under the given circumstances), but in both the action (or action type) and occurrences of it should be brought in. Thus for the first we have a source something like

'$(p)(e)((Ee')(\langle p,\text{Boy}\rangle e'$. e' During e . Day $e) \supset (Ee')(Ea)(Eb)(a$ Des p . b Des e . p Cpbl $e',^\ulcorner\{e_13(e_1 = (\text{Fu}'\{e''3(\langle a,\text{Jump}\rangle e''$. e'' During $b)\})$. $(e_2)(e_2$ During $b \supset (Ee_3)(Ee_4)(e_3$ P e_4 . e_3 During e_2 . $\langle a,\text{Jump}\rangle e_4))$. $(e_2)(e_2$ During $b \supset \sim (Ee_3)(\langle a,\text{Tire}\rangle e_3$. e_3 During $e_2)))\}^\urcorner))$',

and for the second

'$(p)(e)((Ee')(\langle p,\text{Boy}\rangle e'$. e' During e . Day $e) \supset (Ee')(Ea)(Eb)(a$ Des p . b Des e . p Able $e',^\ulcorner\{e_13(e_1 = (\text{Fu}'\{e''3(\langle a,\text{Jump}\rangle e''$. e'' During $b)\})$. $(e_2)(e_2$ During $b \supset (Ee_3)(Ee_4)(e_3$ P e_4 . e_3 During e_2 . $\langle a,\text{Jump}\rangle e_4))$. $(e_2)(e_2$ During $b \supset \sim (Ee_3)(Eq)(\text{Per } q$. $\langle q,\text{Catch},a\rangle e_3$. e_3 During $e_2)))\}^\urcorner))$'.

For the third a suitable form is forthcoming in terms of 'Cpbl'.

Closely related to the notions 'Able' and 'Cpbl' are 'Psbl' for possibility and 'Nec' for necessity—recall (V,H)—'Pmtd' for permission, 'Oblg' for obligation, 'may', 'must', and the like (p. 656). 'He may go' is ambiguous as between 'He is permitted to go' and 'It is possible for him to go', which may have sources

$$\text{`(E}e)he \text{ Pmtd}_{sp} \ e,\text{`}\{e'3\langle he,\text{Go}\rangle e'\}\text{'}\text{''}$$

and

$$\text{`(E}e)he \text{ Psbl}_{sp} \ e,\text{`}\{e'3\langle he,\text{Go}\rangle e'\}\text{'}\text{''}$$

respectively. Similarly 'He must go' is ambiguous as between 'He is obliged to go' and 'It is necessary for him to go', which have the forms respectively

$$\text{`(E}e)he \text{ Oblg}_{sp} \ e,\text{`}\{e'3\langle he,\text{Go}\rangle e'\}\text{'}\text{''}$$

and

$$\text{`(E}e)he \text{ Nec}_{sp} \ e,\text{`}\{e'3\langle he,\text{Go}\rangle e'\}\text{'}\text{''}.$$

'He need go but once' requires an additional uniqueness clause, and is ambiguous as between

$$\text{`(E}e)he \text{ Oblg}_{sp} \ e,\text{`}\{e'3(\langle he,\text{Go}\rangle e' \ . \ (e'')(\langle he,\text{Go}\rangle e'' \supset e' = e''))\}\text{'}$$

and the analogous form with 'Nec' in place of 'Oblg'.

It is interesting to observe that in these various intentional forms involving an *Art des Gegebenseins*, nothing obscure is admitted as a value for the variables. Consider 'p Pmtd$_{sp}$ e,'F'', for example, and observe that it is allowed here that the e be the null event. Person p may be permitted to go but never actually go because of circumstances. In such cases the e is the null entity, taken of course under the suitable description. If this use of the null entity is thought objectionable, it may be avoided by using forms such as

$$\text{`}p \text{ Pmtd}_{sp} \ a\text{'} \quad \text{or} \quad \text{`}p \text{ Psbl}_{sp} \ a\text{'}.$$

as the basic ones. And let 'p Do e' be the basic form for p does e (tenselessly). Then

'p Pmtd$'_{sp}$ e,'F''   may abbreviate   '(Ea)(p Pmtd$_{sp}$ a . 'F'a . a Den e . p Do e)',

where Den is the canonical semantical relation of multiple denotation. This method is suitable irrespective of whether the null entity is available or not. If it is, we would have the meaning postulate that

$$\vdash (p)(e)(p \text{ Do } e \supset \sim e = \text{NE}),$$

where NE is the null act or event. Then the foregoing

'p Pmtd$_{sp}$ e,'F''   may abbreviate   '(p Pmtd$'_{sp}$ e,'F' $\vee$ (p Pmtd$_{sp}$ a . 'F'a . e = NE))'.

Consider now 'likely', 'certain', and 'probable' in suitable contexts. These notions may be construed intentionally and as relative to the speaker. Thus

'e Likely$_{sp}$ 'F'', 'e Certain$_{sp}$ 'F'', and 'e Prob$_{sp}$ 'F''

may express that the speaker takes it as likely, certain, or probable, respectively, that 'F' denotes or applies to e.

'He is likely to see her'

thus, for example, becomes

'(Ee)e Likely$_{sp}$ '$\{e'3\langle he, \text{See}, her \rangle e'\}$''',

and

'I am certain he will come'

becomes

'(Ee)e Certain$_I$ '$\{e'3(\langle he, \text{Come} \rangle e'$. now_{sp} B $e')\}$'''.

"The most difficult search for a predicate source," Harris writes (p. 659), "is in the case of verb operators on nominalized verbs: *have a look, give a look, make a trip*, etc. They almost all have the meaning of some bounded segment of activity. . ." Consider 'I had a walk' or 'I took a walk' as contrasted with 'I walked' or 'My walking took place'. The latter is clearly

'(Ee)($\langle I, \text{Walk} \rangle e$. e B now_{sp})'.

But for the former an intentional mode of construction seems needed in terms of the length of time regarded by the speaker as appropriate for a walk. Let 'a ExtLg e' express that a is the measure of (the extent of) e's length or duration. Then 'I had a walk' becomes

'$(Ee)(Ea)(Ec)(\langle I,\text{Walk}\rangle e$. e B now_{sp} . a ExtLg e . a Approp$_{sp}$ c,'$\{b3(Ee')(\text{Walk } e'$. b ExtLg $e')\}$')'.

This latter entails that I walked but not conversely. I might well have walked without taking a walk.

Let us consider now for a moment verbal moods other than the declarative. "All question forms," Harris writes (p. 662), "both the yes-no form (*Are you going?*) and the *wh*-form (*When are you going? What will you take?*) are paraphrastic transformations of *I ask you whether you are going or not, I ask you when you are going* (or: *whether you are going at time A or. . .or whether you are going at time Z*). . . The imperative, e.g. (*Please*) *go!*, is derived from *I command* (or: *request*) *you that you please go*. The optative *Would that he returned!* is derivable from *I would that he returned, I wish that he would return*. And so on. That is to say, these forms are obtained. . .by paraphrastic transformation from known types of predicate operators." A similar view concerning questions and commands was suggested above in (VI,I). The source form for 'I ask (or question) whether. . .' is no doubt

'p Ask a,q'   or   'p Qstn a,q',

expressing that person p asks person q whether a holds or not, where a is a declarative. It is not clear, however, that the *wh*-form of question may be handled without an additional locution. Let

'p Ask-Which a,q'

express that p asks q which entity (or enties) are denoted by a where a is *a one-place predicate* (or virtual-class abstract). 'When are you going?' then has as its source

'I Ask-Which '$\{e3(Ee')(\langle you,\text{Go}\rangle e'$. e' During $e)\}$',*you*',

to the effect that I ask you which events (as times) are denoted by the predicate (put loosely) 'is such that your going takes place during it'. For further discussion see below. Commands are subject to a similar treatment, as we have seen, where

'p Cmnd a,q'

is the ultimate source form. And likewise for optatives, but without the second person-parameter.

It is curious that Harris makes no mention of allied forms for either assertions or subjunctives, two "moods" along with the others. Clearly

$$\text{'}p \text{ Assrt } a,q\text{'}$$

may provide a source expressing that p asserts a to q, as above. (This form is almost Fregean.) How now about subjunctives? Let, also as above,

$$\text{'}p \text{ Subj } a,q\text{'}$$

express that p *subjunctivises* a to q, or takes a in the subjunctive mood as expressing "a mood. . .the forms of which are employed to denote an action or a state as *conceived* (and not as a fact). . . ," as noted in the *O.E.D.*

Nothing thus far has been said concerning 'and' and 'or'. Harris contends (p. 662) that "one can show that *and* is an operator only on sentences. It is always possible to derive *and* in predicates from *and* or other operators on sentence[s]. And even *and* on nouns can be so derived." This is of course a contention dear to the philosophic logician's heart. Some cases of "N_1 and N_2 can be derived from N_1 *with* N_2 or from *the set consisting of N_1 and N_2.* . . ." The reference to, or need for, a set here is quite unusual in Harris's paper, nor is this use of '*with*' anywhere clarified. Little essential use is made of sets, however, nor does the analysis of 'with' require them. In the case of a collective verb, e.g., 'gather', a collective noun is needed. But we have already seen above, in the discussion of reciprocal verbs as based on symmetric relations, that their effect may be achieved by using logical sums of individuals in the sense of the calculus of individuals. Thus Harris's 'N_1 and (or with) N_2 and N_3 gathered at the corner' becomes

$$\text{'}(Ee)(\langle(N_1 \ \cup \ N_2 \ \cup \ N_3).\text{Gather}\rangle e \ . \ e \text{ B } now_{sp} \ . \ e \text{ At}$$
(the Corner))'.

In this way 'with' in the context 'N_1 with N_2' may be analyzed without reference to any set at all. The avoidance of sets is of course a great advantage, there being no compelling reason to postulate their existence in the report system—nor indeed in the paraphrase system either.

Harris contends (p. 666) that

'I dislike his speaking because she can't'

is two-way ambiguous as between

'His speaking because she can't (speak) is disliked by me'

and

'His speaking is disliked by me because she can't speak'.

But there are other "readings" also, in particular,

'I dislike his speaking because she can't dislike his speaking'

and

'His speaking, because she can't dislike it, is disliked by me',

although these are perhaps less natural. Harris takes the form for his first reading to be

'dislike(I,because(speak(he),not(can(speak(she)))))'

and the second

'because(dislike(I,speak(he)),not(can(speak(she))))'

Suitable forms for these, and for the other two readings, are of course forthcoming on the present basis using the causal relation discussed above.

"Modern linguistic analysis," it is noted (p. 667), "whether descriptive, structural, or transformational, has always sought to remove restrictions. *Of course, the restrictions could not really be removed, but only moved* [italics added]. . ." The source forms in event logic are built up in complete generality without restrictions concerning the intersignificance of predicates and arguments, as is customary in logical systems. The restrictions needed to prohibit certain combinations of words of the natural language (e.g., 'Hitler is a square root of 2') from being sentences are then "moved" into the derivational or transformational rules. Thus "one can carry all the objective information of language in a system containing no. . .restrictions." And later (p. 676), Harris states that in "the present work, we want the source to be as regular as possible, since we want its structure to contain no complexity other than what is required by its informational burden."

Almost all the kinds of English sentences Harris considers have been examined now and source forms for them provided. Some of these forms may be only approximate and may perhaps be improved upon in this way or that.

A word concerning "disambiguation" and the uniqueness of "the" logical form. Each reading of an ambiguous sentence has its logical form. No harm would arise then from regarding the form of the original as merely the disjunction of the forms of the various readings.[9] And in some instances of course the context may serve to rule out some of the disjuncts. Note that a reading may have many logical forms. Presumably, however, these are logically equivalent to each other if the relevant meaning postulates are taken into account.

It is interesting to note again, in conclusion, that Harris makes little if any use or mention of sets or of classes and relations of higher logical type. It looks as though he espouses only first-order logic without abstract objects as the basic one. Secondly, it is interesting that he unabashedly accepts the hierarchy of language, metalanguage, and so on, as built into the source system. And finally, it is notable that he expressly recognizes the existence of source forms, i.e., logical forms, as providing the very bedrock of structural linguistics. Harris is perhaps the most eminent linguist anywhere of whom these three points can be made, and this is of course tremendously to the good. On the other hand, it is regrettable that he has not been more systematic concerning the source-form system. It is difficult to piece together just what he conceives that system to be, what *its* structure is, and so on. Also the character of the metalinguistic part of the source-form system is never clear. If Harris really wishes to employ only first-order logic and still have a semantical metalanguage, he cannot of course have a semantics of

9. A related suggestion is due to Mr. Jonathan Cohen.

Tarskian type. His only recourse would be to do as has been done above, namely, employ a semantics as based upon a special primitive such as 'Den'. Not having an explicit semantics available, Harris confuses use and mention in some formulae. Also he has no method of handling intentional forms, either via the postulation of abstract intensions in some way or (as above) via the Fregean *Arten des Gegebenseins*. Also he seems to miss some of the subtlety concerning the employment of numerosity words. He makes no effort to supply meaning postulates for the primitives of the source system, where presumably vast galaxies of such will be needed once we have gotten to the stage of sorting out primitives. Nor does Harris explicitly recognize acts, states, processes, and events as values for variables, a step that would seem to be all but indispensable for providing the various forms above.

In the foregoing there has been some ambiguity in the use of 'source form', sometimes referring to basic atomic or quasi-atomic sentential forms and sometimes to complex molecular ones. But no harm can arise from this, the latter being built out of the former in the usual fashion.

Finally, a technical point. In some of the formulae above, one and the same pronoun has occurred both in and outside of quotes. It is assumed that rules are available to assure that pronouns used referentially behave very much as individual constants do within a given context. Thus "*I*", for example, is assumed in effect to refer in a formula to the name of the person to whom '*I*' is taken to refer.

CHAPTER IX

ON GENERATIVE SEMANTICS

That logical and grammatical structure are closely related is becoming a commonplace tenet of current linguistics. Thus George Lakoff has noted recently that "for better or worse, most reasoning that is done in the world is done in natural language. And correspondingly, most uses of natural language involve reasoning of some sort. Thus it should not be too surprising to find that the logical structure that is necessary for natural language to be used as a tool for reasoning should correspond in some deep way to the grammatical structure of natural language."[1] The study of this correspondence has developed into what Lakoff calls 'generative semantics', which (p. 11) "claims that the rules of grammar are identical to the rules relating surface forms to their corresponding logical forms." And again (p. 18), "generative semantics claims that the underlying grammatical structure of a sentence *is* the logical

---

1. George Lakoff, *Linguistics and Natural Logic* (Ann Arbor: The University of Michigan, Phonetics Laboratory, *Studies in Generative Semantics*, No. 1, 1970); also available in *Semantics of Natural Language*, ed. by D. Davidson and G. Harman (*Synthese Library*, Dordrecht: Reidel, 1972), pp. 545–665.

form of that sentence, and consequently that the rules relating logical form to surface form are exactly the rules of grammar. If the theory of generative semantics is correct, then it follows that the study of the logical form of English sentences is indistinguishable from the study of grammar."

Details of differences aside, Lakoff's conception of grammar is akin to that of Harris, discussed in the preceding chapter, in emphasizing the very central role of logical form. When we face up to the inventory of kinds of logical forms actually needed to get ahead with the linguistic job at hand, however, Lakoff is rather vague and indefinite just as Harris is. No doubt the inventory is to be supplied by the philosophic logician suitably sensitive to the linguist's needs. Let us try now, on the basis of the foregoing event logic, to provide logical forms for the kinds of sentences Lakoff considers. In so doing, there need not be agreement with the letter of what he has written so much as with its general aim.

Lakoff pitches his discussion to inference, validity of inference depending on logical form and logical form alone.[2] Only after the logical forms have been decided upon, both for premisses and conclusion, can an inference in natural language be tested either for validity or the lack of it.

Consider the example

(1)   The members of the royal family are (now) visiting dignitaries.

(2)   Visiting dignitaries can be boring.

(3a)   Therefore, the members of the royal family can be boring.

(3b)   Therefore, what the members of the royal family are (now) doing can be boring.

For (3a) to be regarded as a consequence of (1) and (2), the phrase 'visiting dignitaries' should be construed as 'visitors and dignitaries'. But if that phrase is regarded rather as denoting the activity of visiting some dignitary or other, (3b) is the appropriate logical consequence of (1) and (2). Even with this ambiguity

2. Cf. the author's "On Stevenson's If-iculties."

settled, however, there is still the use of 'can be' to be accommodated. (1) and (2) may have the forms

(1′) '(p)(RF p ⊃ (Dig p . (Eq)(Per q . p Visit q)))',

(2′) '$(p)(q)$((Dig p . Per q . p Visit q) ⊃ $(Ep')p$ Psbl$_{sp}$ p','$\{q'3(Eq'')q'3$Bore $q''\}$')',

where 'p Psbl$_{sp}$ p','F'' expresses as above that it is possible for p to be a person p' under the description 'F'. Similarly (3a) has the form

(3a′) '(p)(RF p ⊃ $(Ep')p$ Psbl$_{sp}$ p','$\{q'3(Eq'')q'$ Bore $q''\}$')'.

Then clearly (3′) is a logical consequence via quantification theory of (1′) and (2′), and hence (3a) of (1) and (2). Similarly, if (1) and (2) are construed as

(1″) '(p)(RF p ⊃ $(Ee)(Eq)$(Dig q . ⟨p,Visit,q⟩e . e During now_{sp}))'

and

(2″) '$(e)(p)(q)$((Dig q . ⟨p,Visit,q⟩e) ⊃ $(Ee')(Ea)(Eb)(a$ Des e . b Des p . e Psbl$_{sp}$ e',⌜$\{e''3⟨a,$Bore,$b⟩e''\}$⌝))',

and (3b) as

(3b″) '$(e)(p)(q)$((RF p . Dig q . ⟨p,Visit,q⟩e . e During now_{sp}) ⊃ $(Ee')(Ea)(Eb)(a$ Des e . b Des p . e Psbl$_{sp}$ e',⌜$\{e''3⟨a,$Bore,$b⟩e''\}$⌝))',

then likewise (3b″) is a logical consequence of (1″) and (2″). Note that (1″) is tensed in a way that (3a′) is not. However, (3b″) is a little too simple. It does not quite capture the clause 'what the members of the royal family are (now) doing' sufficiently. It is too specific. A better rendition is

(3b‴) '(p)(RF p ⊃ $(Ee)(Ea)(Eb)(p$ Do e . e During now_{sp} . a Des e . b Des p . e Psbl$_{sp}$ e',⌜$\{e''3⟨a,$Bore,$b⟩$ $e''\}$⌝))'.

For this to be a logical consequence of (1″) and (2″), a meaning postulate is needed to the effect that

⊢ $(p)(q)(e)$((Dig q . ⟨p,Visit,q⟩e) ⊃ p Do e),

that every visiting (of a dignitary) is a doing. (3b''') is to the effect that every member of the royal family is now doing something that can bore him. The inference from (1'') and (2'') is enthymematic, according to this analysis, the additional meaning postulate being needed concerning 'Do'.

The logical form for

'I think Sam smokes pot in the evenings'

(p. 4) must clearly differ from

'In the evenings, I think Sam smokes pot'.

Let 'the evenings' be construed as the fusion or logical sum of the evenings under discussion. The first clearly becomes

'I Think Sam,'$\{p3(e)((\text{Evening } e \ . \ e \text{ P (the Evenings)})$
$\supset (\text{E}x)(\text{E}e')(\text{Pot } x \ . \ \langle p, \text{Smoke}, x \rangle e' \ . \ e' \text{ During } e))\}$'',

to the effect that I think the predicate 'is a person who smokes some (bit of) pot during each of the evenings (under discussion)' applies to Sam. On the other hand, the second sentence clearly becomes

'$(e)((\text{Evening } e \ . \ e \text{ P (the Evenings)}) \supset (\text{E}e')(e' \text{ During } e \ . \ \langle I, \text{Think}, \text{Sam},'\{p3(\text{E}x)(\text{Pot } x \ . \ p \text{ Smoke } x)\}'\rangle e'))$',

to the effect that during each one of the evenings an activity of my thinking that Sam smokes pot takes place. Lakoff's other examples of "adverb-preposing," moving an adverb or adverbial phrase to the front of a sentence, may be handled similarly. Especially interesting here of course are adverbials as modifying intentional verbs such as 'think'.

Let us turn to the examples involving the collective or "group" reading of nouns.

'That archeologist discovered nine tablets'

is ambiguous, Lakoff notes (p. 12). It may say that the archeologist discovered a group of nine tablets (all together) or that there are nine tablets that he discovered, not necessarily as a group. And similarly for

'All the boys carried the couch upstairs'.

Lakoff comments (p. 14) that he has "no idea of how the group reading is to be represented formally" and he speaks (p. 17) of "the existence of a group reading for quantifiers of certain sorts, the logical form of which is unknown." It has been noted in the preceding chapter that group readings may be handled, in some cases at least, in terms of logical sums of individuals in the sense of the calculus of individuals. Thus this last sentence becomes in the group reading, where 'the boys' is short for an expression for the fusion or logical sum of the boys under discussion,

'$(Ee)(\langle$(the Boys),Carry,(the Couch)$\rangle e$. e B now_{sp} . Upstairs $e)$'.

On the disjunctive or distributive reading, it becomes rather

'$(p)($(Boy p . p P (the Boys)$)) \supset (Ee)(\langle p,$Carry,(the Couch)$\rangle e$. e B now_{sp} . Upstairs $e))$'.

And similarly for the other examples Lakoff considers.

In the discussion of performative verbs (pp. 18 ff.), such as 'order', 'asks', 'state', or 'say', it is emphasized that "the illocutionary force of a sentence is to be represented in logical form by the presence of a performative verb, which may or may not appear overtly in the surface form of the sentence." Essentially the same point was made in the preceding chapter. It is especially interesting that Lakoff contends that "there is considerable evidence to show that even statements should be represented in logical form by the presence of some performative verb with a meaning like say or state." The use of the forms 'p Utt a,q', 'p Assrt a,q', 'p Ask a,q', and the like, as above, enable us to handle performative verbs in contexts where they are needed. Of this, more in a moment.

Lakoff raises the question as to how presuppositions (pp. 30 ff.) are to be represented in logical form. He toys with the idea of using a "dyadic modal logic" in the manner of von Wright and others, but does not come down firmly in favor of doing so. In fact, the kind of logical framework needed for the study of presuppositions is left open in Lakoff's account. Let us go no deeper into the subject than he does in attempting now to provide logical forms for some of the sentences he considers.

'Sam realizes that Irv is a Martian'

clearly has the structure here

$(Ee)(\langle \text{Sam,Realize,Irv,'Martian'}\rangle e \, . \, e \text{ During } now_{sp})$',

and concerning 'Realize' we have the postulate schema

$(p)(x)(p \text{ Realize } x,\text{'F'} \supset Fx)$'.

But also, Fx even if p does *not* realize that 'F' denotes x. Thus

$(p)(x)(\sim p \text{ Realize } x,\text{'F'} \supset Fx)$'

also holds of 'Realize'.

It is doubtful, however, that analogous principles hold for 'pretend', although Lakoff holds that at least one of them does. Thus Lakoff contends that

'Irv is pretending that he is sick'

presupposes that Irv is not sick. Perhaps, but a general rule here should not be laid down, that the "object complement" of the verb 'pretend' either holds or does not hold. It may or may not. In the *O.E.D.* under 'pretend' we find as a "leading current sense" the entry 'to put forward as an assertion or statement: now *esp.* to allege or declare falsely or with intent to deceive'. This, however, does not justify Lakoff's contention here in general. Thus

'Nixon is pretending that he is a homosexual and that everyone realizes it'

does not seem to have the contradictory presuppositions

'Nixon is not a homosexual'

and

'Nixon is a homosexual',

as Lakoff contends (p. 49).

"Unfortunately," we are told (p. 50), "we have no idea of how to represent embedded presuppositions at present in such a way that the relationship between presuppositions of embedded sentences and presuppositions of entire sentences can be stated naturally." And hence "the question now arises as to how presuppositions are to be represented in terms of logical form." Well, a good approach surely is first to exhibit the logical forms of the various readings, and then to reflect upon the likely meaning postulates concerning the key verbs in their respective meanings. And beyond that, the idiolect of particular speakers may be brought in and, in addition, the peculiarities of a particular speaker's particular usage on a given occasion.

Lakoff distinguishes between "first-order" and "second-order" presuppositions, but the distinction is not really needed. If S_1 presupposes S_2 and S_2 presupposes S_3, S_2 is said to be a first-order presupposition of S_1 and S_3 a second-order presupposition of S_1. There is no need for such a distinction, however, once the various meaning postulates have been suitably arranged. A sentence then has whatever presuppositions it has irrespective of whether it occurs as an embedded sentence or not.

The sentence about Nixon may be given the form

'$(Ee)(\langle$Nixon,Pretend,Nixon,'$\{p3($Homo p . $(q)($Per $q \supset q$ Realize $p,$'Homo'$))\}$'$\rangle e$. e During $now_{sp})$',

but it is not easy to say just what this sentence presupposes without exploring the speaker's use of 'pretend' as well as the truth or falsity of what the speaker is stating about Nixon. In any case, it is doubtful that there is anything Lakoff, or indeed anyone, needs to say about presuppositions that cannot be said within the vocabulary of event logic being used here.

Consider now the ambiguous sentence

'Sam has always loved his wife'.

Lakoff gives this the forms

'SAY(I,you,t_0,($\underset{t<t_0}{\forall}$ t)(LOVE(Sam,($\imath$x . WIFE(x,Sam,t_0)),t)))'
and

'SAY(I,you,t_0,($\underset{t<t_0}{\forall}$ t)(LOVE(Sam,($\imath$x . WIFE(x,Sam,t),t)))'

for the two readings. Here t_0 is the time of utterance and 'LOVE' and 'WIFE' are taken as three-place predicates the third argument of which is a time. The first form gives a structure for

'Sam has always loved the person he is now married to'

and the second for

'Sam has always loved whomever he was married to at that time'.

These two forms are unacceptable for at least five reasons. The embedded clause containing the quantifier has no quotes around it and thus presumably stands for a nonlinguistic entity of some kind, say a proposition. It is far from clear that such additional entities, over and above the other kinds taken as values for variables, are needed or succeed in performing the linguistic tasks required of them. Further, such an entity is one of the arguments for the verb 'SAY'. Now whatever it is that we say, it is never a nonlinguistic entity such as a proposition. We *say* sentences or statements taken as sign events. Thirdly, Lakoff admits variables over times. This is frequently done, and is a method first used by Frege and Peirce. However, in any extended theory, times seem best regarded as constructs in terms of events, as Wesley Salmon has wisely pointed out.[3] Hence the use of unanalyzed times in logical forms seems inappropriate. And further, the universal quantifier '(Vt)' is not suitably restricted even with the underscript '$t < t_0$'. It includes in its range all times prior to t_0, even prehistoric ones and times before Sam's birth. This will never do. Fifthly, it is not clear that the bringing in of 'SAY' here is appropriate. Even if it is, it might be John who says the original sentence to Mary rather than I to you. Lakoff is in effect identifying the logical forms for

'Sam has always loved his wife'

and

'I am now saying to you that Sam has always loved his wife'.

this latter being in disquotational form.[4] This is surely an illegitimate identification. The logical form of a metalinguistic

3. See *Fact and Existence*, ed. by J. Margolis (Oxford: Blackwell's, 1969), pp. 95–97.

4. See the author's "On Disquotation and Intensionality," *Kant-Studien* 65(1974): 111–121, and Nuel Belnap, Jr., "Grammatical Propadeutic," in *The Logical Enterprise*, the Fitch *Festschrift* (New Haven: Yale University Press, 1975).

sentence expressing the illocutionary force of a given sentence is not to be identified with the logical form of that sentence itself.

These difficulties may be avoided by giving the two readings of

'Sam has always loved his wife'

the logical forms

'$(Ep)(Ee)($Per p . $\langle$Sam,Married,$p\rangle e$. e During now_{sp} . $(e')(e'$ During Sam $\supset (Ee'')(\langle$Sam,Love,$p\rangle e''$. e'' During $e')))$'.

and

'$(p)(e)(e')((e'$ During Sam . Per p . $\langle$Sam,Married,$p\rangle e$. e During $e') \supset (Ee'')(\langle$Sam,Love,$p\rangle e''$. e'' During $e))$'.

The clauses containing 'Married' express that e is a state of Sam's being married to p.[5]

Various sentences (pp. 68 ff.) concerning such intentional relations as causing to come about, persuading, intending, believing, causing to intend, causing to believe, accusing, being responsible for, looking for, requiring, permitting, possibility, certainty, and so on, may all be given logical forms in terms of the *Arten des Gegebenseins*, as in the previous chapter. However, Lakoff rightly points out (p. 75) that "providing logical forms is only half the job. At least as much work is involved in finding the right meaning postulates, truth definitions, etc." In addition, of course, there are definitions in terms ultimately of a chosen set of primitives. It should be emphasized that *both* meaning postulates and definitions are needed and that the two are most intimately interdependent. It is not a matter of having one or the other; both are needed fundamental in any system of logical form.

Lakoff suggests an analysis of 'certain', 'possible', and the like, in terms of possible-worlds semantics. He thinks this

---

5. Perhaps we should take into account here Sam's acquaintance with his wife, so as to exclude his loving her even before he met her. Also in the second form it should perhaps be added that Sam is actually now married.

needed for handling pronomial reference, or rather, cross-reference. Consider the example

'It's certain that Sam will find a girl and (it's) possible that he will kiss her'.

To simplify in order to reflect upon one problem at a time let 'a girl' here be replaced by the proper name 'Mary'. And let, essentially as in Chapter VI above,

$$\text{'}sp \ \text{Ref} \ a,x,c\text{'}$$

(with or without the commas) express that the speaker takes a as occurring in the sentence or sentential form c to refer to the entity x. The sentence

'It's certain that Sam will find Mary and (it's) possible that he will kiss her'

then has the form

'$((Ee)e \ \text{Certain}_{sp} \ \text{'}\{e'3(\langle \text{Sam,Find,Mary}\rangle e' \ . \ now_{sp} \ \text{B} \ e')\}$' $. \ (Ee)e \ \text{Psbl}_{sp} \ \text{'}\{e'3(\langle he,\text{Kiss},her\rangle e' \ . \ now_{sp} \ \text{B} \ e')\}$' $. \ sp \ \text{Ref}$ 'he',Sam,'$\langle he,\text{Kiss},her\rangle e$'' $. \ sp \ \text{Ref}$ 'her',Mary,'$\langle he,\text{Kiss},$ $her\rangle e$'')'.

Actually this form is too simple, for the quotation marks here are used in the standard way for sign designs, whereas sign events are relevant. Our sentence may now have the more desirable form

'$(Ea)(Eb)(Ec)(Ed)(Ea')((Ee)(e \ \text{Certain}_{sp} \ a \ . \ \text{'}\{e'3(\langle \text{Sam},$ Find,$\text{Mary}\rangle e' \ . \ now_{sp} \ \text{B} \ e')\}\text{'}a) \ . \ (Ee)(e \ \text{Psbl}_{sp} \ b \ . \ \ulcorner\{e'3$ $(\langle c,\text{Kiss},d\rangle e' \ . \ now_{sp} \ \text{B} \ e')\}\urcorner b) \ . \ \text{'}he\text{'}c \ . \ \text{'}her\text{'}d \ . \ a' \ \text{Seg} \ b \ .$ $\ulcorner\langle c,\text{Kiss},her\rangle\urcorner a' \ . \ sp \ \text{Ref} \ c,\text{Sam},a' \ . \ sp \ \text{Ref} \ d,\text{Mary},a')$'.

Here 'a' Seg b' expresses as above that a' is a segment or continuous portion of b.

We must now consider how 'a girl' is to be handled, as in the original

'It's certain that Sam will find a girl and it's possible that he will kiss her'.

Clearly, although 'a girl' is an indefinite description, 'her' is taken by the speaker to refer to the *one* girl whom he will find and will possibly kiss. There is nothing indefinite about her in this regard nor is any plurality intended. Thus a suitable form for our original sentence may be obtained by replacing 'sp Ref d,Mary,a''' in the foregoing form by

'sp Ref d,($ıp$. $(Ee_1)(Ee_2)(Eb')(Ec')$(Girl p . $\langle$Sam, Find,$p\rangle e_1$. now_{sp} B e_1 . b' Des p . e_2 Psbl$_{sp}$ c' . $\ulcorner\{e_3 3$ ($\langle$Sam,Kiss,$b'\rangle e_3$. now_{sp} B $e_3)\}\urcorner c'$)),a''.

The first conjunct must also be changed to accommodate 'a girl' in

'It's certain Sam will find a girl'.

Thus the entire resulting form is now

'$(Ea)(Eb)(Ec)(Ed)(Ea')((Ee)(e$ Certain$_{sp}$ a . '$\{e'3(Ep)$ (Girl p . $\langle$Sam,Find,$p\rangle e'$. now_{sp} B $e')\}$'$a)$. $(Ee)(e$ Psbl$_{sp}$ b . $\ulcorner\{e'3(\langle c,$Kiss,$d\rangle e'$. now_{sp} B $e')\}\urcorner b)$. 'he'c . 'her'd . a' Seg b . $\ulcorner\langle c,$Kiss,$d\rangle\urcorner a'$. sp Ref c,Sam,a' . sp Ref d,($ıp$. $(Ee_1)(Ee_2)(Eb')(Ec')$(Girl p . $\langle$Sam,Find,$p\rangle e_1$. now_{sp} B e_1 . b' Des p . e_2 Psbl$_{sp}$ c' . $\ulcorner\{e_3 3(\langle$Sam,Kiss,$b'\rangle e_3$. now_{sp} B $e_3)\}\urcorner c'$)),a')'.

Note that it is a logical consequence of this form that Sam will find one and only one girl whom it is possible he will kiss. This seems desirable, for the original sentence seems to have this consequence also, to some ears at least. And although this form might seem long and laborious as a result of the spelling out of detail, actually it is quite simple. The details are in part merely notational, bringing to light explicitly the use made of sign events.

Lakoff's other examples involving pronomial reference may be handled similarly, so that no detour via the semantics of possible worlds is either needed or appropriate.

The difference (p. 101) between Lakoff's

'Sam sliced all the bagels carefully'

and

'Sam carefully sliced all the bagels'

can be brought out by taking into account the fusion of the relevant bagels. The second sentence states that the fusion was sliced carefully in the speaker's Less-Careful-Than scale for a sum of slicings, whereas the first states that each of the bagels was sliced carefully in the scale of Less-Careful-Than for individual slicings. As Lakoff points out, the second is compatible with

'Sam sliced some of the bagels carelessly'.

The various examples concerning 'absolutely' (pp. 103 ff.) can also readily be handled by bringing in the relevant scales, as discussed in the preceding chapter.

Lakoff takes sentences or sentential functions (pp. 109 ff.) as arguments of the Before-Than relation. In the preceding chapters, events, acts, states, and the like have been so taken. Lakoff's procedure here seems based on a confusion of use and mention. To say that S_1 is before S_2, where S_1 and S_2 are sign designs is of course literally meaningless, sign designs being outside of space and time. If S_1 and S_2 are sign events, to say that S_1 is before S_2 is to say that the occurrence of S_1 as a sign event is before that of S_2. But this of course is not what Lakoff intends to say. He wishes 'BEFORE(S_1,S_2)' to say that the event or whatever that S_1 describes or states takes place before that of S_2. This of course is essentially what the notation of event logic enables us to say. All of Lakoff's examples can thus easily be handled in event logic without the confusion of use and mention.

The question of the presuppositions (p. 109) of certain sentences containing 'before', however, is interesting.

'Before Sue punched anyone, she was miserable'

does seem to presuppose that Sue did punch someone. This comes out immediately, however, as a logical consequence, if the sentence is given the form

'$(Ee)(Ee')(Ep)$(Per p . $\langle$Sue,Punch,$p\rangle e$. $\langle$Miserable, Sue$\rangle e'$. e' B e . e B now_{sp})'.

This form also has the consequence that Sue was miserable, which of course it should have. Similarly,

'Before Sue punches anyone, she'll get drunk'

becomes

'(Ee)(Ee')(Ep)(Per p . ⟨Sue,Punch,p⟩e . ⟨Get Drunk, Sue⟩e' . e' B e . e B now_{sp})',

with the logical consequences that Sue will punch someone and that she will get drunk. Note in contrast, that

'Before Sue punches anyone, she gets drunk'

becomes a universal conditional.

The problem arises as to just how one separates those logical consequences one wishes to regard as presuppositions from the others. Lakoff does not consider this problem in any detail. The matter is not simple, and there may well be differences of opinion as to what presupposes what. Thus (p. 109) Lakoff contends that

'Before Sue punched anyone, she left the party'

presupposes that Sue did not punch anyone. But surely now she could have punched someone after she left the party. A better example, to bring out Lakoff's point, is

'Before Sue punched anyone there (at the party), she left the party',

which has the form

'(Ee)(⟨Sue,Leave,(the Party)⟩e . e B now_{sp} . ∼ (Ep)(Ee') (Per p . ⟨Sue,Punch,p⟩e' . e' B e . p At (the Party)))'.

This has as a logical consequence that Sue punched no one at the party, but it is not clear that this need be regarded as a presupposition. It is rather that all the intended informational content of a sentence—recall Harris on this point—should be built into its logical form. Once this is done, it is not clear that we need bother about the notion of presupposition at all.[6]

---

6. In these forms we could read '*she*' for 'Sue' with its intended reference understood.

Consider

'Before Sue punches anyone, she tries to get him to leave'.

Lakoff contends that this presupposes that Sue punches people. He also states that the 'any' or 'anyone' here "might well be said to be understood as a universal quantifier." If we regard this sentence as a universally quantified one with existential import, we gain the form

'$(Ee)(Ep)$(Per p . $\langle$Sue,Punch,$p\rangle e$) . $(p)(e)($(Per p . $\langle$Sue,Punch,$p\rangle e)$ $\supset$ $(Ee')(e'$ B e . $\langle$Sue,Try,p,'$\{q3$Leave $q\}$'$\rangle e'$)'.

This form meets both of Lakoff's requirements and seems eminently natural. And similarly for

'Whenever someone comes to the door, I let him in'.

(Lakoff's puzzles concerning these forms (pp. 112–113) thus seem to be taken care of.)

Consider now

'Before Mary realizes that someone has broken into her room, he'll have stolen her jewels',

which according to Lakoff presupposes both that Mary will realize that someone has broken into her room and this in turn that someone has broken into her room. Let us disregard here any subtleties in the handling of tense, and worry, with Lakoff, only about the quantifier corresponding to 'someone' as occurring (p. 113) "inside the complement of the factive verb 'realize' which is in turn inside a before-clause." The form

'$(Ep)(Ee')(Ee'')$(Per p . $\langle$Mary,Realize,p,'$\{q3(Ee)$(Per q . e B now_{sp} . $\langle q$,Break into,(her Room)$\rangle e)\}$'$\rangle e'$. e'' B e . $\langle p$,Steal,(her Jewels)$\rangle e'')$'

surely now captures the subtlety of the original sentence. Note that no difficulty arises here from having the clause containing 'Realize' here within the scope of '(Ep)' in view of the meaning postulate-schema (R1) above. An alternative form is

'$(Ee)(Ee')(Ee'')(Ee''')(Ep)(\langle$Mary,Realize,$e$,'$\{e_13(Eq)$(Per q . e_1 B now_{sp} . $\langle q$,Break into,(her Room)$\rangle e_1)\}$'$\rangle e'$.

e'' B e' . Per p . $\langle p$,Break into,(her Room)$\rangle e''$. e''' B e' . $\langle p$,Steal,(her Jewels)$\rangle e''')$',

in which the desired reference for 'he' is achieved by reiterating the clauses relevant to 'steal', which are forthcoming anyhow by (R1). This form is roughly to the effect that before Mary realizes of e that it is a breaking into her room by someone, someone who has broken into her room has stolen her jewels.

The following is also of interest (p. 114):

'Before Mary realizes that someone has broken into her room, he will have stolen her jewels and her mother will have reported it to the police.'

Here too the form

'$(Ep)(Ee')(Ee_1)(Ee_2)$(Per p . $\langle$Mary,Realize,p,'$\{q3(Ee)$(Per q . e B now_{sp} . $\langle q$,Break into,(her Room)$\rangle e)\}$'$\rangle e'$. e_1 B e' . e_2 B e' . $\langle p$,Steal,(her Jewels)$\rangle e_1$. $\langle$(her Mother), Report,e_1,'$\{e3(Eq)$(Per q . e B now_{sp} . $\langle q$,Steal,(her Jewels)$\rangle e)\}$'$\rangle e_2)$'

seems a likely one, with an alternative similar to that of the foregoing. Note that the 'it' is taken to refer to someone's stealing her jewels, although it could be taken to refer to someone's breaking in her room, or for that matter to a complex event consisting of one followed by the other.

To some ears

'I dreamt that I was Brigitte Bardot and that I kissed me'

(p. 114) is uncomfortable, contrary to Lakoff, who does not find it so. More natural sentences result from replacing 'me' by 'her' or the third 'I' by 'she'. In any case all of these may be handled in terms of

'p Dream e,'F'',

where 'F' is the mode of description giving the content of the dream. And clearly logically equivalent descriptions need not give the same content. The Lakoff sentence above requires one content and the two alternative sentences suggested two others.

Lakoff brings out an interesting distinction (pp. 116–117) between the participant and the observer. In

'I enjoyed playing the piano'

it is my participation in playing the piano that is discussed. In

'I enjoyed my playing the piano'

it is rather "the fact that I did it," or better, it is myself as observer of my playing. These two sentences may be handled by the following forms respectively,

'$(Ee)(\langle I,\text{Enjoy},e,\text{'}\{e'3(Ex)(\text{Piano } x \ . \ \langle I,\text{Play},x\rangle e')\}\text{'}\rangle e \ . \ e \ B \ now_{sp})$'

and

'$(Ee)(I,\text{Enjoy},I,\text{'}\{p3\text{PianoPlayer } p\}\text{'}\rangle e \ . \ e \ B \ now_{sp})$'.

In the first it is the activity of my piano playing that is enjoyed. In the second, it is rather myself *qua* piano player. Note that 'PianoPlayer' here should presumably represent the predicate 'plays the piano or knows how to play the piano'.

In a somewhat similar way the difference between

'I wanted to be president'

and

'I wanted myself to be president'

may be handled. And likewise for

'Everyone wants to be president'

and

'Everyone wants himself to be president'.

The various examples (pp. 118–120) concerning numerosity present no difficulty if we bear in mind the pragmatics of counting of VII above. "The problem is," Lakoff comments, "how can one represent plural NPs and plural pronouns in such a way as to distinguish reference to individuals from reference to classes [for numerosity words]. . . , while also indicating the appropriate way in which a plural pronoun is related to its antecedent." Consider

'Whenever you put *former servicemen* in a room, *they* start discussing *their* own problems'.

Let '*c* Prob *p*' express that the sentential sign event *c* is a problem to *p*, a problem, that is, as to whether it holds or not. To discuss something or other is to discuss it under a given predicate. Let 'FormerServicemen' denote just the former servicemen being discussed. Our sentence may then be given the form

'$(e)(x)(y)((x$ = (Fu'FormerServicemen) . $\langle you,$Put,$x\rangle e$. Room y . e In $y) \supset (Ee')(Ee'')(Ea)(Eb)(\langle x,$Start,$e''\rangle e'$. b Des x . $\langle x,$Discuss,$a,\ulcorner\{c3c$ Prob $b\}\urcorner\rangle e''$. e'' JustAft $e))$'.

The last clause here expresses that e'' takes place just after e does.

The related sentence

'Whenever you put former servicemen in a room, they start discussing their numerousness'

becomes rather

'$(e)(x)(y)((x$ = (Fu'FormerServicemen) . $\langle you,$Put,$x\rangle e$. Room y . e In $y) \supset (Ee')(Ee'')(Ea)(\langle x,$Start,$e''\rangle e'$. $\langle x,$Discuss,$a,$'$\{c3c$ Num FormerServicemen$\}$'$\rangle e''$. e'' JustAft $e))$'.

The phrase 'FormerServicemen' strictly should be analyzed, and this for two reasons. Not all former servicemen are spoken of but only those intended by the speaker. Further, 'former' is a token-reflexive word, the former servicemen being the intended persons who were servicemen before now but are no longer. Let

'FS^{sp}_{now} p' abbreviate '(Per p . $(Ee')(\langle$Serviceman,$p\rangle e'$. e' B $now_{sp})$. $\sim (Ee'')(\langle$Serviceman,$p\rangle e''$. e'' During $now_{sp}))$',

so that a FormerServiceman now is a person p such that there was a state of his being a serviceman before now but none now.

And since it is the group reading of 'former servicemen' that is needed here, suitable fusions are needed, not of all servicemen but only of those intended by the speaker. Thus in place of the clause 'x = (Fu'FormerServicemen)' the following conjunction is appropriate,

'$((p')(\text{Per } p' \; . \; p' \; \text{P} \; x) \supset \text{FS}^{sp}_{now} \; p') \; . \; \sim (Ey')(y' \; \text{P} \; x \; .$
$\sim (Ez)(z \; \text{P} \; y' \; . \; (Ew)(\text{FS}^{sp}_{now} \; w \; . \; w \; \text{P} \; x \; . \; z \; \text{P} \; w))) \; . \; (y')(q)$
$((y' \; \text{P} \; q \; . \; y' \; \text{P} \; x \; . \; \text{Per } q) \supset q \; \text{P} \; x))$'.

This conjunction states in effect that x is a (not *the*) fusion of former servicemen. The three conjuncts state respectively that every person who is a part of x is a FS^{sp}_{now}, that there is no part of x not being a part of some part of x who is a FS^{sp}_{now}, and that if any part of x is a part of a person that (whole) person is a part of x. Better renditions for the sentences concerning former servicemen are obtained then by replacing 'x = (Fu'Former-Servicemen)' in the two preceding forms by this conjunction.

Little need be said concerning Lakoff's remarks on definite descriptions (pp. 120–122). Many phrases he regards as definite descriptions should not, it would seem, be handled as such.

'The man who doesn't expect it will be elected',

for example, might be regarded as a general sentence to the effect that any man who doesn't expect it will be elected, and should be handled with a definite description only if there is one and only one such man. In its general reading, this sentence has the form

'$(p)(e)(a)((\text{Man } p \; . \; a \; \text{Des } p \; . \; \sim p \; \text{Expt } e,\ulcorner\{e'3\langle a,$
$\text{Elected}\rangle e'\}\urcorner) \supset (Ee')(\langle p,\text{Elected}\rangle e' \; . \; e \; \text{B } e'))$',

and in its descriptional reading the form

'$(Ee)(\langle\text{Elected},(\imath p \; . \; (Ee')(Ea)(a \; \text{Des } p \; . \; \sim p \; \text{Expt}$
$e',\ulcorner\{e''3\langle a,\text{Elected}\rangle e''\}\urcorner))\rangle e \; . \; now_{sp} \; \text{B } e)$'.

In neither example does any grave difficulty arise concerning cross reference and the like, as Lakoff seems to think.

'John and Bill live in the same house'

can be given the form

'(John Lives in ($\imath x$. (House x . John Lives in x . Bill
Lives in x)) . Bill Lives in ($\imath x$. John Lives in x . Bill
Lives in x)))',

so that no difficulty arises here even if descriptions are taken as primitives, contrary to what Lakoff contends.

There is much constructive material in Lakoff's monograph that cannot be commented on here. Nor is there space to consider his running critique of the various methods of giving logical forms to the sentences he considers.

Enough has been shown surely to see that the kinds of sentences Lakoff considers can be given logical forms within event logic, which thus becomes a likely candidate for what he asks for under the guise of "natural logic" (pp. 123 ff.). Of course, "serious grammatical studies are in their infancy" (p. 55), as indeed are serious studies of logical forms and the theory governing them.

CHAPTER X

SOME PREPOSITIONAL RELATIONS

It is characteristic, as Russell noted already in *The Principles of Mathematics* (p. 95), "of a relation of two terms that it proceeds, so to speak, *from* one *to* the other. This is what may be called the *sense* of the relation. . ." The italicized prepositions here are of especial interest, a salient feature of a dyadic relation being its sense. *From* and *to*, along with others, should perhaps themselves be regarded as primitive dyadic relations. If the logic of such relations were fully clarified, no others need then be admitted either primitively or as values for variables. This at least is the thesis to be explored in the present chapter.

According to the *O.E.D.*, a good starting place always in linguistic matters, a *preposition* is a part of speech serving "to mark the relation between two notional words, the latter of which is usually a substantive or pronoun." The confusion of use and mention here need not detain us—prepositions surely are not to be regarded just syntactically as marking relations between mere words. They seem to mark relations rather between or among nonlinguistic entities or things. Just what the "things" are here may include not only substantive individuals but also events, acts, states, processes, and the like. All such entities may be handled within the event logic developed above.

According to another important entry in the *O.E.D.*, a relation in the most general sense is "that feature or attribute of things which is involved in considering them in comparison or contrast with each other; the particular way in which one thing is thought of in connection with another; any connection, correspondence, or association, which can be conceived as naturally existing between things." If prepositions are parts of speech construed as marking relations between things, what prepositions stand for then are the very relations (real or virtual) themselves. Such a relation is called here a *prepositional relation*. Let us reflect upon a few such relations as incorporated within suitable source forms for English sentences.

Consider now

(1)   'John kisses Mary'.

Although the sentence contains no preposition, its logical form or linguistic structure within event logic in fact does. Let

$$\text{'}\langle K\rangle e\text{'}$$

express that e is a kissing act,

$$\text{'}e \text{ By } j\text{'},$$

that j (John) is the *agent* of e,

$$\text{'}e \text{ Of } m\text{'},$$

that m (Mary) is the *recipient* or *patient* of e. Then one reading of (1) is

(1')   '$(Ee)(\langle K\rangle e . e \text{ By } j . e \text{ Of } m)$',

that there is a kissing act by j of m.

There are other readings of (1) to the effect John is *now* kissing Mary or that John *frequently* kisses Mary. The first brings in time and the second the numerosity word 'frequent' as applied to virtual classes of acts. Recall that '$e \text{ During } now_{sp}$' expresses that e is a present event. The second reading of (1) becomes then

(1'') '$(Ee)(\langle K\rangle e . e \text{ During } now_{sp} . e \text{ By } j . e \text{ Of } m)$', and the third,

(1‴) '{e3(⟨K⟩e . e By j . e Of m} Frequent$_{sp}$ '(e'3 (Ep)
(Eq)(⟨K⟩e' . e' By p . e' Of q . Boy p . Girl q)}'',

to the effect that the numerosity of the virtual class of kissings of
Mary by John is frequent for kissings of girls by boys. Other reference predicates would no doubt be equally suitable here also.

The predicate '⟨K⟩' requires comment. Ordinarily one speaks
of the *relation* of kissing, kissing being a "connection, correspondence, or association . . . conceived as naturally existing
between things." The proposal of the present chapter, however,
is to handle all nonprepositional relations rather in terms of
event-descriptive predicates or virtual classes of events, acts,
states, or whatever. The only relations admitted primitively are
thus the prepositional ones. Ultimately of course a complete
list of all prepositional relations should be given, although this
will not be attempted here.

A rather far-reaching change in the logic of relations of
Chapter II ensues. Given any erstwhile nonprepositional relation R, '⟨R⟩e' now expresses that e is an R-event, -state, -act,
or whatever. In some cases one would speak of an act, as above.
In others, of a state, as in loving, The structure, for example, of

'John loves Mary'

is now to the effect that there is a loving state on the part of
John with respect to Mary, with additional clauses if needed, for

'John loves Mary now'

or

'John often loves Mary',

and so on. Every state or act is regarded as an event, in the broad
sense of 'event' being used.

Among nonprepositional relations, monadic ones may be included. A monadic relation is merely a virtual class, and these
likewise may be handled by means of event-descriptive predicates. Where L is the virtual class of living beings, '⟨L⟩e' may
express that e is a living state or process.

(2)   'John is now living'

becomes then

(2′)   '(Ee)($\langle$L$\rangle e$. e During now_{sp} . e Of j)'.

Any one prepositional relation may be used in many different ways. In the structure for (1) 'Of' is used to express patiency, so to speak, whereas in (2′) it is used genitively to express possession. The *O.E.D.* lists *sixty-three* distinct uses of 'of' in English, not all of them perhaps independent and some of them only in the context of a longer (usually prepositional) phrase. In the present chapter all uses of 'of' are to be accommodated by just the one prepositional relation Of. In later chapters, however, various Of-relations will be distinguished and ultimately meaning postulates concerning each should be given. Similar remarks are to be presumed made also with regard to other prepositional relations to be considered.

Prepositions are often used merely as auxiliaries in relational words or phrases, as, for example in 'brother of' or 'greater than'.

(3)   'John is a brother of Mary'

becomes here

(3′)   '(Ee)($\langle$Br$\rangle e$. e By j . e Of m)',

or perhaps

(3″)   '(Ee)($\langle$Br$\rangle e$. e From j . e To m)',

to the effect that there is a brotherhood state going from John to Mary. And

(4)   'John is the one (and only) brother of Mary'

becomes

(4′) '(Ee)($\langle$Br$\rangle e$. e From j . e To m) . $\sim$ (Ep)(Ee') ($\langle$Br$\rangle e'$. e From p . e' To m . Per p . M p . $\sim p = $ j))',

that there is some brotherhood-state from John to Mary but no brotherhood-state to Mary from any male person other than John. (The conjunct 'Per p . M p' here is perhaps not needed.)

The use of 'From' and 'To' here is especially useful in the case of dyadic acts or states, indicating direction or sense, but 'By' and 'Of' could be used also. In a full working-out of prepositional theory, it would be good to settle upon a certain one to designate the relation between the act or state and the agent, another the relation to the patient, another to the direct object, another to the place, another to the time, and so on. Then the structures would be given exclusively in terms of these chosen few, and only these few need then be axiomatized via meaning postulates. The grammatical study of prepositions in English would then center around the formulation of rules of transformation (or paraphrase or translation) of sentences containing them into structures containing only one or more of these chosen few, as noted in the two preceding chapters.

'Jealous of' and 'gives' are usually taken to designate triadic relations.

(5)   'Alys is jealous of Bertrand's love for Ottoline'

would normally be expressed simply as

(5′)   'Jabo'.

But according to the view here, all relations are to be introduced in terms of corresponding relational states, acts, and the like. Thus the structure of (5) is not (5′) but rather something like

(5″) '(Ee)(⟨J⟩e . e From a . e To b . e Of o . e During now_{sp})'.

Then (5′) may be taken as definiendum with (5″) as definiens.

Similarly of course 'Br jm' may be taken as definiendum with (3′) or (3″) as definiens. It seems clear that any erstwhile relational name or constant can be introduced by definition in this way.

(6)   'Angelica gave the book to Henry'

becomes now

(6′) '(Ee)(Ee')(e' During now_{sp} . e B e' . ⟨G⟩e . e By a . e Of (the Book) . e To h)'.

(6) is logically equivalent to

'The book was given by Angelica to Henry',

'The book was given to Henry by Angelica',

'Angelica gave (to) Henry the book',

'Henry was given the book by Angelica',

and to

'Henry was given, by Angelica, the book'.

The structures for all of these may be given merely by commuting various of the conjuncts of (6'). Thus the passive forms of verbs come out very naturally, and therewith all manner of converses of relations. (Note that word order is regarded here as significant in linguistic structures. It is perhaps not necessary to require this, but surely no harm results.)

Incidentally, it is interesting to note that this analysis of sentences containing 'gives' or 'gave' is close to one suggested by Peirce. In 3.492 of the *Collected Papers*, in a paper first published in *The Monist* of 1897, Peirce commented that triadic relations "may be represented with but little violence by means of dyadic relatives [relations] . . . . For instance, A gives B to C, may be represented by saying A is the first party [agent] in the transaction D, B is the subject [object] of D, C is the second party [patient] of D, D is a giving by the first party of the subject to the second party." Strictly all Peirce needs to say here about D is that it is a giving, for it follows from the other clauses that D must be *by* the first party *of* the subject *to* the second party. Peirce does not develop the point further and hence his suggestion remains merely one more of his extraordinary flashes of insight.

The view here concerning prepositions also has some kinship with that of the linguist Charles Fillmore concerning grammatical cases. "I believe," he writes, "that human languages are constrained in such a way that the relations between arguments and predicates fall into a small number of types. In particular, I believe that these role types can be identified with certain quite elementary judgments about the things [events?]

that go on around us: judgments about who does something, who experiences something, who benefits from something, where [and when] something happens, what it is that changes, what it is that moves, where it starts out, and where it ends up. . . ."[1] The chosen few prepositional relations admitted as basic would have to be such as to enable us to specify the various role types to which reference is required for every event-descriptive predicate as occurring in all possible contexts. *De jure* this is simple enough, but vast galaxies of empirical data must be garnered *de facto* to make such specifications adequate.

Intensional relations are to be handled, as above, by bringing in the Fregean *Art des Gegebenseins*. Here the suitable prepositional relation is *Under*, a given entity being taken under a mode of linguistic description. But 'Under' is readily definable in terms of reference. Let 'p Ref ae' express that the person p uses the linguistic expression a to refer to e, as in Chapter VI. Then clearly

$$\text{'}e \text{ Under}_p \text{ } a\text{'} \quad \text{may abbreviate} \quad \text{'}p \text{ Ref } ae\text{'}.$$

An entity e is taken by p under a just where p Ref ae.

Consider 'intends' itself in a suitable context.

(7)   'Oedipus intended to marry Jocasta'

becomes something like

(7′) '$(Ee)(Ee_1)(Ee_2)(Ea)(e_1 \text{ B } e_2 \text{ . } e_2 \text{ During } now_{sp}$. $\langle\text{Intd}\rangle e_1 \text{ . } e_1 \text{ By o . } e_1 \text{ To } e \text{ . } e \text{ Under}_o \text{ } a$. '$\{e'3(\langle\text{Marry}\rangle e' \text{ . } e' \text{ By o . } e' \text{ Of } j)\}$'$a)$',

to the effect that there is some e_1 before some present e_2, namely, an intending by Oedipus to do some e under the linguistic description of its being a marrying by himself of Jocasta. 'Intd' here stands for the intensional relation of intending to do under a given description, and is itself definable in terms of '$\langle\text{Intd}\rangle$' as follows.

1. Charles J. Fillmore, "Lexical Entries for Verbs," *Foundations of Language* 4 (1968): 333–393. Cf. also his "The Case for Case," in *Universals in Linguistic Theory*, ed. by E. Bach and R. Harms (New York: Holt, Rinehart, and Winston, 1968).

'p Intd$_q$ e, a' abbreviates '$(Ee_1)(\langle Intd\rangle e_1$. e_1 By p . e_1 To e . e Under$_q$ a . Per p . q PredConOne $a)$'.

The e_1 here is an intending by person p to do e, where e is taken by q under the description a, q taking a as a one-place predicate constant.

Concerning the relation Intd, a *Principle of Intending under Paraphrastic Descriptions* such as the following presumably obtains.

$(Ec)(Ed)(Ed')(p$ PredConOne a . p PredConOne b . p InCon c . p C dac . p C $d'bc$. p Prphrs $dd') \supset$ (q Intd$_p$ $e,a \equiv q$ Intd$_p$ e,b).

Note the interesting distinction between 'p Intd$_q$ e,a' and 'p Intd$_p$ e,a'. The former expresses that p intends to do e under q's description of e, the latter under p's own description of it. Oedipus intended to marry Jocasta, the object of his intention being expressed in just this way either in his own vocabulary or in that of the speaker. Oedipus presumably did not intend to marry his mother, however, in his own vocabulary, so to speak, although he perhaps did in that of the speaker. The sense in which Oedipus did truly intend to marry his mother may be expressed by taking the object of Oedipus' intention under a description in the speaker's vocabulary. In other words, Oedipus did not intend to marry the person whom *he* refers to as 'Oedipus' mother', but he did intend to marry a certain person whom the *speaker* is privileged to refer to in this way if he wishes. To provide for this difference, in the case of intensional words, is a merit of the present notation.[2] Often to simplify, however, the subscript will be dropped.

Given 'Under$_p$' we can nor do better with (5), for there is no reference to Bertrand's love for Ottoline in (5''). Jealousy may now be construed as essentially quadratic, going from Alys to some state taken under the description of its being Bertrand's

---

2. See the author's "On Truth, Belief, and Modes of Description," in one of the volumes devoted to Bertrand Russell, ed. by George W. Roberts (London: Geo. Allen and Unwin, to appear).

love for Ottoline. Thus

'$(Ee)(Ee')(Ea)(\langle J\rangle e$. e From a . e To e' . e' Under$_{sp}$
a . '$\{e''3(\langle Love\rangle e''$. e'' From b . e'' To o$)\rangle$'a . e
During now_{sp})'

seems better than (5″) as a rendition of (5).

If the foregoing considerations are sound, a very considerable simplification and reduction in the logical theory of relations of Chapter II are achieved. To summarize thus far. It is presupposed that all relations are regarded as virtual and are thus in no way values for variables. But all primitive relations are now prepositional. In place of an erstwhile primitive nonprepositional relation R, an event-descriptive predicate '$\langle R\rangle$' is introduced for the virtual class of all R-happenings, -events, or whatnot. Further, most, perhaps all the primitive prepositional relations seem to be *dyadic* relations between events. (To be sure some such of higher degree might be definable. Another example is 'between', which will be considered in a moment.) Thus all predicates are ultimately definable in terms of one-place event-descriptive predicates for virtual classes, a handful of two-place predicates for prepositional relations, and the resources of event logic. Within such a framework, the full elementary (first-order) logic of relations finds its place, of course, the point being that no specifically nonlogical relational primitives, other than the prepositional ones, are required.

Consider

(8)   'John now sits between Harry and Mary'

and its putative structure

(8′)   '$(Ee)(Ee_1)(Ee_2)(Ee_3)(Ee_4)(Ee_5)(Ee_6)(\langle S\rangle e$. e During
now_{sp} . e By j . $\langle j,At,e_1\rangle e_4$. Pl e_1 . e_1 Bet e_2,e_3 .
$\langle h,At,e_2\rangle e_5$. Pl e_2 . $\langle m,At,e_3\rangle e_6$. Pl e_3 . e_4 During
now_{sp} . e_5 During now_{sp} . e_6 During now_{sp})',

to the effect that a present sitting state by John is such that the place occupied now by John is between the places now occupied by Harry and Mary. Here At is the relation of occupying a place, and Bet is the betweenness relation among places. Clearly, however,

'e' At e_1'   may be regarded as short for   '$(Ee_4)(\langle At \rangle e_4$. e_4 From e' . e_4 To e_1 . Pl $e_1)$'.

And also perhaps

'e_1 Bet e_2,e_3' may be regarded as short for '$(Ee)(\langle Bet \rangle e$. e Of e_1 . e From e_2 . e To e_3 . Pl e_1 . Pl e_2 . Pl $e_3)$'.

Place e_1 is between places e_2 and e_3 provided there is a betweenness state e *of* (or possessed by) e_1 and holding *from e_2 to e_3*. If this definition is feasible, then 'Bet' need not be taken as a relational primitive. And similarly no doubt for Bet taken as a relation among entities other than places.

There is a difference to be noted between (8) and

(9)   'John is now sitting down between Harry and Mary'

or

'John now sits down between Harry and Mary.'

Sitting down is an act, whereas sitting is a state. In any case, '$\langle S \rangle$', denoting states, should be distinguished from '$\langle SD \rangle$', denoting acts of sitting down.

Note that the logical primitives '$=$' for identity, 'P' for the relation of part to whole, and 'B' for the before-than relation, may also be introduced in terms of prepositional relations. Let

$$\langle = \rangle e$$

exposes for the moment that e is an identity state, as in IV. Then

'$e_1 = e_2$' is definable as '$(Ee)(\langle = \rangle e$. e From e_1 . e To $e_2)$'.

And similarly for 'P' and 'B'. There seems to be no cogent reason why identity states, part-whole states, and before-than states should not be admitted along with brother-of states, loving states, sitting states, and the like. (In fact, the distinction between primitive logical and nonlogical predicates has always seemed rather specious anyhow.) On the other hand, there does seem to be a difference in extent of removal from natural language, so to speak, in which nonlogical states and acts are commonly referred to, logical ones (so-called) rarely if ever. The matter need not be decided for the present, closely related as it is with the difficult question as to whether there is any fundamental sense in which logical and nonlogical constants differ.

The whole theory of virtual relations of Chapter II is of course preserved on this basis, relations being now introduced by definition. The various relations of the calculus of individuals, of syntax, of semantics, and of pragmatics, may be handled similarly. The result is of course a very considerable reduction and theoretical simplification of the structure of semiotics or philosophic logic as conceived here.

CHAPTER XI

PREPOSITIONAL PROTOLINGUISTICS I

Simplicity, Ovid's *rara avis*, is surely to be desired in all of our theoretical work, in logic and mathematics as well as in the empirical sciences including linguistics. But it is not easy to attain and, if attained, difficult to be sure of. Some few features of it, however, are obvious and beyond cavil. The simplicity of a theory has to do with its foundations and not with its development or peroration. A constructivistic mathematics is thus presumably simpler than a set-theoretic one, although both may be very complex in peroration. Foundational simplicity is either ontic or postulational and constructivism is surely ahead of set theory in both respects. Ontic simplicity depends upon the kinds of entities condoned as the fundamental ones and as values for variables. All manner of constructs are admitted, of course, and these may be complex to a high degree. It is thus only the fundamental kind of entity admitted that determines simplicity along with the postulates given to cover them.

A high merit of Paul Lorenzen's reflections on logical structure in language is their apparent simplicity. In effect, he classifies expressions as terms, predicators, elementary sentences, and logical particles.[1] So far, so good. We must go on, however, to explore different kinds of terms and predicators and their connection with the "parts of speech" of the traditional grammarians. Proper names and sortal nouns seem better understood than adjectives and adverbs. Concerning these latter some theories have been suggested that seem promising.[2] Less well understood, however, are the little prepositions 'to', 'from', 'with', 'by', and so on, which have not been much studied from a logical point of view. They turn out to be extraordinarily interesting and important, much more so than has traditionally been suspected, as suggested in the preceding chapter.

What amounts essentially to a reconstruction of Harris's system of report, discussed in VIII above, is what is now to be called 'protolinguistics' or 'the protolinguistic system'. It is a system of logical forms constructed out of certain source forms picked out in advance. Out of the source forms, which are always atomic or quasi-atomic, longer molecular ones are constructed in the usual way by means of truth functions and quantifiers. These molecular forms are the *base* or logical forms for the sentences of the natural language.

In a sense, of course, the source and base forms are themselves sentential forms or sentences of the natural language. They are less "natural," however, than sentences ordinarily or colloquially met with and it would be a great error to object to them on such grounds. The protolinguistic system of report is natural only in the sense that all sentences of the ordinary language may be generated out of source or base forms by suitable paraphrastic transformations—by perhaps about a hundred or so altogether, as Harris suggests. And of course the protolinguistic system must include metalinguistic sentences.

In a recent paper, "Positions for Quantifiers," P. F. Strawson discusses the sentence

(1)   'Tom does whatever William does'

----

1. As, e.g., in his *Normative Logic and Ethics*, pp. 14 ff. or *Methodisches Denken*, pp. 70 ff.

2. See, e.g., the material above and in "On How Some Adverbs Work."

in the context of the game follow-my-leader.[3] In the course of
this he remarks casually and almost *sotto voce* (p. 4, typescript)
that "any paraphrase of (1) which mentions expressions is
a poor one," and this is said in a context in which Quine's
"substitutional quantification" is being referred to. There is no
need to consider such quantification here, for it has been well
disposed of elsewhere.[4] It is of interest, however, to ask why
any paraphrase is a "poor" one if someone cares to make it.
The notion of paraphrase is a pragmatic one, as already noted.
If person *p* is able to paraphrase sentence *a* not mentioning
expressions as a sentence *b* that does, nothing is to prevent his
doing so. And *some* sentence clearly would admit of such paraphrases in the most natural way.

"'Mary' contains four letters',

for example, could scarcely be paraphrased without mentioning
expressions. Strawson's casual comment is thus not to be regarded as a general principle—nor indeed does he suggest that
it should be. And Strawson may well be right that any paraphrase of (1) that mentions expressions would somehow be
suspect as rather remote and unnatural, as "unacceptable" or
"uncomfortable."

Incidentally, the sentence (1) can easily be paraphrased in
event logic, without mentioning expressions and without recourse to second-order logic. Let

'*e* KSm *e*''

express that *e* and *e'* are events similar in kind. (See below.)
Also let

'*p* Do *e*'

express merely that person *p* does *e* (in the lexical sense), or
performs *e*. 'KSm' and 'Do' are suitable predicates out of which
Harrisian or protolinguistic source forms are constructed in the

3. Presented at New York University in January 1973.
4. See *Logic Language, and Metaphysics*, Chapter IV, and James Scoggin,
Reference and Ontology.

system of report. Then (1) has as its base something like

(1′) '(e)(Wm Do $e \supset$ (Ee')(e' KSm e' . Tom Do e'))'.

Many kinds of sentences, however, as already suggested, do require mention of expressions in their base forms. Prominent among these are sentences containing intentional verbs, sentences in which objects, events, actions, or whatever are referred to or taken under a given linguistic description. Such verbs have been discussed above, but the theory of them will be developed in a somewhat new way below when we consider one important usage of the preposition 'that' as prefixed to dependent clauses.

According to Quirk, Greenbaum, Leech, and Svartvik, in their monumental *A Grammar of Contemporary English*,[5] "in the most general terms, a preposition expresses a relation between two entities, one being that represented by the prepositional complement." In place of 'expresses' here the semantical word 'designates' would be more strict. Even with this change, however, the definition suggested has too Platonic a tone. It would be still better to speak of a virtual relation rather than a real one. With these two emendations, we end up with essentially the view put forward in the preceding chapters. It is especially interesting to note that prepositions are taken to designate *dyadic* virtual relations, there being apparently no need for any of higher degree among the source forms. Also it should be noted—and this goes far beyond Quirk *et al.* as well as Harris—that no relations other than prepositional ones need then be admitted primitively, all such being definable in terms of the dyadic prepositional ones, expressions for which occur in the source forms. More on this in a moment.

Let us consider now a few further examples of some typical sentences involving prepositional relations.

Take (1) above, or rather its base form (1′), which contains the dyadic-relational predicates 'Do' and 'KSm'. Let now '⟨Do⟩e' express that e is a *doing*, '⟨Do⟩' being an event-descriptive predicate constructed out of the lexical 'Do'. The use of the half-diamond braces enables us to construct a present-

5. (New York and London: Seminar Press, 1972), p. 306.

participial or gerundive predicate out of a lexical verb. Thus

'Doing e'   could be defined as   '$\langle Do \rangle e$',

that e is a doing. And let 'By$_{\text{Agent}}$' be the predicate for the agentive prepositional relation By, discussed above, so that 'e By$_{\text{Agent}}$ Tom' expresses that e is done by Tom as agent.

Dyadic relations have a *sense*—Russell's word—or direction *from* something *to* something, as noted in the preceding chapter. In general 'x R y', where R is a dyadic relation, may be expressed as

(2)   '$(Ee)(\langle R \rangle e \ . \ e$ From $x \ . \ e$ To $y)$',

that there is an R-state, -action, or -event e bearing From to x and To to y. Means are thus at hand for expressing 'e KSm e''' in terms of the prepositional relations. From and To. Thus (1') becomes now, in prepositional protolinguistics,

(1'')   '$(e)((\langle Do \rangle e \ . \ e$ By$_{\text{Agent}}$ Wm) $\supset (Ee')(Ee'')(\langle Do \rangle e' \ . \ e'$ By$_{\text{Agent}}$ Tom $. \ \langle KSm \rangle e'' \ . \ e''$ From $e \ . \ e''$ To $e'))$'.

Let us consider next, just as an interesting example, the "starting rule" of Lorenzen's dialogues,

'The proponent begins by asserting a thesis. The players make their moves alternatively.'[6]

'The proponent' is an anaphoric Russellian description of a human individual, and 'Players' is the predicate for the virtual class of the two players. '$\langle B \rangle e$' expresses that e is a *before-than* state in the simple temporal topology of (IV,D) presupposed and needed here for differences of tense. Then, in accord with (2) above,

'e B e''' is short for '$(Ee'')(\langle B \rangle e'' \ . \ e''$ From $e \ . \ e''$ To $e')$'.

The use of 'By$_{\text{Agent}}$' above is to express agency. Another By-relation is now needed to express *means*, the sense in which something is done (or achieved or takes place) by such and such

---

6. *Normative Logic and Ethics*, p. 27.

a means. Let 'By$_{\text{Means}}$' stand for this second source relation. It is significant in contexts of the form

$$'e \text{ By}_{\text{Means}} \ F',$$

to the effect that an action of the kind F is a means of doing or accomplishing or bringing about e. Let us use an abbreviation similar to that concerning 'B' above, and let '$\langle M \rangle e$' express that e is a dialogic move in Lorenzen's sense and '$\langle \text{Assrt} \rangle e''$ of course that e' is an asserting. Lorenzen's rule now becomes the conjunction,

'$(Ee)(\langle \text{Begin} \rangle e$. e By$_{\text{Agent}}$ (the Proponent) . e By$_{\text{Means}}$ $\{e'\text{3}(Ea)(\text{Thesis } a$. $\langle \text{Assrt} \rangle e'$. e' Of a . e' By$_{\text{Agent}}$ (the Proponent))\}) . $(p)(q)(e)(e')((\text{Player } p$. Player q . $\sim p =$ q . $\langle M \rangle e$. e By$_{\text{Agent}}$ p . $\langle M \rangle e'$. e B e' . $\sim (Ee'')$ $(\langle M \rangle e''$. e B e'' . e'' B $e')) \supset e'$ By$_{\text{Agent}}$ $q)$',

as simple a rendition as one could hope for.

This source form for Lorenzen's rule is of interest in helping to show that no statement, even a statement of procedure or of command, even a statement constituting a recipe, is immune from being generated from a suitable base form by means of rules of paraphrase. It will not do to object that such base forms are not needed or that they are more difficult to understand than the sentences generated, and so on. Such comments would miss the point of protolinguistics and of its role in linguistics generally and of the role of event logic within it. Nothing can escape the tribunal of logic, even recipes, metalinguistic sentences of all kinds, and the like.

The following ten sentences are regarded by Quirk *et al.* (p. 343) as representative types of English sentences in simple declarative form:

(3)   Mary is kind.

(4)   Mary is a nurse.

(5)   Mary is here.

(6)   Mary is in the house.

(7)   The child was laughing.

(8)   Somebody caught the ball.

(9)   We have proved him wrong.

(10)   We have proved him a fool.

(11)   I put the plate on the table.

(12)   She gives me expensive presents.

This is a quite interesting list, involving a considerable variety of linguistic constructions. It will be worthwhile therefore to consider briefly source and base forms for them, to help assure us that protolinguistics can at least get us started. A quick glance reveals that the following must be available: suitable proper names, sortal nouns, the copula, adverbials of place and time, Russellian descriptions of individuals, quantifiers, suitable expressions for differences of tense, demonstratives, pronouns used referentially (and not just cross-referentially), adjectives that may be graded and those that may not, intensional verbs, and dynamic verbs—to mention only the most important. All of these must be provided for, and much else, if protolinguistics is to be adequate to what is expected of it.

(4) may be dispensed with quickly, consisting of a predication between a sortal and the proper name 'Mary'. This latter is an anaphoric proper name, understood by the speaker to designate just such and such a person and no other. (In the case of successful communication, this is also understood by the hearer or hearers.) Thus, where 'Nurse' is a sortal standing for the virtual class of nurses, (4) has

(4′)   'Nurse Mary'

as its source. Then

(8′) '(Ep)(Ee)(Per p . ⟨Catch⟩e . e By$_{\text{Agent}}$ p . e Of$_{\text{Object}}$ (the Ball) . e B now_{sp})'

is a suitable base form for (8). The Of$_{\text{Object}}$ is the *of* for the *direct object* of the action. Similarly (6) and (7) are generable respectively from

(6′)   'Mary At$_{\text{Place}}$ (the House)'

and

(7')   '(Ee)(e B now_{sp} . $\langle$Laugh$\rangle e$. e By$_{\text{Agent}}$ (the Child))'.

'At$_{\text{Place}}$' stands for the propositional relation of being *at* (or in) such and such a place. And where '*here$_{sp}$*' is a demonstrative,

(5')   'Mary At$_{\text{Place}}$ *here$_{sp}$*'

is the form for (5). And

(11')   '(Ee)($\langle$Put$\rangle e$. e By$_{\text{Agent}}$ *me* . e Of$_{\text{Object}}$ (the Plate) . e On$_{\text{Destination}}$ (the Table) . e B now_{sp})'

likewise for (11), where On$_{\text{Destination}}$ is a prepositional relation used to indicate *destination*.

(3) and (12) contain comparative adjectives, i.e., subject to grading, and thus a form such as

'x High$_{sp}$ R,a'

is needed. Thus if R is the relation of *being less kind than*, and if 'F' is short for a shape inscriptions of which stand for the virtual class of human females, i.e., for

$\{p3(\text{Per } p \text{ . Fem } p)\}$,

(3) has

(3')   '(Ea)(Mary High$_{sp}$ R,a . 'F'a)'

as its base form. Similarly (12), construed as

        'Every present she gives (to) me is expensive',

traces back to

(12')   '(x)((Present x . (Ee)($\langle$Give$\rangle e$. e By$_{\text{Agent}}$ *her* . e Of$_{\text{Object}}$ x . e To$_{\text{Patient}}$ *me*)) $\supset$ (Ea)(x High$_{sp}$ Less-Expensive-Than,a . 'Presents'a))'

Here the To$_{\text{Patient}}$ is the relation between e and the *patient* of the action.

We are left now only with (9) and (10), both of which contain the intentional verb 'prove' in its present perfect "aspect." Before forms for these may be given, two or three additional notions are needed.

An interesting propositional relation is 'that' in its use of introducing dependent clauses. Let

$$\text{'}e \text{ That } a\text{'}$$

express now that e is an event to the effect *that a* holds, where a is a sentence. In other words, a is a clause dependent upon e, which ordinarily will be an intentional act, a seeing, a believing, a knowing, or the like. The use of 'That' in suitable contexts will enable us to handle intentional words in a rather novel way.

The following definition is useful.

'e That b,x' may be taken as short for '$(Ea)(Ec)(a$ Des x . e That c . c C b,a . PredConOne $b)$'.

The definiens is to the effect that there is a canonical expression a designating x such that e bears That to the result c of concatenating some one-place canonical predicate constant b with a.

From this definition we see that there is no need for a triadic That, but only a dyadic one, as primitive. Nor is there any need for a triadic relation C of concatenation, for

'a C b,c' may be taken as short for '$(Ee)(\langle C\rangle e$. e Of$_{\text{Object}}$ b . b With$_{\text{Accompaniment}}$ c . e To$_{\text{Result}}$ $a)$'.

The relation To$_{\text{Result}}$ is that between the action and its *result*, and 'b With$_{\text{Accompaniment}}$ c' expresses that b is taken with c as *accompaniment* in that order. And the use of 'Des' and 'C' here is of course legitimate, these notions being available from the underlying inscriptional syntax and semantics of Chapters V and VI above.

We are now equipped to consider the intentional sentences (9) and (10). (9) contains also the nongradable adjective 'wrong' and (10) the object-complement 'a fool'. Let

$$\text{'}\langle Prv\rangle e\text{'}$$

express that e is an act of proving. Then

(10') '$(Ee)(Ea)(\langle Prv\rangle e$. e By$_{\text{Agent}}$ us . e That a,him . 'Fool'a . e B now_{sp} . $(e'')((e$ B e'' . $(e''$ B now_{sp} $\lor$ e'' During $now_{sp}))$ $\supset$ $(Ee')(e'$ During e'' . $\langle Fool\rangle e'$. e' Of$_{\text{Pertaining}}$ $him)))$'

is the base form for (10), where $\text{Of}_{\text{Pertaining}}$ is the prepositional relation for *pertaining to*. Note here the collective use of 'us'. It is we collectively who have done the proving. The final conjunct provides for the perfect aspect of the verb, to the effect that he is *still* a fool and has been all along.

The adjective 'wrong' in (9) seems to be best handled in terms of the relation of *being wrong about*. Thus

$$\text{'}p \text{ Wrong } a\text{'}$$

may express that p is wrong as to whether the sentence a is true or not. And this, in usual fashion, is short for

$$\text{'}(Ee)(\langle\text{Wrong}\rangle e \;.\; e \text{ By}_{\text{Agent}} p \;.\; e \text{ That } a)\text{'}.$$

(9) may then be regarded as ellipsis for

'We have proved him wrong about something (or other)',

with the base form

(9′) '$(Ea)(Eb)(Ee)(\langle\text{Prv}\rangle e \;.\; e \text{ By}_{\text{Agent}} us \;.\; e \text{ B } now_{sp} \;.$ $e \text{ That } a \;.\; \text{Sent } b \;.\; \ulcorner(Ee')(\langle\text{Wrong}\rangle e' \;.\; e' \text{ By}_{\text{Agent}} him \;.$ $e' \text{ That } b)\urcorner a \;.\; (e'')((e \text{ B } e'' \;.\; (e'' \text{ B } now_{sp} \lor e'' \text{ During}$ $now_{sp})) \supset (Ee')(e' \text{ During } e'' \;.\; e' \text{ That } a)))\text{'}.$

This is of course to the effect that there was a proving by us that a, where a is a sentence expressing that there is a wronging by him with respect to a sentence b, and that he is still wrong about b.

It should be observed that, of the forms (3′)–(12′), (3′), (12′), and (9′) and (10′) are metalinguistic, i.e., forms in the metalanguage explicitly involving the mention of expressions. (3′) and (12′) are to be contrasted with (9′) and (10′), however, the reasons for the two uses of the quoted material being different. In (9′) and (10′), the reason is that 'proves' is an intentional verb. To prove someone to be so and so is not necessarily to prove him to be such and such, even if all so and so's are such and such's and conversely. Suppose all and only fools are over seven feet tall. To prove someone a fool is not then to prove him to be over seven feet tall.

The intentional treatment of adverbs is a little more difficult to be sure of. It seems desirable, however, the scales depending not only upon what the speaker *takes* or *regards* the reference predicate as denoting (rather than upon what it actually denotes), but also upon where on the scale he places a given entity. Thus where an instance of

$$\text{`}x \text{ High}_{sp} \text{ R},a\text{'}$$

holds, it is *sp* who places *x* high on *his* R-scale as confined to entities which *he* takes *a* as denoting. Different persons might well place *x* differently for the same *a*. A second level of intentionality concerns the reference predicate *a* itself. It is the *sp* who populates F, where *a* stands for F, with the entities he thinks or imagines to be members of it. Nothing here depends on the *actual* members of F, other than that *x* be in it. For these two reasons, then, it seems best to handle gradable adjectives and adverbs intentionally.

Why not then also handle sortals and verbs intentionally? it might be asked. Well, (4) or (4') are quite independent of the speaker and of *his* "meaning" of 'nurse'. (3) or (3'), on the other hand, do seem to depend upon the speaker rather fundamentally. An inscription of (3') could be true as uttered (or asserted) by one person but false as uttered by another. You might regard Mary as kind and I not and we could both be right. In other words, you place Mary high on your scale of being-less-kind-than, but I do not.

Another way of viewing the matter is to note that gradable adjectives and adverbs are like demonstratives and referential pronouns in occurring only in occasion sentences rather than in eternal ones. They depend fundamentally upon the speaker as well as upon the way he speaks. And the way he speaks involves both his mention and use of expressions.

Another interesting kind of sentence, not provided for above, is that involving an effected object. "An effected object [Quirk *et al.*, p. 355] is one that refers to something which exists only by virtue of the activity indicated by the verb:

Baird invented television,

John has painted a new picture,

(13) I'm writing a letter."

Consider the last. We cannot give this the form

'$(Ea)(Ee)$(Letter a . $\langle$Write$\rangle e$. e By$_{\text{Agent}}$ me . e Of$_{\text{Object}}$ $a)$',

for this would have the false consequence that there is the letter even if I never finish it. What (13) seems to be saying rather is that I am (now) writing something with the intention that a letter results, in other words, I am (now) writing something with the intention that it be part of a letter written (or to be written) by me. (Recall the comments concerning 'Poetry-Write' in VIII above.) Thus

(13')   '$(Ee)(Ea)(Ed)$($\langle$Write$\rangle e$. e By$_{\text{Agent}}$ me . e Of$_{\text{Object}}$ a . e During now_{sp} . I Intd$_I$ a,d . '$\{b3(Ec)(Ee')$(Letter c . b P c . $\langle$Write$\rangle e'$. e' By$_{\text{Agent}}$ me . e' Of$_{\text{Object}}$ $c)\}$'$d)$'

seems an appropriate base form, even though in the meta-metalanguage. (Here 'Intd' is of course a predicate for the relation of intending so and so to have such and such a predicate description apply to it, as above.)

In (13') the intention is that what I am writing be part of a letter (to be) written by me. An alternative is that the intention be rather that my *activity* of writing be a part of my writing a letter. For this

(13'')   '$(Ee)(Ea)(Eb)$($\langle$Write$\rangle e$. e By$_{\text{Agent}}$ me . e Of$_{\text{Object}}$ a . e During now_{sp} . I Intd$_I$ e,b . '$\{e'3(Ec)(Ee_1)$($\langle$Letter$\rangle c$. e' P e_1 . $\langle$Write$\rangle e_1$. e_1 By$_{\text{Agent}}$ me . e_1 Of$_{\text{Object}}$ $c)\}$'$b)$'

seems appropriate.

Is there a difference in "meaning" between (13') and (13'')? Is one a logical consequence of the other? Or are they equivalent in view of suitable meaning postulates concerning 'Intd'? These intriguing questions must be left aside for the present.

Other contexts containing expressions for effected objects may be handled similarly. Consider

(14)   'I gave the door a kick',

where 'kick' is a sortal. This is to be contrasted with

(15)   'I gave the door a kicking'

or

'I kicked the door'.

These latter could be true but (14) false, my activity of kicking not resulting in anything that could legitimately be called 'a kick'. Base forms for these similar to (13′) or (13″) may readily be given.

Consider the predicate 'Intd' for intending, used a moment back. We must be sure that this may be introduced dyadically in terms of prepositional relations. The context

$$\text{'}p \text{ Intd } e,a\text{'}$$

may be regarded as short for

'$(Ee')(\langle \text{Intd} \rangle e'$. e' By_{Agent} p . e' That a,e . PredConOne $a)$',

so that p may be said to intend that the one-place canonical predicate constant a apply to e just where there is some intending by p bearing That to a and e.

The contention now is that the two prepositional relations That and Intd are the two fundamental ones for the theory of intentionality. In other words, it would seem that most if not all intentional notions may be defined with the help of them. Of course all manner of event-descriptive predicates must be available providing for believing, knowing, thinking, perceiving and so on. Thus, in now familiar fashion, where

$$\text{'}\langle \text{Blv} \rangle e\text{'}$$

express that e is a believing, the form

'$(Ee)(\langle \text{Blv} \rangle e$. e By_{Agent} p . e That $a,x)$'

may be abbreviated as

$$\text{'}p \text{ Blv } x,a\text{'},$$

that p believes that the predicate a applies to x.

The word 'intentionality' is being used throughout in a very broad sense embracing both semantical and pragmatico-epistemic matters. For the present there is no need of a narrower construal or of distinguishing different levels of intentionality,

although in a deeper study this would no doubt be desirable. (Also, as in X above, an additional parameter '*sp*' or '*p*' may often be needed to avoid ambiguity.)

A word is in order concerning event identity, the subject having been discussed a good deal in the recent literature.

Consider the individual Socrates, one individual having many properties or attributes—or, one individual being a member of many virtual classes. Socrates drank the hemlock, he married Xantippe, he was a teacher of Plato, and so on. Ordinarily—except perhaps for some specific purpose—we do not divide Socrates up into various "parts," Socrates-the-drinker-of-the-hemlock, Socrates-the-husband-of-Xantippe, Socrates-the-teacher-of-Plato, and so on, and then take Socrates as being the logical sum of all of these. But we can do so if desired. But if we do, the description of each such entity depends upon Socrates as somehow already available as a whole. Thus the preferred procedure is to take Socrates in his full complexity as an individual, allow variables to range over him, and then to ascribe or deny predicates of him.

So likewise now in the theory of actions, events, and the like. Variables are allowed to range over them in their full complexity, and event-descriptive predicates ascribed or denied of them. One and the same event e may be ascribed many such predicates—it may be a strolling, it may be during the evening, it may be by Sebastian, it may be of the streets, it may be in Siena, and so on. But we can also break up such an e into suitable parts, into e-as-a-strolling, e-during-the-evening, and so on, and them sum these to form e. (Note also the comments at the end of XI below.)

In addition to event-identity, the relation KSm of event-similarity, already met with above, is a useful relation. This relation holds between any events to which the same event-descriptive predicate is applicable. Any two strollings bear KSm to each other, any two drinkings, and so on. The most important uses of this relation are in contexts in which one of the events is specified to be of such and such a kind.

Given any propositional relation, there is also a related definable relation of *prepositional similarity*. Then entities e and

e' bear that relation to each other just in case they bear the given prepositional relation to the same entities. Thus, for example

'e On$_{\text{Location}}$Sm e''' may abbreviate '$(x)(e \text{ On}_{\text{Location}} x \equiv e' \text{ On}_{\text{Location}} x)$'

and express that e bear On$_{\text{Location}}$-similarity to e', the On-relation here being that with respect to *location*.

These relations are of interest in helping to explicate the behavior of pro-verbs, pro-adjectives, pro-adverbs, and the like. Consider

'John sits on the grass and so does Mary',

containing 'so' as a pro-adverbial and 'does' as a pro-verb. In the base form for this the 'does' is accommodated by means of 'KSm', John and Mary being said to do the same action-kind. The 'so' is handled by means of 'On$_{\text{Location}}$Sm', whatever it is that John and Mary are doing bearing On$_{\text{Location}}$ to the same entity, the grass. Thus

'$(Ee)(Ee')(\langle \text{Sit} \rangle e \: . \: e \text{ By}_{\text{Agent}} \text{ John} \: . \: e \text{ On}_{\text{Location}}$ (the Grass) $. \: e' \text{ KSm } e \: . \: e' \text{ On}_{\text{Location}}\text{Sm } e \: . \: e' \text{ By}_{\text{Agent}} \text{ Mary})$'

seems suitable on the base form.

The interesting pair of sentences,

'John is ill',

'John has an illness',

merits discussion, the second requiring the notion of event-similarity. Sometimes these sentences are taken as equivalent, perhaps even L-equivalent, perhaps even synonymous.[7] The abstract noun 'illness' seems to carry more information than the adjective 'ill', however, and this suggests that the source forms for them should be quite different. If John has an illness, he is then surely ill, but not necessarily conversely. To have an illness is to be intensely ill *with the same illness* and over some

7. Cf., e.g., R. Posner, *Theorie der Kommentierens* (Athenäum, Frankfurt: 1972), pp.202 ff.

considerable time-span. To report that John is merely ill is for the speaker to place John in the middle or high on his scale for the relation Less-Ill-Than as confined to the predicate 'Per' for human persons. But if John has an illness he is placed high in that scale, for he is probably more intensely ill, as it were. Further, his states of being ill will all be of the same kind of illness, so to speak. The three differences then between these two sentences should be accounted for in their source forms. The first may have

'(John Mid$_{sp}$ Less-Ill-Than,'Per' $\vee$ John High$_{sp}$ Less-Ill-Than,'Per')'

as its form.

Let 'Sh' stand for the relation of being shorter-than in duration between events. Then the second has a form someting like

'(John High$_{sp}$ Less-Ill-Than,'Per' . $(e)(\langle$John,High$_{sp}$,Less-Ill-Than,'Per'$\rangle e \supset (e$ High$_{sp}$ Sh,'$\{e'3(Ep)($Per p . $\langle p,$Mid$_{sp}$, Less-Ill-Than,'Per'$\rangle e' \vee \langle p,$High$_{sp}$,Less-Ill-Than,'Per'$\rangle e')\}$. $(e')((\langle$John,High$_{sp}$,Less-Ill-Than,'Per'$\rangle e'$. e' During $e) \supset e'$ KSm $e))))'$.

Here John is placed high on the appropriate scale, and any state of his being so-placed is high on the speaker's Shorter-Than scale with respect to the predicate for states of being humanly ill. Further, any state of John's being so placed is of the same kind as any state of John's being placed during it. Note that the second form has the first as a logical consequence, as, it seems, it should.

Another interesting kind of sentence to consider are those containing modifiers of modifiers of various kinds. Consider first

'He very nearly strangled me',

with the adverb 'very' modifying the adverb 'nearly'. The adverb 'very' may be characterized in terms of a relation, as in VIII, so that

'e Very$_{sp}$ e',R,a'

expresses that e is taken by the speaker as bearing R to e' very much or to a considerable degree, where e and e' are taken to fall under the one-place predicate a. Also let

$$\text{'} e \text{ Near}_{sp} \text{ } e',a \text{'}$$

express that e is near to e' in being regarded as falling under the one-place predicate a, e' being so regarded.

'He nearly strangled me'

then becomes

'$(Ee)(Ee')(Ea)(e$ By$_{\text{Agent}}$ him . e Of$_{\text{Object}}$ me . e B now_{sp} . e Near$_{sp}$ e',a . '$\{e''3\langle$Strangle$\rangle e''\}$'$a)$'.

Note that this sentence does not have the consequence that I was strangled, but only that something happened to me that is regarded as near to being a strangling. Bringing in now 'Very', we see that

'He very nearly strangled me'

has

'$(Ee)(Ee')(Ea)(e$ By$_{\text{Agent}}$ him . e Of$_{\text{Object}}$ me . e B now_{sp} . e Very$_{sp}$ e',Near$_{sp}$,a . '$\{e''3\langle$Strangle$\rangle e''\}$'$a)$'.

as its base. (The two reference predicates here coalesce to one.) It is also of interest to iterate the 'Very'. Consider first

'John is now walking slowly'

as

'$(Ee)(Ea)(\langle$Walk$\rangle e$. e During now_{sp} . e By$_{\text{Agent}}$ John . e Low$_{sp}$ Sl,a . '$\{e'3(Eq)($Per q . $\langle$Walk$\rangle e'$. e' By$_{\text{Agent}}$ $q)\}$'$a)$',

to the effect that there is some present walking by John that is low on the speaker's Slower-than scale relative to the predicate for human walkings. The idiom 'very slowly' may be accommodated by using 'Very'.

'$(Ee)(Ee')(Ea)(\langle$Walk$\rangle e$. e During now_{sp} . e By$_{\text{Agent}}$ John . e Very$_{sp}$ e',Sl,a . '$\{e'3(Eq)($Per q . $\langle$Walk$\rangle e'$. e' By$_{\text{Agent}}$ $q)\}$'a . e' Low$_{sp}$ Sl,$a)$'

is thus a suitable base for

'John is now walking very slowly'.

Note incidentally that, essentially as in VIII above,

'e VeryLow$_{sp}$ Sl,a'   may presumably be defined as   '(Ee') (e Very$_{sp}$ e',Sl,a . e' Low$_{sp}$ Sl,a)'.

Also

'e VeryVery$_{sp}$ e',Sl,a'   as   '(Ee'')(e Very$_{sp}$ e'',Sl,a . e'' Very$_{sp}$ e',Sl,a)'.

An entity e is taken to be very very much slower than e' relative to a just where it is taken to bear Very to some entity taken to bear Very to e' relative to Sl and a. (Allowance must be made here that e' might be null.)

'John is now walking very very slowly'

thus has

'(Ee)(Ee')(Ea)($\langle$Walk$\rangle e$. e During now_{sp} . e By$_{\text{Agent}}$ John . e VeryVery$_{sp}$ e',Sl,a . '{e'3(Eq)($\langle$Walk$\rangle e'$. Per q . e' By$_{\text{Agent}}$ q)}'a) . e' Low$_{sp}$ Sl,a)'

as a suitable source.

Another interesting kind of construction is that involving modifiers of prepositional phrases, for example (Quirk *et al.*, p. 333),

(16)   'I left it just inside the garage',

'Some people are completely against public ownership',

'Now their footsteps could be heard directly above my head',

and so on. Suppose R is a prepositional relation. then

'e Just R',

'e Completely R',

and

'e Directly R'

may express that e bears the specified adverbial relation to R.

Then (15) has

'(E*e*)(⟨Leave⟩*e* . *e* By$_{Agent}$ *me* . *e* Of$_{Object}$ *it* . *e* B *now$_{sp}$* . *e* Inside (the Garage) . *e* Just Inside)'

as a source, with suitable variants for

'I left it directly inside the garage'

and

'I left it completely inside the garage'.

Note that these modifiers need not be treated intentionally, there being little if any slack in their "meanings". Note also that they may all be explained away or defined prepositionally.[8]

The modifier 'only' is of especial interest, but seems always eliminable. Further, its "meaning" seems to depend in part on stress and intonation. Consider (Quirk *et al.*, pp. 432–433)

(17)   'John only phoned Mary today'.

This sentence is four-way ambiguous as amongst

'Nobody but Mary phoned John today',

'John did nothing else to Mary today but phone her',

'John phoned Mary today but nobody else',

'John phoned Mary today but at no other time'.

Each of these "readings" have base forms with the 'only' explained away. Perhaps this can always be done with 'only', in which case there need be no representative for it among the source forms.

In written language the base forms for (17) should reflect the ambiguity of the original. Fortunately, we have the marvelous little connective ' ∨ ' for disjunction as a fundamental word of protolinguistics. The base form for (17) may perhaps be taken simply as the result of forming the disjunction of the four readings, as we have already noted in VIII above.

---

8. For this some extension of the material of X is needed to allow the To-relation to take on virtual classes or relations as relata.

In oral speech, however, there is the matter of stress, rhythm, and intonation to consider. Perhaps the effect of these is to be achieved somehow by transformational rules. Or perhaps they should be handled in protolinguistics by bringing in some suitable pragmatical primitives. Thus

$$'p \text{ Stress } a,b',$$

$$'p \text{ RisingTone } a,b',$$

and

$$'p \text{ FallingTone } a,b'$$

may express respectively that p *stresses* the word or phrase a in the sentence b, that he gives a a *rising tone* in b, and that he gives a a *falling tone* in b. Matters of rhythm must be spelled out in terms (partly) of the before-then relation, as in music.[9] (Cf. Quirk, *et al.*, App. II., and XV below for further discussion.)

The adverb 'also' seems to share with 'only' these features of eliminability and dependence on stress, intonation, and rhythm.

'John also phoned Mary today'

has a four-way ambiguity, all of the readings having base forms of such a kind that there seems to be no need of having a representative of 'also' among the source forms.

Let us consider a few more sentences that require the mention of expressions in their base forms.

Classic examples are of course.

"All logical consequences of true sentences are true',

'Everything Paul says is true',

'The subject of the sentence "Mary' has four letters' is "Mary"',

'Where 'ist' is a word of German, "ist" is a noun of English',

and so on. Base forms for these may be given in obvious fashion.

---

9. See the author's "On the Proto-Theory of Musical Structure," *Perspectives of New Music* 9 (1970): 68–73. No doubt also numerical measures for stress, intonation, and rhythm should be introduced at some point.

A few less obvious examples are

'Truly he is a good man',

'In other words, he is honest',

'From the point of view of logic, what you say is nonsense',

'Speaking truly, I would urge you to restructure your style of life',

and so on. In the base form for the first, the semantical predicate 'True' is needed; in that for the second, mention of words is needed, that they differ from words already used; in the third and fourth, mention of the expressions constituting the rules of logic or constituting what is spoken freely, are needed.

Some readers may object to the extensive use of quotation marks, of quotes within quotes, of corners, and so on, required in the methods of this chapter and throughout. Such objection would be philistine, however, in view of the vast multiplicity of sentences of natural language that requires such use. And no alternative ways of giving bases for such sentences are known, or even thought possible or desirable. Hence the use of quotation would seem to be a most fundamental protolinguistic procedure on a par with the notions of logic themselves. Hence we are entitled to use them as freely and as fully as we wish.

Another interesting kind of sentence, apparently not heretofore reflected upon in any close logistic detail, is the performative utterance.[10] These may be handled somewhat as follows.

A performative utterance is of course, first of all, an utterance, more specifically, an uttering in the first person singular present indicative active. Hence we shall have an event-descriptive predicate '$\langle \text{Utt} \rangle$' for utterings. But the performative is something more, it is a doing of something other than merely an uttering. Let us consider Austin's example

(18)   'I promise to be there tomorrow'.

The act e of promising is different from an utterance e' of a sentence of the form (18), but is accomplished or put into effect

---

10. See especially J. L. Austin, *How to Do Things with Words* (Oxford: Clarendon Press, 1962).

by *means* of the latter. The sentence (18) has the base form

(18′)   '$(Ee)(Ea)(\langle Promise\rangle e$. e By_{Agent} *me* . e That *I,a* . '$\{p3(Ee')(\langle p, At_{Place}, there_{sp}\rangle e'$. e' During *tomorrow_{sp}*)$\}$'*a*)'.

Let 'Γb' express that a sign event *b* is of the form (18′). We can then say that *e* is an act of my promising to be there tomorrow by means of my utterance of a sign event *b* such that Γ*b*, as follows.

(19)   'e Promise$_{me}$ *b*, '$\{p3(Ee')(\langle p, At_{Place}, there_{sp}\rangle e'$. e' During *tomorrow_{sp}*)$\}$'" may abbreviate '$(Ea)(Ee')$ ($\langle$Promise$\rangle e$. e By_{Agent} *me* . e That *I,a* . '$\{p3(Ee')$ ($\langle p, At_{Place}, there_{sp}\rangle e'$. e' During *tomorrow_{sp}*)$\}$'*a* . e By_{Means} e' . $\langle Utt\rangle e'$. e' By_{Agent} *me* . e' Of_{Object} *b* . Γ*b*)'.

Austin insists that performative utterances (p. 224) "do not themselves report facts [whatever *they* are] and are not themselves true or false". In a way he is right, *b* being an occasion sentence, not an eternal one. Occasion sentences, it will be recalled, are true only relative to the speaker (and perhaps act of utterance). Nonetheless Austin's account is too simple, for sentences of the form of the definiendum of (19) can be true or false in a quite straightforward sense. Either my promise takes place or it does not. Just what the *criterion* for its taking place is, we are not told. "The words have to be said in the appropriate circumstances [p. 223]. . . . But the one thing we must not suppose is that what is needed in addition to the saying of the words in such cases is the performance of some internal spiritual act, of which the words are then to be the report." *No, not the report, but the means.* "It is better . . . to stick to the old saying that our word is our bond." *Yes, but our bond is more than our word, even so.*

Some of Austin's contentions depend upon his inadequate understanding of the semantic predicate 'True', especially as applied to occasion sentences, and his failure to distinguish properly different levels of language.

Other types of performatives may be handled similarly. The whole subject cries out for a fresh looking at *from close to* in the logistic manner.

The roster of types of sentences to be explored on the basis of the foregoing should of course include all types of English sentences, not just declaratives, but questions, commands, subjunctives, and exclamations as well. Each of these calls for a detailed discussion that cannot be given here. Instead, let us look a little more fully than in VIII at some protolinguistic source forms for the handling of some kinds of questions.

These seem to be three basic kinds of questions in English (Quirk *et al.*, pp. 387 ff.), those that take a 'Yes' or 'No' answer, those built with the *wh-* words (*who? what? when?* and so on), and questions asking for an alternative. It seems best to handle the three kinds separately, at least to begin with.

Questions are always directed *to* someone, if to no one else, then to the questioner himself. Thus

(20)   'p Qstn a,q',

defined away prepositionally now as

'$(Ee)(\langle \text{Qstn}\rangle e$. e By$_\text{Agent}$ p . e Of$_\text{Object}$ a . Sent a . e To$_\text{Patient}$ $q)$',

expresses that p *questions* q as to the truth or falsity of the declarative a. The form (20) seems an appropriate source form for handling questions of the first type. And similarly

(21)   'p Answ a,q'

expresses that p answers a to q, where a is the declarative questioned. In place of 'a' in (21), 'Yes' may be inserted, and 'No' for its negation. The words 'Yes' and 'No' are thus in effect pro-sentences, as used in such contexts.

For questions of the second kind, a complete enumeration of the *wh-*words is needed: 'who'-'whom'-'whose', 'what', 'which', 'when', 'where', 'why'. And for each of these a separate source form seems needed. In questions of the first kind, declarative sentences are questioned. What correspondingly are questioned in the second type? One-place predicates (standing for virtual classes), it seems, will suffice. Thus the form for 'who' is

'p WhoQstn a,q',

where the desired answer will be the name of some person who is a member of the virtual class F that a stands for. Note that the form (21) for answering, enables us also to accommodate the answering of *who*-questions, of the second kind, where a is the name (or description) of a person. And similarly for the other *wh*-questions, the answers expected being names (or descriptions) of entities of various sorts, times, places, numbers, processes, and so on.

How-questions are sometimes regarded as questions of the second type. However, the matter is more complicated, for much depends upon what 'how' is combined with. There are at least three kinds of combinations: 'how much', 'how many' and 'how' in the sense of 'in what manner'. Thus we seem to need

(22)   'p HowMuchQstn a,q',

                   'p HowManyQstn a,q',

and

                   'p HowMannerQstn a,q',

defined in the usual prepositional way as source forms. In the second, the a will ordinarily be a count noun or phrase (one-place predicate) and in the third, an event predicate.

In questions of the kind (22), however, a may be a mass noun or phrase or at least a description containing such. 'How much water did you drink?' is a *how-much*-question as to the description

'$(\iota x \; . \; (Ee)(x \; P \; water \; . \; \langle Drink \rangle e \; . \; e \; By_{Agent} \; you \; . \; e \; B$
$now_{sp} \; . \; e \; Of_{Object} \; x))$'

for the part of water drunk by you. 'How much does he care?' is a query for the extent of his caring, that is for

$$(\iota a \; . \; (a \; Ext_{Care} \; e \; . \; \langle Care \rangle e \; . \; e \; By_{Agent} \; him)).$$

The word 'water' here is a mass noun for the whole of the world's water, past, present, and future, P is (as above) the relation of the part to whole, and 'a Ext e' expresses that a is a numeral assigned to e as its numerical measure as a caring.

Questions of the third kind, of alternatives, may be handled by

$$\text{'}p \text{ Qstn } \ulcorner(a \ \lor \ b)\urcorner, q\text{'},$$

that p question q which of a and b holds, a and b being declaratives. The answering of questions of this type may be handled, again, by means of the form (21).

Not very much has been said about *which*-questions, an especially interesting subspecies of questions of the second kind. Above answers to *which*-questions, it will be recalled, were taken to be names (or descriptions) of times, places, numbers, processes, and so on. But *which*-questions might also be construed so that a declarative sentence would constitute the appropriate answer. Thus now in addition to

$$\text{'}p \text{ WhichQstn } a, q\text{'},$$

where the a stands for a virtual class of times, places, or etc., let us admit a second kind of *which*-question, with the form

$$(23) \qquad \text{'}p \text{ WhichQstn } \{a_1, \ldots, a_n\}, q\text{'}.$$

This form is to express that p asks q which member or members of the virtual class whose only members are the declaratives $a_1, \ldots, a_n$, are true. Answers may then be accommodated by means of (21).

If *which*-questions of this second kind are admitted, questions of the first and third kinds may be handled in terms of them. Thus

$$\text{'}p \text{ WhichQstn } \{a, b\}, q\text{'},$$

a special case of (23), provides for questions of the third type. And similarly

$$\text{'}p \text{ WhichQstn } \{a, \ulcorner \sim a\urcorner\}, q\text{'}$$

provides for questions of the first. And these latter still admit of an answer 'Yes' or 'No', if 'Yes' is taken as pro-sentence for the non-negated sentence and 'No' for the negated one. (Double negatives may be excluded in view of the Law of Double Negation.) The logic (or pragmatics or protolinguistics) of questions thus reduces wholly to the *wh*-questions and *how*-questions, provided the two kinds of *which*-questions are admitted.

The pragmatics of questioning and answering must obviously play an important role in the systematic study of human communication, of "dialogues" in both theory and actual practice, and so on.

Finally let us reflect very briefly upon some protolinguistic forms needed for the language of moral theory.

The most casual glance at any paper or treatise on moral philosophy reveals certain kinds of words appearing again and again on almost every page. In the Chapter, "The Foundations of Practical Philosophy," in Lorenzen's *Normative Logic and Ethics*, for example, one finds idioms of which the following are close paraphrases:

'p has the volition to do e',

'p wants to bring about e',

'p wants to bring about the truth of a',

'p intends to do e',

'p has pleasure in doing e',

'p has pain doing e',

'p assents to a',

'p decides in favor of a',

and so on. p here is always a person, the moral agent, e is an action (not an action-type), and a is a sentence (or perhaps state-of-affairs in some unanalyzed sense). This list is not exhaustive, such forms as

'p foresees e (or a)',

'p voluntarily does e',

'p allows (or permits) e to take place',

'p is obliged to do e',

'p is responsible for doing e',

'e is a means of doing e',

'e is a good effect of e',

and so on, also being needed in any extended discussion.

It is interesting to note that event- or action-variables occur in these forms fundamentally. Indeed, it is difficult to imagine suitable forms for the language of moral philosophy without them. Hence it is difficult to conceive of an adequate logic of moral discourse other than in terms of an event logic or some equivalent.

Suitable adaptations of items on the two lists just given, plus others, would be appropriate as source forms for the sentences of moral theory. These adaptations should bring out special features of the idioms involved. For example, the very first mentioned, concerning volition, should no doubt be handled intentionally. The form

'p has the volition to do e'

is too simple. The form should be rather

'p has the volition to do e as described by the predicate a',

a capturing the *content* of the volition. Such intentional forms have been met above and the reason for the need of them is clear. (Person p may have the volition to do e as described in one way but not as described in another.) And similarly for most of the other forms listed.

The language of moral theory is thus shot through with intentional source forms. No wonder then that so little progress has been made to date in formulating it and in characterizing its "logic." The significance of this "logic" has been well stated by Lorenzen himself. "What is of the utmost importance for practical philosophy [*Normative Logic and Ethics.*, p. 81] is theoretical reasoning. Theoretical reasoning is concerned with the truth of sentences [validity of inference?] rather than with the ethical modalities of actions. Practical philosophy has the task of finding principles which allow us to argue for or against an action or . . . . for or against a decision . . . ." It is difficult to see how such reasoning or argumentation can take place rationally other than by means of logical rules and principles, together of course with the meaning postulates characterizing the source forms of the language used.

Almost nothing has been said of meaning postulates in the foregoing. Much needs to be said about them, of course, and a great effort is needed to enunciate them. But this is not a task beyond human capability. The primitive source prepositional relations must be suitably interrelated in all manner of ways, by equivalences, by equivalences under certain circumstances (hypotheses), by one-way implications, and so on. Then sortals are introduced by primitive one-place predicates, and verbs in terms of primitive event-descriptive predicates. Here meaning postulates will lay down fundamental properties of these notions interrelating them suitably. The means of handling gradable adjectives and adverbs is then introduced, these being definable ultimately in terms of event-descriptive predicates and prepositional relations.

Presupposed throughout of course are the resources of Part A, namely, first-order logic with identity, virtual classes and relations, the calculus of of individuals, a theory of the before-than relation, and a first-order syntax and semantics and theory of events grafted onto such a basis. It is difficult to imagine any simpler system that could provide a theory of linguistic structure sufficient for the kinds of sentences considered.

CHAPTER XII

PREPOSITIONAL
PROTOLINGUISTICS II

In the three previous chapters considerable evidence has been amassed that prepositional relations are very useful ones in giving, within protolinguistics, source and base forms for sentences of a natural language such as English. This evidence consists mainly of exhibiting such forms for a great variety of sentences in terms of a systematic semiotical theory concerning their components and how they are interrelated. In this present chapter, let us carry this development further by reflecting more deeply and systematically upon the great variety of prepositional relations needed and upon the general logical theory concerning them. As guides, let us use both the event logic of Part A and the mass of empirical data on prepositions collected in Chapter Six of *A Grammar of Contemporary English* by R. Quirk and his associates. This latter we shall follow rather closely. In this way suitable regard is given to both the logical and empirical facets of structural linguistics. Genuine progress, as in other theoretical sciences, can be made only with due regard to both, but unfortunately usually one or the other is sacrificed.

The main prepositions that any semantics of English should account for in their various contexts of use would seem to be about seventy-five or so in all. These are 'aboard', 'about', 'above', 'across', 'after', 'against', 'along', 'alongside', 'amid(st)', 'among(st)', 'apropos (of)', 'around', 'as', 'at', 'atop', 'before', 'behind', 'below', 'beneath', 'beside', 'besides', 'between', 'beyond', 'but', 'by', 'despite', 'down', 'during', 'for', 'from', 'in', 'inside', 'minus', 'notwithstanding', 'of', 'off', 'on (upon)', 'opposite', 'out', 'outside', 'outwith' (Scots-'except'), 'our', 'past', 'per', 'plus', 'round', 'since', 'than', 'through', 'throughout', 'to', 'toward(s)', 'under', 'underneath', 'until', 'up', 'via', 'with', 'within', 'without'. In addition, the following are also important: 'except', 'excepting', 'bar', 'barring', 'concerning', 'considering', 'following', 'including', 'granted', 'pending', 'less', 'like', 'near', 'save', 'unlike', and 'worth'.

The foregoing prepositions are called 'simple', being single words. In addition there are complex prepositional phrases consisting of more than one word. These may consist of an adverb followed by a preposition ('along with', 'apart from', 'as for', 'as to', 'away from', 'into', 'off of', 'on to', 'together with', 'up to', and so on), a verb or adjective or conjunction followed by a preposition ('except for', 'owing to', 'due to', 'but for', 'because of', and so on), or of a preposition followed by a noun followed by another preposition ('by means of', 'in comparison with', 'instead of', and so on).

This list covers presumably the most used kinds of prepositions and prepositional phrases in English, as well as some of the most used ones within each kind. Some of course are definable or at least paraphrasable in terms of others or in terms of other notions. Thus symbols for all of them need not be taken as fundamental in the protolinguistic source system. For this latter purpose only a handful perhaps is needed, albeit a generous one. A thesis of reducibility is in order: all sentences in English containing prepositions may be reduced to source forms containing one or more of the fundamental ones. And these in turn are definable ultimately in terms of just 'From' and 'To' as the only primitive expressions for prepositional relations. These are needed to indicate the dyadicity of the other prepositional relations needed.

Let us go on now to reflect upon the syntax and semantics of some of the prepositions or prepositional phrases in the list above, by incorporating them appropriately within the proto-linguistic system. Let us consider first prepositional relations of *place* or *position* or *location*. Let

$$\text{`}e \text{ At}_{\text{Position}} \ x\text{'} \quad (\text{or `}e \text{ At}_{\text{Place}} \ x\text{' as above})$$

express that e takes place *at* the place or location of x. The e and x here are events or acts or objects, so that $e \text{ At}_{\text{Position}} \ x$ just where e is at the location of x. The x in particular may be merely a fusion of space-time points. Similarly

$$\text{`}e \text{ On}_{\text{Position}} \ x\text{'} \quad \text{and} \quad \text{`}e \text{ In}_{\text{Position}} \ x\text{'}$$

expresses that e takes place *on* x or *in* x respectively. And similarly for prepositions of *achieved destination*. Let

$$\text{`}e \text{ To}_{\text{AchievedDestination}} \ x\text{'},$$

$$\text{`}e \text{ On}_{\text{AchievedDestination}} \ x\text{'},$$

and

$$\text{`}e \text{ In}_{\text{AchievedDestination}} \ x\text{'}$$

express respectively that e is an act or occasion *to* x as its achieved destination, *on* x as its achieved destination, or *in* x as its achieved destination. (These are to be contrasted with some prepositions of *intended* destination, to be discussed below.)

These six source forms are needed for handling respectively

'Tom was at Cambridge',

'Tom was on the floor',

'Tom was in the water',

'Tom went to Cambridge',

'Tom fell on(to) the floor',

and

'Tom dived in(to) the water'.

The first has as its base form

'$(Ee)(\langle At_{Position}\rangle e$. e From Tom . e To Cambridge . e B $now_{sp})$',

and similarly for the second and third. Here, it is to be observed, the To and From relations indicate the dyadicity of any $At_{Position}$-state. Note that 'was' in these sentences is merely auxiliary, not lexical. The fourth has

'$(Ee)(\langle Go\rangle e$. e From Tom . e To Cambridge . e B $now_{sp})$'

as its base.

We may let

'e AwayFrom$_{Position}$ x'   abbreviate   '$\sim e$ At$_{Position}$ x',

'e Off$_{Position}$ x'   abbreviate   '$\sim e$ On$_{Position}$ x',

and

'e OutOf$_{Position}$ x'   abbreviate   '$\sim e$ In$_{Position}$ x',

so that

'Tom is away from Cambridge',

'The books were off the shelf',

and

'He is out of the office'

may readily be handled, the first and third requiring the present tense.

One can, if thought desirable, specialize 'at', 'on', and 'in' in their positional senses, by introducing the notion of a *dimension type* (Quirk *et al.*, pp. 308–310). Then in place of '$At_{Position}$' we would have three predicates, one for dimension type 0, one for dimension type 1/2, and one for dimension type 2/3. For the present, however this need not be done.

Prominent among prepositions of *relative position* are 'by', 'over', 'under', 'above', 'below', and the like. Let now

$$\text{'}x \ \text{By}_{\text{RelPosition}} \ y\text{'}$$

express that x is by (or at the side of) y,

$$\text{'}x \ \text{Over}_{\text{RelPosition}} \ y\text{'}$$

express that x is over (or above or on top of) y in relative position. And similarly for the others. And some are clearly definable, for example,

'x Under$_{\text{RelPosition}}$ y'   may abbreviate   'y Over$_{\text{RelPosition}}$ x'.

and similarly for 'Above$_{\text{RelPosition}}$' and 'Below$_{\text{RelPosition}}$', one being definable in terms of the other taken as basic. And likewise with 'InFrontOf$_{\text{RelPosition}}$' and 'Behind$_{\text{RelPosition}}$'.

There are also prepositions of *relative destination*, to be accommodated here by 'By$_{\text{RelDestination}}$', 'Over$_{\text{RelDestination}}$', and so on.

As prepositional relation-predicates of passage there are 'By$_{\text{Passage}}$', 'Over$_{\text{Passage}}$', and so on, used in contexts expressing motion. Thus

'He jumped over a ditch'

has

'$(Ee)(Ex)(\langle\text{Jump}\rangle e \ . \ e \ \text{By}_{\text{Agent}} \ him \ . \ e \ \text{Over}_{\text{Passage}} \ x \ .$
Ditch x . e B $now_{sp})$'

as base form. Note that one and the same preposition in English may be ambiguous as to whether it expresses passage or destination. Consider, for example,

'The ball rolled underneath the table',

which is ambiguous as between

'$(Ee)(\langle\text{Roll}\rangle e \ . \ e \ \text{By}_{\text{Subject}}$ (the Ball) . e Underneath$_{\text{Passage}}$
(the Table) . e B now_{sp}'

and

'$(Ee)(\langle\text{Roll}\rangle e \ . \ e \ \text{By}_{\text{Subject}}$ (the Ball) . e
Underneath$_{\text{AchievedDestination}}$ (the Table) . e B $now_{sp})$'.

The former expresses that the ball rolled underneath the table on its way to some other place, whereas the latter states that it rolled underneath and stayed there as its destination.

Note incidentally the use of 'By$_{\text{Subject}}$' in these two forms. This relation is used in place of By$_{\text{Agent}}$ where the relation is not a human agent. Thus 'e By$_{\text{Subject}}$ x' expresses that e takes place or happens to x as subject.

The prepositions 'up', 'down', 'along', 'around', 'towards', and so on, are often used to express along an axis or in a given direction. According 'Up$_{\text{Direction}}$', and so on, are the corresponding notations for *directional* prepositional relations. Thus

'He lived (resided) down the road'

has

'$(Ee)(\langle\text{Reside}\rangle e$. e By$_{\text{Agent}}$ him . e B now_{sp} . e Down$_{\text{Direction}}$ (the Road))'

as base.

The expression 'up and down' is interesting.

'He walked up and down the platform'

does not express that one and the same act of walking was both up and down the platform, but rather that there was a walking by him part of which was a walking up the platform, another part of which was a walking down it, one following another. Thus we have

'$(Ee)(\langle\text{Walk}\rangle e$. e By$_{\text{Agent}}$ *him* . e B now_{sp} . $(Ee')(Ee'')$ $(e'$ TP e . e'' TP e . e' D e'' . e' Up$_{\text{Direction}}$ (the Platform) . e'' Down$_{\text{Direction}}$ (the Platform) . $(e_1)((e_1$ TP e . e_1 Up$_{\text{Direction}}$ (the Platform) . $\sim (Ee_2)(e_2$ TP e_1 . $\sim (Ee_3)$ $(e_3$ TP e . e_2 B $e_3)))$ $\supset (Ee_2)(e_2$ TP e . e_1 ImB e_2 . e_2 Down$_{\text{Direction}}$ (the Platform))) . $(e_1)((e_1$ TP e . e_1 Down$_{\text{Direction}}$ (the Platform) . $\sim (Ee_2)(e_2$ TP e_1 . $\sim (Ee_3)$ $(e_3$ TP e . e_2 B $e_3)))$ $\supset (Ee_2)(e_2$ TP e . e_1 ImB e_2 . e_2 Up$_{\text{Direction}}$ (the Platform))))'.

The last two clauses express that every up-the-platform part of the walking (unless during it the walking is terminated) is immediately followed by a down-the-platform part of it, and that every down-the-platform part of it (unless the walk is terminated during it) is immediately followed by an up-the-platform part of it. (The 'ImB' here is the predicate for the relation of being *immediately before*, 'TP' for that of being a *temporal part* of, and 'D' for discreteness.)

A word or two is needed here concerning the use of 'and'. Note that the sentence is not merely the conjunction of 'He walked up the platform' with 'He walked down the platform'. The phrase 'up and down' suggests a consecutive walking up and down that is not captured simply by 'and'. A good deal of additional spelling out is needed. It has often been contended that the 'and' of English does not always go over into merely a '.' in the logical form. The sentence here is an interesting example of this. And similarly with 'to and fro' and 'here and there' in suitable contexts. The 'and' here clearly carries a much heavier burden than just that of a truth-functional connective, but requires such of course in its explication.

Prepositions such as 'beyond', 'over', 'past', and so on, are often used with static verbs to express *orientation*, and prepositional-relation predicates for them may be symbolized here in the usual way. Thus

'He lived (resided) across the moors'

has something like

'$(Ee)(\langle \text{Reside} \rangle e$. e By_{Agent} *him* . e B now_{sp} . e $\text{Across}_{\text{Orientation}}$ (the Moors))'

or

'$(Ee)(Ex)(\langle \text{Reside} \rangle e$. e By_{Agent} *him* . e B now_{sp} . e $\text{In}_{\text{Position}}$ x . x $\text{Across}_{\text{Orientation}}$ (the Moors))'

as a base form.

When combined with suitable forms of the verb 'be', prepositions such as 'over' or 'out of' are handled by *resultative* prepositions expressing that the state of destination has been reached. Thus

'The horses are over the fence'

becomes merely

'(the Horses) Over$_{\text{AchievedDestination}}$ (the Fence)',

or, with the appropriate tensing and relation elimination,

'(Ee)($\langle$Over$_{\text{AchievedDestination}}\rangle e$. e From (the Horses) . e To (the Fence) . e During now_{sp})'.

'Throughout' is an interesting example of a preposition with *pervasive* meaning, in a context such as

'Chaos reigned throughout the house',

with

'(Ee)(Ee')($\langle$Reign$\rangle e$. $\langle$Chaos$\rangle e'$. e By$_{\text{Subject}}$ e' . e B now_{sp} . e' Throughout$_{\text{Pervasive}}$ (the House))',

as its base, to the effect that there is a reigning of some chaotic state throughout the house. Similarly for 'all through', 'all over', 'all along', 'all around', and the like.

Perhaps 'Throughout$_{\text{Pervasive}}$' is definable in terms of 'pervades' as follows. We might let

'e Throughout$_{\text{Pervasive}}$ x' abbreviate '(Ee')($\langle$Pervade$\rangle e'$. e' By$_{\text{Subject}}$ e . e' Of$_{\text{Patient}}$ x)'.

Here 'From' could replace 'By$_{\text{Subject}}$' and 'To' could replace 'Of$_{\text{Patient}}$'. The clause 'e' Of$_{\text{Patient}}$ x' expresses that x is the *patient* or *recipient* of the pervading e'.

The preposition 'over' may be used in many different senses. The following sentences exhibit seven of these.

'A lamp hung over [positional] the door',

'They threw a blanket over [achieved destination] her',

'They climbed over [passage] the wall',

'They live over (on the far side of) [orientation] the road',

'At last we were over [resultative] the crest of the hill',

'Leaves lay thick (all) over [pervasive (static)] the ground',

and

'They splashed water all over [pervasive (dynamic)] me'.

These may readily be given base forms in terms of the appropriate prepositional relations for 'over'. The difference between the static and the dynamic use of 'over' here comes to light in the respective contexts, one of which contains a static verb, the other a dynamic one.

Some verbs contain within their own meaning, so to speak, the meaning of a preposition following them. Thus 'climb' may be used for 'climb up', 'jump' for 'jump over', and so on. Thus

'They climbed (up) the mountain'

becomes either

$$\text{`}(Ee)(\langle\text{Climb}\rangle e \; . \; e \; \text{By}_{\text{Agent}} \; \textit{them} \; . \; e \; \text{Of}_{\text{Patient}} \text{ (the}$$
$$\text{Mountain)} \; . \; e \; \text{B} \; \textit{now}_{sp})\text{'}$$

or

$$\text{`}(Ee)(\langle\text{Climb}\rangle e \; . \; e \; \text{By}_{\text{Agent}} \; \textit{them} \; . \; e \; \text{Up}_{\text{Direction}} \text{ (the}$$
$$\text{Mountain)} \; . \; e \; \text{B} \; \textit{now}_{sp})\text{'}$$

The '$\text{Of}_{\text{Patient}}$' predicate is used here to indicate the *patient* or direct object of a transitive verb as above. (Sometimes '$\text{Of}_{\text{Object}}$' will be used instead.) The second form no doubt logically implies the first in view of a presumed general principle to the effect that every climbing *up* is a climbing *of*:

$$(e)(x)(y)((\langle\text{Climb}\rangle e \; . \; e \; \text{By}_{\text{Agent}} \; x) \supset (e \; \text{Up}_{\text{Direction}} \; y \supset$$
$$e \; \text{Of}_{\text{Patient}} \; y)).$$

Before considering prepositional relations for handling time, a word or two concerning the *metaphorical* and *abstract* uses of prepositions of place is in order. Predicates for these may be formed by writing the appropriate predicate with 'Metaphor' or 'Abstract' attached as a superscript. Thus '$\text{In}_{\text{Position}}^{\text{Metaphor}}$' is such a predicate, and

'We are in danger'

may be expressed as

$$\text{`}(Ee)(\textit{we} \; \text{In}_{\text{Position}}^{\text{Metaphor}} \; e \; . \; \langle\text{Danger}\rangle e \; . \; e \; \text{During} \; \textit{now}_{sp})\text{'},$$

that there is some present state of danger that we are positionally in, in the metaphorical sense of 'in'. And similarly for expressions such as 'out of trouble', 'in difficulty', and so on.

Let '$\text{In}_{\text{Position}}^{\text{Abstract}}$' be the expression for the relation of being in positionally in the abstract sense. This may be used to handle sentences such as

'We are in the race',

'We were included in the festivities',

and so on.

For some abstract uses of prepositions, Harris's notion of being *appropriate for* seems needed. Recall that we may let

'e Approp$_{sp}$ e',a'

express that e is taken by the speaker as appropriate for e', where e' is taken under the predicate description a. Consider some prepositional relations such as '$\text{Above}_{\text{RelPosition}}^{\text{Abstract}}$', '$\text{Below}_{\text{RelPosition}}^{\text{Abstract}}$', and '$\text{Beneath}_{\text{RelPosition}}^{\text{Abstract}}$' and sentences such as

'He lives above (below) his income',

'Such behavior is beneath him',

and

'He is above such pettyness'.

Note that the 'lives' of the first sentence here is taken not in the biological sense of living but in the social sense of exhibiting such and such a "life style." Thus this sentence becomes something like

'$(Ee)(Ee')(Ea)(\langle \text{LifeStyle} \rangle e$. e By_{Agent} him . $\langle \text{LifeStyle} \rangle e'$. a Des him . $(p)(\text{Per } p \supset (Ed)(e' \text{ Approp}_{sp} p,d$. $\ulcorner\{q3(Eb)$ $(Ec)(b$ Num (the Income of a) . e Num (the Income of q) . $a \approx b)\}^\neg d)) $. e $\text{Above}_{\text{RelPosition}}^{\text{Abstract}} e')$'.

This is to the effect that his life style is "above" the life style appropriate for persons with the (numerically) same income.

In the second and third sentences, the 'such' phrases may be regarded either as involving a demonstrative ('like that behavior') or an anaphoric description ('behavior like that that we have just been discussing'). The second sentence then may be handled as

'Such behavior by him is beneath (in the abstract sense) behavior appropriate for him (as agent)'.

Behavior consists of a fusion of acts, not a fusion of all acts, or course, but a fusion of some acts. Let

'FuActs e'

express that e is a fusion of some human acts, not all necessarily by the same agent. Our sentence then becomes something like

'$(Ee)(Ee')(Ee'')(Ea)($FuActs e . FuActs e' . e' By$_{\text{Agent}}$ him . e' Like$_{\text{Resemblance}}$ (that $\{e\}$) . e' Beneath$^{\text{Abstract}}_{\text{RelPosition}}$ e'' . FuActs e'' . e'' Approp$_{sp}$ him,a . '$\{p3(Ee''')($FuAct e''' . e''' By$_{\text{Agent}}$ $p)\}$'$a)$'.

And somewhat similarly for the third sentence, where 'such pettyness' is construed in terms of 'such petty acts', that is, acts high on the appropriate less-petty-than scale as relativized to human acts. (The predicate 'Like$_{\text{Resemblance}}$' will be commented on below.)

The notion 'FuActs' above needs comment. It and allied notions, in fact, will frequently be useful in what follows. We may let

'FuActs e' abbreviate '$(\sim e = $ NE . $(e')((\text{At } e' . e'$ P $e) \supset (Ee'')(\text{Act } e'' . e''$ P $e . e'$ P $e'')))$',

so that e is a sum or fusion of acts ($e_1 \cup e_2 \cup \ldots$) just where it is non-null and every point event (or atom) that is a part of e is a part of some act that is a part of e. Note that the e's here may overlap in various ways. Sometimes there will be no over-lapping, as in the case of persons and physical objects. The predicate 'FuPer' will be useful below.

Let us turn now to prepositions of time, some of which have already been needed above in the handling of tense. The most useful prepositional relation here is perhaps that of During. But 'On$_{\text{Time}}$' ('on the following day'), 'In$_{\text{Time}}$' ('in the spring'), 'For$_{\text{Time}}$' ('for three months'), and 'At$_{\text{Time}}$' ('at noon') are also legitimate notations. All of these, it would seem, can be accom-modated in terms of 'During'.

'We left on the following day'

becomes

'(Ee)($\langle$Leave$\rangle e$. e By$_{\text{Agent}}$ us . e During (the following Day) . (the following Day) B now_{sp})'.

But

'We left at noon'

becomes

'(Ee)(Ee')($\langle$Leave$\rangle e$. e By$_{\text{Agent}}$ us . e B now_{sp} . e During e' . (Ee''')(Day e''' . (e'')(e'' TP e' $\supset$ e'' Noon e''')))',

in the sense that there was a leaving by us during some e', where there is a day such that every temporal part of e' is the noon of that day. (A better form will be given in a moment.) Another reading is of course that we left at noon each day or always. But these likewise can be handled in terms of 'During'.

The preposition 'at' is useful when a short time interval is pinpointed, perhaps only an instant or perhaps a longer interval.

'We will discuss it at lunch'

involves reference to more than a point event.

'We left exactly at noon'

does single out precisely the split second of noon. On the other hand

'We left at noon'

does not. 'e'' Noon e''''', in the base form just given for this sentence, should be construed as expressing that e'' is a time interval containing the noon but also perhaps a few moments either side of noon. If we left at 12:02 P.M. or 11:59 A.M. we would all be inclined to say that we left at noon and to regard what we say as true. A relation of being *in the environment of* is needed here. Let

'e Env e'''

express that e either is or takes place in the spatial or temporal environment of e'. Then

'e EnvNoon e''' abbreviates '$(Ee'')(Ee''')($Day e'' . e' Noon e'' . e''' Env e' . e During $e''')$'.

A better base form for

'We left at noon'

is then

'$(Ee)(Ee')(\langle$Leave$\rangle e$. e By$_{\text{Agent}}$ us . e B now_{sp} . e EnvNoon $e')$'.

Better yet, where '(that Day)' is a demonstrative for the day under discussion,

'$(Ee)(\langle$Leave$\rangle e$. e By$_{\text{Agent}}$ us . e B now_{sp} . e EnvNoon (that Day)$)$'.

A more thorough discussion of temporal phrases will be given in the next chapter.

Let us now complete the list of types of fundamental prepositional phrases needed. In addition to those required for handling spatial position and time, there are those of *cause*, *reason*, or *motive*, especially 'because of', 'for fear of', 'out of a sense of', 'for' ('for fun'), and the like. To handle these expressions prepositional-relation predicates are needed as follows:

'BecauseOf$_{\text{Cause}}$',   'BecauseOf$_{\text{Motive}}$',   'OnAccountOf$_{\text{Cause}}$',
'OnAccountOf$_{\text{Motive}}$',   'ForFearOf$_{\text{Cause}}$',   'ForFearOf$_{\text{Motive}}$',
'From$_{\text{Cause}}$',   'From$_{\text{Motive}}$',   'OutOf$_{\text{Cause}}$',
'OutOf$_{\text{Motive}}$',   'For$_{\text{Cause}}$',   'For$_{\text{Motive}}$'.

By means of these such sentences as

'The price of bread is high because of the drought',

'I hid the money for fear of being discovered',

'The survivors were weak from exposure',

'He said it for fun',

and so on, may be handled.

Sentences concerned with cause and motive should no doubt be handled intentionally. In the case of 'cause' this has been urged above. It is only an event (or act or whatever) *under a given (predicate) description* that can be said to cause another event (or act or whatever) under a given (predicate) description. The prepositional phrases 'BecauseOf$_{\text{Cause}}$', 'OnAccountOf$_{\text{Cause}}$', and so on, must also be handled intentionally. In fact

'(e,a) BecauseOf$_{\text{Cause}}$ (e',a')'   may immediately abbreviate '(e',a') Cause (e,a)'.

'The price of bread is high because of the drought',

then becomes something like

'$(Ee)(Ea)(Ea')(\langle$bread,High,Less-Expensive-Than, '$\{x3$HumanFood$x\}$'$\rangle e$. '$\{e'3\langle$bread,High,Less-Expensive-Than,'$\{x3$HumanFood$x\}$'$\rangle e'\}$'a . '$\{x3x =$ (the Drought)$\}$'a' . (e,a) BecauseOf$_{\text{Cause}}$ ((the Drought),a'))'.

'ForFearOf$_{\text{Cause}}$' may be handled contextually in terms of 'Cause' or 'BecauseOf$_{\text{Cause}}$'. Thus

'I hid the money for fear of being discovered'

becomes

'$(Ee)(Ee')(Ee'')(Ea)(Eb)(Ea')(\langle I,$Hide,(the Money)$\rangle e$. '$\{e_13\langle I,$Hide,(the Money)$\rangle e_1\}$'a . e B now_{sp} . $\langle I,$Fear,$e',b\rangle e''$. '$\{e_13(Ep)(\langle p,$Discover,$me\rangle e_1$. Per $p)\}$'b . $\ulcorner\{e_13(Ee_2)$ $\langle I,$Fear,$e_2,b\rangle e_1\}\urcorner a'$. (e,a) BecauseOf$_{\text{Cause}}$ $(e'',a'))$'.

'Motive' should presumably be handled similarly so that

'(e,a) Motive (e',a)'

expresses that e under the description a is a motive for e' under the description a'. And then of course

'(e,a) BecauseOf$_{\text{Motive}}$ (e',a')'   may be defined merely as '$(e'a')$ Motive (e,a)'.

Also there are prepositional relations for *purpose* or *intended destination*, handled by 'For$_{\text{Purpose}}$' and 'For$_{\text{IntdDestination}}$'.

'He does anything for (gaining) money',

'Everyone ran for safety',

and

'He died for (benefitting) his country'

may be handled by means of 'For $_{Purpose}$';

'He set out for London',

and the like, in terms of 'For $_{IntdDestination}$'. These notions likewise are to be handled intentionally. Let

p Purps$_{sp}$ e,a' (or   'p Intd$_{sp}$ e,a' as above)

express that person p purposes or intends e to fall under the predicate a.

'He did it for (gaining) money'

is thus

'$(Ee)(Ea)(\langle Do \rangle e$. e By$_{Agent}$ him . e Of$_{Patient}$ it . e B now_{sp} . he Purps$_{sp}$ e,a . '$\{e_1 3\langle he, Gain, money \rangle e_1\}$'$a)$'

or

'$(Ee)(Ea)(\langle he, Do, it \rangle e$. e B now_{sp} . e For$^{sp}_{Purpose}$ a . '$\{e_1 3\langle he, Gains, money \rangle e_1\}$'$a)$',

where

'e For$^{sp}_{Purpose}$ a' may abbreviate '$(Ep)p$ Purps$_{sp}$ e,a'.

Somewhat similarly, where

'x AchvdDestination e'

expresses that x is a or the achieved destination of e,

'x For$^{sp}_{IntdDestination}$ e' may abbreviate '$(Ep)(Ea)(Eb)(a$ Des x . p Purps$_{sp}$ e,b . $\ulcorner\{e'3a$ AchvdDestination $e'\}\urcorner b)$'.

Thus x is an intended destination for e just where someone purposes or intends x to be the actual destination of e.

'He set out for London'

may now be given a suitable form in terms of 'For $_{IntdDestination}$'.

Likewise 'For$_{\text{IntendedRecipient}}$', 'To$_{\text{ActualRecipient}}$', and 'At$_{\text{IntendedGoal}}$' are needed for handling sentences such as

'He laid a trap for his enemies',

'He gave the book to his neighbor',

and

'He shot at the deer'.

The intentional forms here are definable, 'For$_{\text{IntdRecipient}}$' in terms of 'Receives' and 'At$_{\text{IntdGoal}}$' in terms of 'is a goal of'.

Related to To$_{\text{ActualRecipient}}$ is the prepositional relation From$_{\text{Source}}$, as in

'I borrowed the book from him'.

Compare this sentence with

'He loaned the book to me',

which would utilize 'To$_{\text{ActualRecipient}}$'. These relations are not converses of each other (as contended by Quirk, *et al.*), but they are needed in interrelating 'lend' and 'borrow' properly. In general, the principle seems to obtain that

$$(p)(q)(a)(x)((\text{Per } p \,.\, \text{Per } q) \supset ((Ee)(\langle\text{Loan}\rangle e \,.\, e \text{ Of}_{\text{Object}}$$
$$x \,.\, e \text{ By}_{\text{Agent}} p \,.\, e \text{ To}_{\text{ActualRecipient}} q) \equiv (Ee)(\langle\text{Borrow}\rangle e \,.\, e$$
$$\text{Of}_{\text{Object}} x \,.\, e \text{ By}_{\text{Agent}} q \,.\, e \text{ From}_{\text{Source}} p))).$$

Here 'From$_{\text{Source}}$' is presumably definable in terms of 'is a source of'. 'With$_{\text{Manner}}$', 'In$_{\text{Manner}}$', and 'Like$_{\text{Manner}}$' may be used to handle the corresponding prepositions.

'We were received with courtesy'

is paraphrastic of

'We were received in the manner of (some) courteous acts',

and hence may have

$$'(Ee)(Ee')(Ea)(\langle\text{Receive}\rangle e \,.\, e \text{ Of}_{\text{Patient}} us \,.\, e' \text{ High}_{sp}$$
Less-Courteous-Than,$a \,.\, '\{e''3(Ep)(\text{FuPer } p \,.\, \text{Act } e'' \,.\, e''$
$\text{By}_{\text{Agent}} p)\}'a \,.\, e \text{ In}_{\text{Manner}} \{e'\})'$

as a base. Note that 'FuPer p' expresses that p is either a single person or a fusion of persons, to allow for the circumstance that we might have been received by more than one person collectively.

'The army swept through the city like (in the manner of)
a pestilence'

requires 'Like$_{\text{Manner}}$'. 'Like' is also used to express resemblance, so that 'Like$_{\text{Resemblance}}$' must also be introduced and is useful especially with intensive verbs. But clearly

'e Like $_{\text{Resemblance}}$ e'''   is merely short for   '$(Ee'')(\langle\text{Resemble}\rangle$ e'' . e'' From e . e'' To $e')$'.

'Life is like a dream'

becomes simply

'$(Ee)(Ep)(Ee')(\text{Per } p$. $e = (\text{Fu'}\{e''3(\langle\text{Live}\rangle e''$. e'' $\text{Of}_{\text{Patient}} p)\})$. $\text{Dream } e'$. e Like $_{\text{Resemblance}}$ $e')$',

that the fusion of the living states and acts of some one person resembles a dream. (Another possibility here would be in terms of 'Fu$\langle$Live$\rangle e$', expressing that e is the fusion of various acts or states of living. And two others, in terms of *all* persons.)

Consider the difference made by the placement or position of one and the same kind of prepositional phrase.

'He writes poetry like his brother'

requires 'Like$_{\text{Manner}}$' if the *manner* of writing is intended, but 'Like$_{\text{Resemblance}}$', if his poetry is intended to resemble that of his brother. The first thus becomes

'$(Ee)(Ee')(Ee'')(\langle\text{Write}\rangle e$. e By_{Agent} *him* . e $\text{Of}_{\text{Patient}}$ e' . $\text{FuPoetry } e'$. $\langle\text{Write}\rangle e''$. e'' By_{Agent} (his Brother) . (Ee''') $(\text{FuPoetry } e'''$. e'' $\text{Of }_{\text{Patient}} e'''$. e Like $_{\text{Manner}}$ $e''))$'.

On the second reading the last conjunct is rather

'e' Like $_{\text{Resemblance}}$ e'''''.

On the other hand,

'Like his brother, he writes poetry'

states only that he and his brother have the common property of writing poetry, but neither the manner nor results need resemble each other. It has often been observed that any two entities are like each other in having a common property. Here it is the relation of being-alike-as-writers-of-poetry that is relevant. Let 'PR p' be defined to express that p is a poetry writer, that is, that there is a writing by p of a FuPoetry. Then

'p Like$_{PR}$ q' is merely short for '(PR p . PR q)',

and our sentence becomes merely

'he Like$_{PR}$ (his Brother)'

that he is like his brother in being a poetry writer. One could add here a conjunct to the effect that he does write poetry, but it is not needed except for emphasis.

'By' is often short for 'by means of'. Hence 'By$_{Means}$' is the appropriate predicate for handling sentences such as

'I go to work by bus'

and

'By pumping, we kept the ship afloat'.

'With' is often used *instrumentally* rather than to express means, as in

'He caught the ball with his hand',

'He broke the window with a stone',

and the like. Here 'With$_{Instrument}$' is the appropriate preposition-relation predicate. And similarly 'Without$_{Instrument}$'.

There also seems to be an instrumental use of 'by' as in

'The window was broken by a stone',

so that 'By$_{Instrument}$' is also needed. Perhaps the instrumental By is a proper subrelation of the relation By$_{Means}$. Anything done or taking place by so and so as instrument is also presumably done or takes place by means of so and so, but not conversely. If the window was broken by a stone as instrument, it was

broken by the stone as means. But I may go to work by means
of the bus but not by the bus as instrument.

It would seem that 'By$_{\text{Means}}$' should be definable in terms of
'is a means of' and 'With$_{\text{Instrument}}$' in terms of 'is an instrument of'

Consider the difference between

'He was killed by an arrow'

and

'He was killed with an arrow'.

The latter concerns an arrow as an instrument as used by an
agent, the former does not. The former is paraphrastic of

'An arrow killed him',

where the arrow is the agent. These thus have the base

'$(Ee)(Ex)(\langle \text{Kill}\rangle e$. e B now_{sp} . e Of$_{\text{Patient}}$ him . Arrow
x . e By$_{\text{Instrument}}$ $x)$'.

The latter, however, becomes rather

'$(Ee)(Ex)(Ep)(\langle \text{Kill}\rangle e$. Arrow x . Per p . e B now_{sp} . e
Of$_{\text{Patient}}$ him . e By$_{\text{Agent}}$ p . e With$_{\text{Instrument}}$ $x)$'.

The former could be true if he accidentally fell upon the arrow,
or something of the sort; the latter not.

Still another use of 'by' is to indicate the author or maker or
creator, as in 'the works by Tolstoy', 'a painting by Velasquez',
and so on. Here 'By$_{\text{Author}}$' is the appropriate predicate. Again,
this is definable in terms of 'is the author (maker, creator) of'.

'At' is often used to express the *stimulus*, as in

'I was alarmed at his behavior'.

Here again, 'At$_{\text{Stimulus}}$' is definable in terms of 'is a stimulus of'.

In addition to its other uses, 'with' is often used to express
accompaniment, so that

'e With$_{\text{Accompaniment}}$ e''

may be used to express that e is accompanied by e'. Thus

'He is coming with us now'

becomes

'(Ee)(⟨Come⟩e . e By$_{Agent}$ *us* . *we* With$_{Accompaniment}$ *him* . e During *now$_{sp}$*)'.

This of course is very different in meaning from

'He and we are coming now'.

The former has this latter as a logical consequence but not conversely. Similarly for

'Jack, with his friends, was drinking until midnight'

and

'Jack and his friends were drinking until midnight'.

Here again

'x With$_{Accompaniment}$ y' may be regarded as short for 'x Accompanies y' or '(Ee)(⟨Accompany⟩e . e From x . e To y)'.

Similar considerations obtain for 'Without$_{Accompaniment}$' in terms of negation.

'With' and 'for' are often used in certain contexts to express *support*, and 'against' to express *opposition*. Thus

'We are neither for nor against him'

becomes

'(∼ *we* For$_{Support}$ *him* . ∼ *we* Against$_{Opposition}$ *him*)'

in untensed terms, or

'(Ee)(e During *now$_{sp}$* . ∼ ⟨For$_{Support}$⟩e . ∼ ⟨Against$_{Opposition}$⟩e . e From *us* . e To *him*)'

in the present tense. Presumably 'For$_{Support}$' is definable in terms of the verb 'support' in familiar fashion. Thus

'x For$_{Support}$ e' is short for '(Ee')(⟨Support⟩e' . e' From x . e' To e)', and similarly for 'Against$_{\text{Opposition}}$' in terms of 'oppose'. (An alternative to this last form is perhaps

'$\sim$ (Ee)(e During now_{sp} . ($\langle$For$_{\text{Support}}\rangle e$ v $\langle$Against$_{\text{Opposition}}\rangle e$. e From us . e To him)'.

It is often a moot point as to where a '$\sim$' should best be placed.)

The genitive use of 'of' is perhaps its most common, and this is very closely related to the lexical 'have' or 'belongs to'. In fact

'x Of$_{\text{Genitive}}$ y' is perhaps merely short for 'y Have x' or 'x Belong y'.

Other prepositions are also often used genitively, especially 'with'. In fact 'With$_{\text{Genitive}}$' would sometimes seem to stand for the relational converse of 'Of$_{\text{Genitive}}$'.

'The girl with the beret sat in the corner'

would contain

'(the Girl) With$_{\text{Genitive}}$ (the Beret)'

as a conjunct in its base form

'(Ee)($\langle$Sit$\rangle e$. e By$_{\text{Agent}}$ (the Girl) . (the Girl) With$_{\text{Genitive}}$ (the Beret) . e B now_{sp} . e In$_{\text{Position}}$ (the Corner))'.

Incidentally, not very much is being said here concerning the logical consequences of the base forms cited. It is hoped, however, that these are always such as to yield the desired ones— whatever these latter are thought to be. Thus, for example, the preceding form has as consequences formulae to the effect that one and only one girl is under discussion, one and only one beret, one and only one corner, and one and only one girl with the one and only one beret, that there was a sitting going on, that it had the girl as agent, that it took place in the corner, that something was going on having the girl as agent, that something was going on before now, and so on. And all of these would seem to be desirable consequences of the original, some of them too obvious to be spelled out. Also, it would seem, there are no undesirable consequences of the base form given.

'In spite of', 'despite', and 'notwithstanding' are prepositions of *concession*, and are presumably definable in terms of 'concede'.

Sometimes it is the speaker who does the conceding, sometimes the person or entity talked about. In

'I admire him in spite of his faults'

the speaker does the conceding. In

'Despite strong pressure from the government, the unions have refused to order a return to work'.

the conceding is by the unions. 'Conceding' is presumably intentional so that

'p Concede$_{sp}$ e,a'

is the required form, expressing that p concedes e under the predicate description a.

'With reference to', 'with regard to, 'as to', and 'as for' may all be handled by 'With$_{\text{Reference}}$' defined in terms of 'refer', with the speaker usually as subject. And similarly for 'except for', 'with the exception of', 'apart from', 'excepting', 'except', 'but', 'bar', and 'barring', handled in terms of 'But$_{\text{Exception}}$' defined in terms of 'excepts' with the speaker usually doing the excepting under a given predicate description.

The phrase 'but for' is usually used in the sense of a *negative condition*, as in

'But for Gordon, we should have lost the match'.

This seems paraphrastic of

'Gordon caused us to win the match',

which may be handled in terms of 'Cause'.

The prepositions 'about' and 'on' are often used, in suitable contexts of course, to indicate subject matter. These are no doubt definable in terms of 'concerns', this latter handled intentionally. Thus

'e About$^{sp}_{\text{Concern}}$ e',a'   may perhaps be taken as short for '$(Ee_1)(\langle\text{Concern}\rangle e_1 \; . \; e_1 \; \text{By}_{\text{Subject}} \; e \; . \; e_1 \; \text{Of}_{\text{Patient}} \; e' \; . \; e'$ Under$^{sp}_{\text{Description}}$ $a)$'.

The conjunct containing 'Under$_{\text{Description}}$' expresses that e' is taken under the predicate description a.

A reminder is perhaps in order as to why the intentional mode of treatment is desirable here. Compare

'This book is about rational animals'

with

'This book is about featherless bipeds (in a state of nature)'.

It might be that the one is true if and only if the other is, although this is doubtful. (One would not wish to affirm both of St. Augustine's *Confessions*.) Even so, the "cognitive value," in Frege's phrase, of the one differs from that of the other and should be accounted for in the base forms,

'$(Ex)(Ea)(FuRA \ x \ . \ (\text{this Book}) \ \text{About}^{sp}_{\text{Concern}} \ x,a \ .$
$\{y3FuRA \ y\}'a)$'

and

'$(Ex)(Ea)(FuFB \ x \ . \ (\text{this Book}) \ \text{About}^{sp}_{\text{Concern}} \ x,a \ .$
$\{y3FuFB \ y\}'a)$'

respectively. Although

$$(x)(FA \ x \ \equiv \ FB \ x)$$

and hence

$$(x)(FuRA \ x \ \equiv \ FuFB \ x),$$

it is *not* the case of course that

$$(a)('\{y3FuRA \ y\}'a \ \equiv \ '\{y3FuFB \ y\}'a).$$

'With' is often used to indicate an *ingredient* of something made or created, whereas 'of' and 'out of' indicate the entire *material* used. Thus we say

'He made the cake with eggs'

and not

'He made the cake out of eggs'.

This latter would have as a consequence that eggs were the only ingredients used. Both 'With$_{\text{Ingredient}}$' and 'Of$_{\text{Material}}$' (or

'OutOf$_{Material}$') are definable in terms of 'is an ingredient of', symbolized by 'Ingredient'. Clearly

'x With$_{Ingredient}$ y'   is short for   'y Ingredient x'.

But also

'x OutOf$_{Material}$ y'   may abbreviate   '(y Ingredient x . (z)(z Ingredient x $\supset$ z KSm y))',

where KSm, it will be recalled, is the relation of K-similarity, of being of the same kind, here as applied to objects rather than events as above.

'For' is often used to indicate a standard or paradigm, as in

'Mumbo is small for an elephant'.

It will be recalled that 'for' in this sense has been packed into the treatment of scalar adjectives and adverbs above. Incidentally, that treatment well accords with a suggestion of Quirk *et al.* (p. 332): ". . .*big* means something different in *This elephant is big*, *This cat is big*, since 'big for an elephant' presupposes a larger scale, and a larger norm, than 'big for a cat'. We can make the norm explicit by a for phrase. . ." Let us tarry with this a moment with a view to putting the treatment of scalars on a firmer theoretical footing than above or in *Events, Reference, and Logical Form*.

Recall that

'Mumbo is small for an elephant'

is to have a base form something like

'(Ea)(Mumbo Low$_{sp}$ Smaller-Than, a . 'Elephant'a)',

to the effect that Mumbo is placed low on the speaker's smaller-than scale for objects to which he thinks a predicate of the form 'Elephant' ('is an elephant') applies. Let us now analyze this very form itself as follows. Let '$\langle$PlacingLow$\rangle e$' express that e is a *placing-low* (in a suitable scale of entities taken by the speaker to be in the campus or field of a dyadic comparative relation), and '$\langle$Cncv$\rangle e$', that e is an act of *conceiving* such and such. Then our form may be defined as

'$(Ee)(Ea)(Eb)(\langle\text{PlacingLow}\rangle e$. e By_{Agent} sp . e $\text{Of}_{\text{Patient}}$
Mumbo . $\langle\text{Cncv}\rangle e$. $\langle Mumbo,\text{Under}^{sp}_{\text{Destination}},a\rangle e$.
'C'(SmallerThan⌊Elephants)'a . $\langle Mumbo,\text{For}_{\text{Standard}},b\rangle e$.
'Elephants'$b)$'.

This expresses that there is a placing-low of Mumbo by the
speaker, this placing also being describable as a conceiving of
Mumbo under the description of his being a member of the
campus (or field) of the relation of being smaller than as confined to elephants, this placing and conceiving being of Mumbo
relative to the standard for elephants so-called.

$$'e \text{ For}_{\text{Standard}} b'$$

is the new notion here and is given an intentional form. (We
should wish to distinguish being intelligent for a rational animal
from being intelligent for a featherless biped.)

A more general definition is of course needed, as well as
general forms of 'High', 'Middle', and so on, as far as one
wishes to discriminate. The character these would take is clear
enough, however, from the foregoing. (Note that here and
throughout a clause such as

$$'\langle Mumbo,\text{Under}^{sp}_{\text{Description}},a\rangle e'$$

is itself definable in familiar fashion as

'$(\langle\text{Under}^{sp}_{\text{Description}}\rangle e$. e From Mumbo . e To a .
PredConOne $a)$'.)

The preposition 'at' is often used in connection with a scalar
or gradable adjective to indicate the *respect* in which the adjective is supposed to apply, as in

$$\text{'He is bad at games'}$$

or

$$\text{'He is good at administration'.}$$

The respect in these examples is one of degree of goodness or
skillfulness. These we may handle in terms of the relation 'Less-

Good-Than'. The first becomes something like

'$(Ea)(he$ Low$_{sp}$ Less-Good-Than,a . '$\{p3(Ex)($Per p . Game x . p Play $x)\}$'$a)$',

that he is placed low on the speaker's scale of entities in the field of the Less-Good-Than relation relative to the standard (of skillfulness) for players of games. The one-place predicate a here is the *reference predicate*. In the form for

'He is good at administration',

the reference predicate would denote persons who administer, and of course 'High$_{sp}$' would appear in place of 'Low$_{sp}$'. In this way the At of respect may be handled in context.

Another use of 'at' is to indicate *stimulus*, as in 'alarmed at', 'amused at', 'be glad at', and so on. And 'to' is often used for the *reaction*, as in

'To my annoyance, they rejected the offer',

and sometimes for the *reactor*, as in

'To me it sounded absurd'.

Here we need intentional forms such as

'(e,a) At$_{Stimulus}$ (e',b)'   short for   '(e',b) Stimulate (e,a)',

'(e,a) To$_{Reaction}$ (e',b)'   for   '(e,a) React (e',b)',

and

'e,a To$_{Reactor}$ p'   for   'p React e,a'.

Thus

'To my annoyance, they rejected the offer'

becomes something like

'$(Ee)(Ee')(Ea)(Eb)(\langle$Reject$\rangle e$. e By$_{Agent}$ *them* . e Of$_{Patient}$ (the Offer) . e B now_{sp} . $\langle$Annoy$\rangle e'$. e' Of$_{Patient}$ *me* . '$\{e_13(\langle$Reject$\rangle e_1$. e_1 By$_{Agent}$ *them* . e_1 Of$_{Patient}$ (the Offer))$\}$'a . '$\{e_13(\langle$Annoy$\rangle e$. e_1 Of$_{Patient}$ *me*)$\}$'b . (e',b) To$_{Reaction}$ $(e,a))$'.

This base form has the desired consequences to the effect that they rejected the offer, that I was or am annoyed, and that the annoyance is the reaction to the rejection. Presumably

$$`(e',a) \text{ At}_{\text{Stimulus}} (e,a)'$$

could be written here equally well. And similarly for related examples.

It should be mentioned again that the forms given here, either as source or base forms, are in no way intended as final. It is very likely that many of them may be improved upon in various respects. In a base form, some nuance may be sacrificed that perhaps should not be. The guiding spirit here is rather one of discovery and clear formulation as a basis for doing better, as in scientific research generally: tentative formulation and theorizing, followed by error elimination, followed by better formulation and improved theorizing, as Sir Karl Popper has well noted.

Another comment. 'By$_{\text{Agent}}$' and 'Of$_{\text{Patient}}$' have been used in context to express agency and patiency respectively, especially for human agents and patients. Perhaps it would be better to have used 'By$_{\text{Subject}}$' and 'Of$_{\text{Object}}$' instead in the more general sense for the *subjects* and *objects* of acts or events, or whatever, whether human or not.

A final comment about event identity, now that we have an *Überblick* as to the full primitive vocabulary. Necessary conditions for the identity of events have been given above, in (IV,D). Suppose Prep$_1$, . . . , Prep$_k$ are the only prepositional relations needed as primitives. Then the following principle should hold.

EvId3. $\vdash (\langle R \rangle e_1 . \langle S \rangle e_2) \supset (e_1 = e_2 \equiv (R = S .$ $(e')(e_1 \text{ Prep}_1 e' \equiv e_2 \text{ Prep}_1 e') . . . . . (e')(e' \text{ Prep}_k e_1 \equiv$ $e' \text{ Prep}_k e_2) . (a)(b)(sp \text{ Prphs } ab \supset (e_1 \text{ Under}_{sp} a \equiv$ $e_2 \text{ Under}_{sp} b))))$.

But there are of course alternative technical ways of handling event identity that might be preferable.[1]

---

1. See also the author's "Events and Actions: Some Comments on Brand and Kim," in *Action Theory*, ed. by M. Brand and D. Walton (Dordrecht, Reidel: 1976), pp. 179–192. *EvId3* must be broadened somewhat if virtual classes and relations are allowed as relata of some prepositional relations.

It should be evident by now that prepositional relations play a very fundamental role in structural linguistics and are of much greater importance than seems to have been realized heretofore. Even so, the surface has scarcely been scratched. A deeper and more exhaustive analysis is needed of prepositions in general, and of the behavior of each and every particular preposition in its various permissible contexts of use.[2] Once this is done, the task remains of connecting in detail the logistic grammar that results with the morphophonemics of paraphrase and transformation that occupies so much of contemporary linguistics and philosophy of language.

2. See, as interesting examples in this regard, Karl-Gunnar Lindkvist, *Studies on the Local Sense of the Prepositions* In, At, On, *and* To *in Modern English*, *Lund Studies in English* 20 (1950), and *The Local Sense of the Prepositions* Over, Above, *and* Across *Studied in Present-Day English* (Stockholm: 1972).

CHAPTER XIII

SOME TEMPORAL ADVERBS

Any systematic, logico-linguistic theory should, it would seem, take account of the members of four basic classes of temporal adverbs. These are the *when*-adverbs ('today' or 'afterwards'), the *duration*-adverbs ('briefly', 'since'), the *frequency* adverbs (definite: 'daily', 'twice', and indefinite: 'usually', 'always', 'often', 'occasionally', 'never'), and *relationship* adverbs ('already').[1] In the present chapter, some typical sentences containing adverbs of these kinds will be examined in the light of the foregoing.

Then *when*-adverbs divide conveniently into those indicating a "point of time," so to speak, and those that (not only do this but) also indicate in some way the point from which that time is measured or determined. In the first group the following should be placed: 'again', 'early', 'just' ('at this very moment'), 'late', 'now', 'nowadays', 'presently', 'simultaneously', 'then', 'today', 'tomorrow', 'tonight', 'yesterday'. Let us reflect a little upon these before turning to the members of the second group.

---

1. See Quirk, *et al.*, *A Grammar of Contemporary English*, pp. 482 ff.

Of course a suitable method of handling the present must be available. The expression 'now_{sp}' has been used above without analysis. We may now introduce it systematically *in usu* by letting

$$\text{'}sp \text{ Now } e\text{'}$$

express primitively that e takes place during whatever appropriate time-span the speaker wishes (within limits of course) to regard as "now," whether a moment, an hour, a day, and so on. The word 'now' is used with considerable variation in ordinary language, the length of the time-span indicated depending upon the speaker and his occasion of use. (This latter must of course be included in that time-span). The speaker sp is always to be understood as the one uttering an inscription of the form of the parent English sentence under consideration. Strictly another parameter should be given for the occasion of use, but this will be omitted so as not to complicate the notation.

The question arises as to whether the various temporal adverbs to be considered may also be handled wholly in terms of 'B' and 'Now'. Of course suitable expressions for specific times ('8 A.M.'), dates ('18 February 1975'), days ('Monday'), and so on, must be available, together with the system of measuring them. The introduction of these, however, seems to pose no fundamental theoretical problems. The system of Greenwich meridian time may be assumed, so that 'B' is supposed to behave in accord with whatever '(wholly) before than' means within that system. And similarly for the expressions for specific times, dates, and so on. (The International Date Line poses no problem, the use of temporal expressions being relative to the speaker's linguistic acts of utterance, acceptance, belief, and so on, and hence even to his spatial location.) Considerable evidence will be given in this paper to the effect that our question can be answered in the affirmative, and that the whole theory of temporal adverbs may be accommodated in event logic in terms of 'B' and 'Now'. To see this in detail let us examine a good many typical sentences *seriatim*.

Recall from (IV,D) that e_1 temporally overlaps (in the sense of G.M.T.) e_2, e_1 TO e_2, provided neither takes place wholly before the other. Then e_1 may be said to be a temporal part of e_2, e_1 TP e_2, provided every event that temporally overlaps with e_1 also temporally overlaps with e_2. Now another expression for 'TP' is 'During'. Thus we let

'e_1 During e_2' be an alternative notation for 'e_1 TP e_2'.

In the preceding chapters 'During' has been used (without definition) in essentially this sense in helping to provide logical forms for many types of temporal sentences. It will be used also in what follows rather extensively, in the meaning provided by this definition.

In addition to 'During' the temporal prepositional relation At should be introduced, in the sense of 'at a moment'. Strictly an event is a *moment* if it is non-null and is a temporal part of all its non-null temporal parts.[2] A moment in this sense is a specious present. In logico-linguistics, however, the word is often used in a somewhat looser sense, for a small temporal span containing usually at least one second of clock-time. Let 'Mom e' be defined to express that e is a "moment" or "point of time" in this (or some closely related) sense. Then

'e_1 At$_{\text{Time}}$ e_2' may abbreviate '(Mom e_2 . e_1 During e_2)'.

An event e_1 takes place at (the time of) e_2 provided then that e_2 is a moment and e_1 takes place during it.

A few further abbreviations will be useful. Let

'e B now_{sp}' abbreviate '$(Ee')(sp$ Now e' . e B $e')$',

and similarly for 'now_{sp} B e', 'e During now_{sp}', 'e At$_{\text{Time}}$ now_{sp}', and so on.

Let us turn now to some sentences (Quirk, pp. 482 ff.) containing temporal when-adverbs and exhibit suitable logical forms for them in terms of the foregoing.

'They lived (resided) in London during 1970'

clearly has something like

'$(Ee)(\langle$Reside$\rangle e$. e By$_{\text{Agent}}$ *them* . e In$_{\text{Location}}$ London . e B now_{sp} . e During 1970)',

2. Recall (IV,D) above.

as a base form, that there is a residing state *by* (in the agentive sense) them *in* London as location, this residing taking place before the *now* of the speaker's utterance and being during 1970. Similarly

'I will meet you at three P.M.'

becomes

(1) '(Ee)($\langle$Meet$\rangle e$. e By$_{\text{Agent}}$ *me* . e Of$_{\text{Object}}$ *you* . *now$_{sp}$*
B e . e At$_{\text{Time}}$ 3 P.M.)'.

The 'will' here is construed in futurity, not in the sense of intention.

(2)   'I (now) intend to meet you at 3 P.M.'

becomes rather

'(Ee)(Ee')(Ea)($\langle$Intd$\rangle e$. e During *now$_{sp}$* . e By$_{\text{Agent}}$ *me* .
e Of$_{\text{Object}}$ e' . e' Under$_{\text{Description}}$ a . '{e''3($\langle$Meet$\rangle e''$. e''
By$_{\text{Agent}}$ *me* . e'' Of$_{\text{Object}}$ *you* . e'' At$_{\text{Time}}$ 3 P.M.)}'a)'.

Observe that the statement concerning the intending is true of me, of you, and of *now$_{sp}$* if and only if I do actually intend now to meet you at 3 P.M. (2) is thus an occasion sentence, depending for its truth upon the speaker and the now. Further, (2) is intentional and may be true even if the meeting intended never takes place. (1) likewise is an occasion sentence depending for its truth upon you, me, and now. However, it is false if there is no meeting by me of you at 3 P.M. in the future of now. That all of this is the case seems to accord well with what we ordinarily want to say about the truth or falsity of occasion and intentional sentences.

A word or so of additional explanation is needed concerning contexts containing the parameter '*sp*' and one or more egocentric or deictic words. Recall that single quotes are being used throughout in their ordinary sense to indicate shapes or sign designs. Utterances, however, are inscriptions or sign events. A logical form given here as a shape

(4)   '---*sp*---'

is thus intended to indicate some utterance *e* of an inscription *a* by the speaker *sp* of such and such a shape, this shape being of a sentence of English. In place of (4) we could then write

(4') '(---*sp*--- . ⟨Utt⟩*e* . *e* By$_{\text{Agent}}$ *sp* . *e* Of$_{\text{Object}}$ *a* . '·····'*a* . *sp* Now *e*)',

where '·····' is the shape of the parent English sentence, and '*e*' and '*a*' of course do not occur freely in '---*sp*---'. (4') in fact expresses precisely that a shape '---*sp*---' is the logical form of an English inscription *a* of the shape '····' as uttered by the speaker *sp* on a present occasion *e*. Logical forms are thus always *of* inscriptions *of* given shapes as uttered *by* speakers (or writers or whatever) *on* given occasions. Throughout we are using forms such as (4) with the understanding that the corresponding (4') is intended. It could also be added that some *b* of the event-logical form '---*sp*---' would be taken by the speaker as a paraphrase of *a*, provided the speaker understands the logical symbolism.

Consider next (Cf. Quirk)

'I was in New York last year and am now living in Baltimore'.

Let

'(ι*e* . (Year *e* . *e* Before (ι*e'* . (Year *e'* . *now*$_{sp}$ During *e'*))))'

be a Russellian description for the one year before the one year containing *now*$_{sp}$, and be abbreviated as '(*last year*$_{sp}$)'. Then our sentence has a form such as

'(E*e*$_1$)(E*e*$_2$)(⟨In$_{\text{Location}}$⟩*e*$_1$. *e*$_1$ By$_{\text{Agent}}$ *me* . *e*$_1$ Of$_{\text{Object}}$ New York . *e*$_1$ B *now*$_{sp}$. *e*$_1$ During (*last year*$_{sp}$) . ⟨Reside⟩*e*$_2$. *e*$_2$ By$_{\text{Agent}}$ *me* . *e*$_2$ In$_{\text{Location}}$ Baltimore . *e*$_2$ During *now*$_{sp}$)'.

If the 'was in' is construed as 'resided in', then of course another form would be appropriate.

Contexts containing 'again' are of interest in entailing the existence of two similar events. Thus

(3)   'I will kiss you again'

entails that there is a present or past kissing of you by me and also that there is a future one. Thus

'$(Ee_1)(\langle K \rangle e_1 . e_1 \text{ By}_{\text{Agent}} \text{ me} . e_2 \text{ Of}_{\text{Object}} \text{ you} . now_{sp} \text{ B}$
$e_1 . (Ee_2)(\langle K \rangle e_2 . e_2 \text{ By}_{\text{Agent}} \text{ me} . e_2 \text{ Of}_{\text{Patient}} \text{ you} .$
$e_2 \text{ B } e_1))$'

seems to capture what is needed. This form suggests that an adverbial temporal relation Again may be introduced as follows. We may let

'$e_1 \text{ Again}_{\text{Time}} e_2,\text{F}$' abbreviate '$(Fe_1 . Fe_2 . e_2 \text{ B } e_1)$'.

The F here is a virtual class of events, so that e_1 is *again* an F relative to e_2 provided e_1 is a member of F and e_2 is a prior member of F. In the example, we could then replace the conjunct beginning '(Ee_2)' by

'$(Ee_2)(e_1 \text{ Again}_{\text{Time}} e_2,\{e3(\langle K \rangle e . e \text{ By}_{\text{Agent}} \text{ me} . e$
$\text{Of}_{\text{Patient}} \text{ you})\}$'

without loss. An equivalent form for (3) in fact is

'$(Ee_1)(Ee_2)(now_{sp} \text{ B } e_1 . e_1 \text{ Again}_{\text{Time}} e_2,\{e3(\langle K \rangle e . e$
$\text{By}_{\text{Agent}} \text{ me} . e \text{ Of}_{\text{Patient}} \text{ you})\})$'.

Note here that '$\text{Of}_{\text{Patient}}$' is used in place of '$\text{Of}_{\text{Object}}$' where a human patient is involved.

The adverb 'just' in the sense of 'at such and such a moment' may be handled in terms of 'At_{Time}'. In fact

'$e_1 \text{ Just}_{\text{Mom}} e_2$' may be defined as '$(e_1 \text{ At}_{\text{Time}} e_2 .$
$\text{Mom } e_2)$'

(4)   'I am just (now) finishing my homework'

becomes

'$(Ee)(\langle \text{Finish} \rangle e . e \text{ By}_{\text{Agent}} \text{ me} . e \text{ Of}_{\text{Object}} (\text{my Homework})$
$. e \text{ Just}_{\text{Mom}} now_{sp})$'.

(4) might also be construed as

'I am (now) finishing my homework and finishing nothing else'

or as

'I am (now) finishing my homework and doing nothing else to it', and perhaps even as (although less likely)

'I am (now) finishing my homework and doing nothing else at all'.

All of these may readily be handled here. The second, for example becomes, where 'p Do e' expresses that person p does e in the lexical sense,

'$(Ee)(\langle\text{Finish}\rangle e$. e By$_{\text{Agent}}$ *me* . e Of$_{\text{Object}}$ (my Homework) . e During *now$_{sp}$* . $\sim$ $(Ee')(Ee'')(\langle\text{Do}\rangle e'$. $\sim$ (Ee''') $(\langle\text{Finish}\rangle e'''$. $e' = e''')$. e' By$_{\text{Agent}}$ *me* . e' Of$_{\text{Object}}$ e'' . $e'' = $ (my Homework) . e' During *now$_{sp}$*$))$'.

But these variant construals of (4) do not involve a temporal use of 'just'.

The notion 'throughout' (in the temporal sense) seems to be readily definable. For e_1 to take place throughout the duration of e_2 is merely for e_1 to take place during e_2 and conversely. Thus we may let

'e_1 Throughout$_{\text{Time}}$ e_2' abbreviate '$(e_1$ During e_2 . e_2 During $e_1)$'.

The adverb 'then', it seems, is always used to refer to something either before or after what is taking place in the present. Thus we may let

'sp Then e' abbreviate '$(Ee')(sp$ Now e' . $(e$ B e' $\vee$ e' B $e))$'.

Some uses of 'then' are of course cross-referential, in which cases the time or event referred to must be brought in by means of some additional clause. Consider 'then' in the context

'They lived (resided) in London during 1970 and were then self-employed'.

Clearly 'then' here is cross-referential to '1970'. This may be handled in terms of 'Then' somewhat as follows.

'$(Ee)(\langle\text{Reside}\rangle e$. e By$_{\text{Agent}}$ *them* . e In$_{\text{Location}}$ London . e B *now$_{sp}$* . e During 1970 . $(Ee')(\langle\text{Employ}\rangle e'$. e' By$_{\text{Agent}}$ *them* . e' Of$_{\text{Patient}}$ *them* . sp Then e' . e' Throughout$_{\text{Time}}$ $e))$'.

The cross-referentiality is accommodated here by the through-out-clause.

Consider now the when-adverb 'when' in the context

'I will tell you the news when I meet you tomorrow'.

A form for this is something like

'$(Ee)(Ee')(\langle\text{Tell}\rangle e$. e By$_{\text{Agent}}$ *me* . e To$_{\text{Patient}}$ *you* . e Of$_{\text{Object}}$ (the News) . *now$_{sp}$* B e . $\langle\text{Meet}\rangle e'$. e' By$_{\text{Agent}}$ *me* . e' To$_{\text{Patient}}$ *you* . e' During *tomorrow$_{sp}$* . e When e')'.

Just how is 'e When e'' to be construed? It is to express that e takes place when e' does. Perhaps we may let

'e When e'' abbreviate '(e During e' ∨ e Throughout$_{\text{Time}}$ e')'.

The definiens here seems to capture pretty well what is desired. Also we may let

'*sp* Tomorrow e' abbreviate '(Day e . $(Ee_1)(Ee_2)$(Day e_1 . *sp* Now e_2 . e_2 TP e_1 . e_1 B e . ∼ (Ee_3)(Day e_3 . e_1 B e_3 . e_3 B e)))'.

And similarly of course for 'Today' and 'Yesterday'. Then, as above with '*now$_{sp}$*' and the like,

'e During *tomorrow$_{sp}$*' may abbreviate '(Ee')(*sp* Tomorrow e' . e During e')'.

Or we could let

'*tomorrow$_{sp}$*' abbreviate '(ιe . *sp* Tomorrow e)',

and so on, so that contexts containing these deitic words are easily provided for.

Let us turn now to some *when*-adverbs in the second group, those indicating "a point of time but also implying the point from which that time is measured." Some typical adverbs here are 'afterwards', 'before', 'earlier', 'eventually', 'finally', 'first', 'formerly', 'immediately', 'initially', 'instantly', 'just' ('a very short time ago'), 'last', 'lately', 'later', 'momentarily', 'next', 'originally', 'previously', 'presently', 'recently', 'shortly', 'since', 'soon', 'subsequently', 'then' ('after that').

Clearly

'He is (now) going to the barber shop but will return here later'

may have as a form

'$(Ee)(\langle Go \rangle e$. e By$_{Agent}$ *him* . e To$_{Destination}$ (the Barber Shop) . e During now_{sp} . $(Ee')(\langle Return \rangle e'$. e' By$_{Agent}$ *him* . e' To$_{Destination}$ $here_{sp}$. now_{sp} B e' . e B $e'))$'.

The '$here_{sp}$' is of course a demonstrative for whatever place or location the speaker intends. More specifically, where 'sp Here x' expresses that the speaker takes the place x as here, in familiar fashion

'e To$_{Destination}$ $here_{sp}$' may be short for '$(Ex)(sp$ Here x . e To$_{Destination}$ $x)$'.

Also the final 'e B e'' could be written as 'e' Later e', this latter being obviously definable merely as the former.

Next consider

'I went into my room and immediately started to work'.

Clearly the 'immediately' here may be handled in terms of 'B' by utilizing a clause to the effect that no time (other perhaps than a moment) elapsed after I went into my room and before I started to work. Thus

'e ImmediatelyAfter e''' may abbreviate '$(e'$ B e . $(e'')((e'$ B e'' . e'' B $e) \supset$ Mom $e''))$'.

The sentence

'I haven't got any time at the moment but I'll see you soon'

involves the special pragmatical word 'soon', the designation of which may vary from person to person and from occasion of use to occasion of use. Presumably, however 'soon' means merely 'after a short time span', and hence is relative to the speaker's use of 'short'. To accommodate 'soon' in the sense of 'soon after', we may let

'e_1 SoonAfter$_{sp}$ e_2' abbreviate '$(e_2$ B e_1 . $(Ea)(Eb)(Ee)$ $(e = (Fu'\{e'3(Mom$ e' . e_2 B e . e B $e_1)\})$. a Des e_1 .

b Des e_2 . *e* Low$_{sp}$ Shorter-Than, $\ulcorner\{e'3(Ee_3)(Ee_4)(Ep)$
$(e_4$ Like *b* . e_3 Like *a* . $e' = (Fu'\{e_53(Mom$ e_5 . e_4 B
e_5 . e_5 B $e_3)\})$. e_3 By$_{Agent}$ *p* . e_4 By$_{Agent}$ *p* . *p* Like
$sp)\}\urcorner))$'.

The definiens is to the effect that e_2 is before e_1 and the fusion
of all moments between them is low on the speaker's scale of
the comparative relation Shorter-Than as confined to fusions of
moments between acts or events like e_2 where e_1 as performed
by agents like the speaker. A good deal is packed into this
definiens, but its intent should be clear enough.

Similarly 'just' in the sense of 'a very short time ago' may be
defined. We may let

$$\text{'}e_1 \text{ JustBefore}_{sp} \ e_2\text{'}$$

express that e_1 took place "a very short time before" e_2 on the
speaker's scale for Shorter-Than. Note that 'very' is involved
here, so that a suitable fusion of moments is placed very low
in the speaker's scale.

Consider now

'She once owned a dog',

which does not imply that she either does or does not now own
a dog, nor that she twice owned a dog, nor that she twice has
not owned a dog. It merely states that there is at least one past
state or occasion in which she did own a dog. Thus

'$(Ee)(Ex)(\langle Own \rangle e$. *e* By$_{Agent}$ *her* . *e* Of$_{Object}$ *x* . Dog *x* .
e B now_{sp})'

seems to capture what is needed, 'once' being construed as
'at some time in the past'.

'Then' as construed in the sense of 'and then' may obviously
be handled in terms of '.', 'Then', and 'ImmediatelyAfter'. Thus

'I went home and then went to bed'

becomes something like

'$(Ee)(Ee')(Ee'')(\langle Go \rangle e$. *e* By$_{Agent}$ *me* . *e* To$_{Destination}$
(my Home) . *e* B now_{sp} . $\langle$Go-to-Bed$\rangle e'$. e' By$_{Agent}$
me . e' Then e'' . e'' ImmediatelyAfter *e*)'.

In a somewhat similar way other temporal adverbs of this second kind may be handled.

Quirk *et al.* point out (Note [a], p. 484) the interesting difference between 'earlier' (or 'earlier than') and 'later' ('later than') as synonyms respectively of 'before' (B) and 'after' (After), and 'earlier' and 'later' as the comparative forms of the adverbs 'early' and 'late'. This difference is accommodated here by taking 'B' as a nonpragmatical predicate. 'Early' and 'late' are pragmatical words depending upon the speaker. Just how early early is depends upon the speaker and some suitable reference class.

$$\text{'I am eating (a meal) late today'}$$

becomes something like

$$\text{'(E}e)(\text{E}x)(\langle\text{Eat}\rangle e\ .\ e\ \text{By}_{\text{Agent}}\ me\ .\ e\ \text{Of}_{\text{Object}}\ x\ .\ \text{Meal}\ x\ .}$$
$$e\ \text{High}_{sp}\ \text{B,'}\{e'3(\text{E}x)(\langle\text{Eat}\rangle e'\ .\ e'\ \text{By}_{\text{Agent}}\ me\ .\ e'\ \text{Of}_{\text{Object}}}$$
$$x\ .\ e\ \text{During}\ today_{sp})\}\text{')',}$$

to the effect that an eating by me of a meal is placed high on my before-than scale (the *sp* here is myself) as confined to my eatings of meals today. (The subjective scales, it will be recalled, start at the small or low end at the bottom, so that 'High' here indicates late on the speaker's B-scale.) In general, it would seem,

$$\text{'}e\ \text{Late}_{sp}\ \text{'F'' could be defined as}\quad\text{'}e\ \text{High}_{sp}\ \text{B,'F''}$$

and

$$\text{'}e\ \text{Early}_{sp}\ \text{'F'' as}\quad\text{'}e\ \text{Low}_{sp}\ \text{B,'F''.}$$

And analogously for 'VeryEarly' or 'VeryLate', where of course the relation Very is used.

It is interesting to note, incidentally, the extremely important role played by the connective '.' for 'and' in the various forms given. In spelling out the various conjuncts needed, we in effect provide a full semantics of the sentence, a full anatomy of it, getting down to the bare bones constituting its skeletal structure. It may well be that '.' is the most needed connective for this purpose. We merely spell out clause after clause, being sure of course that the proper quantificational structure is exhibited.

No other single connective seems to play so significant a role in protolinguistics.

Let us turn now to the frequency adverbs and recall that these may be either definite or indefinite. The definite ones indicate "explicitly the times by which the frequency is measured." Commonly occurring adverbs of this kind are 'hourly', 'daily', 'nightly', and so on. Contexts containing these adverbs might be thought to pose no problems, and to be handled in terms of the appropriate quantifiers. Thus

'The sun rises daily'

becomes merely

'(e)(Day $e \supset$ (Ee')($\langle$Rise$\rangle e'$. e' By$_{\text{Agent}}$ (the Sun) . e' During e))'.

A sentence such as

(5)   'Each summer I spend my vacation in Bermuda',

however, does pose the problem that not every summer in the history of the cosmos is being covered but only a few. This and similar examples such as

'Committee meetings take place weekly'

or

'I shall be in my office every other day'

show that some additional construction is needed to restrict the range of the relevant quantifiers. (5) may be paraphrased as

'Every summer during which it is appropriate that I have a vacation I spend it in Bermuda',

where Harris's notion of *being appropriate for* is used. Let, essentially as in VIII,

'e Approp$_{sp}$ e','F''

express that the speaker takes it as appropriate for e to be an e' such that the predicate 'F' denotes it. Our example then becomes something like

$(e)(e_3)((\text{Summer } e \, . \, e \text{ Approp}_{sp} \, e_3\{e_1 3(\text{Summer } e_1 \, .$
$(Ee')(\text{Vacation } e' \, . \, e' \text{ During } e_1 \, . \, e' \text{ Of}_{\text{Genitive}} me \, . \, \sim (Ee'')$
$(\text{Vacation } e'' \, . \sim e' = e'' \, . \, e'' \text{ During } e_1 \, . \, e' \text{ Of}_{\text{Genitive}}$
$me))\}') \supset (Ee_2)(Ee')((\langle\text{Spend}\rangle e_2 \, . \, e_2 \text{ By}_{\text{Agent}} me \, . \, e_2$
$\text{Of}_{\text{Object}} e' \, . \text{ Vacation } e' \, . \, e' \text{ During } e \, . \, e' \text{ Of}_{\text{Genitive}} me \, .$
$\sim (Ee'')(\text{Vacation } e'' \, . \sim e' = e'' \, . \, e'' \text{ During } e \, . \, e'$
$\text{Of}_{\text{Genitive}} me) \, . \, e_2 \text{ In}_{\text{Location}} \text{Bermuda}))'.$

This expresses that every summer during which it is appropriate that I have one and only one vacation, I spend one and only one vacation during it in Bermuda. Note that if in (5) 'vacation' were in the plural, the uniqueness clause here would not be needed. The other examples may be handled similarly in terms of 'Approp'.

The adverbs of indefinite frequency require fundamental reference to the speaker and perhaps also to his appropriate comparative scales. Adverbs of this kind may be subdivided into those indicating *usual* occurrence ('commonly', 'customarily', 'generally', 'habitually', 'invariably', 'normally', 'ordinarily', 'usually'), *continuous* or *continual* occurrence ('always', 'constantly', 'continually', 'continuously', 'ever' ('always'), 'incessantly', 'permanently', 'perpetually'), *high frequency* ('often', 'frequently', 'regularly', 'repeatedly'), and *low or zero frequency* ('infrequently', 'irregularly', 'occasionally', 'periodically', 'rarely', 'seldom', 'sometimes', 'never', 'ever' ('at any time')). Frequency adverbs of usual occurrence seem to depend upon the speaker's scales, as do those of high or low frequency; those of continuous or continual occurrence or of zero frequency do not but seem rather to require 'Approp' to restrict the range of the relevant quantifiers. An example of each must suffice for the present.

'We normally go to bed at midnight'

becomes

$(e)(e')((\langle\text{Go-to-Bed}\rangle e \, . \, e \text{ By}_{\text{Agent}} us \, . \text{ Day } e' \, . \, (Ee'')(e''$
$\text{Midnight } e' \, . \, e \text{ At}_{\text{Time}} e'')) \supset e \text{ Mid}_{sp} \text{ LessNormalThan,}$
$\{e_1 3(\langle\text{Do}\rangle e_1 \, . \, e_1 \text{ By}_{\text{Agent}} us)\}')',$

to the effect that all goings to bed by us at midnight of any day are placed by the speaker (one of us) middling on his scale of LessNormalThan relative to the predicate for our doings.

'He is continually complaining about the noise'

becomes rather

'$(e)(e')(e$ Approp$_{sp}$ e','$\{e_1 3(Ep)(\langle$Complain$\rangle e_1$. Per p . e_1 By$_{Agent}$ p . e_1 Of$_{Object}$ (the Noise))$\}$' $\supset$ $(Ee_1)(Ee_2)$ $(\langle$Complain$\rangle e_1$. e_1 By$_{Agent}$ him . e_1 Of$_{Object}$ (the Noise) . e_2 TP e_1 . e_2 During e))'.

Here '(the Noise)' is an anaphoric description, and the form is to the effect that whenever it is taken as appropriate for there to be a complaint about the noise, a temporal part of a complaining by him about it is taking place.

On the other hand

'We frequently go to bed at midnight'

involves the numerical word 'frequent'. Where, as above, the form

'F Frequent$_{sp}$ 'G''

is available, we have

'$\{e3(Ee')(Ee'')(e''$ Midnight e' . e At$_{Time}$ e'' . Day e' . $\langle$Go-to-Bed$\rangle e$. e By$_{Agent}$ us)$\}$ Frequent$_{sp}$ '$\{e3(Ep)($Per p . $\langle$Go-to-Bed$\rangle e$. e By$_{Agent}$ p)$\}$''

as a suitable form. The virtual class of our goings-to-bed at midnights is frequent with respect to the virtual predicate for all human goings-to-bed.

Consider now an adverb indicating zero frequency.

'He has never resided in Singapore'

can be handled in terms of an unrestricted quantifier, as

'$\sim (Ee)(Ee')(\langle$Reside$\rangle e'$. e' During e . e' By$_{Agent}$ him . e' In$_{Location}$ Singapore)'.

There is much more to be said of course concerning these various frequency adverbs. It would seem, however, that most of this—perhaps all—can be said in terms of the framework provided here.

Quirk *et al.* regard as "equivalent" or as "very similar" sentences such as

> 'Sailors often drink rum'

and

> 'Many sailors drink rum',

or

> 'A dog is sometimes a dangerous animal'

and

> 'Some dogs are dangerous animals'.

But we should not be too hasty to equate these, and should be able to provide different logical forms for them. Clearly

$$\text{'}(Ex)(\text{Dog } x \,.\, x \text{ High}_{sp} \text{ Less-Dangerous-Than,'Animal'})\text{'}$$

says something very different from

$$\text{'}(x)(\text{Dog } x \supset (Ee)(Ee')(\langle x, \text{High}_{sp}, \text{Less-Dangerous-Than,}$$
$$\text{'Animal'}\rangle e \,.\, e \text{ At}_{\text{Time}} e'))\text{'}.$$

There may well be a dog high on the speaker's Less-Dangerous-Than scale for animals without its being the case that all dogs are on some occasions in a state the speaker places high on his Less-Dangerous-Than scale for animals.

Commonly occurring adverbs indicating time relationships include, in addition to those already considered, 'afterwards, 'eventually', 'finally', 'first', 'next', 'originally', 'previously', 'subsequently', 'already', 'yet', and 'still'. The various contexts containing them are not dissimilar to ones already considered, and may be handled essentially as above.

Let us consider finally some commonly occurring time-duration adverbs, both those indicating some specific duration or length of time as well as those indicating a duration relative to some preceding point of time [Quirk, pp. 486 ff.]. Among the first are 'always', 'awhile', 'briefly', 'indefinitely', 'long', 'momentarily', 'permanently', 'temporarily', and among the second, 'lately', 'recently', 'since'. Most of these are pragmatical, except 'since' (in the sense of 'from some time in the past' or 'after that'). Even 'always' does not always mean at all times whatsoever, past, present, or future. It enables us rather to achieve a certain kind of generality in context. For example

'I have always resided here'

may be paraphrased as

'All my residings have taken place here and I am still residing here'

or as

'All my places of residence have been here and still are'.

Also

'I have always had that scar on my face'

states merely that all my life I have had that scar on my face. The other time-duration adverbs may be introduced in terms of the speaker's appropriate scales, so that no new theoretical problems remain in accommodating them.

Suitable constraints or meaning postulates concerning 'B' and 'Now' must of course be laid down. (Some of these have been suggested in IV above and more will be said concerning 'Now' in the next chapter.) And although the evidence here is by no means exhaustive, it does lend some support to the thesis that most—perhaps all—temporal adverbs in English may be handled in terms of these two primitives, and that the various contexts of use containing them may be given suitable logical forms within event logic.

CHAPTER XIV

'NOW'

It was suggested in the previous chapter that the logic of many temporal adverbs may be handled in terms of 'B' for the relation of occurring wholly before-than as between events, and 'Now' for the deictic relation between speaker and event of taking the event as now. The form 'sp Now e' expresses that the speaker takes event e to occur now. It was mentioned that this form actually is too simple and that the occasion of use should also be brought in. And not only the occasion of use but also the particular sign-event for now being used as well as the sentence in which it occurs. Thus a better form is no doubt

$$\text{'}sp \text{ Now } e_1,a,b,e_2\text{'},$$

expressing that the speaker uses the sign-event or inscription a as occurring in the sentence b to refer to event e_1 as one that is occurring now, whatever the now is taken to be.

Ordinarily the inscription a will itself be a sign-event of the form 'now'. If we use quotation marks in their usual sense,

$$\text{"now'}a\text{'}$$

expresses that a is a sign-event of the form 'now'. Thus the effect of saying that sp Now e_1,a,b,e_2 is merely that the speaker *refers* to e_1 as now. In fact, where 'a Occ b' expresses, as in the syntax of sign events, that a occurs in b, (1) may be defined merely as

'('now'a . Sent b . a Occ b . sp Ref' $e_1,a,b,e_2)$'.

Here 'sp Ref' e_1,a,b,e_2' expresses that the speaker uses the sign-event a as occurring in b to refer (in his use e_2 of b) to entity e_1. (It is readily definable in terms of the Ref' of VI.) Whenever this obtains, b is a sentence so that 'Sent b' may be dropped in the definiens. Also whenever sp Ref' e_1,a,b,e_2, the speaker uses the sentence b in some very broad sense—he utters it to himself or apprehends it or asserts it or questions it, and so on. Let 'sp Use b' express that the speaker uses b in one or another of these ways. Thus whenever sp Ref' e_1,a,b,e_2, it holds that $\langle sp, \text{Use}, b \rangle e_2$.

Many uses of 'now'[1] are such that if sp Now e_1,a,b,e_2 the act e_2 of the speaker's using b occurs during e_1. Uses of this kind are probably the most frequent ones. Let us call them *primary*. To capture this notion let us define

'sp PrNow e_1,a,b,e_2'   as short for   '(sp Now e_1,a,b,e_2 . e_2 During e_1)'.

Thus the speaker takes an inscription of 'now' as occurring in a sentence b in use e_2 as primary and as referring to e_1 provided e_2 takes place during e_1.

All the uses of 'now' considered in the preceding chapter were primary, as in

'I am now living in Baltimore',

'John is now finishing his homework',

and so on. No problems seem to arise concerning primary uses of 'now' not considered there. Hence let us move on to the secondary uses.

---

1. In speaking of the word 'now' a certain ambiguity may be allowed. Sometimes the shape is being referred to, and sometimes inscriptions of that shape. And similarly for other words, clauses, and even full sentences.

By definition the secondary uses are those wherein the speaker refers to events *not* containing the duration of the relevant sentence of use. Thus

'*sp* SecNow e_1,a,b,e_2' is short for '(*sp* Now e_1,a,b,e_2 . $\sim e_2$ During e_1)'.

Secondary uses of inscriptions of the form 'now' occur in sentences such as

(1)   'Night had now approached',

and

(2)   'He visited us now and then'.

Secondary uses are frequently, perhaps always, in contexts concerning the past or future. There are other uses of 'now' that are not primary, however, and these need not be secondary either. For example,

(3)   'Now he speaks to me, now he doesn't',

(4)   'Now that you are here, you will help me',

(5)   'I do not believe anything he says now',

and

(6)   'Between the now and the then a chasm arose'.

Let us consider now structures or logical forms for the sentences (1)–(6). These logical forms are to be of inscriptions of sentences as used by someone, the speaker, on given occasions, these sentences containing inscriptions of the deictic word 'now'. Hence they will all contain parameters for the speaker, the occasion of use, the sentence used, and the word. For (1) we then have something like

(1') '((1)b . 'now'a . a Occ b . $\langle sp,\text{Use},b\rangle e$. $(Ee')(Ee'')$ ($\langle\text{Approach}\rangle e'$. e' By$_{\text{Agent}}$ night . e' B e . sp SecNow e'',a,b,e . e' B e''))'.

Note that the clause '$\langle sp,\text{Use},b\rangle e'$ may be dropped, but its inclusion is a useful reminder. The first four clauses of this form are boundary conditions, as it were, the remainder spelling out the suitable logical paraphrase of what (1) is supposed to convey. (Note that 'night' here is left unanalyzed, such analysis being irrelevant for present purposes.)

(1′) is not quite adequate, however, no constraints being placed upon the length of the duration of the now. Clearly the now must be taken as having the duration associated with or appropriate to approachings of night. To handle this, let 'c MD e'''' express that c is the measure of the duration of e'', c being a numerical expression. And let

$$\text{'}c \; \text{Approp}_{sp} \; \delta\text{'}$$

express that it is *appropriate* for the one-place predicate δ (a meta-meta-linguistic predicate) to denote c. To assure then that e'' in (1′) be of the appropriate duration,

'$(Ec)(E\delta)(c$ MD e'' . e Approp$_{sp}$ δ . '$\{d3(Ee_1)$ $(\langle$Approach$\rangle e_1$. e_1 By$_{\text{Agent}}$ night . d MD $e_1\}$'$\delta)$'

is to be added as a conjunct after 'e B e'''' in (1). All uses of 'now', it may well be, need an appropriateness clause tacked on in somewhat this way.

(2) contains in addition to an occurrence of 'now' a second deictic word 'then', which needs analysis. We may let

'sp PrThen e,b' abbreviates '$(Ee')(\langle sp,\text{Use},b\rangle e'$. (e' B e ∨ e B e'))'.

so that the speaker takes e as a then in sentence b just where e occurs before or after his act of use of b. This of course gives us only a *primary* use of 'then', taken to refer to some event before or after the span of use. The use of 'then' in (3), however, is not of this kind. Here the 'then' refers to some event occurring before or after whatever is taken as now. Thus

'sp SecThen e_1,e_2,b' abbreviates '$(Ee)(Ea)(sp$ Now e_1,a,b,e . (e_2 B e_1 ∨ e_1 B e_2))',

and expresses that the speaker takes an occurrence e_1 of 'now' to be secondary relative to e_2 provided e_2 occurs before e_1 or

e_1 before e_2. For (2), then, we have something like

(2′) '((2)b . 'now'a . a Occ b . $\langle sp, \text{Use}, b\rangle e$. $(\text{E}e_1)(\text{E}e_2)$ $(\langle\text{Visit}\rangle e_1$. e_1 By$_{\text{Agent}}$ him . e_1 B e . e_1 Of$_{\text{Patient}}$ us . sp SecNow e_1, a, b, e . $\langle\text{Visit}\rangle e_2$. e_2 By$_{\text{Agent}}$ him . e_2 B e . sp SecThen e_2, e_1, b))'.

Note that from (2) it does not follow that he visited us now (dubious English at best) nor that he visited us then, the use of 'then' here being secondary. Here too appropriateness conjuncts are needed, namely,

'$(\text{E}c)(\text{E}\delta)(c$ MD e_1 . e Approp$_{sp}$ δ . '$\{d3(\text{E}e')(\langle\text{Visit}\rangle e'$. e' By$_{\text{Agent}}$ him . e' Of$_{\text{Patient}}$ us . d MD $e')\}$'δ) . $(\text{E}c)(\text{E}\delta)(c$ MD e_2 . e Approp$_{sp}$ δ . '$\{d3(\text{E}e')(\langle\text{Visit}\rangle e'$. e' By$_{\text{Agent}}$ him . e' Of$_{\text{Patient}}$ us . d MD $e')\}$'δ)'

under the scope of '$(\text{E}e_2)$'.

It might be thought that there is overelaboration here and that 'now and then' means merely occasionally. True perhaps, but even so the form for (2) should be spelled out, then the form for

'He visited us occasionally'

also, so that the exact interrelations of the two sentences may be studied. Perhaps not all speakers would paraphrase one as the other on all occasions. The logical form should mirror as closely as possible the "meaning" of the original, and should contain logical representatives of the main words it contains but with the full logical skeleton exhibited. (Note that in (2′) the sp is a person who is a part of the *sum* of persons ($p_1 \cup \ldots \cup p_n$) constituting *us*.)

In (3) the two occurrences of 'now' introduce contrastive clauses. The two may be distinguished syntactically by letting 'a_1 Left a_2, b' express that a_1 falls to the left of a_2 in the sentence b, this locution being readily definable in inscriptional syntax in terms of concatenation. We then have something like

(3′) '((3)b . 'now'a_1 . 'now'a_2 . a_1 Left a_2, b . $(\text{E}e)(\text{E}e_1)$ $(\text{E}e_3)(\text{E}e_4)(\langle\text{Speak}\rangle e_1$. e_1 By$_{\text{Agent}}$ him . e_1 To$_{\text{Patient}}$ me . sp Now e_3, a_1, b, e . $(\text{E}c)(\text{E}\delta)(c$ MD e_1 . c Approp$_{sp}$ δ .

'$\{d3(Ee')(\langle\text{Speak}\rangle e'$. e' By_{Agent} him . e_1 $\text{To}_{\text{Patient}}$ $me)\}'\delta)$.
e_1 During e_3 . $\sim (Ee_2)(\langle\text{Speak}\rangle e_2$. e_2 By_{Agent} him . e_2
$\text{To}_{\text{Patient}}$ me . sp Now e_4,a_2,b,e . $(Ec)(E\delta)(c$ MD e_2 . c
Approp_{sp} δ . '$\{d3(Ee')(\langle\text{Speak}\rangle e'$. e' By_{Agent} him . e_1
$\text{To}_{\text{Patient}}$ $me)\}'\delta)$. e_2 During $e_4)))$'

as a structure for (3). Note that uses of 'now' here are not
required to be either primary or secondary, but may be either.
Note also that this structure does not have the consequence that
he speaks to me now (in a primary sense of 'now') nor that he
does not speak to me now (in the primary sense). It does follow,
however, as it should, that he does speak to me at some time(s)
and that he does not speak to me at some time(s). Of course
this latter is presumably trivially true. What is intended is rather
that there are times when he does not speak to me when I
regard it as appropriate for him to do so. Here still another
appropriateness clause, of a somewhat different kind, is needed.
Let

$$'he\ \text{Approp}_{sp}\ a'$$

express that it is appropriate for the one-place predicate a to
denote him, the person referred to as 'he'. The relevant predicate
here is for the (virtual) of people who speak to me during
e_4. To provide for this we add after 'e_2 During e_4'

' . $(Ec)(E\delta)(c$ Des e_4 . he Approp_{sp} δ . $\ulcorner\{p3(Ee_5)$
$(\langle\text{Speak}\rangle e_5$. e_5 By_{Agent} p . e_5 $\text{To}_{\text{Patient}}$ me . e_5 During
$c)\}\urcorner\delta)$'.

It might be thought that there is more innuendo in (3) than
is captured in this form. In particular, (3) might be taken as
stating that he first spoke to me, then didn't, then did, and so
on, or that he spoke to me several times, then failed to speak to
me several times when it would have been appropriate for him
to do so. Such additional matters may be added *ad libitum* to
provide alternative "readings" of (3). (Note here that the speaker
and I are of course the same person.)

The 'now that' phrase in (4) is somewhat idiomatic, equivalent
perhaps to 'since'. Let 'e Since e''' express that e occurs since

e' does. This is not quite equivalent perhaps to saying that e' causes e. (Perhaps the Fregean *Art des Gegebenseins* should be brought in here, but to simplify this will be disregarded.) (4) has as consequences that you are now here and that you will help, and that you will help while being here. Thus we have a form something like

(4′) '((4)b . 'now'a . a Occ b . (Ee')(Ee_1)(Ee_2)(sp PrNow e',a,b,e . $\langle you,At_{Location},here_{sp}\rangle e_1$. $\langle you,Help\rangle e_2$. e_2 Since e_1 . e_2 During e_1 . (Ec)(Eδ)(c MD e' . e Approp$_{sp}$ δ . '{$d3$(Ee_3)($\langle you,At_{Location},here_{sp}\rangle e_3$. d MD e_3)}'δ)))'.

In (5) the 'now' has the effect of 'under the circumstances' or 'in view of the circumstances'. Here the compound prepositional relation InViewOf is needed. The phrase 'the circumstances' is an anaphoric Russellian description, the reference of which is presumed understood by the hearer. Even so, the work 'now' occurs, but structurally in such a way that the speaker takes it to imply (materially) the appropriate InViewOf-clause. Thus our form would seem to be

(5′) '((5)b . 'now'a . a Occ b . $\sim$ (Ec)(Ee')(he Say c . Sent c . $\langle I,Believe,c\rangle e'$. sp SecNow e',a,b,e . (sp SecNow e',a,b,e $\supset$ e' InViewOf (the Circumstances))))'.

Note that no appropriateness clause seems needed here. (Here also the speaker and I are the same person.)

In (6), 'the now' and 'the then' may be regarded as fusions of virtual classes of simultaneous events. Let

'e_1 Simul e_2' abbreviate '(e_1 During e_2 . e_2 During e_1)'.

Then our sentence becomes something like

'((6)b . 'now'a . a Occ b . (Ee')(Ex)(Ee_1)...(Ee_4) ($\langle Arise\rangle e'$. Chasm x . e' By$_{Agent}$ x . e' Bet e_1,e_2 . sp Now e_3,a,b,e . e' B e_3 . sp SecThen e_4,e_3,b . $e_3 =$ (Fu'{$e_5 3 e_5$ Simul e_3}) . $e_4 =$ (Fu'{$e_5 3 e_5$ Simul e_4})))'.

(The appropriate appropriateness-clauses are ommitted here, being somewhat complicated.)

There are of course other uses of 'now' than those considered.[2] It would seem, however, that all of these are reducible to the foregoing or at least can be handled within the protolinguistic resources available.

Nothing has been said about equivalent logical forms, or L-equivalent ones—or ones having some Carnapian intensions or the same Fregean *Sinne*, if sense can be made of these latter notions. Also *word-order* in a natural language is often of the very essence of what is said, whereas many variant orders are permissible in the logical form provided the results are L-equivalent. It is often thought that the logical form or structure of a sentence of natural language should mirror its syntactic structure. The difficulty with this contention is that some *theory* of syntactic structure is needed, and about all that can be supplied in this direction is a rather traditionalistic one based on the outmoded and threadbare doctrine of the parts of speech and of the old-fashioned distinction between subject and predicate. The only really acceptable syntax we have—for inscriptions anyhow—however, is *logical* syntax as based on concatenation and shape-descriptive predicates. Nonetheless, the demand implicit in the doctrine that semantic structure mirror syntactic form seems a legitimate one and may be met to a large extent by wedding the logical form as closely as possible to the given word-order of the parent sentence. If we do this, we then in effect abandon the notion that any form L-equivalent to a given logical form is a logical form of the original. Such a doctrine needs working out on the basis of the foregoing, and it seems likely that this could be done without too much difficulty. We should then be able to read off the logical form from the parent sentence in a more or less exact way, as in the next chapter.

Some constraints upon 'now' have been built into the forms given above, for example, the requirements concerning appropriateness. There is also the constraint that

$$\vdash (sp \ \text{PrNow} \ e_1,a,b,e_2 \ . \ sp \ \text{PrNow} \ e_3,a,b,e_2) \supset e_1 = e_3,$$

---

2. It is interesting to reflect upon the entries under 'now' in the *O.E.D.* Note, incidentally, that 'Simul' as just defined is identified with 'Throughout$_{\text{Time}}$', an identification perhaps not wholly desirable.

but this is provable from the Rule of Reference that

$$\vdash (sp \ \text{Ref} \ e_1,a,b,e_2 \ . \ sp \ \text{Ref} \ e_3,a,b,e_2) \supset e_1 = e_3.$$

It is not clear that there are further constraints needed. In any case it is interesting to note that there are no object-language axioms or meaning postulates for 'now' and the other deictic words, such constraints as are needed being forthcoming from rules of reference or from requisite additional clauses built into the logical forms.

CHAPTER XV

THE VERY IDEA OF
A LOGICAL FORM

Although many logical forms have been discussed and exhibited in the foregoing chapters, little attempt has been made to state in any precise way just what they are. Gilbert Harman's recent discussion[1] is welcome as an attempt to state in general terms what a "theory of logical form" is and in putting forward five useful principles for evaluating such theories. Summarily, a "theory of logical form for a natural language must do three things," Harman notes. "First, it must assign a logical form to every interpretation of every sentence. . . . Second, it must state rules of logical implication. And third, it must provide a finite list of obvious truths or axioms. A minimal condition of adequacy is that the theory account for all obvious implications in the language."

The five principles for evaluating theories of logical form are: "(P1) A theory of logical form must assign forms to sentences in a way that permits a (finite) theory of truth for the language. . . . (P2) A theory of logical form should minimize novel rules of logic. In practice, this means that rules of logical implication

1. "Logical Form," *Foundations of Language* 9 (1972): 38–65.

should be kept as close as possible to the rules of ordinary (first order) quantificational logic. . .[with identity]. . . . (P3) A theory of logical form should minimize [nonlogical] axioms. Other things being equal, it is better to account for obvious implications by rules of logic alone than by rules of logic alone plus non-logical axioms. (P4) A theory of logical form should avoid ascribing unnecessary ontological commitment to sentences of the language. . . . (P5) A theory of logical form must be compatible with syntax. . . ."

Valuable as these "principles" are, additional ones are needed as follows, to accord with protolinguistics as conceived here. (P6) A theory of logical form must be based upon the syntax and semantics of sign events or inscriptions rather than upon that of sign-designs or shapes, in order to handle the notion of truth for occasion sentences containing one or more indexical or deictic words, as in VI above. Shapes are then handled in terms of suitable predicates, so that the semantical theory needed must part rather considerably from that of Tarski.

(P7) A theory of logical form should avoid unnecessary *ontic involvement*.[2] In other words, the metalanguage should be of order no higher than that of the object language. Here too there must be a very considerable departure, as in VI, from the semantics of Tarski.

(P8) A theory of logical form must admit as values for variables such entities as events, acts, states, and processes in one fashion or another, as in IV. If the underlying logic is to be of first order, in accord with requirement (2), such entities must be regarded as individuals or entities of lowest type level.[3]

(P9) A theory of logical form must itself incorporate the heirarchy of languages, with an object language, its metalanguage, its metametalanguage, and so on. Given any part of a

---

2. See *Belief, Existence, and Meaning*, Chapter II.

3. This principle rules out the earlier analysis of events in the author's "On Events and Event-Descriptions," in *Fact and Existence*, pp. 63–74, as well as that of Jaegwon Kim. See especially his recent "Events as Property Exemplifications," in *Action Theory*, and the author's "Some Comments on Events and Actions," *ibid*. In effect, (P8) rules out all platonistic methods of handling events.

natural language of a given level, its metalanguage is also a part of that language. All natural languages of sufficient complexity contain metalinguistic sentences of various orders.

(P10) A theory of logical form must contain a pragmatics in the guise of a theory of reference. Certain words (shapes) are such that different speakers on different occasions use them to refer to different objects. The logical form of a sentence will contain one or more clauses indicating that the speaker or user on the given occasion of use uses the relevant inscriptions of those shapes to refer to such and such objects. A logical form is thus, so to speak, a function of speaker, sentence, and occasion of use.

(P11) A theory of logical form must incorporate a theory of intentionality in a most concrete way, to accord with (P2), (P3), and (P4). The only way of doing this developed to date seems to be that of employing Fregean *Arten des Gegebenseins* as handled in terms of designation or denotation, as above.

(P12) A theory of logical form must include a theory of the part-whole relation as between its individuals, just as it must include a theory of identity in accord with (P2). This is presumably best supplied by incorporating within it the calculus of individuals or mereology, as in III.

(P13) A theory of logical form must contain a logically sound, noncircular *lexicon*, or ordered list of definitions of expressions in terms of those picked out as primitive or "source" forms (in Harris's sense). The compilation of the lexicon is thus part and parcel of the theory and not a mere adjunct.

(P14) A theory of logical form cannot be developed piecemeal, but must be a *holistic structure* of considerable complexity. We must be wary, as George Lakoff has suggested, "of studying small fragments [of language] or just looking at a handful of sentences. . . . Studying a single phenomenon, or even a single word, in a natural language is like fooling with a giant delicately balanced mobile. Touch one piece and the whole thing moves."[4]

---

4. G. Lakoff, "Notes on What It would Take to Understand How One Adverb Works," *The Monist* 57 (1973): 328–343. See also Chapter VI of *Events, Reference, and Logical Form* for commentary on Lakoff's paper.

Nothing less than a fully developed logical theory of very great breadth will do. This must include not only the logic of (2), the calculus of individuals, a theory of events, but a suitable semiotics as well, as already noted.

(P15) A theory of logical form must be developed in accord with an attitude of respect for natural language *precisely as it is*. It should not seek to "regiment" it or make it behave in any other way than it actually does. Every sentence of natural language is sacred, with its own special structure including *word order*. The logical form of a sentence will mirror this structure, ideally perhaps containing a separate clause *for every word*, perhaps even several such clauses for a single word. Here word order is essential, and the logical form should mirror this as closely as possible. The logical form, in other words, will be of just the given sentence, and not of some paraphrase or grammatical transform of it.

All of these fifteen requirements are in need of further elaboration. Their general intent, however, should be clear enough in view of the preceding chapters and in view of what follows.

Harman remarks that the "principles (P1)–(P5), when taken together, put nontrivial constraints on a theory of logical form. Almost any theory can be modified so as to satisfy any one principle; and many theories can be modified to satisfy several of the principles simultaneously. What is nontrivial is getting a theory that does well with respect to all five principles." *A fortiori* of course with the addition of (P6)–(P15). Logical forms for many kinds of English sentences have been given above in accord with (P1)–(P14), but the requirement (P15) has been neglected. In this present chapter the attempt is made to undertake some first steps towards remedying this defect.

To see more clearly the purport of (P15), let us consider the sentence

(1)   'Socrates is a man'.

This sentence is often taken as merely of the form 'Ms', or 'sM' if we follow the English order of writing the subject first followed by the predicate. This latter, incidentally, is not a bad practice, extending easily to 'x R y' for dyadic relations and 'x Q yz' for triadic ones. Let us adopt it now. The 'is a' in (1) is then often regarded as a single notion. It is also of interest, however, to regard the 'is a' here as consisting of 'is' followed by 'a' and to give the structure of (1) accordingly. If we do this, the 'is' may be taken as the 'is' of identity and the 'a' as characterized by a selective-description operator. Let '(εM)' symbolize 'a man'.[5] Then (1) has the form rather

(1′)   '$s = (\varepsilon M)$'

that Socrates is identical to a man. Where

'$(\varepsilon M)G$'   is short for   '$(Ex)(xG \; . \; xM)$'

and G is the virtual class $\{p3s = p\}$, then (1′) is merely short for

(1″)   '$(Ex)(s = x \; . \; xM)$'.

We see this by noting that (1′) is, in view of the theory of virtual classes, logically equivalent to

(1‴)   '$(\varepsilon M)\{p3s = p\}$',

where, again, the predicate or virtual-class abstract follows the subject.

Now of course any one of these three forms, as well as 'sM' itself, could be taken as *the* logical form of (1). However, it would seem that (1′) is the most appropriate, mirroring as it does the precise word-order of (1) itself. Also the 'a' in (1) is given its proper semantical role to play, and the 'is' is taken in the very natural sense as the 'is' of identity.

A diagram may be helpful in showing how (1) is related to its preferred form (1′).

'Socrates is a man'

'$s = (\varepsilon M)$',

---

5. Cf. D12 of Chapter I above, but note the slight difference.

the arrows associating 'Socrates' with the individual constant 's', the 'is' with ' = ', 'a' with 'ε', and 'man' with 'M', the parentheses being needed for grouping.

The question of tense immediately arises. How would

(2)   'Socrates was a man'

be handled? Well, even the 'is' of identity may be tensed. In other words, identity-states are recognized, in addition to acts and processes, and given appropriate temporal location. Where From and To are the fundamental prepositional relations, a sentence of the form '$x = y$' is merely short for

$$\text{'(E}e)(e\langle=\rangle \ . \ e \text{ From } x \ . \ e \text{ To } y)',$$

as in X above. The e here may be tensed by locating it as earlier than, during, or later than the now.

The problem then is to gain a logical form for (2) akin to (1′) for (1). Clearly the parameter 'e', to be quantified existentially, is needed as well as some interpolated material indicating the semantic role of the various words occurring. This we may achieve as follows.

'Socrates was a man'

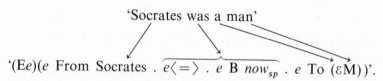

$$\text{'(E}e)(e \text{ From Socrates } . \ e\langle=\rangle \ . \ e \text{ B } now_{sp} \ . \ e \text{ To } (\varepsilon\text{M}))'.$$

The interpolated material here indicates that s plays the semantic role of having e bear From to it, that e is a member of $\langle=\rangle$, the class of all identity states, that e occurs before or earlier than now, and that (εM) is such that e bears To to it. The 'e' functions merely as an auxiliary variable, as a semantic connective, as it were, enabling us to associate the various clauses together in the required way, and is quantified existentially at the extreme left. The whole form may be abbreviated as

(2′)   '$s =_{past} (\varepsilon\text{M})$'.

It must not be supposed of course that all uses of the English 'a' (or 'an') are to be handled in this way in terms of 'ε'. There is, in addition, the *generic* use of 'a', equivalent to 'any', as in

(3)   'A horse is an animal'

and similar sentences. This may be construed either *per accidens* or *per necessitatem*, and thus may be "disambiguated" in (at least) two ways. A theory of virtual classes of virtual classes has not been needed up to this point in the various grammatical studies based on event logic. However, they may easily be introduced without fanfare if needed and it will be convenient to have them available now.

Let

(4) $\quad\quad\quad\quad\quad\quad\quad$ '$\{F3(--F--)\}G$'

be defined to express that the virtual class G is a member of the virtual class of all virtual classes F such that $(--F--)$.[6] (4) could also be written as

$\quad\quad$ '$G \; \varepsilon \; \{F3(--F--)\}$' $\quad$ or $\quad$ '$G\{F3(--F--)\}$',

but it is desirable at the moment to write it in just the way given. The generic use of 'a' *per accidens* may be defined as follows.

$\quad\quad$ '(ΣG)' $\quad$ abbreviates $\quad$ '$\{F3(x)(xG \supset x = (\varepsilon F))\}$',

so that 'a G (generically) is a' is short for an expression for the class of all virtual classes F such that every member of G is identical with a (or some) member of F. (3) then has as its form

(3') $\quad$ '$(\Sigma H)A$' $\quad$ or $\quad$ '$\{F3(x)(xH \supset x = (\varepsilon F))\}A$',

where of course 'H' designates the virtual class of horses and 'A' that of animals. Diagrammatically we have

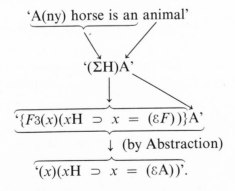

$$\text{'A(ny) horse is an animal'}$$

$$\text{'}(\Sigma H)A\text{'}$$

$$\text{'}\{F3(x)(xH \supset x = (\varepsilon F))\}A\text{'}$$

$$\downarrow \text{ (by Abstraction)}$$

$$\text{'}(x)(xH \supset x = (\varepsilon A))\text{'}.$$

6. As in *Belief, Existence, and Meaning*, pp. 130 ff.

Note again that '(ΣH)' strictly is short, not just for 'any horse', but for 'any horse is a', the 'is a' being accommodated in the '=' clause.

Construed *per necessitatem*, (3) may be handled in terms of the notion of analytic or necessary truth, essentially as

'Anlytc '(ΣH)A''.

To bring this closer to the ordinary English

'A horse is necessarily an animal',

we may define

'(ΣG) Nec F'   or   'Nec (ΣG) F' as short for   '(Ea)(Eb)(a LDes (ΣG) . b LDes F . Anlytc $\ulcorner(a\frown b)\urcorner)$',

in terms of L-designation.[7] Note that the use of the relation LDes here is in effect to make use of the device of disquotation.[8] Thus (3) construed *per necessitatem* has the form

(3″)   '(ΣH) Nec A'.

Some uses of the generic 'a' may have existential import, others not. The foregoing uses do have it, although this circumstance is not built into the forms. An existence clause may of course easily be added if it is needed.

The definite article 'the' has both a singular (Russellian) use as well as a generic one. The former may be handled here in familiar ways and the latter is essentially like the generic uses of 'a'.

Let us reflect now upon some of the sentences considered by Harman.

(5)   'Jack walked in the street',

(6)   'Jack walked',

(7)   'Jack walked slowly',

(8)   'Jack walked intentionally',

---

7. See *ibid.*, pp. 140 and 183. Recall also (V,G) above for a related notion.
8. See the author's "On Disquotation and Intensionality."

(9)   'Necessarily Jack walked',

(10) 'Necessarily Jack intentionally walked slowly in the street at 10 o'clock.'

These sentences contain quite a variety for any theory of logical form to assimilate.

Clearly, for (6), we have

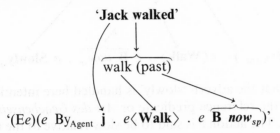

'$(Ee)(e$ **By**$_{Agent}$ **j** . $e\langle$**Walk**$\rangle$. e **B** $\overbrace{now_{sp}})$'.

(5) arises from this by the addition of a clause for location,

'e **In**$_{Location}$ **(the Street)**'.

Let us follow the convention hereafter, as here, of putting English sentences, and the logical correlates of their words in the logical forms, in bold face. This will help us to read off the English sentence from the logical form, as well as to help us in formulating the latter given the former. The other signs in the logical forms, those that are not in bold face, are then merely logical (or other) auxiliaries.

For (7), let

'e **Slowly**$_{sp}$ 'F'' be short for 'e **Low**$_{sp}$ Less-Slow-Than,'F'',

essentially as above, so that e is said to occur slowly relative to the reference predicate 'F', just where e is placed *low* in the scale of entities ordered by the Less-Slow-Than relation to which 'F' is supposed to apply.[9] The relevant reference predicate here is one for human walkings (perhaps for human walkings of persons roughly like Jack, of his same age, etc.). The virtual

---

9. Perhaps the parameter for the speaker may be omitted here. This would constitute a deviation from the treatment in the preceding chapters. It is a moot point anyhow as to where and when such parameters are needed.

class of human walkings, HW, is merely the class

$$\{e\exists(Ep)(\text{Per } p \;.\; e\langle\text{Walk}\rangle \;.\; e \text{ By}_{\text{Agent}} p)\}.$$

The form for (7) is then

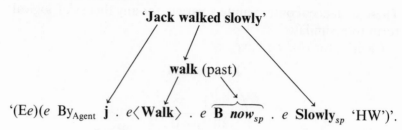

'**Jack walked slowly**'

walk (past)

'$(Ee)(e \text{ By}_{\text{Agent}} \mathbf{j} \;.\; e\langle\mathbf{Walk}\rangle \;.\; e \; \overline{\mathbf{B} \; \mathbf{now}_{sp}} \;.\; e \; \mathbf{Slowly}_{sp} \text{ 'HW')'}.$

Note that the adverb 'slowly' is handled here intentionally in terms of the reference predicate or *Art des Gegebenseins* 'HW', as above. The action *e* is said to be slow relative to the reference *predicate* for human walkings, not relative to the *class* of human walkings. This latter might be identical with some class, slow relative to which would be very different from slow for human walkings. Slow for a mermaid is not the same as slow for a unicorn. And similarly for 'big', 'beautiful', and so on.

(8) involves 'intentional' itself, which likewise must be handled intentionally, as in X. Let Less-Intentional-Than be a scalar relation such that

'e Less-Intentional-Than$_{sp}$ e','F''

expresses that *e* is less intentional than e' with respect to the predicate 'F'. In the present case the 'F' here will be the predicate for Jack's walkings. Then

'e High$_{sp}$ Less-Intentional-Than,'F''

expresses that *e* is placed *high* in the scale of entities in the field of the Less-Intentional-Than relation to which 'F' is supposed to apply. To say now that Jack walked intentionally is to say that there is a past walking by Jack placed high in the Less-Intentional-Than scale relative to the predicate for Jack's walkings. Let now

'e Intentionally$_{sp}$ 'F'' abbreviate 'e High$_{sp}$ Less-Intentional-Than,'F''.

Then our logical-form diagram or tree-structure is

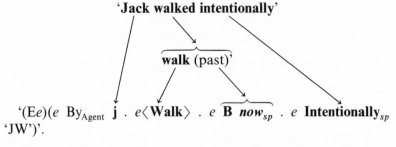

'(E*e*)(*e* By$_\text{Agent}$ **j** . *e*⟨**Walk**⟩ . *e* **B** $\overline{now_{sp}}$. *e* **Intentionally**$_{sp}$
'JW')'.

(9) may be handled in a manner somewhat similar to (3). Thus

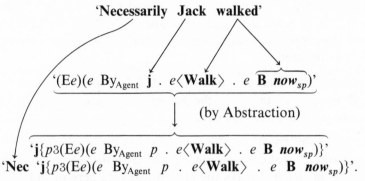

'(E*e*)(*e* By$_\text{Agent}$ **j** . *e*⟨**Walk**⟩ . *e* **B** $\overline{now_{sp}}$)'

↓ (by Abstraction)

'**j**{*p*3(E*e*)(*e* By$_\text{Agent}$ *p* . *e*⟨**Walk**⟩ . *e* **B** $\overline{now_{sp}}$)}'
'**Nec** '**j**{*p*3(E*e*)(*e* By$_\text{Agent}$ *p* . *e*⟨**Walk**⟩ . *e* **B** $\overline{now_{sp}}$)}'.

The logical form for (10) requires nested *Arten des Gegebenseins*, which, however, poses no essential difficulties. Just how
should we construe the reference predicate for 'intentionally' in
(10)? Is it just his walking that is done intentionally, or his
walking slowly, or his walking slowly in the street, or his walking
slowly in the street at 10 o'clock? Presumably the last is the
best candidate here. If so, we may let the virtual class of such
walkings by Jack be designated by 'JWSST'. This is then short for

'{*e*3(⟨**Walk**⟩*e* . *e* By$_\text{Agent}$ *j* . *e* Slowly 'JW' . *e* In$_\text{Location}$
(the Street) . *e* At$_\text{Time}$ (10 o'clock))}'.

The form for (10) is then, in now familiar fashion but with the
arrows omitted,

'**Nec** '(E*e*)(*e* By$_\text{Agent}$ **j** . *e* **Intentionally**$_{sp}$ 'JWSST' .
e⟨**Walk**⟩ . *e* **B** $\overline{now_{sp}}$. *e* **Slowly** 'JW' . *e* **In**$_\text{Location}$
(**the Street**) . *e* **At**$_\text{Time}$ (**10 o'clock**))''.

As in (9) this form may be reduced by Abstraction and disquotation to one of the form 'Nec jF' for a suitable 'F'.

Let us consider, by way of further illustration of the methods being used, a few more of the sentences mentioned by Harman.

(11)   'That John walked in the street upset Mabel'

differs from

(12)   'John's walk in the street upset Mabel'.

both syntactically and semantically. In (11) it is the fact or occurrence of John's walking in the street, perhaps several times or habitually or frequently, that is said to have upset Mabel; in (12) it is some one and only one walk itself. For (11) we need the prepositional relation for 'that'. Thus for (11) we have (arrows omitted)

'$(Ee)(Ea)(e$ **That** a . a'$(Ee')(e'$ By$_{\text{Agent}}$ **John** . $e'\langle$**Walk**$\rangle$. e' **B** now_{sp} . e' **In**$_{\text{Location}}$ (**the Street**))$)'$. $e\langle$**Upset**$\rangle$. e **B** now_{sp} . e Object **Mabel**)'.

In (12) 'John's walk in the street' is an elliptic description for some one of John's walkings. Note that the apostrophe and final 's' in 'John's' plays the semantical role here of indicating possession, or better, agency. Thus 'John's walk in the street' has the form

'$(\imath e$. $(e$ By$_{\text{Agent}}$ **John** . $e\langle$**Walk**$\rangle$. e B now_{sp} . e In$_{\text{Location}}$ (the Street))$)'$.

These various renditions part very considerably from Harman's account, which does not accord with principles (P6), (P7), (P9), (P11), and (P12).

Let us go on now to reflect for a moment upon

(13)   'Ralph does not believe of Ortcutt that he is a spy',

much discussed by Harman, David Kaplan, and others. This is of course a very different sentence from

(14)   'Raph does not believe that Ortcutt is a spy',

both syntactically and semantically. Harman and Kaplan think that (13) is three-way ambiguous. However, the analysis here would reveal that it is at least thirteen-way ambiguous, depending upon where the negation sign is placed. And even (14) is twelve-way ambiguous. (14) being a little simpler, let us consider only it. Its "disambiguations" may have the form

(14.1)   '$\sim$ (Ee)(Ea)(Ralph Do e . $e\langle$Blv$\rangle$. e That a . a'Ortcutt = (εSpy)')',

(14.2)   '(Ee)(Ea) $\sim$ (Ralph Do e . $e\langle$Blv$\rangle$. e That a . a'Ortcutt = (εSpy)')',

(14.3)   '(Ee)(Ea)($\sim$ Ralph Do e . $e\langle$Blv$\rangle$. e That a . a'Ortcutt = (εSpy)')',

(14.4)   '(Ee)(Ea)(Ralph Do e . $\sim$ $e\langle$Blv$\rangle$. e That a . a'Ortcutt = (εSpy)')',

(14.5)   '(Ee)(Ea)(Ralph Do e . $e\langle$Blv$\rangle$. $\sim$ e That a . a'Ortcutt = (εSpy)')',

(14.6)   '(Ee)(Ea)(Ralph Do e . $e\langle$Blv$\rangle$. e That a . a'$\sim$ Ortcutt = (εSpy)')'.

(14.3) and (14.4) correspond with the English sentence stressed as

'RALPH does not believe that Ortcutt is a spy',

'Ralph does not BELIEVE that Ortcutt is a spy',

and (14.6) with

'Ralph does not believe that ORTCUTT IS A SPY'.

There are three more readings, corresponding with

'Ralph does not believe that ORTCUTT is a spy',

'Ralph does not believe that Ortcutt IS a spy',

and

'Ralph does not believe that Ortcutt is a SPY'.

These we may gain by analyzing 'Ortcutt is a spy' as

'(Ee)(e' From Ortcutt . $e'\langle=\rangle$. e' To (εSpy))'.

There are then the three internal clauses to negate, resulting respectively in

(14.7) '(E*e*)(E*a*)(Ralph Do *e* . *e*⟨Blv⟩ . *e* That *a* . *a*'(E*e*')(∼ *e*' From Ortcutt . *e*'⟨=⟩ . *e*' To (εSpy))')',

(14.8) '(E*e*)(E*a*)(Ralph Do *e* . *e*⟨Blv⟩ . *e* That *a* . *a*'(E*e*')(*e*' From Ortcutt . ∼ *e*'⟨=⟩ . *e*' To (εSpy))')',

and

(14.9) '(E*e*)(E*a*)(Ralph Do *e* . *e*⟨Blv⟩ . *e* That *a* . *a*'(E*e*')(*e*' From Ortcutt . *e*'⟨=⟩ . ∼ *e*' To (εSpy))')'.

The readings for (14.1) and (14.2) seem to be unstressed. Also there would seem to be no reading with stress on 'that'. For the stressed sentences, something more is suggested, e.g., (14.3) seems to suggest that someone other than Ralph does believe that Ortcutt is a spy, (14.4), that Ralph knows or thinks (or whatever) that Ortcutt is a spy. It does not seem necessary to build such "pragmatic consequences" into the forms, although this may easily be done if it is thought desirable.

There is still another reading of (14), namely

(14.10) '(E*e*)(E*a*)(Ralph Do *e* . *e*⟨Blv⟩ . *e* That *a* . *a*'(E*e*') ∼ (*e*' From Ortcutt . *e*'⟨=⟩ . *e*' To (εSpy))')'.

And still further renditions or "disambiguations" of (14) result where more than one negation sign is allowed in the scope of '(E*a*)' and also in the scope of '(E*e*')'. All of these would seem to be captured, however, by (14.2) and (14.6). Note that (14.3), (14.4), (14.5), and (14.6) all have (14.2) as a logical consequence but not conversely. Also (14.7), (14.8), and (14.9) perhaps have (14.10) as a logical consequence but not conversely. We say "perhaps" here, pending meaning postulates for the prepositional relation That sufficient to justify that

(*e* That *a* . *b* LogConseq *a*) ⊃ *e* That *b*,

where LogConseq is the relation of first-order logical consequence (with identity), in the present context for suitable *a* and *b*.

In none of the renditions given of (14) has 'believe' been explicitly tensed. It is natural to read it in the present tense, in which case 'e During now_{sp}' may be added as a conjunct in the scope of '(Ea)' immediately before '$e\langle\mathrm{Blv}\rangle$'. A further reading then results, with this clause negated, corresponding to the English

'Ralph does not NOW believe that Ortcutt is a spy'.

Note that this sentence is very different semantically from

'Ralph does not believe NOW that Ortcutt is a spy'.

The former clearly tenses the believing as taking place now. In the latter, however, the 'now' is tantamount to 'under the circumstances'. This is a secondary use of 'now', as in the preceding chapter. Similarly the 'is' in 'Ortcutt is a spy' is understood as in the present tense, so that 'e' During now_{sp}' should be added as a conjunct under the scope of '(Ee')' immediately after '$e'\langle=\rangle$'. When negated, this gives a still further rendition: that Ortcutt is NOW a spy. ('that NOW Ortcutt is a spy' and 'that Ortcutt NOW is a spy' seem, again, to mean that under the circumstances Ortcutt is a spy.) We are not to read (14) as containing any secondary uses of 'now', for if we were 'now' should occur in it at the appropriate places, and we would no longer be considering (14) but some different, albeit closely related, sentence. It is natural, however, to read (14) as tensed in both the ways suggested, in which case two additional readings come to light, summing to twelve in all, two or three of them being perhaps a bit remote.

Note that the content of these disambiguations is easily grasped if word stress is brought in. There seems to be no reason why subtleties due to stress, rhythm, and intonation should not be brought in explicitly in the logical form. In fact this would seem a desideratum, so that we have another addendum to Harman's list of "principles:" (P16) A theory of logical form must be sufficiently rich as to accommodate all differences in spoken sentences due to differences in stress, rhythm, and intonation.[10]

---

10. See Quirk *et al.*, *A Grammar of Contemporary English*, Appendix II.

In a similar vein (13) may be handled.

To bring the foregoing forms in line with (P10), some additional clauses concerning the speaker and the occasion of use are needed, especially for sentences containing deictic words. This may readily be done in the manner of the preceding chapters.

What do we conclude from this analysis? Merely that English sentences are more subtle and complex than is dreamt of in most logical discussions of them. One is tempted to add a seventeenth "principle" to the list above: (P17) Given any two theories of logical form, one should be judged superior to the other if *ceteris paribus* it has greater resources than the other for isolating ambiguities and providing alternative "disambiguated" forms. (It is not clear that any theory of logical form suggested heretofore can bring to light the various ambiguities discussed above.) Of course a theory should not be judged merely upon its capacity to disambiguate. Some disambiguations may be mere curiousities of little linguistic interest, but it is important that the theory be able to characterize them if needed. A theory of logical form must be like a vast iceberg with only a small portion of it of immediate use to the linguistic, its greater portion always floating beneath the surface. The whole logic of Chapters I–VII, with its great panoply of notions, is available for use in protolinguistics as occasion demands.

It is interesting to note that the logical forms here and throughout are gained merely by interpolating logical details between the words of the English sentence. Put the other way around, the English sentence may be said to result from the logical form by deletion of logical detail. The logical form suffices for all purposes of report, as Zellig Harris has noted, and the English sentence results from it by paraphrase or other grammatical transformations. Strictly all the English sentence does is to shorten and abbreviate, man being a lazy animal. We have then an eighteenth principle: (P18) The only essential difference between a sentence of a natural language and its logical form must be that the latter contains interpolated, including prefixed or suffixed, logical and other notations between the words or syllables of the former. All other differences are mere accidents or unimportant minutiae. One interrupts the sentence here or there for explicitness and to spell out in full detail just what one wishes to say. Henry James, in his convoluted prose, is said to have "interrupted himself fifty times in any sentence *because he wanted to be clear.*"[11]

There is of course much more to be said here. All manner of other kinds of sentences should be examined. Also much more needs to be said concerning pragmatic consequences. Given certain meaning or other postulates, the sentences with stresses may be said not merely to suggest but to have such and such as logical consequences. For example, (14.3) above has the logical consequence that there is a believing that Ortcutt is a spy. If a meaning postulate or theorem is available that all believings have a human agent, then it is a logical consequence of (14.3) that someone other than Ralph does believe that Ortcutt is a spy. In addition to matters of primary stress, there are of course secondary stresses, the falling tone, the rising tone, and so on, all of which influence meaning and hence logical form.

It should be observed that nothing whatsoever of the traditional grammar of the parts of speech is presupposed in the foregoing. There is no need of a theory of noun phrases, verb phrases, adjectives, adverbs, and the like. This is in marked contrast with most other theories of logical form. The only syntax recognized here is *logical* syntax, i.e., the theory of shape-descriptive predicates and concatenation as applied to the letters, morphemes, words, sentences, texts, and discourses of natural language. In this observation there is implicit a nineteenth principle: (P19) A theory of logical form should in no way presuppose the traditional doctrine of the parts of speech, which is itself in need of a complete overhauling, as has frequently been observed by writers so disparate as Russell, Reichenbach, Carnap, Zellig Harris, and others.

We have not yet finished. Having come this far, we may without too much risk take a further step, a twentieth one. (P20) Logical forms are themselves to be regarded as being

11. By Louis Szathmary, as quoted in *The New York Times*, 24 May 1975, p. 42.

contained in natural language. They are not forms in some other language of a different kind. The symbolic notations introduced for them are merely for convenience and shorthand. Everything that is said with symbols and special abbreviations may be said without them. The theory of logical form is thus merely the theory of language itself. Hence the fundamental parts of speech required are merely those of the latter: connectives, variables, quantifiers, individual constants, the identity sign, the sign for the part-whole relation, various expressions for virtual classes and relations, shape-descriptive predicates, a sign for the concatenation relation, expressions for various semantical relations, event-descriptive predicates, expressions for various prepositional relations, and so on. The traditional parts of speech are then to be characterized in terms of these. The study of so-called surface grammar is thus merely a development or extension of protolinguistics and not something presupposed by it.

(P20) carries with it a twenty-first and final principle. (P21) Logical forms are not in general to be given to sentences singly or as isolated from the wider linguistic contexts in which they occur. (This point is due essentially to Henry Hiż.) In some cases, it will do no harm to consider a sentence in isolation, but often this cannot be done satisfactorily. The logical form of a sentence may depend upon sentences that precede or follow it in the given "text." Just how wide the text is to be taken depends of course upon all manner of special circumstances. Ultimately the whole discourse should be subjected to analysis, the analysis of the parts depending often most intimately upon the whole. This does not mean that analysis can never get started; it means rather that once started it must not stop until the relevant parts are given their proper structures.

With the addition of (P6)–(P21) we end up with a conception of linguistic structure rather far removed from any that has been suggested heretofore, it would seem. No doubt there is much in the foregoing that will need improvement and development before we are done. Perhaps some of (P1)–(P21) will have to be given up or modified in one way or another. Even so, it is hoped that they have served as useful guides, in our voyage of discovery, in getting us started on the right track.

There are occasional discrepancies of treatment of essentially the same kind of sentence as between what has been said here and what has been said in one or more of the chapters above. Such discrepancies may be viewed as allowing for alternatives. In general, however, those given later are presumably the preferable ones. It is hoped that there has been gain in profundity and adequacy of analysis from chapter to chapter.

The study of logical form or linguistic structure is still in its infancy. It is by now surely clear, however, that the riches of first-order logic as extended in various appropriate directions can no longer be disregarded by the philosophical analyst interested in language or by the professional linguist. Whatever its defects or shortcomings, the system of linguistic structure sketched in the preceding chapters is probably the simplest and most extensive that has yet been forward. In any case, it is hoped that it will be useful as a basis for further study, extension, and improvement.

INDEX

abstraction 6ff, 21ff
acceptance 113ff
Ackermann, W. 3
acts, states, processes 69ff
adjectives 227, 268f
adverbs 152f, 155f, 226f, 273ff
apprehension 113f
appropriateness relations 169, 254, 284f, 292, 294
arithmetic 126ff, 167f
Art des Gegebenseins 122, 157f, 167, 170, 178, 184, 193, 211ff, 258f, 295, 301
assertion 133ff, 181
atomic summation 32ff
Austin, J. L. 237f

Bar-Hillel, Y 150
Before-than relations 60, 66ff, 221
belief 115f, 229
Belnap, N., Jr. 192
Bernays, P. 3ff, 15

calculus of individuals 41ff, 60
cardinal pairs 29f
cardination 123ff
Carnap, R. xiv, xix, 66, 78, 150, 296, 315
causal relations 165, 257f
characters 77ff
Cohen, Jonathan 183
collective plurals 173, 176, 200ff
commands 116ff, 180f

concatenation 78ff, 225
conceptualistic syntax 95ff
converses 25f, 36f
counterdomains 24f, 36f

Davidson, D. 165
demonstratives 101ff
denotation 7, 108ff
descriptions 17ff, 27ff, 38, 51
designation 108f
determination 109f
discreteness relation 43
domains 24f, 36ff

exclamations 116ff
existence 18, 39, 48ff
event-descriptive predicates 58ff
events 57ff

fields 25, 36f
Fillmore, C. 210f
'formula' 7, 42, 44, 61, 83ff
framed ingredients 86, 90
Frege, G. xi, 4, 114, 116, 122, 192, 267, 296, 301
fusions 52f, 201f, 255, 267

geometry 131ff
Goodman, N. 41, 73
Gurwitsch, A. xx, 128

Harman, G. 299f, 310, 313
Harris, Z. xvii, 149ff, 186, 197, 218, 284, 314f

Hilbert, D. 3, 15
Hiż, H. xx, 121, 156, 316

identity 10ff, 15f, 22ff, 61ff, 214, 230, 271
inclusion 11, 22ff
intransitive relations 33
irreflexive relations 33f

James, H. 315
Jespersen, O. 70

Kaplan, D. 310
Kim, J. 300
knowledge 115f, 120

Lakoff, G. xvii, 185ff, 301
Leonard, H. 41
Leśniewski, S. xii
Lindkvist, K.-G. 272
logical form 145ff, 299ff
Lorenzen, P. 217f, 221f, 242f

many-one relations 31ff
measurement 141ff
moments 68
Morris, C. xiv
Moutafakis, N. 118

necessity 95, 117f, 306f
negatives 10ff, 23f, 46f, 69
nuclei 52
null event 63ff
null individual 46f, 53ff
nullity 12ff, 23ff, 69, 179

one-many relations 31ff
one-one relations 32
ordered pairs and triples 30f
ordination 128ff
overlapping relations 43, 67

paraphrase 121f, 150
part-whole relations 42ff, 68
Peano, G. 7

Peirce, C. S. xi, xiv, xvi, 36, 192, 210
performative utterances 237ff
Popper, K. 271
Posner, R. 231
possibility 95, 177f
predicates 3, 58ff, 74ff, 149
prepositions 205ff, 217ff, 245ff
products 12ff, 23f, 46f, 69
pronouns 100ff

quantifiers 3ff, 54f
quasi-quotes 4, 156
questions 115ff, 180, 239ff
Quine, W. V. 4, 73, 97, 110f, 156, 219, 310
Quirk, R. and associates xviii, 220, 222ff, 245ff, 273ff, 313

real numbers 136ff
reference 99, 194f, 290
reflexive relations 33f
Reichenbach, H. 62, 173, 315
relative products 25f, 37f
Russell, B. xiv, 18, 157, 172, 205, 221, 295, 315

St. Augustine 267
satisfaction 109
Scoggin, J. 55, 219
Sellars, W. 74
'sentence' 87ff
serial relations 34f
shape-descriptive predicates 74ff
similarity 84, 219, 230f, 262
Smaby, R. 121
Strawson, P. 218ff
stress, rising tone, falling tone 236
subjunctives 116ff, 133ff, 181
sums 12ff, 23f, 46f, 69
symmetric relations 33f
synonymy 121f

Tarski, A. xiv, 41, 184, 300
tense 154, 156, 274ff, 289ff
'theorem' 89ff

transitive relations 33f
triadic relations 35ff
'truth' 100ff, 118ff
truth functions 3ff

understanding 115f
unit virtual classes 29ff
universality 12ff, 23f, 69
utterance 113ff

virtual classes 3ff
virtual relations 21ff

Weinreich, U. xiii
Whitehead, A. N. xv, 136
Woodger, J. H. 41
world individual 46f